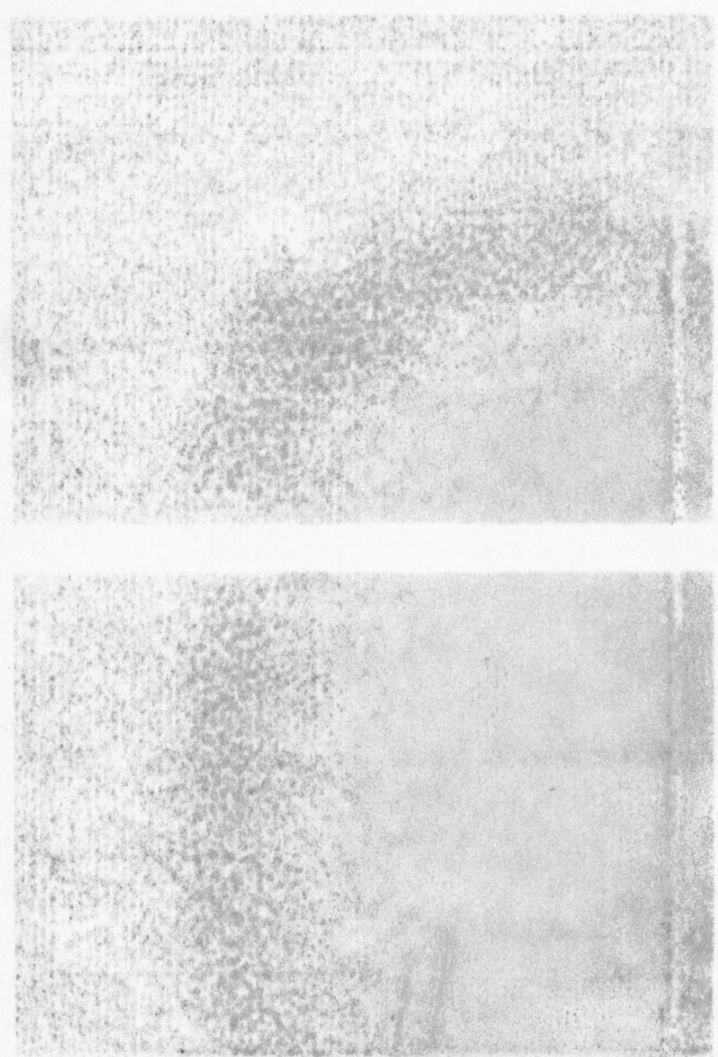

ENGLISH RECUSANT LITERATURE
1558–1640

Selected and Edited by
D. M. ROGERS

Volume 165

PATRICK ANDERSON
The Ground of the Catholike and Roman Religion
1623

PIETRO TERAMANO
Esmudiad Eglwys . . . Loreto
1635

PATRICK ANDERSON

The Ground of the Catholike and Roman Religion
1623

The Scolar Press
1973

ISBN 0 85967 131 3

Published and Printed in Great Britain by The Scolar Press Limited, 20 Main Street, Menston, Yorkshire, England

NOTE

The following works are reproduced (original size), with permission:

1) Patrick Anderson, *The ground of the catholike and Roman religion*, 1623, from a copy in the library of the Abbey, Fort Augustus, by permission of the Prior. In this copy leaves *–*2 of Part 3 have been misbound before section B; in the facsimile these two leaves are in their correct position.

References: Allison and Rogers 20; STC 575.

2) Pietro Teramano, *Esmudiad eglwys . . . Loreto*, 1635, from the unique copy in the British Museum, by permission of the Trustees.

Reference: Allison and Rogers 808; not in STC.

THE GROVND OF THE CATHOLIKE AND ROMAN RELIGION IN THE WORD OF GOD.

With the Antiquity and Continuance therof, throughout all Kingdomes and Ages.

COLLECTED

Out of diuers Conferences, Discourses, and Disputes, which M. *Patricke Anderson* of the Society of IESVS, had at seuerall tymes, with sundry Bishops and Ministers of Scotland, at his last imprisonment in *Edenburgh*, for the Catholike Faith, in the yeares of our Lord 1620. and 1621.

Sent vnto an Honourable Personage, by the Compyler, and Prisoner himselfe.

The first Part, or Introduction.

Philip. 1. Vers. 12. & 13.

And I will haue you know, Brethren, that the thinges about me, are come to the more furtherance of the Ghospell: so that my bandes were made manifest in all the Court &c.

Permissu Superiorum, Anno M. DC. XXIII.

TO THE RIGHT HONORABLE REVEREND, VVISE, AND GRAVE LORDS

of his Maieſties priuy Counſell of Scotland.

MAny & iuſt are the conſideratiõs (Noble, Graue, Wiſe, and Learned) which haue induced me to dedicate theſe Works of *M. Patrick Anderſon* to your Lordſhips. Firſt becauſe one of his Diſputes (which was an happy diſpute for me, & diuers others) was made before ſome of your Honours. Secondly becauſe the order & methode which he hath kept in theſe Works, is euery day practiſed in your ſeſſiõhouſe of Scotlãd; for in Law-matters you giue place in your ſeſſiõhouſe to the *Confeſſion of the party*. And truly the parties owne acknowledgment of his offence is a ſufficient proof amongſt all Nations. Heere your Lordſhips ſhal ſee in like mãner how the very Proteſtants thẽſelues auow, that in the Catholike Roman Church & Religion, Saluation vndoubtedly is to be found. 2. If you make great accõpt of *faithfull & honeſt witneſſes* in proofe of maters in Law, you ſhall find likewyſe alledged faithfully in the first, second, third, fourth, & insuing Ages the ancient and holy Fathers, euery one in his owne Age & Century giuing ful and cleer testimony for vs Catholiks against the Ministry; which holy Fathers did not forsee any debats amongst vs; (a) *Nor yet were angry neither at you, nor at vs* (sayth S. Augustine:) *What they haue found in the Church, that they haue held; they haue taught that wh they haue learned; & what they haue receaued from their Forfathers they haue deliuered to vs their posterity*. 3. *If Priority of possession* be of any regard (as questionles it is) among you, it is heer plentifully set down, that we Catholiks are first in possession, & that it is but a few yeares since we Catholiks of these three Kingdome were thrust out, by the Ministers, of our former rightfull, and so long continued possession of fifteen hundreth yeares; and condemned by those who had no power, authority, nor commission to accuse or condemne vs; not so much as hauing our accusers before vs, nor place to defend vs. 4. *If Prescription* be a matter of great Importance in proofe amongst you, you shal then heere find our Catholike Religiō, for which we now suffer in Scotland, England, & Ireland, deduced frō the tyme of the Apostles, from Age to Age, to these our very dayes, giuing in further proof that the Protestant & Puritan Ministers, who (against all Law hauing bereft vs of our prescription & possession) haue been condemned in all Ages, by the Church of God then apparent, as manifest Heretiques, in the persons of the Arians, Pelagians, Nouatians, Waldenses, Albigenses &c. 5. *If cōtinual clayme* be a sufficiciēt way amongst you to preserue right & title, it is more then euidēt that our Catholike Pastours haue beene euermore waking to preserue our right, and Religion, as the Prophet fortold thus: (b) *Vpon thy walles O Hierusalem haue I set watch men, all the day & all the night*

(a) *Aug. aduers. Iulim Pelag. l. 1. prope finem & l. 3. cap. 17.*

(b) *Esa. 62. 6.*

for

for euer they shall not be silent. But your Protestant Church hath (to the contrary) been so farre from performing the like, that it hath been inuisible, latent, and vnknowne to the world the space of fifteen hūdreth yeares. (c) *Gods true Church* (sayth M. Napper) *most certainly aboad so long latent and inuisible* 6. If whē the letter of the law being foūd in some cases doubtful, ought (cōforme to your coustome in Scotlād) to be interpreted according to the *answerable practise of ensuing tymes*; you shall in like maner find heer the doubtfull letter of the Scriptur, and obscure sayings of the Fathers made plaine on our part, by the answerable practise of all succeding tymes & ages. 7. If the iudgment and *resolution of most Ancient & wyse Iudges and Presidents* giuen in former Ages in your Countrey, be authentical or of credit in your Sessionhouse; heer then you shall see the graue and wholsome Iudgments giuen for vs Catholiks by the most famous, learned and holy Iudges & Presidēts of all Kingdoms & Ages for these 1500. yeares, cōdēning the Puritan, & the Protestāt Ministry of manifest Heresy and Errour, in the persons of *Aerius, Vigilantius, Nouatus* & such other Heretiks. Finally, if the Ministers would free thēselues (cōtrary to all Law) from all these precedēt proofes and Iudgments, appealing to the only written Law, & to the expresse word of God (as they do, & must needs do,) first it is easie to be seen by the ensuing Treatises; That all the Ministers togeather shall not, or cannot shew, no not one debatable point of their Religion, to be conteyned in the expresse word. 2. They shall not be able to improue any debatable point of our Religion as being against the expresse word. 3. It is shewed that they haue falsified and corrupted the word of God miserably & ignorātly, making it therby not the word of God, but their owne word, & inuention.

(c) *In his Treatise vpon the reuelation.*

By al which it appeareth sufficiētly, that our Catholike Faith & Religion (for the which now presently we suffer persecution in Scotland) is that selfesame Religion, and Faith wherunto our Scotish Nation was, aboue fourteen hundreth yeares since, confessedly first conuerted: That religion also which euen then, so longe since, and now is professed throughout the Christian world: That Religion also, which was then confirmed to vs, and other Nations from heauen with the testimony of vndoubted miracles: That religion which hath founded your ancient Municipall Lawes, Courts of Iudgement, erected & builded your most famous Churches of Elgene, of Murray, Glasco, Paslay, S. Giles in Edenburgh, Holyrood-house, the Chaunry of Rosse, and many others: That Religion finally which hath erected your Bishops Seas, Religious houses, and Abbayes, Colledges, Vniuersities, and many other knowne Royall monuments of Piety, in your most Noble, and ancient Kingdome of Scotland.

To the reading therfore of these insuing Parts & Treatises, I earnestly and humbly exhort your Lordships, euen by the infinit multitude of benefits which God hath bestowed vpon yow, by the pretious Bloud of Christ who hath redeemed vs all, by the tēder care of your own saluation, and by whatsoeuer els is sacred and holy; to the which end I will continue my dayly prayers to God, and remaine alwaies,

Your Lordships most humble Seruant.

M. I. L.

The Preface to the Christian Reader.

IT is, Christian Reader, the ancient and iust complaint of our holy, & wise Forefathers, that Man of his weakenes affect the knowledge of certayne forraine, childish and fruitlesse thinges, & not to apply earnestly his mind to the *Consideration* of that *Punctum vnde pendet Æternitas*, of that wherupon eternall saluation relyeth, which is only the *true Fayth & Religion*. The consideration of the subtill course of the seas, of the perpetuall motion of Planets, of the inestimable riches of the whole materiall world is but beggery, and misery in respect of the diligent search and consideration of the true Church & Religion. What Monarch had euer such Embassadours as are the fiue senses of man? Or such Solicitors as are his desires? or such Executioners as are his passiõs? or such a Lord Steward of his house as is Reason? or such a Secretary of State as his discretion? or such a Treasurer as is his memory? or such a president or cõmander as is his Will? all which inuiteth him to imploy whatsoeuer he hath in earnest, graue, & wise *Consideration*, to find out the true religion, out of the which there is nothing but eternall misery & damnation.

Those Creaturs which want reason go towards their end, through a meere naturall Inclination, which is, as if they were moued by another & not by thẽselues, because they consider not the reason of their end; & that eyther to an end apprehended, as it hapneth in the case of beasts, or not apprehended, as it is with inanimate creatures, which want all kind of knowledge & *Consideration*.

But man who is not a meere materiall creature as others are, but is spirituall & immortall, as he hath a more eleuated & noble end; so also must he needs haue a more noble means, for the reaching & arriuing to so excellent an end, which is only *Consideration*.

Since then *Consideration* in it selfe is so noble & excellent a thing in man, I haue set downe heer of set purpose the meanes to attayne to the true Religion, & the Grounds therof by way of *Consideration*. For as in matters of great consequence & moment, *Consideration* specially should be imployed; the finding of the true Religion being a matter aboue all others of moment and great consequence, I could not vse a fitter means to attayne so noble a treasure, as is that, wherupon relyeth our eternall saluatiõ. To this end I haue set down in this first Part & Treatise twenty foure *Considerations*, wherby it shalbe easy to the vnpassionate & indifferent Reader, to find out, by the grace of God, the true Church and Religion.

Of

Of set purpose I haue omitted to requite some Minister his bitter words in my behalfe, his Paradoxes, Vntruths, Impertinencyes, Paralogismes, Ignorance, Immodesty, Folly, & Scurrility specifyed in a misconstrued letter of his vnworthy to be refuted, known well to such as best know me, not to be so much subiect to such bitternes and insultatiõ of speach, which *non parit victoria laudem*, not intending to encounter him in the lik stile with *maledictum pro maledicto*, leauing that as hereditary to such a Puritan Minister: my wordes shall still beseeme my selfe, shal haue modesty & truth for their characters, they shall offẽd no chast eares, and shall not proceed of any like blacke Hypocondriall humour, giuing alwaies this, as a Caueat to such a Minister ———

——— *Capere vel noli nostra, vel ede tua.*

Yet if once againe I be stirred vp by such men to obserue & keep *legem talionis*, let them thanke themselues, who, without any occasion offered, do prouoke me against my nature & inclination *paribus concurrere telis:* Yet in such a requytall I shall euer obserue the admonition of the Comicke *Ne quid nimis*, to shoot rather too short thẽ too far at such rouers, knowing well such sharpnes in wordes to be the whetstone of dissention, by which mens myndes are soone moued but hardly reconciled: wishing alwayes that such a Minister should not haue forgot that rule of S. Ambrose: (a) *Veritatis* (sayth this Father) *ea est regula, vt nihil facias commendandi tui causa, quo minor alius fiat*, that is the rule of truth, that you do nothing in your own commendation, wherby another may be abased.

(a) *l. 1. de offic. c. 24.*

The painted wordes of such men, their lyes & vntruthes serue to no other end, then to make the simpler sort to swallow down more gredily their poysoned pills: of these thrids is the Net wouen, which catcheth so many of the weaker people, much like as S. Hierome sayth of the web of spiders, that catcheth weak flyes, & by birds & beasts is broken asũder. *The* (b) *Heretiks*, saith he, *weaue a spiders web, which is able to catch little & light creatures, as flyes, gnats, or the like, but by others of more strength is broken in peeces. The light & more simple sort in the Church are deceaued by their errors, whẽ as they cãnot seduce such as are strõg in the truth of fayth. Such Ministers are not conuinced* (saith (c) S. Bernard) *by reasons, because they vnderstand them not, nor amended by authorities, because they regard them not, nor mooued by persuasions, because they are subuerted:* nec rationibus conuincuntur, quia non intelligunt: nec auctoritatibus corriguntur, quia non recipiunt: nec flectuntur suasionibus, quia subuersi sunt. But let vs come to the matter in hand, my selfe resting alwayes,

(b) *Ep. ad Cipr. presb.*

(c) *ser. 66. in Cãtica.*

Thy humble seruant,

P. A. S. I.

THE GROVND OF THE CATHOLIKE AND ROMAN RELGION IN THE WORD OF GOD.

VVith the Antiquity & Continuance thereof throughout all Kingdomes & Ages.

The First Consideration.

That true Fayth is absolutely necessary to saluation: and that it must be only one Fayth.

WHOSOEVER hath a true desire to please God, and an earnest care to saue his owne soule (which should be the chiefest desire, and care of euery good Christian,) he must resolue and settle himselfe in a sound beliefe of matters of fayth, holding it for a most assured ground, That there is a fayth, which whosoeuer wanteth cannot please God, nor consequently be saued; according to the saying of S. Paul: (a) *Without Fayth it is impossible to please God.* Which saying S. Augustine confirmeth: (b) *It is certayne* (sayth he) *that none can come to true happines, except he please God, and that none can please God but by fayth: for faith is the foundation of all good thinges, fayth is the beginning of mans saluation:* (a) Heb. 11. v. 6. (b) Augu. serm. 18. de tempore.

 without

without faith none came come to the fellowship of the children of God: because without it, neither in this world doth any mā obteine the grace of iustification, neyther in the next world shall he possesse eternall life.

This Faytħ so absolutly necessary, must only be one, as S. Paul saith: (c) *There is but one Lord, one baptisme, & one faith:* Yea, (d) *except it be one it is not fayth.* This fayth is that, (e) *which the Church spread ouer the whole world, doth diligently keep, as dwelling in one house, and doth beleeue in one like maner al points of fayth, as hauing one soule, and one heart, and doth preache, and teach, and deliuer by tradition those things after one manner, as possessing one mouth: for albeyt there be diuers and different languages in the world, yet the vertue of tradition is the same.* By which wordes it is playne, not only that there is but one fayth, but also how it is sayd to be one: which might seeme not to be one, cōsidering there are so many points, which we beleeue by our Faith, and so many seuerall men who haue in them this faith; yet it ceaseth not to be one, because the whole Church belieueth those points in a like manner: neyther the beliefe of one man differeth from the beliefe of another; neyther the beliefe of the Catholikes of France, Spaine, Italy, Germany, Flāders, of the Indians, of Scotlād, England, & Ireland, differ in any essential point of Religiō.

(c) Ephes. 4. v. 5.
(d) Leo ser. 4. in natiuit. Dom.
(e) Iran. lib. 2. c. 3.

Contrary the Puritane Ministers excommunicate and wholly condemne the Protestant Ministers of Scotland, for receauing of the ceremonies of England. Heare the very words of the Puritane Ministers against Protestant Ministers: (f) *The Protestant Ministers haue imbraced that doctrine which is a hotch-potch of Christ and Antichrist, of God and the diuell; and such a Minister may iustly suspect himselfe to be a halting Neutrall, who seeketh nothing but like a greedy dog to fill his owne paunche, a desperate and forlorne Atheist, of a cursed, vncircumcised generation.* Heare I pray thee (gentle reader) what the Puritan Ministers say of the Protestants in general: (g) *The Protestants prescript forme of prayer and seruice is all full of corruption, in all the order of their seruice, there is no edification but confusion, and many things in the Communion booke are contrary and agaynst the word of God. They put no difference betwixt truth and falsehood, betwixt Christ and Antichrist, betwixt God and the diuell. Their*

(f) Dangerous positions lib. 2 c. 9. & 13.
(g) Dangerous positions lib. 2. c. 9. & 11. Gilby. p. 29

Clergy

Clergy are an Antichristian swynish rable, enemies of the Gospel, Beelzebub of Canterbury the chiefe of the diuels. And M. Bernard a famous Minister in England enobleth the Protestant Ministers with these glorious titles: (h) *Ministers of the Church of England are Ægyptian Enchanters, limmes of the diuell, Sicophants, Angells of hell.* Now what the Protestants say of the Puritan Ministers in M. Iohn Caluin his person, is easie to be seene by two famous Protestants: the first Franciscus Stancarus who writeth thus: (i) *Beware o Christian Reader, and chiefly all you Ministers, beware of Caluins bugges, specially of the Articles of the Trinity, Incarnatiō &c. for they contein impious doctrine, & Arriā Blasphemies.* (k) Schlusselburge sayth worse of the Puritan Ministers, if worse may be sayd. Whereby it is easie to be seene that there is no vnity of fayth amongst the Protestants & Puritans, yea in essentiall poynts of Religion, since the one condemneth the other so horribly.

(h) Bernard Minister of Worsop in his book of the Separistes Schisme. pag. 71.
(i) *Franciscus Stācarus lib. 4. contra Caluin. n. 4.*
(k) *Lib. 2. art. 9. The. Caluin. fol. 71.*

The second Consideration.

That this one Fayth, must needes be infallible and entiere.

THis one Fayth, without which we cannot be saued, must be infallible and most certaine. This is cleare, because, *Fayth is that Credit, or inward assent of mind, which we giue to that which God hath reuealed vnto vs, by meanes of the preaching or teaching of the true Church.* For as S. Chrysostome saith: (a) *It cannot be called fayth, vnles a man be more certayne of those things which are not seene, then of those things which are seene.* And agayne: (b) *We cannot be deceaued by Gods wordes, but our sense is most easily deceaued.* Seeing then our Fayth is grounded on the word of God, reuealed to vs by Iesus-Christ our Lord, speaking by the mouth of the Church, as he sayth himselfe, (c) *He that heareth you, heareth me*; we ought to receaue the word of Fayth, preached by the true Church, not as the word of man, but as it is truly the word of God, and consequently we must accompt it a thing most certayne & absolutly infallible. Which doctrine should be well remarked as the only ground of true Religion, yea the infallible way to

(a) *Chrys. Hom. 12. in ep. ad Heb.*
(b) *Hom. 83. in Mat.*
(c) *Luk. 10 v. 16.*

to discerne the true Religion from the false. The infallibility therfore, which I require in true fayth is the highest degree of certainty, excluding not only actual & deliberate doubt (for vndeliberate doubt taketh not away fayth) but also possibility of deliberate doubt, or feare of being deceaued, which infallible assurance all faithful Christians haue, so long as they haue fayth.

This infallible faith must be entiere, whole, and sound in all points; neyther is it sufficient to belieue stedfastly some points, misbelieuing, or obstinatly not belieuing som other, or any one: because euery point of doctrine, yea euery word that God hath reuealed, and by his Church proposed to vs to be belieued, must vnder paine of damnation be belieued: for (d) *He that shall not belieue, shall be condẽned.* And S. Iohn saith: (e) *He that belieueth not, is already iudged.* For not to belieue any one poynt whatsoeuer, which God by reuealing of it testifieth to be true, and which by his Church he hath commaũded vs to belieue, must needs be damnable as being a notable iniury to Gods verity, & a great disobedience to his will. But all essential poynts of fayth are thus testifyed by God, and commanded to be belieued, otherwise they be not points of fayth, but opinion or some other kind of knowledge. Therefore all essentiall poynts of faith vnder payne of damnation must be belieued, I meane eyther expresly or implicitly, it being not necessary to vnderstand and know in particular euery thing which we belieue.

(d) *Matth.* 2. v. 19. *Mark.* 16. v. 16.
(e) *Iohn.* 3. v. 18.

The third Consideration.

That there must be some meanes prouided by Almighty God, by which all sorts of men may learne this Fayth, which is necessary to saluation: & what conditions are requisite therto.

AS this one, infallible, and entiere fayth is necessary to saluation in all sorts of men, as well vnlearned al learned: so we must say that Almighty God, (a) *who would haue all men to be saued, and to come to the knowledge of the truth,* hath pro-

(a) *Tim.* 2. v. 4.

prouided ſome Rule and meanes wherby euery man in all queſtions and doubts of fayth, may be infallibly inſtructed and taught what is to be holden for the true fayth: and that the only cauſe why any man miſſeth of the true faith, is eyther becauſe he doth not ſeeke out, and find this rule and meanes, or hauing found it, he will not vſe it, and in all poynts ſubmit himſelfe to it, as the nature of diuine fayth, and the duty of euery Chriſtian bindeth him to do. To this purpoſe ſayth S. Auguſtine: (b) *If Gods Prouidence rule & gouerne humane matters, we may not deſpayre, but that there is a certayne authority appointed by the ſame God, vpon which ſtaying our ſelues, as vpon a ſure ſtep, we may be lifted vp to God*: which lifting vp to God is firſt begun by true fayth: for the finding of which, God hath prouided a certayne authority and meanes, wherby men may come to the knowledge of the diuine myſteryes of fayth.

(b) *Aug. de vtilit. credendi.*

This rule and meanes to find out the true fayth neceſſary to ſaluation, muſt haue the propertyes following. 1. It muſt be certayne and infallible, for otherwiſe it cannot be a ſufficient foundation wherevpon we ſhould build our fayth, which is abſolutly infallible. 2. It muſt be eaſy and playne to be knowen of all men, for if to any one ſort it could not be knowen, or not certaynly knowen, it could not be to them a rule or meanes wherby they might direct themſelues to the certayne knowledge of the true fayth. 3. It muſt be vniuerſal, that it may not only make vs to know certainly what is the true fayth in ſome points, but abſolutly in all points of fayth. Otherwiſe it were not a ſufficient meanes, wherby we might attayne to an entiere & whole fayth, which abſolutly is neceſſary. 4. It muſt be continual, and neuer interrupted to the end of the world: for euen as fayth, and the Church do alwaies endure and continue, ſo muſt alſo the ground of fayth, ſeeing that nothing can conſiſt without this foundation and ground. 5. It muſt be vnchangeable, for otherwiſe truth would ſomtymes periſh, and there would ariſe ſome errour againſt fayth, ſeeing that nothing can endure and conſiſt, except it haue ſufficient ground and foundation.

The fourth Consideration.

That the Scripture, or expresse written Word alone, cannot be this Rule of Fayth.

THat the expresse written Word alone is not the rule of our fayth, is euident, because it wanteth perpetuall duration and continuance. For it began first vnder the old Law in Moyses time, so that before Moyses for the space of two thousand yeares, there was both true beleuers and a true Church, & yet the writtē Word was not in like mãner in the new Law which the Apostles began to wryte some yeares after they had receaued the holy Ghost. So as it is cleer, that the Christian faith doth not necessarily & wholy depend vpon the Scripture & written Word of God only.

As for the English translated Bibles, they cannot be the only ground and rule of Faith. First, because they are not infallible, for neyther were they written in this language immediatly, neither were the translatours therof assisted by the holy Spirit infallibly: for the ministers themselues confesse, that in their translation they might erre, being men. Sith therfore the translatours as being but men, may erre, how can a simple vnlearned man be infallibly sure that this particular translation which he hath, doth not erre?

Secondly, the English Bibles cannot be the rule of faith because they are obscure and hard to be vnderstood, at least by vnlearned men, who cannot read them: and therefore they can not be a sufficient rule to instruct all men, in all points of fayth. For vnlearned men must needs be saued, but they cannot be saued without an entiere and infallible faith, which they cãnot haue without some rule or meanes meet for their capacity to teach them the same, which rule in no wise can be the English Bibles, seeing they cannot read, much lesse vnderstand the same. Yea the learnedst men cannot by only reading the Scriptures in whatsoeuer language be infallibly sure that they rightly vnderstand them: for whilst they vnderstand one way, perhaps they ought

ought to vnderstood another way: and that which they vnderstand plainly and litterally, ought perhaps to be vnderstood figuratiuely and mystically: and contrary, that which they vnderstand figuratiuely, ought perhaps to be vnderstood playnly and properly. Seeing then, that expositions are diuers, according to the diuers opinions of men, how shall any man be sure, which is the right exposition, hauing nothing to assure him, but his owne sense and reason, which is vncertayne and fallible, and therefore cannot be this rule of fayth, which we seach for.

Thirdly, the English or Scottish Bibles cannot be the Rule of Fayth, because they are not vniuersall, that is to say, able absolutly to resolue all doubts and questions, which either haue bene, are presently, or may herafter come in Controuersy: for there be diuers questions and doubtes moued now a dayes, and those also touching very substantiall matters, which are not expressely set downe, nor determined by only Scripture. For where haue we any Scripture sufficient to proue, that al those, & only those bookes which Catholikes or Puritās hold for Scripture, are indeed Gods Word, & true Scripture? This we shall not find set downe in any part of Scripture. So as it is euident that the English Bibles cannot be the infallible rule of our Faith.

Finally because the ignorant who doe not vnderstand the Greeke and Hebrew, connot discerne infallibly whether the English Bible be well translated or no; yea many Ministers, not being skillfull in the said Greeke & Hebrew languages, cannot be infallibly sure of the English translation.

Some obiect that place of S. Paul, (a) *All Scripture is giuen by inspiration of God, and is proffitable for doctrine, for reproofe, for correction, for instruction in righteousnes, that the man of God may be perfect; throughly furnished vnto all good werkes.* But it proueth nothing for them. Because it sayth not, that the Scripture is alone sufficient to instruct a man to perfection, but that it is profitable for this purpose. For there is a great difference betwixt a thing that is proffitable, and a thing that is fully and only sufficient. For example, Stones and

(a) Tim. 3. v. 16.

Timber

Timber be profitable to the building of a house, yet they are not of thēselues fully & only sufficient to build a house, for the hand of a skilfull workeman to prepare them, and set them together in order, is also required.

The fifth Consideration.

That neyther naturall Wit, nor Learning, or Consequences drawen out of the Word of God, can be the Rule of Fayth.

THat no naturall Wit, or Learning, or necessary Consequences drawen out of the Bible, eyther of one man or of any company of men (only as they are learned men, and not infallibly assisted by the holy Spirit of God) can be this rule of faith, is manifest. Because all their consequences wit, and learning, be they neuer so exquisite and rare, are humane, naturall, and fallible; and therfore cannot be a sufficient foundation, whereupon to build a diuine and infallible Faith; seing it can haue no more certainty, then the wit & learning of man, who proponeth it, which is subiect both to deceaue, and be deceaued; according to the saying of the Apostle, (a) *All men are lyars.* Therefore the beliefe which is only grounded vpon the bare word, consequences, and learning of man, is subiect to falshood, neyther can be a true and Christian Fayth, which alwayes is most certayne and infallible.

(a) *Rom.* 3. *v.* 4.

Besides, this Rule of Fayth must be able to propose to vs infallibly, not only the letters, and sense that seeme true to vs, but the very true sense of Gods Word intended by the holy Ghost, who is the author of this Word. Otherwise it cannot be a sufficient meanes to breed in vs, an infallible Christian Fayth and beliefe, which is only grounded vpon the true sense intended by Almighty God, who is the speaker of this Word. But no man, nor company of men can by their naturall Wit, consequences, and learning tell infallibly what is the true intended sense of Gods Word, For as S. Paul sayth, (b) *Who hath knowen the sense of our Lord?* And Againe: (c) *Those things which are of God, no mā hath knowen but the*

(b) 1. *Cor.* 2. *v.* 16.
(c) 1. *Cor.* 2. *v.* 11.

but the Spirit of God. And therefore that knowledge which the Apostle himselfe had of diuine matters, came not from any naturall wit of man, but (as he playnly affirmeth) from the spirit of God: *God hath reuealed to vs,* (sayth he) *by his Spirit.* Therfore we may well conclude that no one man, nor no one company of men, without the assistance of Gods spirit, can be the rule of fayth, eyther by interpreting Scripture, or by gathering consequences out of the same.

The sixt Consideration.

That the priuate Spirit of euery Minister, is not the Ground or Rule of Fayth.

NO priuate man who persuadeth himselfe to be particularly instructed by the Spirit (as the most part of our inspired Puritans doe) can be this rule of fayth, in so farre forth as he belieueth, or teacheth contrary to the generall doctrine of the Catholike Church. First, because S. Paul (a) *Gal. 1. v. 9.*
sayth: (a) *If any man preach to yow any other Ghospell, then that which yee haue receaued, let him be accursed.*

Secondly, because the rule of Fayth must be infallible, such as this priuat spirit is not. For whosoeuer vaunteth himselfe to haue this Spirit, is not infallibly sure that he hath the same in particular, much lesse can assure others in points of Faith: for it is impossible for him to proue by any passage of Scripture an infallible assurance that he is taught by the holy Spirit, neyther by naturall reason can the same be verified. For albeyt he find in himselfe extraordinary motions, illuminations, feelings, and such like (of which those high spirited Brethren do much boast,) yet neyther by Scripture, nor reason, can he infallibly conclude, that those motions are of God, because the Scripture most plainly affirmeth, (b) *That the diuell doth change himselfe into an Angell of light.* (b) *1. Cor. 11. v. 14.*
Wherfore S. Iohn, as it would seeme, forseeing these spirituall Puritanes, that were to come in these later dayes, forbiddeth vs, (c) *To belieue euery Spirit, but to try the* (c) *Iohn. 4. v. 1.*
Spirits

Spirits whether they be of God or no. Neyther can any man, trying the Spirit by his owne priuate iudgement, or by any inward motions, incontinently affirme, that it is the Spirit of God, because this his tryall is subiect to errour: for our iudgements are easily deceaued, and the diuel can cunningly couer himselfe vnder the shape of a good Angell, & colour his wicked designes vnder pretense of good, (d) *Going about like a roaring lyon seeking whome he may deuoure.* Wherfore the safest way were to try these Spirits by the touchestone of the true Pastours of the Catholike Church, who may say with S. Paul, (e) *We are not ignorant of the cogitations of Sathan.* And who may also say with S. Iohn, (f) *We are of God, he that knoweth God, heareth vs, he that is not of God, doth not heare vs. In this we know the Spirit of truth, and the Spirit of errour.* Now if men will not admit this manner of trying and discerning the Spirit of truth, from the Spirit of errour, but wil trust to their owne iudgement alone in this matter they may be sure that in their thoughts they worship the Angell of darknes, insteed of the Angell of light, which doing will be the cause of their endles damnation.

(d) 1. Pet. 5. v. 8.

(e) 2. Cor. 2. v. 11.

(f) 1 Iohn 4. v. 6.

Thirdly, this priuate Spirit cannot be the rule of faith, because it is variable & vnconstant, & is subiect to errour: first in euery person and company of men in particular; for our Aduersaries themselues confesse that they may erre, & experience teacheth vs, that they oftentymes change their opinions, teaching whyles one thing, whiles another according to their owne fantasie. Secondly, it is manifestly subiect to errour, seeing that all men challenge this Spirit. For if a man were bound to belieue all those that affirme themselus to haue the Spirit, of necessity he would belieue infinite contradictions. For the Lutherans, Caluinists, Brownists, Puritanes and the rest of that holy band, all affirme that they haue this Spirit, notwithstanding the great difference that is betwixt them, shewes that they haue not all the same selfe Spirit. For there is but one holy Spirit, the Spirit of truth, which whilest euery one chalenges to himselfe, he doeth great iniury to the Church of God, to whom the infallible assistance of holy Spirit was promised, and

and not to euery one in particular. Neyther is there any of those new spirited Gospellers that can shew any good reason, why they rather haue the true Spirit, then their neighbours. But suppose one could assure himselfe, that he were taught by Gods Spirit immediatly what is the true fayth in all points, in such sort, that he could erre in none, (as it is not the mãner of God to teach men immediatly by himself alone, or by an Angell, for (g) *fayth cometh by hearing*, & is to be required (h) *at the mouth of the Priests*, and is to be learned of Pastors and Doctours, whome God hath appoynted in his Church, of purpose to instruct vs, and to continue vs in the true fayth:) Suppose I say one could assuredly perswade himselfe to be immediatly taught of God what is the truth in al points, how should he giue assurance to others that he is thus taught, specially when he teacheth contrary to the Catholike Church, which by playne promises and testimonies of Scripture we know to be taught of God? What arguments should he vse against others, that sayes they haue the same Spirit?

(g) *Rom. 10. v. 17.*
(h) *Malac. 2. v. 7.*

It may be he wil alledg that general promise of Scripture (i) *Euery man that seeketh, receaueth*. He will say, that hauing sought earnestly for the true Spirit, he hath infallibly receaued the same. But I answere, that this promise of our Sauiour is to be vnderstood in this manner: Euery mã that seeketh things lawfull to be sought, in due time and place, and according to the pleasure of God, & profitable to their owne saluation, receaueth the same. Otherwise it cometh to passe that, as S. Iames sayth, (k) *They aske and receaue not, because they aske wrongly*. So that to haue sought this Spirit in prayer, is no sure signe to haue obteyned the same, seeing that there is no heretike, but he will affirme, that he hath sought for, yea and therefore obteyned the spirit: albeyt by the contraryeties betwixt him and his brethren it is manifest, that eyther he, or they, or both must be destitute of the true Spirit: For (l) *God is not the author of contention, but of peace*. What assurãce then can we haue that their new Gospellers and Fathers of new opinions haue the true spirit? Forsooth they will giue you a marke, or token as vncertayne, and dif-

(i) *Matth. 7. v. 8.*
(k) *Iames 4. v. 3.*
(l) *1. Cor. 14. v. 13.*

ficile to be known, as the Spirit it selfe. Yee may be assured say they, that they haue the true Spirit, who preach nothing but the pure written word of God, euer still, for euery poynt of doctrine, alledging Scripture. But this their marke cannot be sufficient; for first, insteed of Scripture they bring forth their own translations in many places corrupted, and subiect to errour as translated by men. Secōdly, albeit they did alwayes alledge the true words of Scripture, yet they are not certayne that at all times, & in all points of doctrine they alledge them rightly. For as S. Peter sayth; (m) *The vnlearned & vnstable* (such as most part of our Puritans be) *wrest the Scriptures, to their owne damnation.* And S. Augustine: (n) *A carnall and sensuall mynd turneth all the mysteries and words of holy bookes vnto his owne imaginations and fansies.* Whereupon it cometh to passe, as the same S. Augustin saith, (o) *That all heretikes that admit the authority of Scriptures, seeme to themselues to follow only Scripture, when in the meane tyme they follow their owne errours.* And as they seeme to themselues to follow only the Scriptures, when they follow their owne errours, so they may seeme (specially to simple people, and those who being seduced by them, wholy build their beliefe vpon them) to preach nothing but Scripture, when indeed they preach their owne erroneous opinions, coloured & painted with words of Scripture: for such is the mãner of new vpstart preachers, to confirme their errours with words of Scripture, eyther falsly translated, or els falsly applyed. So the diuell for his purpose falsly applyed the words of the Prophet *Dauid*, against our blessed Sauiour, as S. Matthew testifieth.

(m) 2. Pet. 3. v. 16.

(n) *Aug.* lib. 3. de baptis. cont. Donat. c. 19.

(o) Augu. ep. 222.

Math. 4. v. 6.

Wherefore there is no reason whereby we may be assured that such men haue the Spirit of God: but we may find many reasons to conuince them that they haue not this Spirit; yea the only particularity and priuatnesse of their Spirit is sufficient to mooue to suspect it, & to assure vs that it is not the Spirit of truth. For as S. Augustin sayth: (p) *Whosoeuer he be that challengeth to himselfe priuatly, that which God hath proposed publickly to be enioyed of all, and taketh to himselfe that which is common to all, he is driuen from the common to his own particular*

(p) *Augu.* lib. 12. cōf. c. 25.

particular, that is to say, from verity to falshood and lyes. Seeing then this Spirit is so vncertaine, it is good for all those who desire their owne saluation, to vse the counsell of S. Peter saying, (q) *Yee therfore beloued, seeing yee know these thinges before, beware least yee also being led away with the errour of the wicked, fall from your owne stedfastnesse:* For all those that vaunt themselues of this Spirit, are no other then licentious Libertines, who (r) *Whiles they promise liberty to others, they themselues are the seruants of corruption; for whom it had bene better not to haue known the way of righteousnes, then after they haue known it, to turn from the holy cõmandments, which were deliuered to them.*

(q) 2. Pet. 2. v. 17.

(r) 2. Pet. 2. v. 19.

It may also mooue vs to suspect this Spirit when we see euery one to boast of the same. For as S. Hierome sayth of the Scripture, so may we say of the Spirit, which euery Minister so boasteth of: (s) *This the pratling old wife vaunteth her-selfe to haue, this the doating old man ascribeth to himselfe, this the clattering sophist laboureth to persuade, finally this only Spirit by euery sort is arrogãtly challenged.* Which in our Countrey most euidently appeareth by the first vnordered preachers of this fifth Euangell. Such spirituall inspired brethren were *Paul Mephen* Baker, *William Harlaw* Tailour, *William Aird* Maison, *Iohn Cayrus* skinner. I omit *Iohn Knox* a renegate priest, *William Willoks*, and Mayster *Iohn Craig* Apostata Fryars, who as they were somewhat more learned then the fornamed crafteimen (yet nothing in comparison of the holy Catholike Church, whose belly like venemous vipers they laboured violently to rent in peeces,) so they were also in their assertions and opinions more impudent and shamelesse, (t) *hauing only an outward forme and shape of godlynes, but in their life and doctrine, denying the power and vertue thereof.*

(s) Hier. in Ep. ad Paulinum.

(t) 2. Tim. 3. v. 5.

The seauenth Consideration.

That the Doctrine and teaching of the true Church, is the Rule of Fayth.

Hitherto we haue shewed what is not the Rule of Faith; it remayneth that we shew what is the Rule of of fayth according to the properties required in the sayd Rule. We proue then, that this Rule of Fayth can be no other, then the doctrine, and teaching of the true Church, or company of the true faythfull of Christ. Because if our Sauiour Christ hath promised to any company of men, the presence of himselfe, who it truth it selfe, and the assistance of his holy Spirit, of purpose to instruct and teach them al truth, giuing withall peculiar charge and commission to them to teach all nations, and to preach to euery creature; giuing also warrant to all men that they may safely heare them; giuing also Commaundement, whereby he bindeth all, to do in al things according to their saying; and threatning greatly those who will not heare and belieue them: Then certaynly the doctrine and teaching of those men is in all poynts most true, and such as may well be proposed to all sorts, as an assured ground, wherupon they may safely build an infallible Christian fayth. For looke what our Sauiour Christ hath promised, must needs be performed, & whatsoeuer he warranteth or commaundeth, may safely, and without danger of errour be done, nay of necessity must be done, specially when he threatneth those that will not do it: and consequently if he haue promised to send his holy Spirit, to teach any company of men all truth, it is not to be doubted, but that he sendeth this his holy Spirit, and by him teacheth them all truth: and sith the teaching of this Spirit is infallible, we are not to doubt but that this company is in all points infallibly taught the truth.

If also our Sauiour gaue warrant & commandement, that they should teach vs, & that we should heare thẽ, & do in al things according to their saying: we may not likewise doubt, but that they shalbe able to teach all sorts of men, in all points, the infallible truth; and that all sorts of men may, if they will, learne of that company, what is in all points to be belieued. For otherwise by this generall commandement of hearing them, and doing according to their saying, we should be sometymes bound to heare and belieue an vntruth, and to do that which were not vpright

and

and good, which without blasphemy to Christs verity and goodnesse, can no wise be taught.

But so it is that our Sauiour hath promised, giuen commission, warranted, commanded, and threatned in manner aforesayd: Therfore we cannot doubt but there is a certayne company (the which is called the true Church of Christ, which both is in all points of fayth infallibly taught by the holy spirit, and is likewise to teach all sorts of men in all points of Fayth, what is the infallible truth; and therfore the teaching of this company may well be assigned & proposed to all men, as a sufficient Rule of Fayth, and as a sufficient meanes to instruct all, in all matters of Fayth.

Now, let vs proue euery part of this conclusion out of the written word of God. And first, that our Sauiour promised his owne presence to this company of men, called
the Church of God, is euident by these most playne words: (a) *Math.*
(a) *I am with you* (sayth he) *all dayes, euen to the end of the world.* 28. v. 20.
That he promised the holy Ghost to the same company of
men, is testified thus: (b) *I will aske my Father, and he will giue* (b) *Iohn.*
you another Comforter, the Spirit of truth, that he may remayne 14. v. 16.
with you for euer, he shall teach you all things. And againe: (c) (c) *Iohn* 16
When that Spirit of truth shall teach you all truth. The charge & v. 13.
commission is thus set down: (d) *Going, teach all nations, and* (d) Math.
preach the Gospell to euery creature. The warrãt is in S. Luke: (e) 28. v. 19.
He that heareth you, heareth me. The commaundement is ex- *Mark.* 16.
presse in S. Matthew: (f) *The Scribes and Pharisies sit in Moyses* v. 15. (e) *Luk* 10
seat, whatsoeuer therfore they shall say to you, do you. Out of which v. 16.
words we may gather that we are bound in all points, to (f) *Math.*
do according to the doctrine of the Prelates of the Catho- 23. v. 2.
like Church: yea although it should happen, that their lyues were not laudable, but bad. For although our Sauiour in this place, doth only in expresse words make mention of the chayre of Moyses, in which the Priests of the old Law did sit; yet he is to be vnderstood to speake also of the chayre of S. Peter, in which the Priests of the new Law do succeed. Because we may rather thinke that our Sauiour intended in his doctrine to giue Rules to the Priests and people of his new Law, which was presently to beginne,

and to continue, till the worlds end ; then only to giue documents to those of the old Law , which were shortly to cease. And this to be the true sense of that place , S. Augustin testifyeth: (g) *Into that order of Bishops which is deryued frō* S. Peter *vnto* Anastasius, *who now sitteth vpon the same chaire, although some Traytour had crept in, in those tymes, he should nothing hurt the Church and innocent Christians, for whome our Lord prouiding, sayth, What they say, do , what they do , do not.* The threats that our Sauiour vseth against them that will not heare his Church are these, (h) *He that despiseth you despiseth me.* And agayne : (i) *He that will not heare the Church, account him as an Ethnick and publican.* Finally after he had giuen charge & commission to preach the Gospell , he pronounceth this threat against those that will not belieue : (k) *He that will not belieue , shall be damned.*

(g) *Aug. ep.* 165.

(h) *Luk.* 10. *v.* 16.

(i) *Math.* 18. *v.* 17.

(k) *Mark.* 16. *v.* 16.

By these testimonies it is euident that it appertayneth to the Church to instruct vs in all points of Fayth, and that of it we ought to learne in all matters of Religion, what is the infallible truth; and consequently it is manifest , that the doctrine of this Church is the rule of Fayth. Worthily therfore doth S. Paul call this Church , (l) *The pillar and ground of truth* : For the foundation of any building , hath two offices , one to vphold the building , another to strenghthen it, both which the Apostle attributeth to the Church, when he calleth it , *The pillar and ground of truth.*

(l) 1. *Tim.* 3. *v.* 15.

Therfore I conclude, that neither the writtē Word alone, nor consequences drawen out of the same , nor naturall wit, and learning , nor the priuate Spirit , nor any thinge els, except only the teaching of the true Church of Christ, is the ordinary meanes which God hath prouided, wherby all men may learne that one, infallible, entiere Faith, which is necessary to saluation.

The eight Conſideration.

That this Church, or Company of men muſt alwayes continue.

THat this Church, whoſe doctrine is the rule of our
Fayth, muſt euer continue without interruption to (a) *Math.*
the worlds end, is proued by theſe words: (a) *I will be with* 28. v. 20.
you all dayes, euen till the end of the world. And agayne ſpeaking
of the Church: (b) *The gates of hell shall not preuayle againſt it.* (b) *Matth.*
For how is it true that the gates of hell ſhall not preuayle, 16. v. 18.
if they haue preuayled ſo much, as vtterly to aboliſh the
Church, or at leaſt to baniſh it quite out of the world for (c) *Pſal.* 48
a long ſpace? Of this Church it is ſayd: (c) *God hath eſtablish-* v. 8.
ed it for euer, according as S. Auguſtine expoundeth: & the
Prophet Daniel calleth it, a kingdome (d) *which shall not be* (d) *Daniel.*
broken in peeces, for euer: and S. Luke: (e) *There shalbe no end* (e) *Luk.* 1.
of his kingdome. By which it is manifeſt that the true Church v. 33.
of Chriſt was not only to continue, for foure or fiue hundreth yeares, but for euer vnto the worlds end.

The ninth Conſideration.

That this Church, or Company of men, muſt be Viſible.

THis is proued firſt, becauſe the Church is Chriſts body: but the body of Chriſt was viſible, for the Apo-
ſtle ſpake to viſible men when he ſayd: (a) *Yee are the body of* (a) 1. *Cor.*
Chriſt. Moreouer we are made the body of Chriſt by bap- 12. v. 27.
tiſme and the receauing of our Lords body, as the Apoſtle
teſtifieth. Alſo in this body of Chriſt, there are doctours &
Paſtours vntill the Conſumation of Saintes, vntill we meet
with Chriſt, but ſuch perſons are alſo viſible. The building alſo of the Church is viſible, the conſumatiō of Saints
is viſible, the worke of miniſtry is viſible, which the Apoſtle ſayth ſhall continue vntill the coming of Chriſt.

Secondly, this Church is the Kingdome of Chriſt, but
euery kingdom comprehendeth in it a viſible company of

subiects that obey one king. Hence it is that Ieremy sayth: (b) *Euen as the starres of heauen cannot be numbred, and the sands of the sea measured; so will I multiply the seed of my seruant Dauid, and the Leuits my seruants:* but such and so great a multitude of men cannot be inuisible. In like manner the Prophet Isay describing the sayd kingdome of Christ, and the coueuant of God with it, sayth thus: (c) *I will make a perpetuall league with them, and their seed shall be knowen in all nations, and their of-spring in the midst of people; all that shall see them, shal know them, because this is the seed that God hath blessed.* Where he saith manifestly, that all nations, euen the Infidels, assoone as they shall behold and see the Church, they shall easely know her, by the benefits of God bestowed vpon her. This kingdom also is cōpared to the Sunne & full Moone which are very visible planets, and easy to be seene of all men.

(b) *Ierem.* 33. v. 22.

(c) *Isa.* 61. v. 8.

Thirdly, the Church is a Citty which is scituate vpon high mountayne, which is placed vpon the top of Mountaynes, the which our Lord will strengthen for euer, whereof Christ himselfe sayth: (d) *A Citty placed vpon a Mountayne cannot be hid.* Christ therefore hath made this Church not to hide it, but that it might be cleere & manifest. Wherfore S. Augustin sayth: (e) *What more shall I say, but that they are blind who doe not see so great a Mountayne, who shut their eyes agaynst a candle placed vpon a candlestick.*

(d) Math. 5. v. 14.

(e) *Augu. tom.* 9. *in ep. Ioan tract.* 2.

Fourthly, if the Church were inuisible, in vayne should we say in our beliefe, *I belieue the Catholike*, or vniuersall Church: for if the Church be vniuersal & spread abroad ouer the whole world, she cannot be but very visible as also we shalbe forced to deny another article of our beliefe; to wit, *The Communion of Saints*, vnlesse the sayd Saints be visible & manifest one to another, seeing that this Communiō, as the Apostle saith, consisteth in the continual help, which one mēber maketh to another; but help cannot be made to one that is not visible. Therfore the Church and Communion of Saints must be visible.

Fifthly, our Sauiour hath ordained this Church to be the light of the world, according as he sayth: (f) *Yee are the light of the world:* and to be a rule or meanes wherby all men, at all

(f) Math. 5. v. 14.

all times, may come to the knowledg of that one infallible & entiere fayth, which is necessary to saluation. But how can it be the light of the world, if it be inuisible? How can it be a meanes wherby men shall know the truth, if it cannot be seeene nor knowne? If we say it fayled, we must then also say, that all that tyme men wanted sufficient meanes to attayne to the knowledge of the truth, and so were destitute of the true way to come to their saluation: which if it were true, of necessity it would follow that God should haue permitted men to be destitute of meanes necessary to their saluation, and so suffred them to be damned, contrary to the saying of holy Scripture: (g) *God would haue all men saued, and to come to the knowledge of the truth.* Wherefore to verify that God would haue all men saued, we must needes say that he hath prouided a necessary meanes for all men, by which they may come to the knowledge of true fayth, and therby to saluation: which meanes is a visible Church, of which they must heare & learne the true fayth. Therfore the Church must alwayes be visible.

(g) 1. *Tim.* 2. *v.* 4.

Sixtly, if the vniuersall Church of Christ should for any space be inuisible, it should for that space cease to professe outwardly that fayth, which in hart it did belieue: for if it did outwardly professe, it would haue bene visible; if it did not professe, then hell gates did preuayle against it, contrary to Christs owne promise.

Seauenthly, if the Church were inuisible, we could not fulfill the commandment of Christ, wherin he sayd: (h) *Tell the Church.* For how can we tell the Church any thing, if we know not how, nor where to find it? Neither if by châce we did meet it, could we know it, to be the Church.

(h) *Math.* 18. *v.* 17.

Eightly, it is certayne that once the true Church of Christ was visible, to wit, when it began first in Hierusalem in the Apostles and Disciples of our Sauiour, and in that number, which by their preaching was conuerted to the Christian Fayth. But there can no reason be shewed why it should be visible then, and not euer since.

Ninthly, the chiefe ground and reason why the Puritanes hold the Church to be inuisible is, because they imagine

gine the Church to consist only of the elect, or only of the good: But this ground is false, as appeareth by the name of the Church, in greeke ἐκκλησία, which signifieth, not a company of the elect or chosen, but a company that is called: so that in it are both good and bad, for as our Sauiour sayth: (i) *Many are called but few are chosen*. Therefore the Church is cōpared to a floore wherein wheat and chaffe is mixt: to a mariage feast, to which came good and bad: to a net wherin are gathered all sorts of fish both good and bad: Finally to ten virgins, wherof fiue were foolish, and excluded from the heauenly mariage.

(i) *Matth* 20 v. 16. *Math.* 3. v. 12. *Matth*, 22 v. 10. *Matth*, 13 v. 47. *Matth.* 25. v. 1.

As for testimonies of the Fathers, there is nothing more plainly expressed by them, thē this visibility of the Church. I will only alledge one or two exemples, remitting the curious Reader to search further in the sayd Fathers works. S. Chrysostome sayth (k) *It is more easy that the Sunne should be extinguished, then that the Church should be obscured.* To whome agreeth S. Augustin: (l) *The Church* (sayth he) *being built vpon a Mountayne, cannot be hid.*

(k) *Chrys. in cap.* 8. *Isaiæ.*
(l) *Augu. lib.* 3. *con. ep. Parm.* c. 4.

The tenth Consideration.

How we should discerne and know, which is the visible Church of Christ.

Hitherto I haue shewed that no other thing els is, or can be the Rule of Fayth, but the doctrine of Christs Church, which must continue alwayes, and euer be visible. It resteth that I shew how this true Church shall be discerned and knowen, from false and hereticall companyes, which falsly vsurpe the title & name of the Church; who notwithstanding do in no wise pertayne to the true Church, being only couered with the name of Christians. The way then to find out this Church is first to set downe, which be the certayne markes whereby the true Church is knowen; next to examine, to what company those marks doe agree.

It is therfore to be noted. First, that a true mark cannot

be

be common to many, but must agree only to the thinge whereof it is the marke. Secondly, it must be more euidēt and easy to be knowen, then the thing which it signifieth. Wherfore, when we will assigne some good markes, by which all sorts of men may in some sort discerne which particular company of men is the true Church: we must haue speciall regard to assigne those things which in some manner may be apparent to all sorts of men, since all sorts of men haue need to seeke out, & according to their capacity discerne which is the true Church. We must also assigne those things, which are known to agree to the true Church at this tyme, and to no other company, but that which is the true Church, to the intent, that a man seeing all those things, which be assigned as markes, to agree to any company, he may straightwayes conclude, that company to be the true Church: as on the contrary side, if he perceaue eyther all, or any of them to be wanting in any company, he may be sure, that that company is not the true Church.

The eleuenth Consideration.

That the marks of the Church which the Puritanes giue, are not the true markes of the Church.

THe markes assigned by the Puritanes to discerne and know the true Church, are two. True Fayth or the preaching of the word, and the right vse of the Sacramēts, which are no sufficient marks, by which the true Church may be knowen, but rather are meanes to beguyle the simple, knowing well that they can easily turne all the Sacraments and words of holy Scripture vnto their owne fantasticall, opinions. These I say, are not true marks. For first, by the true Fayth and preaching of the word, they eyther meane true doctrine in some points or els in all. If they meane true doctrine in some points only, it is no good marke: For heretiks teach the truth in some points. Therfore it is not proper only to the Church, and so can be no marke therof. If they meane true doctrine in all points, it is not

not sufficient, because it wanteth the second condition, to wit, it is not easy to be knowne, because it would require a very learned man to examine if that doctrine were true in all points, as also that he were assisted with the infallible assurance of Gods Spirit, least in his examination and tryall of his doctrine he should erre. As for the Sacraments, it is very hard for a man of himselfe to iudge which vse of Sacraments is right, if he be not first taught by the Church. Therfore it is necessary before he know the right vse of the Sacraments, that he know the Church, which is more easy to find out, as being that direct way wherof *Isay*
(a) *Isa.* 35. speaketh: (a) *This shall be to you a direct way, so that euen fooles*
v. 8. *may not erre in it.*

Secondly, their two markes are not sufficient. Because when we seek for the true Church, we seek it principally to the end, that by it, as by necessary and infallible meanes, we may heare and learne of it the true Faith in all points, which otherwise in it selfe is hidden and obscure, accor-
(b) 1. *Cor.* ding to that saying of S. Paul: (b) *The sensuall man doth not per-*
2. *v.* 14. *ceaue those things which are of the Spirit of God.* For sith none by the only power of naturall wit, can obteyne the supernaturall knowledge of diuine mysteries which we belieue by our Fayth, neyther doth the Spirit of God now adayes ordinarily instruct any man in the knowledge of true Fayth immediatly by himselfe, or by an Angell sent from heauen: we must needes if we will haue true Fayth, seek it by that meanes that God hath ordayned: which meanes is no other then the teaching of the true Church, according to
(c) *Rom* S. Paul his saying: (c) *How shall they belieue him whome they haue*
10. *v.* 14. *not heard? How shall they heare without a preacher? How shall they preach vnles they be sent?* Therfore the true Church, which only hath preachers truly sent of God, must first be found out, that by it we may heare and know which is the true Fayth. Therfore this marke of Faith is no wise sufficient to discerne the true Church by, yea rather contrary, the true Church is a marke wherby we may know the true Fayth.

Thirdly, true Fayth is included in the true Church, & as it were inclosed in her belly, as S. Augustine sayth:

(d) *Truth*

(d) *Truth remayneth in the belly of the Church, from which whosoeuer is separate must needs speake false.* Therfore, like as if a man had gold in his belly, we must first find the man, before we can come to see the gold it selfe; so we must first by other markes find out the true Church, which hath the gold of true Fayth hidden in her belly, before we come to see to gold of true Fayth it self; sith specially we cannot see it, vnlesse she open her mouth and deliuer it vnto vs; neyther can we certaynly know it to be true, and not coũterfayte, but by giuing credit to her testimony of it, according to the saying of S. Augustine: (e) *I would not belieue the Ghospell it selfe, except I were moued therto by the authority of the Church.* For if we had not the authority of the Church, how should we be infallibly sure that there were any gospell at all? Or how should we haue knowen that some books are Gospell and others not?

(d) *Aug. in Psal.* 57.

(e) *Augu. lib. con. ep. Fund. c.* 5.

Fourthly, if the true doctrine of Fayth in all particular poynts must be first knowen, as a marke wherby to know the true Church: then (contrary to that which before we proued) the authority of the Church should not be a necessary meanes wherby men must come to the knowledge of the true Fayth. For if before we come to know which is the true Church, we must by other meanes haue knowne which is the true Fayth: what need is there for to find out true Fayth which already we haue, to bring in the authority of the true Church?

Fifthly, if before we giue absolute and full credit to the true Church, we must examine and iudge whether euery particular point of doctrine which it holdeth, be the truth, with authority or liberty to accept only that which we like or which seemeth in our conceyt right and conformable to Scripture, and to reiect whatsoeuer we mislike, or which in our priuate iudgement seemeth not so right and conformable, then we make our selues examiners and iudges ouer the Church, and consequently we preferre our lyking or dislyking, our iudgement of the interpretation and sense of Scriptures, before the iudgement of the Church of God. But it is absurd both in reason and Religion to preferre one priuate

priuate mans iudgement, to the iudgement and sentence of the whole Church of God, which is a company of men for the most part vertuous, wise & learned, & which vndoubtedly hath the holy Spirit to guide them in all truth, not suffering them to erre.

But some man will say, that the Scripture forbiddeth vs to belieue euery Spirit, but to try the Spirits if they be of God, therfore we must examine the Spirit of the Church, by examining in particular the doctrine thereof. I answere, that in that place of Scripture, it is not meant, that it apperteineth to euery man to try all Spirits, but generally the Scripture warneth the Church, not to accept of euery one that boasteth himselfe to haue the Spirit, and willeth those Spirits to be tryed: not that euery simple and vnlearned man should take vpon him to try them, but that those of the Church, to whome it apperteyneth to try Spirits, should do the same, to wit the Doctours & Pastours which God hath placed in his Church, to the end we may not be caried away with euery wind of Doctrine, & that we may not be lyke litle ones, wandring with euery blast of those that boast themselues to be particularly taught by the Spirit. So that this trying of Spirits, is only meant of those Spirits, of which men may well doubt whether they be of God or no, and then this tryall belōgeth to the Pastours of the true Church. But when it is certayne that the Spirit is of God, we neyther need nor ought doubtfully to examine, or presumptuously iudge of it; but submitting obediently the iudgement of our owne sense and reason, we must belieue the teaching of it in euery point. Now we haue sufficiētly proued before out of the writtē word, that the Spirit of the true visible Church is of God: Therfore our only care should be to seeke out those markes by which all men may know, which particular company of men is the true Church of Christ, whose doctrine we neither need, nor lawfully may examine in doubtfull manner, but must obediently and vndoubtedly in all points belieue, as the only assured and infallible truth, which is to be belieued by Christians.

The twelueth Consideration.

That the marks of the Church are foure, to wit, One, Holy, Catholike, *and* Apostolike : *and first of* Vnity.

NOw hauing shewed the properties of a true marke, & token by which the true Church is knowen, from al false and hereticall Congregations ; as also in the precedent consideration hauing proued euidently and clearly, that the markes assigned by Protestants and Puritanes, are not sufficient to discerne the true Church among so many sects and opinions ; It remayneth, that I proue the foure marks assigned by the Catholike Roman Church, to be good and sufficient, and only to apperteyne to the sayd Roman Church, and nowise to any hereticall Congregation.

That there must be manifest markes wherby the true Church must be knowen, the holy Scripture it selfe most manifestly declareth in these wordes : (a) *Their seed shalbe knowen to the nations, and their of-spring in the midst of people : all that shall see them, shall know them, because they are that seed which our Lord hath blessed:* As if he would say, the true Church shall haue such manifest marks, that it shalbe easy for euery one to know it.

The Confession of Fayth of the Hugenots in France art. 5.

The true markes then of the true Church are foure, to wit, *One, Holy, Catholike,* and *Apostolike* : which markes are set downe in the Nicene Creed which the Protestants themselues admitte. And first that the true Church of God must be *One*, the Scripture clearly sheweth : (b) *My Doue is one* : and our Sauiour calleth his Church (c) *One sheepfold* : and S. Paul calleth it, (d) *One body.* This vnity our Sauiour did pray for and vndoubtedly for his reuerence was heard, (e) *Neyther pray I for those alone, but for them also which shall beleeue in me through their word, that they al may be one, as thou Father art in me & I in thee, that they also may be one in vs.* Which request the Scripture sheweth he obteyned when it maketh mention that, (f) *the multitude of them that beleeued, were of one heart, and*

(b) *Cant.* 6. v. 8.
(c) *Iohn.* 10 v 16.
(d) *Rom.* 12. v. 5.
(e) *Iohn.* 17. v. 20.
(f) *Act.* 4. v. 32.

and one soule. This vnity S. Peter recõmendeth to vs saying: (g) *Be yee all of one mynd; hauing compassion one of another.*

(g) 1. Pet. 3. v. 8.

There is a threefold vnity preached in the Church of Christ. First an vnity of all the members with Christ, who is the supreme head of the Church, which is wrought by Fayth; wherevpon it followeth, that the members of the Church so vnited together, must haue only one Fayth, according to the saying of the Apostle: (h) *There is one Lord, one Baptisme, one Fayth.* Secondly, there is an Vnity of the members among themselues, which vnity whosoeuer breaketh is a Schismatike, euẽ as he who breaketh the first vnity is an Heretike. This vnity our Sauiour affirmeth to be a speciall token wherby to know his Church, when he saith: (i) *In this shall all men know that you are my Disciples, if you loue one another.* Thirdly, there is an vnity betwixt the faythfull people and their Pastours by obedience, which whosoeuer breaketh, is also a Schismatike. This vnity the Apostle commandeth to be kept, when he sayth: (k) *Obey your Prelates and be subiect to them.*

(h) Ephes. 4. v. 5.

(i) Iohn 13. v. 35.

(k) Heb. 13. v. 17.

That this vnity is a true marke, is euident, because it hath the two properties of a true marke. First, *It is euident to all men:* For if there be disagreement in doctrine, it is easily perceaued, if there be contentions betwixt the people and their Pastors, it is easily heard of. Secondly, it is proper only to the true Church, because (as Tertullian well obserueth:) (l) *All heresies are found to differ in many things from their first founders; and heretiks among themselues do differ, while euery one taketh vpon him to fashion the Fayth which he rceaued, according to his owne pleasure, euen as the first inuentour thereof did make the same according his fansie.*

(l) Tertul. de praescr.

The thirteenth Consideration.

Of the second Marke of the true Church, which is Holynesse.

THis title is attributed to the Church by S. Paul: (a) *The Church of God is holy, which you are:* & S. Peter calleth the Church

(a) 1. Cor. 3. v. 17.

Church: (b) *A holy nation.* By which it is not meant, that (b) 1. Pet. 2. v. 9.
there are none in this company but those which be holy:
for the Apostle sheweth, that in the same true Church, and
amongst the said company (c) *There is plainly Fornication heard* (c) 1. Cor. 5 v. 1.
of, yea such as the like is not euen among Heathens. Yea therfore the
Church is compared to a *Net*, wherein are gathered both
good and bad fishes; to a *floore* wherein wheat and chaffe
is mixt, to a *field* wherein wheat and darnell groweth, as
in the ninth Consideration before is declared. But this title
of *Holinesse* is giuen properly to the true Church, because this
company which is called the Church is dedicated to God,
and the profession and doctrine thereof withdraweth men
from all vice, and instructeth them in all vertue; and the
holy Sacraments, as conducts of grace, worke in vs true
and inward holynesse.

This marke so confirmed by Scripture, hath the two
propertyes assigned to a true marke; for first there is no man
but he may cleerly see the good workes, holy doctrine,
good lyfe, & miracles of some of Gods seruants. For our Sa-
uiour promised, (d) *That those that belieue, these signes shall follow* (d) Mark. 16. v. 17.
*the͂, in my name they shal cast out diuels, they shal speak with new ton-
gues, they shal take vp serpents, & if they drink any deadly thing, it shal
not hurt them, they shall lay hands on the sicke, and they shall recouer:*
All which are visible signes; and as they were promised
by our Sauiour, so a little after his ascension they were most
faythfully performed by some members of the Church, as
in the Acts of the Apostles manifestly appeareth. Secondly
this marke of holinesse is only proper to the Church of God
(e) *For which Christ gaue himself, that he might sanctify and cleanse* (e) Ephes. 5. v. 26.
*it with the washing of water, by the word, that he might present it
to himselfe a glorious Church, not hauing spot or wrinkle, or any such
thing, but that it should be holy and without blemish.* Whereas the (f) 1. Tim. 3. v. 3.
Apostle calleth Heretiks, (f) *Vnholy louers of pleasures more then
louers of God, hauing a forme of godlynes but denying the power therof.* Which is easy to be seene in the Heretiks of our tyme.

The fourteenth Consideration.

Of the third marke of the Church, which is Catholike, *or* Vniuersall.

THe third marke of the Church is, that it is *Catholike*, or *Vniuersall*, aswell in tyme & place, as in points of doctrine. And first that the Church is vniuersall in tyme, and continueth perpetually, is sufficiently proued out of the Scriptures cited aboue in the eight Consideration. Second-
(a) Psal. 22 ly, that the Church is vniuersall in place, is expresly set
v. 27. downe in the Bible: (a) *All the bounds of the earth shalbe conuer-*
(b) Psal. *ted vnto our Lord.* And agayne: (b) *His dominion shalbe also from*
72. v. 8. *sea to sea, and from the riuer to the ends of the earth.* And our Sa-
(c) Luk. 24 uiour sayth: (c) *That it was needfull that he should suffer and ryse*
v. 46. *agayne from the dead the third day, and that pennance and remission of sinnes should be preached in his name throughout all nations, beginning at Hierusalem.* Thirdly, it is manifest that the true Church is vniuersall, in respect of Doctrine, holding vniuersally in all ages and in all countreys the selfe same points of doctrine (as the Centuries following witnes largely) without interruption or change, which from the
(d) 2. Thes. Apostles partly by word and partly by writing it receaued,
2. v. 14. according to the commaundement of S. Paul: (d) *Hold the traditions which you haue learned eyther by word, or by our Epistle.* Which commaundement S. Augustine declareth to haue
(e) Augu. bene obserued by the Catholike Pastours of the primitiue
lib. 1. con. Church, for thus he sayth: (e) *whatsoeuer they found in the Church*
Iulian. *that they held, whatsoeuer they learned that they taught, whatsoeuer they receaued of their Fathers that they deliuered to vs their children.*

The contrary whereof is verified of all Heretiks, and specially of the Puritanes and Protestants of Scotland, for their Congregation is not vniuersall in tyme, because they
Matth. 13. are new come. For first the true doctrine was plāted, euen
v. 25. as the good seed was sowen in the field, and afterward the darnell, that is false doctrine, was oversowen by the enemy of Gods Church. And S. Paul hauing taught the Ephesians

ſians the true doctrine of Fayth, ſayd, that after his departure, *He knew that rauenous wolues wold enter in among them, not ſparing the flock*; and, *that amongſt themſelues there would aryſe men ſpeaking peruerſe things, that they might lead away diſciples after them.* Neyther is the Proteſtants Congregation vniuerſall in reſpect of place. For it is proper to all heretiks to ſay, Heere is Chriſt, there is Chriſt, that is to ſay, Chriſt is only truly preached in this Countrey of Scotland, or that countrey of England; and therfore our Sauiour fortold vs of them, and commanded vs not to belieue them. For as S Auguſtin ſayth: (f) *Whatſoeuer hereticall company ſitteth in corners* (that is to ſay in a few particuler Prouinces of the World) *is a Concubine, not a Matrone*; that is, ſhe is not the ſpouſe of Chriſt, nor the lawful mother of Gods children. And this vniuerſality is aſſigned by the ſayd S. Auguſtin as a proper token to diſcerne true Chriſtian Religion from hereſy: (g) *For hereſies are not found* (ſayth he) *in many nations, where the Church is* (as in Spayne and Italy,) *but the Church, which is in all places, is found euen in thoſe natiōs where hereſies are* (as in Scotland, England, and Ireland.) Neyther doe the Proteſtants and Puritanes hold vniuerſally one manner and forme of doctrine, chopping and changing, adding and detracting continually ſome thinges perteyning to the ſubſtance of doctrine.

Actes 20. v. 29. *Matth. 24. v. 23.*

(f) *Augu. lib. 4. de Symbol. c. 10.*

(g) *Aug. lib. de vnit. Eccleſ. c. 3.*

This marke hath the two propertyes perteyning to a true marke: firſt it is euident and cleare, euer to be ſeene in the Church of God, becauſe that which is in all places and at all tymes, cannot be hid from the eyes of al men. Secondly, it is only proper to the Church: for hereſies and falſe opiniōs endure only for ſhort tyme, neither are they ſpread through the whole world, but only in particular kingdoms and Prouinces thereof.

The fifteenth Consideration.

Of the fourth Marke, that the true Church is Apostolicall.

THE fourth and last marke is, that the Church of God is Apostolicall. So witnesseth S. Paul: (a) *You are not strangers & forreiners, but cittizẽs of the Saints, & the houshold children of God, built vpon the foundation of the Apostles and Prophets, Iesus-Christ himselfe being the corner stone.* For the Apostles wẽt frõ Citty to Citty planting Churchs & preaching the word of God, as in the Acts of the Apostles is clearly expressed. The which also S. Paul testifieth of himselfe, and by his Epistles written to diuers nations euidently appeareth. As for the Protestants, they are not able to shew of their opiniõ any one Apostolike man, who did perseuere in the doctrine & place of the Apostles: as by the contraryes hereafter following appeareth.

(a) *Ephes.* 2. v. 19.

This marke also is euident and cleare to be seene by the succession of Pastours in Gods Church. For except this continuall succession were, the true Church of God should altogether perish, all honour of God should be ouerthrowen, and no way should remayne for men to know the true and perfect way to their saluation. This marke is only proper to the true Church, for all heresies and new-fangled opinions are forced to acknowledg some particular author and beginner, of whom it did both receaue their first begining, and also the name. So we see Lutherans named from Luther, Caluinists from Caluin &c. For as Vincentius Lyrinensis sayth: (b) *There was neuer any heresy yet arose, but vnder a certayne particular name, in a particular place, & certayne time.* And this is a way to discern the true Church frõ the false. (c) *Wherseouer thou hearest* (sayth S. Hierome) *those that are called Christians not to be named from Iesus-Christ our Lord, but from some particular person, as Marcionists, Valentinians,* (Caluinists, Lutherans) *know thou most certainly, that the Church of Christ is not there, but the Synagogue of Antichrist.*

(b) *Vincẽt Lyrinens. aduers. hæ.*

(c) *Hieron. cont. Lucifer. in fine.*

The

The sixteenth Consideration.

A particular application of the foresayd markes of the Church to the Catholike, Apostolike and Roman Church, and to the Protestants Congregation; and first of the marke Vnity.

IT is most manifest that the Protestants Congregation is not the true Church of Christ, because the true and proper marks aboue rehearsed do in no wise agree vnto it. As by the contrary the Roman Church is proued to be the only true Church, because in it only are to be found the sayd markes. First then it is cleere, that the Protestants Church can in no wise be called *One*, such as the true Church should be. For in the Protestants Church there is no vnity im matters of Fayth, as fully in the first Consideration is declared; it being very hard to find three of them in all points of one mynd and opinion. Neyther haue they any meanes to end their controuersies, and to returne to vnity and continue therein. For while they admit no rule of Fayth, but only the Bible, which euery one according to his fantasie doth expound, not submitting themselues to any one superiour guyded by the holy ghost to the end that all occasion of cōtrouersies & diuision may be taken away: while, I say, they do thus, it is impossible that they should all agree in one Fayth and beliefe.

Contrarywise, the Roman Church is alwayes *One*, neuer changing any poynt of Doctrine, contrary to that which from the beginning it did belieue. Yea if at any time any controuersy cōcerning any point of Doctrine do arise, the same is easily ended, in respect that the Roman Church doth acknowledge one chiefe Pastour, appointed for that end by our Sauiour Christ Iesus, who commaunded all Christians to obey the same Church. This difference therefore may be assigned betwixt the Roman Church, and all heretikes Congregations, that the Roman Church, is (a) *A people ioyned to their Priest, and a flock cleauing to their Pastour, whome whilest it heareth, it is not possible but that it should hold fast the*

(a) *Cyp. lib. 1. epist. 3.*

the vnity of Fayth. Wheras Heretikes are not vnited amongst themselues, but rather contrary one to another, not considering, ([b]) *That in the Church of God there is one Priest* (as S. Cyprian saith) *and one iudge for the time, in Christs steed.*

(b) *Cypriã loco citato.*

The seauenteenth Consideration.

That the Roman Church only, is Holy.

THe second marke to wit of Holynesse, can no wise be applyed to the Protestants Congregation. For first there is no holynesse of life among them: ([a]) The most part of them, by Luthers owne testimony, *being more wicked more reuengefull, more couetous, more vnmercifull, more vnmodest, and vnruly then when they were papists.* As for their Doctrine, it leadeth men wholly to liberty and loosnes of life, commanding men to breake fasting-daies prescribed by the Church, to cast away Confession of sinnes to a Priest, to neglect good workes; teaching that Gods commaundements cannot be kept, that the perfectest worke that a man doth is sinne, that all sins are equall; which blasphemous poynts together with innumerable others, which for breuityes sake I do omit, do mak a man to cast away all care of auoiding sinne and vice, so that we may iudge of the Protestants, conforme to their fruite, according to the saying of our Sauiour: ([b]) *By their fruites yee shall know them, for a good tree bringeth forth good fruit, but a corrupted tree cannot bring forth good fruit.*

(a) Luther *in postilla sup. Euãg. dom. 1. Aduent.*

(b) *Math. 7. v. 16.*

As for the Roman Church, it cannot be denyed, but in it some sinfull folks are mixt with the good, as in the ninth Consideration is aboundantly declared. Yet betwixt the sinfull in the Roman Church, and those among Heretiks, there are two differences. The first is, that there are none among Heretikes which may truely be called *Holy*, from whome, as from the better part, their congregation may be named *Holy*. For albeyt we find some among them who absteyne from sinnes most apparent to the eyes of man, as stealing, swearing, and such lyke, and who do exercise some morall workes, as giuing of almes, liuing temperatly and moderatly &c. Yet those are not sufficient signes of *Holinesse*, because the same, & much more was practised by the heathē Philosophers, and did proceed rather of naturall wit, and learning, then of charity and deuotion, in which true holynesse doth consist: For as S. Paul sayth: (c) *Although a man bestow all his goods to feed the poore, and giue his body to be burned, yet not hauing Charity it should profit him nothing*. Which Charity must proceed (d) *out of a pure heart, and good conscience, & an vnfained Faith*. Which things because they are inward, are very hard to be knowē, except it please God to reueale them by miracle, or some other certayne way to vs. But hertofore it hath not bene heard that *Luther* or *Caluin*, or any of their followers confirmed by miracles their fayned holynesse, but rather it pleased God, by giuing euil successe to their enterprises, to shew that in thē there was no holinesse. Wheras in the Roman Church God hath euer giuen testimony by miracles, of the Fayth and holynesse of diuers Professours thereof, as the Protestants of Scotland must needes confesse of sundry of our holy Kings, as King *Malcolme Kenmor*, Queene *Margaret*, King *William*, King *Dauid*, and of others as *S. Mongo*, *S. Ninian*, *S. Serfe*, *S. Padie*, *S. Columbane*, *S. Baldred*, *S. Patrike*, whose miracles and holynesse of lyfe to this day are with one assent acknowledged in Scoland.

(c) 1. Cor. 13. v. 3.

(d) 1. Tim. 1. v. 5.

The second difference betwixt the bad Catholiks & best Protestants is, that the Protestant Doctrine doth lead the Protestants to all sort of liberty, as is notorious by the grounds of their Religion: wheras the Roman Fayth both expressly forbiddeth all vice, and prescribeth Lawes contrary to liberty and loosnes of life, and conteyneth most soueraygne meanes, to incite and mooue men to all perfect vertue and holynesse of life. So that those which be sinfull in the Roman Church, cannot in any sort ascribe their sins to any defect or want of the doctrine of the Church; but rather to their owne frailty or malice, contrary to the teaching of the Church, and sometymes contrary to their owne conscience and knowledge.

Wherof it followeth, that albeyt there be some sinfull

men in the Roman Church, yet it may well be called *Holy* becauſe the doctrine which it profeſſeth, directeth & leadeth men to all holyneſſe, many of the profeſſours thereof being moſt manifeſtly knowen to haue excelled in piety and good workes, whome God alſo of his infinite bounty hath vouchſafed to declare, by manifold and cleare miracles to haue bene holy.

The eighteenth Conſideration.

That the Roman Church only, is Catholike.

THis Title in no wiſe can be applyed vnto the Proteſtant Congregation, for it is not Catholike, neyther in time, in place, nor in doctrine. Firſt for tyme, it is confeſſed by themſelues that Luther was the firſt preacher therof. Neyther can the Proteſtants ſhew by any good teſtimony, any one man or company, that did profeſſe and belieue in all points thoſe opinions, which ſince Luthers reuolt from the Catholike Church, they haue profeſſed. Secondly for place, it is not vniuerſall, for as before Luther and Caluin the Proteſtant Religion was not, ſo now preſently there is no kingdome or nation that maketh wholly profeſſion of Proteſtancy. Not England, wherein there are diuers Puritans, many of the Family of Loue, many Atheiſts, and of no Religion. Not Scotland, wherein likewiſe there be many Puritans, yea many of the Biſhops are Puritans in their hart, and likewyſe many Atheiſts. Thirdly, for doctrine, it is not vniuerſall, because their whole doctrine conſiſteth of negatiues, in denying diuers points which haue beene generally belieued in all former ages, as Purgatory praying to Saints, and ſuch lyke: for which cauſe the Puritanes thinke the Proteſtant Paſtours to be Antichriſtian Miniſters, by reaſon that Antichriſt ſhall conteyne in his name *666.* which number is wholly conteyned in the word ἀρνοῦμαι, I deny: the Proteſtants Religion not being any other thing then a heap of denials.

Whereas on the contrairy ſide, the Roman Church may

may only take vnto it selfe as proper & peculiar, the name of Catholike, both in tyme and place, it hauing been first planted and preached by the Apostles through the whole world, & so still visibly vntill these our dayes hath endured, and shall to the end of the world continue. And also hauing euer in all places, where there be any Christians, some visible professours of the same. As also it is vniuersall in doctrine, teaching in all points the selfe same doctrine which by lineall succession of Pastours it hath receaued from Christ and his Apostles. Wherefore let the Protestants who affirme that Christs Church hath erred, let them I say, shew in what age, vnder what Pope, by what way, with what violence and force, with what increase did a strange Religion ouerflow Rome, and the whole world? What speaches or rumors there were? What tumultes and troubles, what lamentations did such a nouelty breed? Was all the rest of the world asleepe, when Rome, the head seat of the Empire, and mother Citty of Christians did forge and make vp new Sacraments, a new sacrifice, a new doctrine of Fayth and Religion? Was there no history-writer neyther Latin nor Greeke, neyther far nor neer, who would, if not playnly, yet at least obscurely mak some mention in writing of such a notable euent, as this should haue beene, if it had fallen out? We find mutations of kingdomes, deaths of Princes, changing of Lawes, alterations of Commonwelthes, and the very least introductions of any new thing faythfully to haue beene obserued, and committed to writing by those who at that tyme lyued: But as for this mutation of Religion in the Romā Church, which the Protestants so maliciously obiect to couer only the newfandglednes of their yesterday-Religion, I find no mention therof at all: I find no history writer of England, Scotland, France, or any other kingdome, who euer did make mention before Luther, of Protestants or Protestant Religion, or of any one man who before Luther made profession of such a Religion.

The ninteenth Consideration.

That the Roman Church only, is Apostolike.

THe fourth and last marke of the true Church is, that it should be *Apostolike*, which marke cannot be found in the Protestant Congregation, but by the contrary they shew euidently, that they are not Apostolike, when as they are forced to acknowledg some other beginner and Father of their Fayth then Christ and his Apostles, to wit, Luther and Caluin, whome they in no wise can proue to haue succeeded lawfully to Christ and his Apostles; neither to haue bene sent to teach this new doctrine by any lawfull Bishop or Pastor of Christs Church. Which Luther himselfe not only confesseth, but braggeth thereof: (a) *We dare glory and bragge in this* (sayth he) *that Christ was first published by vs.* And Melancthon speaking of his maister Luther, sayth: (b) *God by him restored the Gospell vnto vs.* For which bragging and bosting it may be sayd of him, as Optatus sayd of Victor the first Bishop of the Donatists; (c) *That he was a sonne without a Father, a disciple without a maister.*

(a) *Luther in epist. ad Argent. tom. 7.*
(b) Melāct *præf. in tom. 12. Lutheri.*
(c) *Optat. cōt. Parm.*

As for the Roman Church, there is and euer hath bene in it a continuall succession of Bishops without interruption, since the tyme of the Apostles, as hereafter I shall set down and proue, which succession as a most forcible argument the holy Fathers vsed against all heretiks. So Irenæus: (d) *By shewing the tradition from the Apostles, & the Faith coming to vs by succession of Bishops, we confound all them who any way through euill flattering of themselues, or vainglory, or through peruerse opinion do collect otherwise then they ought.* And S. Augustin: (e) *The succession of Priests from the very seat of Peter the Apostle, to whome our Lord commended his sheep to be fed, vntill this present Bishop, doth hold me in the Catholike Church.* Wherefore we may say to the Protestants, that which S. Augustine sayd to the Donatists: (f) *Number the Priests from the seat it selfe of Peter, and behold in that order of Fathers who they were that succeeded to others.* And with

(d) *Iræn. 3. cap. 3*
(e) *Aug. cont. ep. Fundam. cap. 4.*
(f) *Augu. in Psal. cōt. part. Don.*

with Irenæus: (g) *By this orderly succession of Bishops, the tradition of Apostles hath come to vs, and it is a most full demonstration that the Fayth which from the Apostles is confirmed euen till now, is one and the same.* (g) *Iræn. lib. 3. c. 3.*

It is euident then by the examination of the foure marks aboue written, that the Roman Church is the only true Church of Christ, whose doctrine is the infallibly rule of Christian Fayth; and the Protestants Congregation is nothing els but a company without a head, whose opinions consist in denying the doctrine professed by the Church of Christ, without interruption this sixteene hundred yeares.

The twentith Consideration.

That out of the Roman Catholike Church there is no participation of the merits of the Passion, and precious Bloud of Christ Iesus, and consequently no Saluation.

SVndry of the most learned Protestants considering with themselues without passion, the holynes, antiquity, succession, vnity of fayth, miracles, and the infinite multitude of most holy and famous persons, of Kings, Princes, & others of all sorts, who haue liued and dyed in the Catholike and Roman Church, auow constantly, that the Roman Catholikes may worke assuredly their saluation, remayning Papists & Catholikes. So writeth D. Couell: (a) *We gladly acknowledg thē of Rome to be of the family of Iesus Christ &c.* The same auoweth M. Hooker saying: (b) *The Church of Rome is of the family of Iesus-Christ, a part of the house of God, a lymme of the visible Church of Christ.* The same sayth D. Barrow: (c) *The learned writers acknowledge the Church of Rome to be the Church of God.* The same affirmeth George Cassander: (d) *The Church of Rome is to be reuerenced, as being the true Church and temple of God.* In lyke sort M. Moreton a prime Protestant affirmeth: (e) *That Papists are to be accompted the Church of God, because they do hold the foundation of the Ghospell, which is Fayth in Christ Iesus, sonne of God and Sauiour of the world.* Finally

(a) *In his defence of M. Hooker pag. 68.*
(b) *In his Ecclesiasticall Policy lib. 3. sect. 1. p. 130.*
(c) *In his foure Sermons and two questions, ser. 3.*
(d) *Lib de officio pij viri pag. 14.*
(e) *In his*

treatise of the Kingdome of Israel, and of the Church p 94.

(f) *In his late treatise to the Archbishop of Canterb.*

ly D. Couell affirmeth in playne termes: (f) *That those that lyue and dye in the Church of Rome are saued.* Yet notwithstanding this constant doctrine of the most learned Protestãts, the Parliamentary Protestants of Scotland, England and Ireland persecute the Catholikes euen to death, not for any zeale of their owne Religion, but rather to take hold of the goods, landes and possessions of the poore Catholikes. The most learned sort then of the Protestants auow constantly, that the Papists and the Catholikes remayning constant in their owne Religion shall be saued.

Now it resteth to shew that there is no saluation out of this Catholike and Roman Church, as witnesseth the word of God by the Prophets Ioel and Isaias: (g) *In Mount Sion, and in Ierusalem shalbe saluation* (which word, *Saluation*, the Ministers in their corrupted Bibles haue taken away) *as our Lord hath sayd, and in the residue whome our Lord shall cal.* (h) *The nation and kingdome that shall not serue thee, shall perish.* For the which cause, the Church of God is called, *the City of refuge, the sanctuary of God, the spirituall seed,* and *of-spring of Abraham, the Father of the faithfull, the spouse of God*, out of which whosoeuer eateth the Paschall Lãbe, *is a prophane person, and stranger from the merits of Christ.* The Church lykewyse is called the Arke of *Noe*; out of the which there was nothing but death and perdition, saith Gaudentius, whose words are: (i) *It is manifest that all men of those tymes perished, excepting only such as deserued to be found within the Arke, bearing a type or figure of the Church: for in lyke manner they cannot be saued who are separated from the Apostolike fayth & Catholike Church.* Lykewise the Church of God is called the *body of Christ*, to signify that no man can enioy the benefit of lyfe and saluation, vnles he be a member of this mysticall body So S. Augustine: (k) *The Catholike Church only is the body of Christ, whereof he is head: out of this body the holy Ghost quikneth noman &c. Therfore he that will haue the holy Ghost, let him beware he remayne not out of the Church; let him beware he enter not faynedly into it.* And agayne: (l) *To saluation it selfe, and to eternall lyfe no man arriueth, but he that hath Christ his head But no man can haue Christ his head, vnles he be in his body, which is the Church.* Conforme

(h) *Ioel* 2. *v.* 32.

(h) *Isa.* 60 *v.* 12.

(i) *Tract.* 2. *de lect. Euang.*

(k) *Aug. epist.* 50. *ad Bonif. prope finẽ*

(l) *De vnitat. Eccles. c.* 16.

forme to this doctrine of S. Augustine the Church is called *the Mother of the faythfull*, because none can receaue lyfe except he be conceaued in her wombe: which gaue occasion to ancient S. Cyprian to say: (m) *No man can haue God for his Father, vnles he haue the Church for his Mother.* Which sentence hath bene famous amongst all the auncient Fathers vntill this our age. The Church is called *the kingdome of Christ*: out of which whosoeuer be, are rebels and traytours to God. True it is, that sundry heretikes Protestants and Puritanes may lead a good morall lyfe to the eye of man, giue some almes to the poore, be ciuill in conuersation, read the Bible, haue the Sacrament of Baptisme, sing the Psalmes, yet being out of the Church, there is no saluatiō for them saith S. Augustin: (n) *Out of the Catholike Church a man may haue all things except saluation, he may haue orders, he may haue Sacramēts, he may sing* Alleluia, *he may answere* Amen, *he may haue the Gospell, he may haue and preach the fayth in the name of the Father, and of the Sonne, and of the holy Ghost, but he can by no meanes obteyne saluation, but in the Catholike Church.* Which doctrine of S. Augustin, hath euer bene in the Church of God an essentiall point of Religion, yea as an infallible doctrine it was auowed, sworne and subscribed to by the three Estates of Scotland: (o) *Out of the which Kirke there is neyther lyfe nor eternall felicity, and therfore we vtterly abhorre the blasphemy of thē who affirme, that men who lyue according to equity and iustice shall be saued, what Religion that euer they haue professed.* The Generall Councell of Lateran auerreth the same to be a poynt of saluation: (p) *There is one vniuersall Church of the faythfull, out of the which no man is saued.* The reason of this doctrine is, the secret will of God, who did send his sonne Christ Iesus into the world to erect and build one Church, one Fayth, one Religion, one chosen company, which he hath purchased with his precious blood; for the which he delyuered himselue to sanctify her with the lauer of water. In this only Church he hath appointed Apostles, Prophets, and Doctours to the end of the world: to this only Church he giueth his Spirit, promiseth his assistance, imparteth his grace and spirituall gifts: wherfore whosoeuer is deuided, or separa-

(m) *De simplic. Prael.*

(n) *Tom. 7. conc. ad plebem de Emerita. post med.*

(o) *In the Parlament holden at Edēburgh anno 1560.*

(p) *Conc. Later. cā. 1.*

parated from this Church, is wholly bereft of Gods celestiall comfort, as witnesseth the Ministers of Scotland themselues in playne termes: (q) *No man can receaue forgiuenes of his sinnes vntill he be ioined in the fellowship of Gods people & Church, and so continue in the vnity of Christs body euer to the end, lyke a trew member of his Church.* Wherefore I conclude, that whosoeuer liueth and dyeth out of the Catholike Church, not hauing any vse of the Sacraments thereof, of the true word of God preached therein, of the good workes and prayers proceding from the members thereof, cannot iustly hope for any saluation, yea rather maketh himselfe guilty of eternall Damnation.

(q) *In the articles of Fayth. 16. Sonday.*

The twentith one Consideration.

That euery man cannot be saued, of whatsoeuer Religion he make profession.

THere be many Libertines in Scotland, England, and Ireland, & elswhere who do thinke foolishly that euery man may be saued in any kind of Religion: which opinion as it is most false and erroneous, so is it most foolish and dangerous, bringing a man thereby to acknowledge no Religion at all, which is the way & path to Atheisme. The reason wherfore this opinion is most erroneous and false is, because in euery act of Fayth, we must not only regard what we doe belieue, but also (and that principally) vpon what ground and motiue we belieue it, or what is the reason of our beliefe. For of what kind the motiue, or reason of our beliefe is, of the same kynd is our Fayth, beliefe, & Religion. So that if the ground, motiue, or reason (called *Ratio formalis Fidei*) wherfore we beleeue any thing, be most certayne and infallible, our Fayth lykewise is certayne and infallible: if it be vncertayne, our Fayth also is vncertayne, fallible and subiect to errour, and consequently not a *diuine*, but a *humane Fayth*. As for example: The Turke beleeueth, that there is one God, Creator of all things, because he is so taught by his *Alcoran*, which he thin-

thinketh (being persuaded by the inward Spirit, sayth he) to be written by the Spirit of God. But his fayth (albeyt he belieue that which is true) relyeth, and is grounded vpon a deceitfull reason and motiue, that is, vpon his *Alcoran* or false Bible, by the force whereof he is moued to belieue many false and blasphemous things, as, That there are not three persons in the Blessed Trinity, that Christ is inferiour to Mahomet, & many such: wherfore that fayth of his by reason of the foundation and motiue is deceitful and erroneous, leading a man to eternall damnation. Euen so the Protestants belieue: (a) *That Christ his soule was put in the graue*: (b) *That Christ feared the paynes of hell*; and many such heads of Religion, because they find (say they) those heads of Religion in the Bible translated by their owne Ministers, whome they must auow to haue erred in the translation thereof, and consequently must needes auow not to be the infallible word of God. For asmuch then as this their fayth relyeth vpon a deceitfull ground and motiue, that is, vpon their corrupted Bible, not vpon an infallible and sure ground, it cannot be diuine but humane Fayth. Hence I inferre this argument. That Fayth which relyeth vpon a false foundation and ground (albeyt it belieue somethings which are true) cannot be sufficient to saluation or diuine Fayth. But the Fayth and Religion of sundry sectes and heresies of other ages, and of this our corrupted age relyeth vpon a false foundation. *Ergo*, they cannot be sufficient to saluation.

(a) *Act* 2. v. 27.

(b *Heb.* 5. v. 7.

As for example. The yeare of our Lord two hundreth, there were certaine Heretikes called *Symmachians* who belieued the blessed Trinity, the true Messias, receaued the Scripture, and the Bible as the word of God, exponing it alwayes according to their owne fansie and priuat Spirit, but because they denyed or misbeleeued the day of the vniuersall iudgement, they were condemned as Heretykes by the Church of God. Because the ground and motiue of their Religion was not in effect the *Word of God*, but the word of God interpreted according to their owne fansie & & Imagination. Likewise the *Valesians*, *Nouatians*, *Angeliques*, *Apo-*

Epiphanius lib. de mens. & pond.

Apostoliques receaued the Scripture as the word of God, exponing the same according to their owne fansie, to proue therby their heresies and errours; yet because the ground & lastresolution of their Religiō was not in the true word of God, but rather in their owne fansie and imagination, against the consent of the vniuersall Church, they were condemned by the auncient Fathers, as Heretikes & members of the Diuell. Euen so it is with our Protestants, who belieue not the word of God, as it is precisely the word of God, but as it is viciously translated by the Ministers, and as it is erroneously explicated conforme to their owne fansie, and against the consent of the vniuersall Church of God, which hath bene these sixteene hūdreth yeares; which doctrine I will mak more manifest by this argument. *Those who belieue many heads of Religion which are not conteyned in the expresse word of God, and misbelieue other heads of Religion, which are conteyned in the expresse word of God; are not grounded in their beliefe vpon the only expresse word of God, or are not moued to belieue or misbelieue by the authority of the expresse word of God only, as it is manifest: But thus belieue the Ministers of Scotland and England.* Ergo. I proue the *Minor*. The Ministers belieue. 1. That there be only two Sacraments. 2. That the supper of the Lord should be receaued with kneeling. 3. That the best worke a man can do, conteineth deadly sinne. 4. That children may be saued without Baptisme &c. Which are no wise cōteyned in the expresse word of God: yet they misbelieue these heads of the Catholik Religiō. 1. (c) *This is my body which is giuen for you.* 2. (d) *He that sayth I know him and keepeth not his commaundments, is a lyar, and the truth is not in him.* 3. (e) *Yee see then how that through workes a man is iustified, & not by Fayth only.* And many such sentences which are conteyned in the expresse words of the Bible. *Ergo,* the Ministers are not moued to belieue or misbelieue by reasō of the authority of the expresse word of God only, (otherwise they would belieue all alyke) but because they are so persuaded in their conscience to belieue the one, and misbelieue the other, and in a word, because it pleaseth them to belieue the one, and not the other.

(c) Matth. 26. v. 26.
(d) 1. Iohn. 2. v. 3.
(e) Iames 2. v. 24.

Of

Of the which doctrine I inferre. First that the last resolution of the Protestant Religion is in one of these two grounds; first they belieue this or that to be a poynt of fayth because they find it(say they)in their corrupted Bible(thogh they shall neuer be able to proue any debatable poynt out of the expresse word of the Bible) belieuing neuerthelesse many other things which are not conteyned expressely in their owne corrupted Bible, but it cannot be a sincere faith which is groũded vpon such a corrupted Bible. 2. They belieue this or that head of Religion, not because it is conteyned in the word of God expressely, otherwise they would belieue all therin conteyned alyke, but because it pleaseth them to expone the expresse word of God to their fansie, and iudgement, which they call *the inward persuasion of the holy Ghost*; the which is the last *Rendeuous*, and resolution of the Protestants Religion, as the Hugenots in France witnesse plainly in their confession of Fayth: (f) *Nous cognoissons ces liures estre Canoniques, & regle de nostre foy, non pas tant par le commun accord, & consentement de l'Eglise, que par le tesmoignage & persuasion interieur du S. Esprit, qui nous les fait discerner d'auec les autres liures Ecclesiastiques.* That is: *we acknowledg these books to be Canonicall and the rule of our Fayth, not in regard of the common agreement and consent of the Kirke, but rather in regard of the testimony and persuasion of the holy Ghost, who maketh vs to discerne these from other Ecclesiasticall books.* The same teach the Ministers of our Iland in their articles of Fayth, where the Minister asketh: (g) *M. How must we vse this Word, to haue this profit by it? C. We must receaue it being perfectly persuaded thereof in our conscience, as of an vndoubted truth sent downe from heauen.* Wherfore if yee aske of a Minister why he belieueth the prophesy of Ieremy to be Canonicall, and the bookes of the Machabees not to be? he must needs answere at last after much idle talke: *Because the inward persuasion of the holy Ghost doth thus persuade me, though the common consent of the vniuersall Church be against me.* If yee aske of a Minister why doth he interpret and translate those plaine wordes of the Bible: (h) *Thou shalt not leaue my soule in hell*, contrary to the Church of God, and all the holy Fathers? he will answere at last, if yee vrge him

(f) *In the confession of Fayth of the Hugenots in France. artic. 4.*

(g) *In the articles of Fayth set down in the Scots Catechisme. 45. Sunday.*

(h) *Act. 2. v. 27.*

him, *because the inward persuasion of the Spirit doth thus persuade him.* What is this I pray yow, but abhominable & manifest heresy, the selfe same fashion which all heretikes euer vsed, and in a word the doctrine of the deuills, preached vnder the pretext of the word of God, by the Ministers, of whom S. Paul fortold: (i) *In the last dayes there shall some depart from the Fayth, attending to the Spirit of errour, and doctrine of deuills.*

(i) 1. Tim. 4. v. 1.

Secondly I inferre, that though the Protestants agree in some poynts of Religion with vs Catholikes, yet their fayth is not diuine and infallible, but rather humane, fallible and diuerse from ours, euen as the Donatists heretykes, sayth S. Augustine, beleeued one God with the Catholikes, belieued in the same Christ, they had the same Gospell, song the lyke psalmes &c. yet because they erred in one, they erred in all; (k) *In those* (sayth S. Augustin) *they are with me, and yet not altogether with me, in schisme not with me, in heresy not with me, in many things with me, in a few not with me, by reason of those few wherby they were not with me, the many could not help them, in which they were with me.* The which few things wherein the Donatists dissented from the Catholikes were some vnwritten Traditions, sayth the same S. Augustine: (l) *This neyther you, nor I do read in expresse words &c.* Yet because the Church of God beleeuing those vnwritten traditions, & the Donatists refusing to beleeue the same, they were condemned as heretikes, as witnesseth the same holy Father: (m) *Although no example of this mater be found in holy Scriptures, yet do we follow in this the truth of the Scriptures, when we do that which is agreable to the vniuersall Church, commended vnto vs by the authority of the same Scriptures.* And againe: (n) *The Apostles haue commanded nothing concerning this matter: But the custome which was alledged agaynst S. Cyprian is to be thought to haue descended from their tradition, as diuers other things haue done, which the vniuersall Church doth obserue, and are therfore with great reason belieued to haue bene commanded by the Apostles, although they be not written.* The reason of this is, because the true Fayth must needes be one and the same, in all the faythfull; for truth is one, vniforme and constant: falsity and errour is various, discordant, and changeable; and the reason wherfore

(k) Aug. in explic. psal. 54.

(l) De vnitat. Eccles. c. 19.

(m) Lib. 1. cont. Crescon. c. 33.

(n) Lib. 2. de Bapt. cont. Don. & lib. 5. c. 24.

fore Fayth must be full and entiere, is the infallible authority of God, vpon whose testimony we belieue, which authority being once suspected or doubted of in any poynt of Religion, be it neuer of so small importance, the like doubt and suspition may creep into others, & consequently shake the foundation of Christian Religion. Wherby it is euidēt, that the Ministers belieuing some articles of faith according to their fansie, and not belieuing others, belieue not at all, as wisely disputeth Tertullian agaynst Valentine the heretike, saying: (o) *Some things of the Law and Prophets* Valentine *approueth, some things he disalloweth, that is, he disalloweth all, whilest he disproueth some.* And S. Athanasius: (p) *Whosoeuer doth not hold the Catholike Fayth whole and inuolate, he shall perish for euer.* The same auoweth S. Hierome: (q) *That for one word or two contrary to the Fayth, many heresies haue bene cast out of the Church.* The same S. Gregory: (r) *Nothing can be more dangerous then those Heretikes, who when as they runne through all things vprightly, yet with one word, as with a drop of poyson, corrupt and stayne the true and sincere Fayth of our Lord, and of Apostolicall tradition.* S. Basil: (s) *Such as are instructed in the diuine doctrine, do not suffer any sillable of the diuine decrees to be depraued, but for the defence thereof, if need require, willingly imbrace any kind of death.* Truly if one word, one sillable may make a man to loose the true Fayth, much more one errour and deprauation in the Scottish Bible, may take away from it the authority of the word of God.

(o) *De praescript.*
(p) *Atha. in simbolo.*
(q) *Lib. 3. de Apolog. cont. Ruf.*
(r) *Greg. Nazianz. tract. de fide.*
(s) *Apud Theodoret. lib. 4. hist. c. 17.*

Finally it is not inough for a Catholike to belieue al the heads of the Catholike Fayth, but he must also communicate and ioyne in the vse of Sacraments, together with the Catholiks. Therfore though some indifferent and worldly men belieue all things which the true Church belieueth, fearing to professe outwardly that inward beliefe for worldly respectes: Yet as long as they separate themselues from outward communion of the Catholike Church; that very separation & that dissention alone is sufficient to cast them headlong into euerlasting fyre: (t) *For he that doeth not gather with me, scattereth; he that is not with me, is agaynst me*, sayth Christ. Wherby it appeareth first, how much they are deceaued

(t) *Math. 12. v. 30.*

ceaued who thinke it to be sufficient to saluation, to belieue the common principles and heads of our Religion conteyned in the Creed, not submitting themselues to belieue all and whatsoeuer the holy Church belieueth. 2. It appeareth lykewise how foolishly the Protestants flatter themselues, crying out agaynst vs Catholikes for want of charity, because we condemne (say they) so many morall and good men of other Religions then of ours, such men being in conuersation modest, blameles in their lyues, zealous in praier, almes, hospitality, and many other vertuous works. Whereunto I answere, that it is no want of charity in vs to speake the truth without dissimulatiõ in a matter of so great importance, whereupon relyeth eternall saluation, but rather an euident token of perfect charity, in forwarning the Protestants of the perill of damnation wherein they are: following in that the holy exãple of S. Paul, who without

(u) 1. Cor. 6. v. 9. flatterie wrot vnto the Corinthiãs: (u) *Do not erre: Neyther fornicatours, nor seruers of Idolls, nor adulterers, nor the effeminate &c. shall possesse the kingdome of God.* So the Catholikes, zealous of Gods honour, & saluation of soules purchased with the blood of Christ, doe charitably, in forwarning the Protestants of their dangerous estate in the sight of God; notwithstanding the outward morall lyfe, modest carriage, prayers and almes deeds, which will auayle them nothing to the gaining of heauẽ, being out of the Catholik Church.

(x) Augu. lib. 4. con. Donat. c. 8 S. Augustine sayth: (x) *Let vs suppose a man to be chast, continẽt, not couetous, not seruing Idols, ministring hospitality to the needy, enemy to none, sober, frugall, but yet an Heretike: truly no man maketh doubt, but for this alone that he is an heretike, he shall not possesse the kingdome of God.* And all those be heretikes who with contumacy and pertinacy manteyne their peruerse opinions against the Church of God, which hath bene this sixteene hundreth yeares: yea those Protestants who wilfully follow the heresies of others, who slouthfully deferre to imbrace the true Religion, who fearfully put of to accept the same whẽ it is sufficiently proposed vnto them, all those in the sight of God be manifest heretikes, & belieue not in the true God, the true Messias, but forge vnto themselues theſelues another God, another Meſſias. Now, (y) *Whoſoeuer imagineth God ſuch as God is not, he caryeth euery where another God, a falſe God in his mind*, ſayth S. Auguſtine. (y) *Aug. q. 29. ſup. Ioſue.*

True it is, that there are many amongſt the Proteſtants who haue no fit occaſion to be inſtructed in the Catholike Religion, yea who neuer hauing heard any thing at all of it, thinke that there is no other Religion except the Puritanes and Proteſtants, leade lykewiſe to the eye of men a good morall lyfe: All thoſe I confeſſe are not ſo guilty before God, of the crime of hereſie, as the Miniſters, as ſundry Noble and Gentlemen be, who know in their conſcience the Catholike Religion to be the only Religion, yet for feare of the world, of neceſſity, and perſecution, remayne ſtill in the eſtate of perditiō. Neuertheles thoſe ſimple ones are in a very hard caſe, by reaſon that falling into deadly ſins eyther by thought, word, or deed, they haue not the meanes of the holy Sacraments (which are only in the true Church) wherby they may ryſe from that damnable eſtate. Beſides that, the very grounds of the Proteſtant Religion, to wit, *That a man continually tranſgreſſeth the commaundements of God; Man hath not freewill to worke his ſaluation; There is no merit of good workes; Fayth only is neceſſary to ſaluation*, and ſuch like: Theſe damnable grounds (I ſay) often beaten in the eares of the ſimple people, make them careleſſe to withſtand tentation, to ouercome ſinne, to do good workes, to be ſory for their ſinnes committed, and conſequently make them to be without excuſe in the ſight of God.

Happy be they then, who hauing heard of the Catholike Fayth, are carefull in ſearching and finding it out: Happy are they who hauing found it, do ſincerely imbrace and intierly belieue it: happy are they who doe communicate in outward profeſſion and participation of the Sacraments, with the members of the Catholike Church: happy are they who by the often vſe of the Sacraments doe renew their life in ſanctification and holineſſe, and that conſtantly, till they heare thoſe bleſſed words: (z) *Come yee bleſſed of my Father, take inheritance of the Kingdome prepared for you, from the beginning of the world.* (z) *Mat. 25. v. 34.*

The

The twentith two Consideration.

What disposition is requisite to him, who by reading the foresayd Considerations, should imbrace the Catholike, Apostolike, and Roman Religion.

BEsides the forsayd Considerations, which are sufficiẽt to mooue any wise man to imbrace the Catholike, Astolike, Roman Religiõ, we haue many others, as in al ages & kingdoms innumerable visible professours, innumerable learned and wise, men; yea of our Scottish Nation we haue had as many holy, wise and valiant Kings as any externe Nation, and more in number then diuers other Nations, as *S. Malcolme* called *Kenmor*, and *S. Margaret* Queen, *S. Dauid* King, *Constantin* the Martyr, *S. William* King, King *Malcolme* the Virgin, *Conuallus* King, *S. Vdelina* Queen, *S. Mathilda* Queen, *S. Richarda* Empresse, Blessed *Queen Marie* the Martyr our Soueraigne King Iames the sixt his mother, *S. Alexander*, S. *Colomannus* patron of Austria in Germany, *S. Mungo*, S. *Fridelinus*, S. *Edmũdus*, S. *Fiacre*, S. *Syra*, S. *Romualdus* Martyr, S. *Drõstan*, *S. Oda*, S. *Maxentia*, S. *Florentine*, S. *Clarus* & sundry others, famous to this day amongst forrayne nations, & acknowledged to haue descended of the Royall bloud of Scotland, being all Papists, and Roman Catholikes, whose holy conuersation & lyfe I am to set out, God willing in my *Menalogy of the Saints of Scotland*. We haue had in like mãner millions of most cõstant Martirs, who moued only with the Loue of God alone, haue contemned al temporall things, riches, liberty, yea life it selfe; liuing innocently, and shedding their blood constantly for defence of the Catholike Religion. We haue had innumerable holy Confessours and Virgins, who in vertue of our Religion haue made great mutation in their liues, in changing frõ an imperfect degree of vertue to the very top of perfection: and who in proofe of their Religion haue wrought many miracles. Which motiues to our Religion cannot with any colour of truth, be pretended by the Protestants and Puritanes

tanes, who can not proue one debatable poynt of Religion by the expresse word of the Bible. 2. Who cannot improue, no not one poynt of the Catholike Religion by the expresse word. 3. Who cannot name any man, who before Caluin was of their Religiō. 4. Who cannot name any nation which maketh accompt of the Bible now presently vsed in Scotland, Latin or Scottish, as of the word of God. 5. Who cannot shew any monument, as Churches, Chappells, or such, builded by any of their Religion, before the cōming of Iohn Caluin the Sophist. 6. Who cannot name any king in Christendome to haue bene of their Religion, before the coming of Caluin and Luther.

Notwithstanding all these most weighty and forcible Considerations, sundry Protestants through the liberty of their Freewil, and specially through want of pious affection to imbrace the truth, for worldly respects, or fleshly liberty, doe not suffer their minds to consider earnestly (as the importance of the matter requireth) these forsayd motiues, doe not permit their will to make election of the true and sincere Religion, and that by reason of a preiudicate erroneous conceit, which is setled in their mind, with pride and obstinacy, which is common to all Heretikes; to which end the Ministers without any conscience intertayne the people with preiudicate and preocupied opinions, yea blasphemies agaynst the Catholike Religion: as that the Catholikes adore Images, put all their trust in their good workes, pray to stocks and stones, and such blasphemies which were tedious to me to rehearse. The other Impediment which hindreth men to imbrace the true Religion, notwithstādīg the foresayd Considerations, is a spirituall slouth, carelesnes, and neglect of heauenly thinges necessary to our saluation. This impediment is remarkable in many Protestants, specially in those who are giuen to honours, pleasures, and commodities of this world, who hauing little feeling of any Religion, no apprehension of things to come, of Gods Iudgments, of death, of the eternall paynes of hell, of the losse of that eternall blisse, haue chiefly fleshly pleasures, worldly honours, or both in mind

(a) *Iohn.* 5. *v.* 44. and hart, of whome our Sauiour foretold: (a) *How can yow beleiue, who do receaue glory one from another, and doe not seeke the glory which is from God alone?* And S. Paul: (b) *The fleshly man perceaueth not the things of the Spirit of God, for they are foolishnes to him.* (c) *Such men,* sayth the Apostle, *are without all feare, feeding themselues, they are lyke wandring starres to whome is reserued the darknes for euer.* If yow talke with such men of matters of Religion, yow shall see them turne all the places of the Scripture, yea can cite to their owne fansie, humor, and bad disposition, not making any accompt of the exposition of the holy Fathers, of generall Councels, nor of the whole body of the Catholike Church: which is no new forme of dealing amongst heretikes, since it was vsed by the Donatists, as wisely remarketh S. Augustine: (d) *The Donatists* (sayth he) *conuerted all the mysteries, and words of the holy books of the Scripture, vnto the images of those their fansies, which hauing done, they seemed to themselues to follow the very Scriptures, when indeed they followed their owne errours.* Doe not the Protestants and Puritanes the same in explicating the Bible to their owne imagination and fansie?

(b) 1. *Cor.* 2. *v.* 14.

(c) *Iude v.* 12. 13.

(d) *Lib.* 3. *cont. Donatist. cap.* 1. *& epi.* 222.

He then who desyreth to saue his soule eternally, to enioy the blessings of heauen eternally, to see God, and the Saints of heauen eternally, must needes set aside all worldly Consideration, in seeking out the true Religion, set aside passion and obstinacy which are infallible tokens of a diuellish Spirit; and desyre to seeke out, search, and diligently to inquire the true Religion, *with humility of will and docility of vnderstandinge*, which are opposite to obstinacy and pryde, the very rootes and grounds of all heresie. This humility in hart is one of the greatest dispositions to find out the true Religion, as witnesseth the Prophet who sayth: (e) *To whome shall I haue respect, but to the poore litle one, and the contrite of Spirit, and to him that trembleth at my words.* And our Sauiour Christ Iesus: (f) *Learne of me, because I am meeke & hüble in hart* Yea the want of this humility only is the cause that many do not find out the true Religion, because, (g) *God doeth withstand the proude, and lofty mynded, and giueth his grace and fauour to the humble in mind.* Docility of vnderstanding

(e) *Isa.* 66. *v.* 2.

(f) *Matth.* 11. *v.* 29.

(g) *Iam.* 4. *v.* 6.

derstanding is likewise requisite, wherby a man yieldeth willingly to reason without further obstinacy, setting aside contention of idle wordes, which alwayes doe accompany heresy, and is a worke of the flesh, sayth S. Paul: (h) *The works of the flesh are manifest &c. wrath, contentions, seditions, heresies.* Finally frequent prayer made to God, with a humble mind, & earnest affection to find out the true Religion is a most fit and necessary meanes to obtayne the same; for true Religion is a special gift of God, which is giuen by instant and feruent prayer.

The three & twentith Consideration.

Certayne Notes and Animaduersions, which the wise and learned Protestant, is to obserue, in seeking out the true Religion.

FIrst of all, yow are to apprehend this mater of Religion as a point of great moment and importance, and wherupon dependeth eternall felicity, and consequently yow should not read Controuersie-books eyther for curiosity, as many doe, or negligently and to passe your time only, nor with the Spirit of contradiction (which is familiar to the Protestants and Puritans) to find out faultes, and quarrell without iust occasion, the Catholikes sayings: But rather yow should read sincerely and in conscience making God himselfe the iudge of your reading, proposing for end only to find out the true Religion, the true fayth and profession for the sauing of your soules: for by this meanes you shall, as it were, oblige God to giue you light and assistance to discerne the true Religion from the false; which to obteyne you haue great need to be hūble in mind, deuout in praier, and indifferent to imbrace the truth only, to pray to God often, saying with the Prophet Dauid: *O Lord teach me to fulfill thy will, because thou art my God.*

2. When yow beginne to read any controuersy, endeauour first to apprehend well the true state of the Question, not belieuing one side only, but rather searching out what euery syde, Catholik & Protestant holdeth therin, & in this

poynt, besids many others, yow shall find amongst the Protestant-writers great fraud and deceit vsed, by reason that they propone the questions not sincerely as we Catholikes do hold and belieue them, but as they would haue the Reader vnderstand them to their owne aduantage. As for example: The Protestants propose that question thus, *Whether a man may be saued by workes without grace?* Which is easy for the Protestants to impugne, by reason that it is false. But the true state of the question, and as the Catholikes do belieue it, is this: *Whether by good workes that proceed from the grace of God, and true Fayth, a Christian may be saued?* And so in all the rest, yow shall find great fraud amongst the Protestant-writers in proposing the true state of the question, as yow shal see specially in *M. Perkins* book called, *The reformed Catholike*, who almost neuer doth propose the true state of the question: which deceitfull proceedings *Iohn Fox* also vseth in the booke of his Actes and Monuments printed at London anno 1596. Where in his preamble to the same pag. 22. setting downe differences in doctrine betwixt the Catholik & Protestant Church, is conuinced to haue made aboue an hundreth & twẽty lyes, in lesse then three leaues.

3. When yow haue found the true state of the Question, yow must be very carefull to hold the same continually in your mynd, considering attentiuely whether the discourse which yow shall read in your Author be to the purpose, & doe leuell right at the marke or no, or runne aside to impertinent matters, as often yow shall find the Protestants to doe; and specially *D. Whitaker* in his controuersies, who doeth fill vp leaues with many wordes, but to little purpose, playing alwayes the Oratour, but not the Deuine & Doctour. In lyke manner yow shall find many Protestant-writers in these our dayes who slip asyde, and will dryue yow into many by-matters to confound your iudgment and memory, weary your patience, and therby make all your reading vnprofitable: and thus yow shall find in those Protestant-writers, who haue more words then wit, passion then learning, deceit then truth.

4. Yow must remark diligently how that the Protestãt

writers

writers doe promise nothing but *Scripture*, nothing but *the pure word of God, the expresse words of the Bible*; yet in effect yee shall find that they giue for Scripture, their owne inuentions, for the word of God, their owne expositions, & for the true text of the Bible, a most corrupted and falsified translation, as yow will see in the booke followinge. Moreouer you must remarke, that when the Protestants doe cite Scripture, and their owne corrupted Bible, you must consider I say, how that place cited by them was vnderstood and interpreted by auncient Fathers, of whome the Protestants themselues make great accompt, and who were many hundreth yeares before those our controuersies did aryse. As for example: We Catholikes doe alledge for proofe of *purging fire* after this lyfe, those words of S. Paul: (a) *He shalbe saued, but so as by fire*, as S. Augustin in sundry places of his workes witnesseth, and before him Origen, and after him S. Gregory, and sundry others. The Protestants agaynst *Purgatory*, alledge vpon their side the saying of Salomon: (b) *Where the tree falleth, there it lyeth*. No man shall find that this place was euer alledged in this sense by any auncient Father, which is so certayne and infallible, that the Protestants in citing the Scripture for their heresies & opinions, cannot possibly name not only one auncient Father who hath interpreted those places of the Scripture as they doe; which sheweth the Protestãts to be manifest Heretikes in explicating the Scripture agaynst the streame and multitude of all the learned holy men, who were frõ Christ to Luther his time, and since.

(k) 1. Cor. 3.

(b) Ecclesi. 11.

5. As for the holy Fathers themselues, when they are alledged, it is to be considered in what age they wrote, and whether that which they say was euer found to be contradicted by other Fathers of that age, or after them. For whẽ no contradiction is found (though any Fathers sentence doth not make a matter fully *de fide*, or of necessity vnder payne of sinne, or heresie to be absolutly belieued,) it is a weighty and infallible proofe, that the thing which the Father affirmeth, was so belieued by the whole Church of God, in his dayes, and consequently it were great temerity

y not to belieue the same. As for example, S. Augustins [ex]plication of the foresayd place, *he shall be saued, but so as by [fi]re*, in proofe of Purgatory, was neuer contradicted by a[n]y Father of his age, yea or before or after him, which is an infallible marke that the fayth of the Catholike Church cōcerning Purgatory was then vniuersally in vse, and before S. Augustine, yea and after him. And forasmuch as that Church and Religion which was in S. Augustines tyme, was, and is acknowledged by all to haue bene the true Catholike Church, it must needs be presumed to haue held nothing generally, which the Catholike knowne Church of the precedent age before S. Augustine did not also belieue and teach, and so from one age to another, vpward and downward may this demonstration be made, which ought to be a great motiue to any discreet and vnpassionate Reader. Whereof the contrary is manifest in sundry expositions of the Scripture by Origen, Tertullian, and such, whose partiall and erroneous expositions were contradicted by those of their tyme, and after them.

6. Yow must needes in lyke manner remarke the double dealing of the Protestants in writing and preaching: by reason that in generall, and publickly they will say and protest the holy and auncient Fathers to be of their Religion, of their Faith, and profession, to the end that they may bleare the eyes of the ignorant. But if any Catholike cite for him any manifest place in particular of any auncient Father, as of S. Augustine for Purgatory, & praying to Saints in heauen, S. Ambrose for the Reall Presence, and sacrifice of the Masse, and such like; then yow shall see the Ministers answere that the holy Fathers were men, might erre, and lye, deceaue and be deceaued; as if the Ministers were not men, yea lying and erroneous men, since *they can doe no good, say they, but continually, do transgresse Gods commaundments*, teaching alway two seuerall sorts of doctrine, one in publicke the other in particular. In lyke manner when the holy Fathers are brought agaynst their damnable opinions, they will answere euer with shift and guyle, *that there is no comparison betwixt the Fathers and the Scripture*; *that*

they

they should not be believed except they bring Scripture with them. But if the Catholike aske Scripture of the Minister, and the expresse word of the Bible for his opinions, the Minister being guilty, and certayne that he cannot proue any debatable poynt of his Religion by the expresse word, nor yet impugne any of our Religion, will giue yow, insteed of the expresse word of the Bible, his consequences and deductions, that is, his owne expositions, explications, superstitious damnable heresies, and doctrines of the deuill, which he giueth and preacheth to the ignorant people, as if they were the word of God. After the same manner, if the Ministers alledge any places out of any auncient Father, sounding to the fauour of any poynt of their Religion, if yow demand of them, whether they will stand absolutly to such a Fathers doctrine and determination in that, and all other controuersies which he handleth, they will refuse it assuredly. But we not, if it be a matter not censured by any other Father, or by the holy Church at that tyme. As for example, when the Ministers do alledge S. Augustine agaynst *Freewill,* if yow aske them whether they will stand absolutly to S. Augustines iudgment in this poynt, and in all other poynts of controuersy betwixt vs and them, as *Purgatory, Prayer to Saints, prayer for the dead &c.* they dare in no wise accept thereof: But we Catholikes haue no difficulty to admit S. Augustin concerning all controuersed points. Finally if yow cite playne and manifest sentences of the Fathers agaynst Protestants, they will answere that they speake figuratiuely. Thus *M. Andrew Ramsey* being asked of me, then in prison in *Edenburgh*, whether S. Augustine had not in his workes, sundry prayers directed to the Saints in heauen? he answered as a playne Atheist, That *S. Augustine* prayed *per prosopopeiam.* Could any Turke or Iew answere more Sophistically or Atheistically?

7. By reason that the Controuersies be so many and the discourse so large vpon euery Controuersy, and the shifts so innumerable, it will be impossible for yow, to quyet and settle your iudgement by only reading of diuers books. And though it were possible for yow, yet it could

not

not be possible for thousands of others who cannot read, nor haue the commodity of books: for which cause you must haue a more sure and infallible rule, to find out the true Religion, then reading; which is, *the Resolution* of the vniuersall Christian Church in euery age concerning matters of Religion. This is the only sure, short, and infallible way, to find out the true Religion: which way S. Augustin teacheth and setteth down plentifully, in his booke against *Cresconius* the heretike saying: (c) *Quisquis falli metuit huius obscuritate Quæstionis, Ecclesiam de ea consulat* That is; *Whosoeuer feareth to be deceaued by the obscurity of this Question let him go, and aske the Church thereof*. And this same infallible way our Sauiour commaunded vs to follow, when we are in doubt of any poynt of Religion, saying: *Tell the Church of it: He that will not heare the Church, let him be to thee as a heathen and publican.* For the which cause S. Augustin sayd wisely: (d) *I truly would not belieue the Ghospell, except the authority of the Church did induce me therto.* To which testimony of S. Augustin, I might ioyne the testimonyes of the holy Fathers, who with one consent doe appoint, as an infallible rule to find out the true Religion, to try and search diligently, *which is the true Church*. For, *Seeing the Controuersies of Religion* (sayth a Protestant in our tyme) *are growen in number so many, and in nature so intricate, that few haue tyme and leasure, fewer strength of vnderstanding to examine them; what remayneth for men desirous of satisfaction in things of such consequence, but diligently to search out which among all the societies of men in the world, is that blessed company of holy ones, that houshould of Fayth, that spouse of Christ, & Church of the liuing God, which is the pillar & ground of truth; that so they may imbrace her communion, follow her directions, and rest in her iudgement, and consequently ioyne themselues to that happy company of the triumphing Church in heauen.* I wish from my hart that my deare countrymen in Scotland, England and Ireland would yield to this Protestant-writers counsell, in seeking out the true Church of God. To which end I haue set downe these foresayd Considerations to the glory of the blessed Trinity, the proffit of the Protestants and Puritans, and the comfort of the Roman Catholikes.

(c) *Lib. cont. Crescon. c. 33.*

(d) *Cont. Epist. Manich. c. 3.*

(e) *M. Field in his Epistle dedicatory.*

The

The foure and twentith Consideration.

The Conclusion of this first Part, or Introduction.

HAuing set down at length the infallible meanes wherby we may find out the true Religion, Church, and Profession: hauing lykewise proued the true markes of the true Church, and those to be only proper to the Catholike and Roman Church, and consequently hauing proued that for the space of fifteene hundreth yeares the Protestants and Puritanes had no Church at all, no Religion, no Fayth, no outward profession knowen to God, or the world, yea no professours of their Religion except two, to wit, *Nullus* and *Nemo*, that is to say in truth, *none at all*: It followeth then of necessity, that the Protestants Religion before the comming of Caluin & Luther was nothing els, but a plain Platonicall or Poeticall Chymera, that is a meere imaginary fiction inuented by seditious Puritanes, to change the Politicall State (vnder the pretext of a reformed Religion) of Scotland, England and Ireland, that thereby they might more freely inuade the lands and possessions of Catholikes, take to their own vses the rents and temporall goods of the Church liuings, ouerthrow the auncient Nobility of those three auncient kingdomes, casting down their houses, banishing them from their natiue Countrey, imprisoning their persons, and vsing all sort of barbarity, which the furyes of hell could inuent, against them.

Now it followeth to set down in these sixteen following Ages or Cēturies, first the names of the chiefe Pastors in euery Centurie, as being the principall members of the visible Church. 2. The names of the Kings of Scotland (the same is easy to be done of the Emperours, of the Kings of Frāce, England, Ireland, Spayne, Poland, Denmarke, Sweden, and other Princes, all Catholiks, who did raygne in all Christendom before the coming of Luther & Caluin) who happily haue raygned & professed the Catholike Religion to this our Age & Century. 3. To set downe the doctrine,

Fayth, and Religion of the most holy, famous, and learned Fathers, who were in euery age and Century, vsing the very words of those holy Fathers with all fidelity, that thereby the Catholike Reader may see manifestly, that the Catholike and Romane Religion (for the which we are now persecuted by the Protestants and Puritanes in Scotland, England, and Ireland) is the selfe same Religion which was professed by the holy Apostles, & which from them hath visibly without any interruption continued frō age to age to these our dayes. To which end I haue made choyce of twenty fyue articles of the Catholike Religion, which, (as the chiefest of all the rest) I proue first by Scripture and good Reason, called *probatio de iure*. Then, by the consequences & doctrine of the holy Fathers of euery age, called *probatio de facto*. Thirdly, I set downe the places of the Bible concerning those articles, falsified by the Ministers of Scotland and England. Finally, I shew, cleerly in my opinion, that the Protestants and Puritanes haue neyther for thē the expresse word of the Bible, nor the plaine text therof, eyther to proue any debatable point of their Religiō, or to improue any of ours; nor any groūd in the Scripture, nor antiquity, nor succession, nor vnion, nor meanes to manteine the same; and finally that their Religion is nothing els but a meere inuention of the Ministers.

Now, I challenge the Protestants, if they can, to deuise & set downe a catalogue sufficient to confront this of mine. I challenge them to set down the Professors of their Relgion in euery age, as I doe the Professours of our Catholike, and Roman Religion; to set down their very words, and & plaine sentences faithfully: which they not being able to do, are obliged in conscience (if they haue any conscience) to auow plainly the truth in so weighty a poynt; that is, That they are childrē without Fathers, & schollers without Maisters; That they are the first professours of this new deformed Religion, & that they cannot name any professour of their Religion in all essential points, before Luther and Caluin, the former two alwaies excepted, *Nullus* and *Nemo*.

A deuout Prayer, to conforme our selues to the Will of God.

GRaunt me, O most mercifull God, feruently to desire such things as may be most acceptable & pleasing vnto thy diuine Maiesty, with wisdome to search after them, not to be deceaued in the knowledg of them, & vnfaynedly to accomplish the performing of the same, to the prayse & glory of thy holy Name. Direct so my life, and graunt, I humbly beseech thee, that I may haue both knowledge, wil & power, to do that which thou requirest, & wouldest haue me to do, & in such manner, as is most behoofull, and expedient for my soule. *Ex Diuo Thoma Aquinat. & aliis.*

Graunt me, O Lord God, vnderstanding to know thee, wisdome to find thee, conuersation to please thee, perseuerance to expect thee; & finally through hope to imbrace thee, and through thy Grace to enioy the benefits of this transitory life, and in the world to come, be made partaker of the reward and heauenly ioy, through the precious bloud of that immaculate Lambe our only Sauiour Iesus-Christ; to whom with the Father and the holy Ghost, three persons & one God, be all honour & glory, world without end. Amen.

Another Prayer.

OMnipotent, & most benigne, and mercifull Father, I most humbly beseech thee, that it may please thy diuine Maiesty to visit with thy Fatherly affection, all such as are any way fallen, or departed from the pure Catholik & Apostolike Church, or haue doubt in any article of the Faith & doctrine therof, or be seduced & deceaued through any false persuasion; & to illuminate their harts & vnderstanding, with the beames of thy diuine light. Stay them O Lord, and bring them backe to acknowledge their errour, that being truly conuerted, and vnited to the Catholike Church, they may confesse with mouth, and shew in workes, one true Catholike & Christian Fayth; and by remayning in it, worke their owne saluation; that so both we and they, being of one mind & wil, & dwelling togeather in one fould, may heare & follow thee O Lord, our true sheepheard, through the merits of thy precious bloud & passion. Who liuest & raygnest world without end. Amen.

A Prayer for the imbracing of the true, Catholike, and Roman Fayth.

OMnipotent, & most mercifull God, wheras without true Fayth no man can be saued, or please thee, but comming vnto thee (as the Apostle sayth) he must belieue; I most humbly beseech thee to giue vnto me the true, right, & Catholike Fayth, which is not stayned with any spot of peruersenesse, nor inuolued in any errour, but in euery part pure and sincere.

Ex S. Dionysio & alijs.

Graunt O Lord, that I may follow & imbrace that Faith only, which the holy, Catholike & Roman Church doth teach & professe; she being the pillar & firmamēt of Verity, & so guided & grounded by thy holy Spirit, that in Faith and doctrine she cannot erre.

Giue me Grace, O Lord, that whatsoeuer shalbe conforme, & consonant to this orthodoxe & Catholike Faith, I may imbrace, and approue the same; & detest & abhorre what shall be contrary therunto: that al my works, words, & deeds may be answerable to this Fayth, least by my bad life & example, I may seeme to deny thee, whome with a true & sincere Fayth I confesse.

Increase, O most mercifull Father, and so confirme this true Fayth in me, that neither man, nor diuell may be euer able to take the same away from me: but that both in word & worke, I may alwayes professe, & confesse the same; yea and if need be, to seale this truth with the sheeding of my bloud, and death it selfe, in testimony therof. Confirme O Lord God, this my will & desire, through Christ Iesus thy only Sonne, & our Iudge, who liueth and raygneth, with thee and the holy Ghost, in perfect Trinity, world without end. Amen.

The end of the first Part.

THE GROVND OF THE CATHOLIKE AND ROMAN RELIGION IN THE WORD *OF GOD.*

With the Antiquity and Continuance therof, throughout all Kingdomes and Ages.

COLLECTED

Out of diuers Conferences, Discourses, and Disputes, which M. *Patricke Anderson* of the Society of IESVS, had at seuerall tymes, with sundry Bishops and Ministers of Scotland, at his last imprisonment in *Edenburgh*, for the Catholike Faith, in the yeares of our Lord 1620. and 1621.

Sent vnto an Honourable Personage, by the Compyler, and Prisoner himselfe.

The second Part, & first Century.

Philip. 1. *Vers.* 12. & 13.

And I will haue you know, Brethren, that the thinges about me, are come to the more furtherance of the Ghospell: so that my bandes were made manifest in all the Court &c.

Permissu Superiorum, Anno M. DC. XXIII.

TO THE

RIGHT VVORTHY STVDENTS

Of the foure famous Vniuersities of Scotland, S. Andrewes, Glasco, Aberdine, and Edenburgh.

ARISTOTLE that famous Philosopher in penning his morall Philosophy thought all his labours wel imployed if he could proffit any one therby: how happy then may *M. P. Anderson* thinke his labours imployed, the tyme of his hard and rude impersonmēt in Edenburgh spent in Disputes, & Conferences with the Ministers, hauing wonne therby sundry to the light of the true Ghospell, to the loue and feare of God, from whence the hope of all Eternity dependeth? And as you are the Fountaines of which many must drinke, the seeds from whence many must proceed, the lightes of the Kingdome, and the Mynes, whose treasure of learning is to be deriued to the whole body of the Kingdome of Scotland: So are there opened vnto you in this second Part those veines of gold, cōteyned in the expresse Word of God, and in the testimonies *Lib. 1. Eth. c. 1.*

of the holy Fathers, and Writers of the first hundreth yeares after Christ; which Testimonies I will intreate you to peruse with an indifferent and single eye, with a great zeale of imbracing Truth frõ the mouth of Christ, and from those Honorable, Learned, and holy Fathers of the first age, *Quorum testimonia sunt omni exceptione maiora.*

Truly, if yee would heare none but those, in whose bosomes yee haue been bred, and consequently to be so farre enamoured of your Ministers doctrine, without any ground in the expresse Word of God, or al Antiquity; the more yee should be blamed, that being amongst all Nations held of witty & quicke Iudgment, fit for all sort of Sciences, yet yee would willingly, & wittingly preferre the counterfeit drosse of the Ministers, before the true & perfect Mettal of the holy Word, and testimonies of all antiquity. Or can you but imagin, that men of such life and conuersation, as your Ministers be, could find out any holsome doctrine, (a) *Qua tot latuerit Sanctos, tot praterierit sapientes?*

(a) *Bern. Ep.* 190.

S. Augustine remarketh, that (b) *Faustus Manichaus* and the ancient Heretiques of his sect, in their preaching and discourses promised nothing more thẽ Truth, Truth, the word of God, the Scripture, the Bible: yet he found, as he witnesseth no truth amõgst them, yea nothĩg but lies, vanities, and new inuented superstitions.

(b) *Lib.* 5. *Confess. c.* 2

The same shall you discerne in the Ministers of our tyme: for although they bragge, and boast of the pure Word of God, the Bible, the written Word; yet in effect they cannot shew, no not one debatable point of their Religion to be cõteyned in the expresse Word of God. 2. They cãnot possible improue any point of the Catholike Religion out of the same expresse Word. 3. They cannot name

name any Nation vnder the heauens, which auoweth their Scots Bible to be the Word of God. 4. They cannot name any forraine Doctour, or Doctours, who doe free their owne Scots Bible from falsifications, lyes, and errours. Finally, (c) *By the Word of the law they impugne the law, framing their priuate sense and construction to countenãce the peruersity of their mynds, by the authority of the law:* making by their peruerse Interpretation, (d) *The Ghospell of Christ, the Ghospell of man, or which is worse, the Ghospell of the Diuell.*

(c) *Amb. in c. 3. Ep. ad Titum.*
(d) *Hier. l. 1 in c. 1. Ep. ad Galat.*

They boast of the pure preaching of the Word of God, yet in effect they haue no Cõmission, no Authority to preach, no Vocation at all, but are (e) *Theues who enter not by the dore, but climbe another way, to steale, kill, and destroy* your soules. They are the false Prophets who cry, (f) *Thus sayth the Lord, when the Lord said it not, nor sent them.* They glory to haue reformed the Church of God; wheras you shall easily perceaue how miserable, and deformed Scotland is become by their reformed Religion: and their owne formes and fashions do witnes the same plentifullie, as a famous, yea a Protestant-Writer called *Zanchius* doth testify thus of them: (g) *We Protestants of the reformed Church* (sayth he) *often of set purpose ouercloud the state of the question with darknes; things which are manifest we impudẽtly deny; things false without shame we auouch; things plainly impious we propose as the first principles of Faith; things orthodoxall we condemne of heresy; Scriptures at our owne pleasure we detorte to our owne dreames; we boast of Fathers whom we will follow nothing less then their doctrine; to deceaue, to calumniate, to raile is familiar with vs &c.*

(e) *Ioa. 10. v. 2. 10.*
(f) *Ezech. 13. v. 3. 6. 7.*
(g) *Ep. ad Ioan. Sturmi. Habetur in fine l. 7. & 8. Miscellan.*

O yee flourishing Academians, O Scotland my dearest Countrey, consider wisely, & in the presence of God, I beseech thee, how thou hast damned vp the passage, by which the cleere waters of al antiquity ſhould flow vnto thy kingdome, and thou haſt opened the ſluſe to the Puddels of the Miniſters new doctrine, new fayned Sacraments, new Articles of faith, new Bible, and Scripture vnknowne as yet to all other Kingdoms, and Nations: Conſider, I ſay, how God therefore hath puniſhed thee, yea now of late with extraordinary Indigency; and abandon theſe new, and vnwonted doctrines, and imbrace againe that ancient Faith which once thy Noble, Ancient, and Princly Kingdome, Daughter of God, deuoutly ſucked from the breaſts of the Apoſtles, which all thy former Kings, and Princes, from King *Donald* the firſt, vntil Bleſſed Queen Mary, conſtantly profeſſed, thy Lawes eſtabliſhed, thy People honoured, thy Vniuerſities defẽded. To this end I will not ceaſe to ſacrifice vnto God my continuall prayers, and reſt alwaies,

Your moſt humble Seruant.

P. A. S. I.

To the Christian Reader.

BECAVSE the visible successiõn of lawfull Pastours, and the perpetuall pedegree of zealous belieuers is an infallible marke of Christs chosen Church, I haue heere presented to thy view: First the supreme Heads and Gouernours of the Roman Church. 2. The chiefe professours, yea of our own Nation of Scotland, by which it hath been taught & cõtinued. 3. I shew the pedegree of the Kings of Scotland, all Roman Catholikes, from Donald the first vntill B. Queene Mary the Martyr, our Gracious soueraygne his Mother, few other Mothers in our age being worthy of such a Sonne, few other Sonnes worthy of such a Mother. 4. I prooue by the Scripture twentyfoure substantiall points of our Catholike fayth the rest being easily deduced out of those, & the Churches authority, which I prooue at length. 5. I chalenge the Ministers to improue any of those 24. articles, and to be contrary to the expresse word of the Bible, which they shall neuer be able to do. 6. I challeng them likewise to proue any one point of their Religion, as set downe in the expresse word of their own Bible, which being impossible for them to do, I force them to auow that they preach not the Bible, not the expresse word, not the Scripture, but their owne fancies, yea old rotten & condemned heresies, which they call their consequences drawne out of the Bible. 7. I set downe those same 24. substantiall points of our Catholike Religion proued by the holy Fathers of the first hundred yeares, putting downe most faithfully their owne words, sayings, & consequences drawne out of the expresse word of the Bible; being a thing so notorious, that a man who hath any reason, iudgmẽt, or vnderstanding, any feeling of God, or care of his conscience, should willingly prefer the consequences of these holy, wise, learned & ancient Fathers before the stinking puddle of cõsequences of the Ministers, who are children without Fathers, & preachers without commission, or any warrant in the word of God 8. I shew how the ministers haue falsified the Bible in all those places which make for vs Catholiks against thẽ. Finally & last of all, I proue that the Church of God in this & the other ensuing Ages, was a known generation, society & congregation of Pastours & people, Parents & Children, Heades and members successiuely propagated & iointly vnited without interruptiõ one frõ the other; which must needs still perseuere constant & faithful, what opposition soeuer be made against it. And on the contrary I shew, that the Ministers of Scotlãd, England, or Ireland can shew no such pre-

decessours

deceſſors of their religion, no not one before Luther & Caluin, who do agree with them in all eſſentiall points of fayth, concluding therby that they are vnkind ſlipps grafted by Sathan, of whom the Wiſeman ſaith:
(a) Sap. v. 3. 4. (a) *Baſtard plants ſhall not take deep roote, nor lay ſure foundation: & if in the boughes for a time they ſhall ſpring, being weakly ſet, they ſhall be moued of the wind, & by the vehemency of the winds they ſhall be rooted out.*

Conſider Chriſtian Reader I pray thee, if in the caſe of ſome tēporall State any Lord or Earle of Scotland to prooue the tytle of the lands he holds, ſhould produce the publike ſentence, not only of all the Iudges of Scotland for the ſpace of fourteen hundred yeares, but of all the world for the ſpace of fifteen hundred years: the ſentence, I ſay, iudicially decided in the preſence of all thoſe Kinges, & of the three Eſtates of all thoſe Chriſtian Kingdomes in fauour of the true Poſſeſſour of the land, condē-ning the aduerſe party of impoſture & intruſion: & this their deciſion, ſentence & condemnation in diuers recordes amongſt the publike monuments not only of that one Kingdom, but likwiſe of the whole world to be extant: And on the other ſide the aduerſe party could bring forth none of former tymes to ſpeake in his fauour, alledging only that all his Forefathers & keepers of the land, were & had been inuiſible, vnknown & latent; what Iudge, I pray you, what reaſonable Man would make doubt who had the better right in Law? So it is betwixt vs Catholiks & the Proteſtants: for we produce for our Religion the Iudiciall ſentence not only of all the Kings & ſpirituall Iudges of our Kingdom of Scotland iudicially pronounced, but of the whole world, and that not at one tyme but at ſeueral, for the ſpace of fifteen hundred years: iudicially I ſay, pronounced, & all accepted, ratifyed, executed, & by publike monuments teſtified. The Miniſters in the contrary can name no viſible predeceſſors for their Religion, yea bring nothing but their own phancies & inuentiōs, vnder the Childiſh pretext of the word of God; bring no Iudiciall ſē-tence giuen in their behalfe by either Coūſell, or Parlament, or Publike monument, ſhew vs no Author, name vs no writter, ſpecifie no marke or token of the being of their Religion before Luther and Caluin: ſhall then any reaſonable Man thinke ſuch Miniſters & preachers to haue any Right or Commiſſion to preach, to haue any ground in the word of God, any warrant for their religion, any antiquity or lineall ſucceſſion?

Wherfore I earneſtly intreate the Chriſtian Reader to giue place to reaſon, & to eſchew their new Religion & profeſſion, if he will auoyd his eternall ruine, & loſſe of euerlaſting ſaluation, which is the due & ineuitable reward allotted for misbelieuers: from the which Chriſt Ieſus free all them who are effectually deſirous to liue, & dye in the true and Catholike Church, Amen. With the which deſire, I reſt alwayes,

Thy humble ſeruant
P. A. S. I.

THE FIRST AGE, OR CENTVRY.

A Table, or Catalogue of the Names of ſome Roman Catholiks, which ſhew that the Roman Church hath byn continually in all ages ſince Chriſt & his Apoſtles, vntill our dayes, & ſhall continue to the end of the world.

CHAP. I.

The yeare of our Lord.	The chiefe Paſtours of the Roman Church.	Paſtours, Doctours, & Profeſſours of the Roman Faith.	Kings of Scotland from the yeare of Chriſt 30. vntill 100.
30.	*Ieſus Chriſt God and Man borne of the Bleſſed Virgin Mary the 25. of December, from the Creation of the world 4022. yeares*	The Bleſſed Virgin Mary, S. Iohn the Baptiſt, S. Iohn the Apoſtle & Euãgeliſt, with the reſt of the Apoſtles, and Euangeliſts, S. Martha, S. Mary Magdalen,	*Before the comming of Chriſt the ſpace of 330. yeares, the firſt Scottiſh King was* Ferguſius *ſonne to* Ferchard, *to whome lineally did ſucceed* Feritharis, Mainus, Dornadilla, Notharus, Reuther, *Reu-*

yeares, did suffer Death vpon the Croße the 34 yeare of his age. He is our Soueraigne Lord, Redeemer, and Pastour, who hath left in his Church for the consolation of the Faythfull, and to keep peace and vnion, in matters of Religion, a Vicar vnder him.

34. *S. Peter Apostle, to whome succeeded,*

69. *Linus.*

80. *Cletus.*

83. *Clemens.*

len, S. Paul, S. Stephen the first Martyr, Timothy, Barnabas, Dionysius Areopagita, Martialis.

And of our Scottish Nation S. Mansuetus Bishop of Toul in Lorraine & disciple to S. Peter, of whome Demochares in *Catalog ep. Tullensium.* Frãciscus du Rosiers *Tom.* 2. *Stemmat. Lotharing. ad ann.* 62. and others wryte thus: *S. Mansuetus discipulus S. Petri, socius S. Clementis Episcopi Metensis, Natione Scotus &c.*

Lykewyse of our Scottish Nation famous in this age were the SS. Barinthus Priest, Paschasius Abbot sent by King Donaldus to Pope *Victor* in the yeare of Christ 99. B. Claudia wife to S. Pudens Senatour of Rome, and mother to Timotheus, Nouatus, Praxedis, & Pudẽtiana: as witnesseth *Romanum Martyrologiũ.* Finally S. Beatus, S. Peter his Disciple.

Reutha, Thereus, Iosina, Finnanus, Durstus, Euenus 1. Gillus, Euenus 2. Ederus, Euenus 3. to whome succeeded Metellanus who was crowned King 5. yeares before the comming of Christ, and dyed the yeare of Christ 29. to him succeeded Caratacus, Corbredus, of whome thus reporteth du Rosiers *Tom.* 6. Corbredus licèt à Romanis sæpius superatus esset, eos tamen cruentissimis prælijs superatos, ex Scotorum & Pictonum depulit agris. *Dardanus, Galcus, or Galcacus, of whom sayth the same* du Rosiers *Tom.* 6. Galcacus Rex optimus egregiè Romanos debellauit. *Of this king Galcacus (whom others do call* Galdus, *as brought vp amõg strãgers, for he was brought vp amõg the Brittõs) maketh mentiõ* Tacitus in vita Agricolæ, *which Agricola did make warre against the Scots, or Caledonians, about the yeare of Christ* 82. *as witnesseth* Dio.

But

But King Galcacus *did manfully stand against the power of* Agricola, *and of the Romans.* Tacitus *maketh mention of a most eloquent Oration of* Galcacus *to the Scots, to the end they should keepe their naturall liberty. Of which Oration* Lipsius *in his Annotations vpon that place giueth this iudgement:* Moriar, si quid meo sensu prudentiùs, disertiùs, argutiùs est in omni Romana lingua. *I might easily in lyke sort set downe the names of the Kings of* England, Ireland, France, Spayne, Dennemarke, Poland, Sueden, *and diuers other Kingdomes, all Catholike Romans: prouing therby the antiquity and vniuersality in tyme, place, and persons of our Religion, which notwithstanding I will heere omit, to be short.*

The holy Apostles wrote the new Testament in this first Age: and because the Puritans blinde and abuse the poore people in *Scotland*, saying, that their Religion is the self-same Religion which the Apostles professed: I will set downe heer some chiefe heads of the Puritans and Protestants Religion, drawne out of their owne Confession of Fayth, which the three Estates of *Scotland* at seuerall Parlaments haue solemnely sworne, auowed and subscribed. And on the other syde I will set downe how such poynts of their Religion be directly against the old and new Testament, and consequently that their Religion is far different from the Apostles Religion, yea is nothing els but a new inuention of the Ministers.

That the Puritans and Protestants Religion, is not the Religion of the holy Apostles.

The first Section.

1. THE Puritanes doe belieue that the commandements of God are impossible to be kept, yea though a man haue the grace of God: (a) *For the flesh (say they) euermore rebelleth against the spirit, whereby we continually transgresse thy holy Precepts, and Commandements, and so purchase to our selues, through thy iust iudgement, death & damnation.* If continually the Puritanes transgresse them, *Ergo,* in

(a) *In a prayer vsed in Scotlād called the* Confessiō of sinnes, *set downe in their Psalm-booke.*

in no moment of their whole lyfe, do they, or can they keep them, though assisted by the grace of God.

The Apostles, and the Bible affirme the contrary: (b) *For my yoke is easy and my burthen light*. Againe: (c) *I am able to do all things through the help of Christ, which strengthneth me*. And in another place: (d) *For this is the loue of God, that we keep his Commandements, and his Commandements are not grieuous*. And againe: (e) *Heereby we are sure that we know him, if we keep his Commandements. He that sayth I know him, and keepeth not his Commandements is a lyar, and the truth is not in him*. And our Sauiour sayth: (f) *If thou wilt enter into lyfe keep the Commandements*. And S. Luke sayth of Zacharias and Elizabeth Father and Mother of S. Iohn Baptist: (g) *That both were iust before God, and walked in all the Commandements and Ordinances of our Lord, without reproofe*. Can the Ministers belieue the Bible, who belieue not so manifest and expresse words of the Bible? Can their Religion be Apostolicall, who bely so euidently the Apostles and Christ himself?

(b) *Matth.* 11. v. 30.
(c) *Philip.* 4. v. 13.
(d) *Ioan.* 5. v. 3.
(e) *Ioan.* 2. v. 3.
(f) Matth. 19. v. 17.
(g) *Luc.* 1. v. 6.

2. Puritanes doe belieue that Catholikes are the limmes of the Diuell; their words be: (h) *The defence of the Church appertayneth to the Christian Magistrats, against all Idolaters and Hereticks, as Papists, Anabaptists, with such lyke limmes of Antichrist, to roote out all doctrine of Diuels and men, as the Masse, Purgatory, Limbus Patrum, Prayer to Saints, and for the Dead, Freewill, Distinction of meats, apparel, and dayes, Vowes of single lyfe, Presence at Idol-seruice, mans Merits, with such lyke*.

(h) *In the Confession of Fayth sworne by the Ministers at their admission.*

Contrary, I find not one expresse word of all their blasphemies in the Bible, or Doctrine of the Apostles, yea the Protestants against their solemne Oath, haue now receaued apparel and festiual dayes, and kneeling at Idol-seruice, that is, at the receauing of their Bakers bread and winy supper: as in his Maiesties 23. Parlament act. 1. holden at Edenburgh anno 1621 appeareth.

For praying for the Dead, I find in their owne Bible: (i) *And he (to wit* Iudas Machabæus*) hauing made a gathering through the company, sent to Ierusalem about two thowsand drachmes of siluer, to offer a sinne-offering, doing very well and honestly, that he thought*

(i) 2. *Machab.* 12. v. 43.

thought of the Resurrection; for if he had not hoped that they who were slaine should ryse againe, it had byn superfluous and vayne to pray for the dead. And therfore he perceaued that there was great fauour layed vp for those that dyed godly (it was a holy & good thought.) So he made a reconciliation for the dead, that they might be deliuered from sinne. This place sheweth that it was at least a custome among the Iewes to pray for the dead. And S. *Augustin* (whose opinion is to be preferred to all the *Ephemerian* Ministers) assureth vs, that not the Iewes but the Church of God euer did hold those book as Canonicall. The Ministers shall neuer be able to giue vs expresse words of the Bible which deny praying for the dead. *Aug. lib. 18 de ciuit. c. 36.*

3. The Puritanes belieue that the sicke should not be anoynted with oyle, and remission of sinnes giuen to them by men.

The Apostles contrary: (k) *Is any sick among you? Let him bring in the Priests of the Church, and let them pray ouer him, & anoynt him with oyle in the name of our Lord, and the prayer of Fayth shall saue the sick, and our Lord shall rayse him vp: and if he haue committed sinne, it shall be forgiuen him.* Which place the Ministers haue corrupted, as prouing clearly the Sacrament of Extreme Vnction. (k) *Ioan. 5. v. 14.*

4. The Puritanes belieue that no sort of sinne is done against the will of God, and that he vseth the Diuell but as an instrument: so that in their Religion al sorts of sinnes and abhominations, should rather be imputed to God the chiefe Author, then to the Diuell the instrument, conforme to the common saying, *Qui est causa causæ, est causa causati.* The fault is more to be imputed to the Maister, who commaundeth the seruant, then to the seruant who is but an instrument: Heare the Ministers owne words: (l) *That God is the Authour of Heauen and Earth, that is to say, that the Heauen and earth, and the contents therof are so in his hands, that there is nothing done without his knowledge, neyther yet against his will: & so we confesse and belieue that neyther the Diuels, nor yet the wicked of the world haue any power to molest or trouble the chosen children of God, but so far as it pleaseth him to vse* (l) *In the order of Baptisme.*

(m) The Articles of Fayth set downe in the Scots Cathechisme 45. Sunday.

to vse them as instruments. And agayne: (m) *God of his infinite mercy doth preserue his faythfull, not suffering the Diuell to lead them out of the way, neyther permitting that sinne haue the vpper hand of them: so lykewyse he doth not only giue vp, cast off, and withdraw his grace from such as he will punish, but also he deliuereth them to the Diuell, committing them to his tyranny; he stryketh them with blindnes, and giueth them vp to reprobat mynds, that they become vtterly slaues to sinne, and subiect to all tentations.* Againe: (n) *So then by this saying, the power of God is not idle, but continually exercised; so that nothing is done but by him, and by his ordinance.* Againe: (o) *The knowledge hereof doth wonderfully comfort vs, for we might thinke our selues in a miserable case, if the Diuels and the wicked had power to do any thing contrary to Gods will.*

(n) In the 3 Sunday.
(o) In the 4. Sunday.

The whole Bible is against this blasphemy, as by the Texts following may appeare: (p) *God is true, and without wickednesse, iust and righteous is he.* (q) *The Scepter of thy Kingdome is a scepter of righteousnes. Thou louest righteousnes, and hatest wickednes.* And againe: (r) *Let no man say when he is tempted, I am tempted of God, for God cannot be a tempter of euill, neyther tempteth he any man.*

(p) Deut. 32. v. 4.
(q) Psalm. 44. v. 6.
(r) Ioan. I. v. 13.

5. The Puritanes belieue, that for all those who kneele or worship the Supper of the Lord, there is nothing but eternall damnation; which poynt of Fayth the Parlament, holden almost these 40. yeares ago, did sweare solemnely and subscribe: (s) *Neyther must we in the administration of those Sacraments* (say the Ministers) *follow mans fantasy, but as Christ himself hath ordayned, so must they be ministred, and by such as by ordinary vocation are thereunto called. Therefore whosoeuer reserueth and worshippeth those Sacraments, or contrarywise contemneth them in tyme and place, procureth to himself damnation.*

(s) In the Confession of Fayth.

Notwithstanding this, kneeling at the Lords Supper is now receaued, commanded, and by Parlament confirmed. The words be: (t) *Considering that there is no part of Diuine Worship more heauenly and spirituall, then is the holy receauing of the blessed Body and Bloud of our Lord & Sauiour Iesus Christ; the Assembly thinketh good, that that blessed Sacrament*

(t) In his Maiesties 23. Parlament holdē at Edenburgh an. 1621. act. I.

cramment be celebrated hereafter meekely and reuerently vpon their knees.

6. The Puritanes do excommunicate Kings & Princes, and the ciuill Magistrats: let vs the͂ giue credit to their owne words, which the Ministers vse: (u) *And therfore in the name and authority of the Eternall God, and of his Sonne Iesus Christ, I excommunicate from this Table all Blasphemers of God, all Idolaters, all Murmurers, all Adulterers, and all that be in Malice and Enuy, all Disobedient persons to Father and Mother, Princes or Magistrats, Pastors or Preachers, all Theeues and Deceauers of their Neighbours, and finally all such as lead a lyfe directly fighting against the will of God.*

(u) *In the manner of the administration of th Lords Supper.*

Now the Ministers belieue, that in Kings and Princes (x) *The flesh euermore rebelleth against the spirit, wherby they doe continually transgresse the precepts of God, and his holy Commandements.* Since then the Ministers do excommunicate all those that lead a lyfe against Gods Commandements, and since no man can keep the Commandements of God, and all sinnes are mortall and against the Commandements; it followeth of necessity, that all perso͂s who receaue the Supper of the Lord, are excommunicate, and consequently receaue the Supper of the Lord vnworthily, and to their owne damnation.

(x) *In a prayer called the Co͂fession of sinnes.*

7. The Puritanes belieue that: (a) *Christ suffered his Humanity to be punished with most cruel death, feeling in himself the anger and seuere Iudgment of God, euen as if he had byn in the extreme torments of Hel.* And againe: (b) *Christ did not only suffer naturall death, which is a separation of the soule from the body, but also his soule was in wonderfull distresse enduring grieuous torments, which S. Peter calleth the sorowes of death.* And againe: (c) *Heereby we see the difference betweene that grief of mynd, which Christ did suffer, and that which the impenitent sinners do abyde, whom God doth punish in his terrible Wrath: for that very payne which Christ sustayned for a tyme, the wicked must endure continually, and that which to Christ was but a prick, is to the wicked insteed of a glaiue to wound them to death.*

(a) *In the Confession of Fayth.*
(b) *In the Catechisme, the 10. Sunday.*
(c) *In the said Cathechisme.*

Contrary, the Apostles belieued, that the blessed Soule of Christ descended to the Hell where the Soules of the ancient Fathers, Abraham, Isaac, Iacob, Noe &c. were, to wit *Limbus Patrum*, and not to the Hel of the damned and reprobate, out of the which there is no redemption.

8. The Puritanes belieue, that in the Sacrament of the Lords Supper, the Body of Christ is not contayned, but only a signe and figure therof.

(d) *Matth.* 26. v. 26. (e) *Ioan.* 6. v. 51.

Contrary-wise our Sauiour sayth in expresse wordes: (d) *This is my Body*. And agayne: (e) *The bread that I will giue, is my Flesh*.

9. The Puritanes belieue, that Priests cannot forgiue sinnes on earth.

(f) *Ioan.* 20 v. 23.

Contrary to our Sauiour his commission and power granted to his Apostles, and their Successours: (f) *Whose sinnes you forgiue, they are forgiuen, whose sinnes you retayne they are retayned*.

10. The Puritanes belieue, that it is not lawfull to make Vowes, and if they be made, they may be broken.

(g) *Psalm.* 76. v. 11.

Contrary to the expresse words of the Bible: (g) *Vow you, and render your Vowes.*

The

The first & second Article.

1. *That the Catholike Roman Church vniuersally believed in this first Age, the Reall Presence of Christs Body in the blessed Sacrament, after the words of Consecration.*

2. *That saying of Masse, was vniuersally in vse in this Age.*

CHAP. II.

BEFORE I come to the testimony of the holy Fathers of this Age, I will proue these two verities by the expresse words of the Bible. First then, Christ promised to giue his Flesh to his Disciples & their Successours: (a) *The bread that I will giue is my Flesh, which I will giue for the lyfe of the world*. And againe: (b) *My Flesh is meat indeed, and my Bloud is drinke indeed*, in the Greeke it is, *my Flesh is meat truly*, ἀληθῶς: if truely, then not *figuratiuely*, but *really*, for *Veritas & Realitas conuertuntur*. Our Sauiour sayth, *My Flesh is meat truly*; The Ministers say, *Christs Flesh is meat figuratiuely*. Which of the two should be more belieued, Christ, or the Ephemerian Ministers of Scotland?

(a) Ioan 6. v. 51.
(b) Ioan. 6. v. 55.

2. Secondly our Sauiour sayth: (c) *Verily, verily I say vnto you, except yee eat the Flesh of the Sonne of Man, and drinke his Bloud, yee haue no lyfe in you*. Our Sauiour sayth not, except ye eat my flesh *by Fayth*, except ye eat the *figure* of my flesh. Now if they who eat not the Flesh of Christ, cannot go to Heauen, how can the Puritanes go thither, who will not belieue the plaine and manifest words of Christ? yea how can the Ministers belieue in Christ, who bely him speaking so plainly, cleerly, and manifestly? In this whole Chapter our Sauiour neuer sayth, *I will giue a figure of my Flesh for the*

(c) Ioan 6, v. 53.

the lyfe of the World: nor yet, *Except yee eat my Flesh by Fayth, yee haue no lyfe in you.* He then who desireth to saue his own soule, must needes rather belieue the plaine and manifest words of Christ, then the Ministers expositions, yea new inuentions and dreames: since all the holy, learned, and wise Fathers did euer expone these words of our Sauiour, as the Roman Catholikes belieue at this present.

3. Thirdly, let euery man consider in the presence of God, and without passion, and as he will answere at the day of Iudgement, those most playne words of our Sauiour in the institution of this Sacrament: (d) *Take, eate, this is my Body which is giuen for you: This do in remembrance of me.* First, Christ in his latter Supper made his Testament, and last will, at which tyme euery wyse man is obliged to speak plainly and not figuratiuely. 2. Our Sauiour spake only heer to his twelue Apostles, to whome alone he was not accustomed to speake in figures and parables. (e) *Vnto you it is giuen to know the mysteries of the Kingdome of God, but to others in parables.* And plainly S. Matthew witnesseth that Christ was not accustomed to speak to his Apostles alone in parables and figures: (f) *Then the Disciples came and sayd to him, why speakest thou to them in parables: and he answered and sayd to them, Because it is giuen to you, to know the secrets of the Kingdome of Heauen, but to them it is not giuen.* 3. Christ sayth, *This is*, he sayth not, *This signifieth my Body, this is a figure of my Body.* 4. Christ sayth: *My Body which is giuen for you:* that is, *which is giuen for you as the pryce of your redemption.* But bread cannot be the pryce of our Redemption, lykewise a figure of the body of Christ cannot be the pryce of our Redemption. 5. Christ sayth, *which is giuen*, in the present sense, and not *which shalbe giuen*, in the future. 6. Christ sayth, *Which is giuen for you*, and not, *which is giuen to you*, because it was giuen for the remission of our sinnes. 7. Christ sayth, *This is my Bloud which is shed for many, for the remission of sinnes:* but pure wyne, & the figure of his bloud, cannot be the remission of our sinnes. 8. Christ sayth in the present sense, *which is shed*, which words cannot be referred to the bloudy shedding vpon the Crosse, but to the

(d) Matt 26. v. 26. Marc. 14. v. 22. Luc. 22. v. 19

(e) *Luc* 8. v. 10.

(f) Matth. 13. v. 10.

vnbloudy shedding in the holy Sacrifice of the Masse. As for the words that follow, *But I say to you, that I will not drinck henceforth of this fruite of the vyne, vntill that day when I shall drinck it new with you in my Fathers Kingdome*, Christ spake them at the eating of the Paschal Lambe, as S. Luke witnesseth plainly, and not at the institution of the blessed Sacrament. 9. Christ sayth *Do this*: Wherby he gaue power to his Apostles, and their lawfull successours to do the same thing which he did, that is, as he by his Almighty power and word created the world of nothing, turned wyne into water, turned Moyses rod into a serpent, and infinite such things: So the same God by his Almighty word and power at his last Supper turned bread into his precious Body, and wyne into his precious Bloud to the consolation of the faythfull Catholiks, and gaue power to do the same to his Apostles, and all their lawfull successours. So that whatsoeuer is in this Sacrament aboue our capacity & vnderstanding, is done by the Almighty power of God, wherunto we should submit our iudgements, since the Almighty power of God is infinite, & the iudgement of man so weak, blinded, erroneous, and inconstant, that it cannot conceaue sufficiently naturall and common things, much lesse supernaturall and heauenly. 10. Remarke the words, *Do this*, τοῦτο ποιεῖτε, that is: *Sacrifice this, offer vp this.* The Syriak words which our Sauiour vsed are playne, *Hodo hauaithun*, that is, *Sacrifice this*, for the word and radix, *Hauad*, signifieth plainly *to sacrifice*, as (g) *Let my people go, that they may serue me in the wildernesse*. In the Hebrew Bible the self same word, *Vera habduni*, is thus, word by word, *Let my people go, that they may do to me, or sacrifice to me in the wildernesse*. And the Greek word ποιέω, *I doe*, is sundry tymes in the Bible taken for, *to Sacrifice*, as in these places: (h) *And the Priest shall make of one of them a sinne-offering*. In the Greek, καὶ ποιήσει αὐτὰ ὁ ἱερεύς. And againe: (i) *After this maner ye shall prepare throughout all the seauen dayes for the mentayning of the offering made by fyre, for a sweet sauour to our Lord; it shalbe done besides the continuall brunt-offering, and drinck-offering thereof.* And againe: (k) *This is the thing which our Lord commanded*, *that*

Luc. 22. v. 18.

Gen. 1. v. 1. Ioa. 2. v. 9. Exod. 4. v. 3.

(g) Exod. 7. v. 16.

(h) Leuit. 15. v. 15.

(i) Numb. 28. v. 24.

(k) Leuit. 9. v. 6.

that yee should doe, and the glory of our Lord shall appeare to you. Besides this, *Pagan* wryters doe chalenge our Ministers of intollerable ignorance, for asmuch as they teach, that the word *Facio*, is sundry tymes taken for to *Sacrifice*, as witnesseth Virgil: *Cum faciam vitula pro frugibus ipse venito.* Plautus, *Faciam tibi fideliam.* Cicero, *Iuno sospita cui omnes Consules facere necesse est.* Iuuenal, *Pro populo faciens:* and sundry others. Lykewise Greeke holy Fathers who did vnderstand better the force of their owne naturall tongue then all the Ministers doe, plentifully witnesse that our Sauiour offered vp in his later Supper, *An vnbloudy Sacrifice for vs,* which Sacrifice we do call, *the Masse,* from *Messias,* because we belieue that the true Messias is offered therin. See S. Chrysostome, S. Basil, S. Cyprian, S. Ambrose, S. Augustin, with many others, who plainly say, that our Sauiour did offer vp, *an vnbloudy Sacrifice for vs, in his last Supper:* and cōmanded his Apostles and their Successours, to offer vp the same dayly: Which Sacrifice S. Ambrose, and other holy and learned ancient Fathers call *the Masse.* I will heer omit to bring other places of the Scripture to proue the holy Sacrifice of the Masse, and the verity of the blessed Sacramēt, reseruing the same to euery Age in particuler, where I will also shew, how manifestly the Ministers haue corrupted their owne Bibles in all debatable points of Religion, but specially in this of the holy *Masse.*

Virgil in Buc. *Plaut. in Aul.* *Cice. pro Mur.*

Chrysost. hom. de ieiunio Dauid. *Basil. in orat. suæ Liturgiæ.* *Cypr. l. 2. ep. 3 secundū alios 63.* *Ambro. in exhort. ad Virgines.* *Aug. l. 10. de ciuit. c. 20.*

4. Now I will intreat the Reader to consider without passion, how that those expresse and formal words of the Bible aforerehearsed do make for vs Catholiks, and no wyse for the Ministers, who grant willingly that these poynts and articles of their Religion, *This is a figure of my Body; This signifieth my Body; we take the Body of Christ by fayth only, and not really,* are not in playne termes & expresse words to be found in their owne Bible: But they will proue, say they, these articles by necessary consequence out of the Bible: As M. *Andrew Ramsey* granted, in disputing at seuerall tymes with me in prison, and before some Lords of the Councel of Scotland; he granted (I say) that he could not proue that there were only two Sacraments out of the expresse

presse words of the Bible, eyther Hebrew, Greek, or Scottish, and such other debatable poynts; but that he could proue it (said he) by necessary consequence: and yet could he neuer make a necessary consequence. To the which saying of M. *Andrew Ramsey*, I replyed then, and now reply thus: 1. M. *Andrew Ramsey* must needes then auow, that he cannot proue, not one debatable poynt of his Religion by the expresse word, the formall text, the pure word of God; or if he can, I challenge him heer before the whole world to do the same, and to set out in print his necessarie consequences, to the end the world may see them. 2. That M. *Andrew* his consequences cānot be called the Word of God, and consequently cannot be the ground of a poynt of Religion, which must needs be *infallible*. 3. Eyther *Maister Ramsey* Minister of *Edenburgh* may erre in making of his consequences, or no? If he grant that he may erre, how then can his consequences be *infallible*, as an article of Fayth must be. If he say he cannot erre in making his consequences: who is so sensles to think, that the true Church of God hath erred, and may erre (as the Ministers belieue) seing *Maister Andrew Ramsey* (who is but a sinfull man, an ignorant Minister) cannot erre in making his consequences, which are no other thing but his owne inuentions, dreames, expositions, and plaine heresies, which the ignorāt people of *Edenburgh* thinke foolishly to be the Word of God. 4. The conclusion of a Syllogisme, as drawne out of the premisses, *sub illa formalitate*, cannot be a poynt of Fayth; for as it is drawen out, *vi formæ*, of the premisses, it is grounded vpon Logike, or the Syllogisticall forme of Logik, which is an inuention of man, and consequently it cannot be the ground of true Religiō which must needs be *infallible*. Let *Maister Ramsey* then remark this poynt of Philosophy: *Conclusio vt formaliter deducta nunquam est de fide, id est, vt deducitur vi forma, in modo & figura*. 5. All Heretiks haue vsed the Scripture to confirme their heresies and blasphemies. As *Arius* out of these wordes, (l) *Thou shall haue no other Gods before me*, made this consequence, *Ergo*, God the Sonne is not God: yea out of these words of the Psalme: (l) Exod. 10. v. 3.

(m) *For*

(m) Psal. 91. v. 11. (m) *For he shall giue his Angels charge ouer thee, to keep thee in all thy wayes; they shall beare thee in their hands, that thou hurt not thy foot against a stone:* The Diuell drew this consequence against

(n) Matth. 4. v. 6. Luc. 4. v. 9. our Blessed Sauiour, *Ergo*, (n) *Cast thy selfe downe*. 6. Albeit *Maister Ramsey* made a Syllogisme, wherof the *maior* & *minor* propositions were playne and expresse words of the Bible, which he shall not be able to do to his aduantage; yet the conclusion or consequēce needeth not to be a point of Religion. The reason of this is, because *Conclusio sequitur debiliorem partem*, and the Syllogisticall forme of an argument is a part, and the weakest in that case, and consequently erroneous, and not infallible. 7. If the one proposition be in expresse words in the Bible, and the other not, though true, then the conclusion can no wyse be infallible, and a poynt of *Diuine Fayth*, which is *infallible*. The reason is: *Quia conclusio sequitur debiliorem partem*. 8. The ground of al Syllogismes and arguments are. 1. It is impossible that the same thing be, and be not. 2. Euery thing is, or is not. 3. One verity cannot gaynstand another. 4. *Conclusio sequitur debiliorem partem*. 5. *Ex puris negatiuis nihil infertur*, and such others, which though most true, yet as they are not in expresse words in the Bible, so they cannot be an infallible ground of the true Religion: because they are humane grounds, subiect to errour, instability, and changing. Contrary, the ground of the true Religion, must needs be infallible. Let not then the Ministers make any accompt of their consequences made against the blessed Sacrament, against the holy Sacrifice of the Masse, against any other poynt of our Religion, because they are erroneous and fallible; which gaue occasion to our Sauiour to command vs to beware of the necessary consequences of

(o) Matth. 15. v. 9. Marc. 7. v. 7. the Ministers: (o) *In vayne do they worship me, teaching for Doctrines the Commandements of men*. S. Paul lykewyse forwarneth vs to beware of the Ministers consequences: (p) *Let no*

(p) Ephes. 5. v. 6. *man deceaue you with vayne words*. And againe: (q) *Beware lest*

(q) Coloss. 2. v. 8. *there be any man that spoyle you through Philosophy*. For all the Ministers consequences and arguments are nothing els, but their owne traditions, dreames, Philosophicall sophismes, and inuentions without any infallible ground of the Word of God.

5. Now as I haue set downe before, the playne and manifest words of the Bible, to confirme the verity of the Blessed Sacrament, and of the holy Sacrifice of the Masse: so I will set downe the consequences drawne out of those foresayd words of the Bible by the holy Fathers of the first Age, and consequently the constant and infallible belief of the Church of God in this first hundreth yeares. And in my opinion there is no man so sensles, so foolish, and soe careles of his owne saluation, who will not prefer and make greater account of the cõsequẽces of the holy Church, and of the holy Fathers, then of these our *Ephemerian* Ministers, who haue no vnion amongst themselues, who are come in at their owne hand, without authority, without power and commission, whose lyues, behauiour, and carriage, as it is presently well knowne throughout all Brittaine, so in no wise can they be compared to our Ancestors, and holy Fore-fathers, whose deep learning, heauenly wisdome, godly conuersation, charitable and vertuous behauiour, doth vtterly confound, specially our Scottish Ministers ignorance, worldly greedynes, bad conuersation, and most vicious behauiour. The very auncient monumẽts and princely buildings of our Fore-fathers shew manifestly their great charity, angelicall lyfe, and profound humility, plaine contrary to the intollerable pryde, filthy auarice, and lewd conuersation of our Ministers.

Testimonyes of the holy Fathers of this first Age, or hundreth yeares, concerning the Real Presence, *and holy* Sacrifice of the Masse.

The first Section.

THis witnesseth S. Denys of Areopagita (of whome S. Luke maketh mention) who belieuing constantly that Christ Iesus God and man, was conteyned in the Blessed Hoste, prayed therto after this forme: (a) *O Diuinissimum & Sanctum*

Act 17. v. 34.

(a) *Eccl. Hierar. c. 3*

Sanctum Sacramentum obducta tibi symbolice operimenta ænigmatis reuelans, dilucide nobis fac vt appareas, ac spiritales nostros oculos singulari apertoq; lumine imple. That is: O most Diuine & most holy Sacrament, vouchsafe to remoue from the veyles or couerings of those signifying signes, and appeare to vs perspicuously, and fill our spirituall eyes with a singular and cleare resplendency of thy light. How could S. Denys pray to the Blessed Sacramēt, if he had not belieued Christ to be contayned therein, really, and truely? And a little after he maketh mention in playne termes of Altars, wherupon the Masse was said, of the prayers vsed at the Masse, of the lifting vp of the precious Body of Iesus Christ to be adored by the people at the Masse, of the Incense, of the Priests kissing the Altar in token of reuerence, of the Priests blessing the people, and saying, *Dominus vobiscum*, of the Euangel read at the holy Masse. Truly since S. Denys was S. Pauls Disciple, no wyse man will doubt, but that which the Disciple testifieth to vs, was taught and practised by S. Paul his Maister.

2. S. Ignatius Martyr, Disciple to S. Iohn the Euangelist: (b) *Non gaudio nutrimento corruptionis, nec voluptatibus vitæ huius &c. Panem vitæ volo, quæ est caro Christi filij Dei, qui factus est posterioribus temporibus ex semine Dauid & Abrahæ; & potum volo sanguinem illius.* That is: I take no delight in coruptible food, nor in the pleasures of this lyfe; but I desire rather to haue the bread of lyfe, which is the Flesh of Christ, the Sonne of God, who was made of the seed of Dauid & Abraham: I desire for drinke, his Bloud. And plainly the same holy Father calleth the Eucharist: (c) *Carnem Saluatoris, quæ pro peccatis nostris passa est, quam Pater sua benignitate suscitauit.* That is: The Flesh of our Sauiour which suffered for our sinnes, which the Father by his bounty raysed vp. So that by this holy Fathers consequences drawne out of the Bible, the selfe same flesh of our Sauiour, which suffered for our sinnes, is in the Eucharist or Blessed Sacrament; the selfe same Christ God and man, who was made of the seed of Dauid is contayned in the Blessed Sacrament. And towards the midst of the same letter to the people of *Smyrna*,

(b) *Epist. ad Rom. post. med.*

(c) *Epist. ad Smyrn.*

na, he witnesseth, that no man should offer vp sacrifice, or baptize without the Bishops authority and ordination. *Non licet sine Episcopo baptizare, neq; offerre, neq; sacrificium immolare.* It is not lawfull without the Bishop to baptize, neyther to offer, or sacrifice.

3. S. Andrew the holy and ancient Patron of Scotland, witnesseth clearly, how that he euery day said the holy Masse, and receaued the precious Body of Christ. (d) *Ego Omnipotenti Deo immaculatum agnum quotidie sacrifico, qui cùm verè sit sacrificatus, & verè à populo carnes eius manducatæ, integer perseuerat & viuus.* That is: I sacrifice dayly to the Almighty the vnspotted Lamb, who albeit truely sacrificed, and his flesh truely eaten by the people, yet continueth whole and lyuely.

(d) *Lib. poss. S. Andreæ.*

4. S. Clement, S. Pauls Disciples of whom in his Epistle to the Philippians he maketh mention, plainly vseth the word *Masse*, saying: (e) *The faythfull & specially Priests, Deacons, and other Church-men should beware to do any thing without the licence of the Bishop: Yea the Priests in their own Parish should neyther say Masse, nor baptize without the Bishops authority.* The words be: *A cunctis fidelibus & summopere omnibus Presbyteris & Diaconis, ac reliquis Clericis attendendum est, vt nihil absq; Episcopi proprij licentia agant, non vtiq; Missas sine eius iussu quispiam Presbyterorum in sua parœcia agat, non baptizet.* And a little below: *Quoniam in alijs locis sacrificare, & missas celebrare non licet nisi in his in quibus Episcopus proprius iusserit &c. Hæc Apostoli a Domino acceperunt & nobis tradiderunt, hæc nos docemus, vobisq; & omnibus absq; reprehensione tenere & docere quibus agendum est, mandamus.* That is: It is not lawfull to sacrifice, and say Masse but in those places, where the Bishop of the same place commandeth.

(e) *Philipp. 4. v. 3.*

5. Besides these most plentifull and manifest words of the holy Fathers of this Age, sundry holy Fathers make mention of the changing and transubstantiation of the bread and wyne in the body and bloud of Iesus Christ by vertue of the Sacramentall words: yea the Fathers do further wryte, that our senses are heer deceaued, for though the eye seeth only the shapes of bread and wyne in the Eucharist,

rist, yet they say plainly, that there is neyther bread nor wyne. So Eusebius Emissenus: (f) *The inuisible Priest doth change, through a secret power of his Word, the visible creatures into the substance of his body and bloud.* Declaring therby that Christ the inuisible Priest is Author of all that which is done in this holy Sacrament: Againe, the same holy Father sayth more plainly: *Quando benedicenda &c. When the Creatures (which are to be blessed) are placed vpon the Altars, before they be consecrated with the inuocation of the highest power, they are the substance of bread and wyne; but after the words of Christ, they are the*
" *body and bloud of Christ.* What meruaile is it, if those things
" which he could creat by his word, he can change being al-
" ready created? Be not these words playne and sufficient to moue any vnpassionate mynd? S. Augustin: (g) *Non omnis panis &c Not euery bread, but that only which receaueth the Benediction*, fit Corpus Christi, *is made the Body of Christ.* S. Chrysostome: (h) *Num vides panem, num vinum? &c. Doest thou see bread? Doest thou see wyne? Doe those things passe into the common passage as other meats do? Let it be far from thee to thinke so, for euen as wax cast into the fyre doth assimulate or change it selfe to it, nothing of the substance therof remayning, or superfluously redounding, so mayst thou suppose the Mysteries heer to be consumed by the substance of the body.* S. Gregory Nyssene: (i) *Quamobrem recte, &c. Wherfore we now truely belieue euen by the Word of God, that the sanctified bread is changed by the Word of God &c That those things which are seene (to wit, bread and wyne) are changed into the body of our Lord, is to be attributed to the vertue of the benediction.*

(f) *Euseb. Emiss. serm de corp. Domin.*

(g) *Aug. serm quem citat Beda in c. 10. prior. ad Corinth.*

(h) *Hom 83. in Matt & Homil. de Euchar in Encaen.*

(i) *Orat. Catech. c. 37.*

6. I will supersede to cyte other authorities of the Fathers, who make amply mention of the transubstantiation or change, which is wroght by the power of God in this holy Sacrament and Sacrifice; contenting my self to shew, how that these holy Fathers do witnesse, that the custome of the primitiue Church, was to adore and worship with *Latria* the Blessed Sacramēt, belieuing that Christ true God and Man was contayned therin. S. Augustin exponing those words, *Adorate scabellum pedum eius*, wryteth thus: (k) *Fluctuans conuerto me ad Christum &c. I doubting doe turne*

(k) *In Psa. 98.*

turne my selfe to Christ, because I seeke him heer, and doe find how without impiety the earth may be adored, the footstoole of his feete may be adored; for he did take earth from earth, because flesh commeth of the earth, and he tooke flesh of the flesh of Marie: and because he did heer walke in that flesh, and gaue that flesh to be eaten by vs, for our health, now no man doth eat that flesh, except he adore it before. Heer then it is found how such a footstoole of the feet of our Lord may be adored; so as that heere we not only do not sinne in adoring, but we sinne in not adoring. And wryting to *Honoratus* he witnesseth, that the vncleane receaue and adore the Body of Christ, though not to their saluation: (l) *Adducti sunt ad mensam Domini & accipiunt de corpore & sanguine eius, sed adorant tantùm, non etiam saturantur, quia non inuitantur.* The same holy Father warneth most earnestly the Catholiks, and especially Priests to be carefull, that no part of the Host or blessed Sacrament fall vpon the ground.

(l) *Epist.* 120. c. 27.

7. As for the holy Masse if any man will aske, whether or no the holy Apostles sayd Masse? I answere, that sundry holy Fathers (whose authority is to be preferred to all the ministry for learning, antiquity, piety, and godlinesse.) witnesse the same plentifully; as S. Isidorus Hispalensis twelue hundreth yeares ago: (m) *Ordo autem Missæ vel orationum quibus oblata Deo sacrificia consecrantur, primùm à S. Petro est institutus, cuius celebrationem vno eodemq; modo vniuersus peragit orbis.* The same witnesseth (n) *Paschasius*, (o) *Epiphanius*, (p) *Lindanus*, and sundry others which I omit. Yea the self same Masse which S. *Peter* vsed, is yet extant, as the forenamed Authors and sundry others witnesse, in the which holy Apostles Masse, are contayned the selfe same prayers and ceremonies, which the Roman Catholik Priests vse in this Age: as, the *Kyrie eleison, Dominus vobiscum, Credo in vnum Deum Patrem Omnipotentem &c. Lauabo inter innocentes manus meas. &c. Sursum habeamus corda nostra. Verè dignum & iustum est Te igitur clementissime Pater &c. Memento Domine famulorum tuorum &c. Communicantes & memoriam venerantes &c. Qui pridie eius diei &c. Supplices te rogamus &c. Pater Noster &c. Agnus Dei qui tollis peccata mundi &c.* And

(m) *In 2. off. lib. c. de Missa.*
(n) *in l. de corp. & sang. prope finem.*
(o) *Hæres.* 79. *ante med.*
(p) *Apol.* c. 17. p. 97.

And sundry others particularities which I refer to the reading of the diligent Reader in (q) Baronius, and (r) Turrianus. Lykewise the Masse which S. Iames the Apostle called *maior*, was accustomed to say, is yet extant, and hath been famous in Christian Kingdomes this sixteenth hundreth yeares, as witnesseth after many others, (s) Genebrardus. S. Matthew the Apostle his Masse is yet extant, as witnesse (t) Socrates, and (u) Baronius, which Masse is called commonly in the Æthiopian language, *Corbon*, that is, a voluntary Free-gift, or Sacrifice, and with vs in Europe the word *Missa*, or *Masse*, signifieth a voluntary Sacrifice, drawne from the Hebrew word, *Missah*, as the Bible witnesseth, (x) *And thou shall keep the Feast of weekes vnto the Lord thy God, euen a free gift of thy hand*, yea the Apostle calleth the Sacrifice of Christ vpon the Crosse, a voluntary Sacrifice: (y) *Oblatus est quia ipse voluit*.

(q) *In Annal. ad annum 44.*
(r) *In 3. character. dogmatic. libro post medium.*
(s) *In Chro. in fine primi sæculi.*
(t) *Lib. 1. hist. c. 15.*
(u) *Ad an. 44. nu 35.*
(x) *Deut. 16 v. 10.*
(y) *See this place in the Bible.*

8. Truly it is a great comfort and consolation to vs Catholiks, to see the holy Apostles and ancient Fathers of this first Age, so constant in this poynt of the blessed *Sacrament*, and of the *Masse*. For it is most cleare, that those holy Fathers so neere to the Apostles, yea Disciples to the Apostles, so learned in all Doctrines, so addicted to Heauenly things, so deare and familiar to God, could not be but inspired by the spirit of God, in so weighty a matter, wherfore we Catholiks securely follow such Captaynes and guydes, who haue byn sixteene hundreth yeares before vs.

That the Ministers haue corrupted the Bible in sundry places, which proue the Reall Presence, and holy Sacrifice of the Masse.

The second Section.

EVen as in this our corrupted Age, there be many and diuers Sects and Religions (yet but one true Religion Fayth, and Profession) in Germany & Holland specially, in Scotland, England, Denmarke, and Sueden; so there be many diuers Bibles, euery Religion forging and making

a Bible

a Bible to proue and mantayne the errours, heresies, and blasphemies therof. And this with that pretext, which by inuentours of heresies is vsed in euery Age, saying alwayes to the poore ignorant people, that they preached nothing but the expresse Word of God, the playne Scripture, the formall text of the Bible. Notwithstanding in effect they preached nothing but their owne fantasies, inuentions, dreames, expositions, yea in a word, heresies and blasphemies. To the which end it hath bene euer the custome of new Religion-makers to corrupt the Bible, to falsify the word of God, committing therby Lese-Maiesty Diuine. So the Puritane Ministers in Scotland haue euery where corrupted the Bible, and that in such sorte, that there is not one debatable poynt of Religion, betwixt vs and them, wherin they haue not most blasphemously and impiously corrupted the Bible.

2. As for example, our Sauiour Christ Iesus in Saint Matthew, in that short prayer called the Lords prayer, teacheth vs to aske specially not only corruptible bread, *but the bread of Lyfe*, that is, his owne flesh contayned in the blessed Sacrament, vnder the shape of bread, for the which cause our Sauiour called it (a) *Supersubstantiall* (because one substance is changed in another substance) *or supernaturall bread*, for so it is in the Greeke, τὸν ἄρτον ἡμῶν τὸν ἐπιούσιον δὸς ἡμῖν σήμερον, that is, *Giue vs this day our supersubstantiall bread*, which word: (b) S. Hierome expoundeth plainly of the blessed Sacrament. Likewise, (c) S. Ambrose, (d) S. Athanasius, (e) S. Augustin, and (f) S. Cyprian, whose words are; *Sicut enim dicitur Pater noster, quia credentium Pater est: sic panis noster, quia in Sacramento nobis datur*. That is: *Euen as God is called our Father, because he is God of the faythfull: so he is called, our Bread, because he is giuen to vs in the blessed Sacrament*. Damascenus confirmeth the same with sundry other holy Fathers, who all expone those words of the Lords prayer, specially of the Blessed Sacrament, and Reall Presence.

3. And notwithstanding that in all the Greek Bibles, it is, τὸν ἐπιούσιον ἄρτον, *supersubstantiall bread*, yet neuer a one of the Scottish Bibles hath followed the Greek text heer, because

(a) *Matth. 6. v. 11.*

(b) *In Cōment. in hunc locū & in epist. ad Titum c. 2. & in Ezech. c. 18*

(c) *Lib. 3. de fide cont. Arri. c. 7.*

(d) *Lib. de Incarnat. Christi.*

(e) *Ep. 121.*

(f) *In orat. Domini.*

cause it is a disaduantage, against them, and for vs Catholiks. And the word ἐπιούσιος, not only is in S. Luke, but also the same is craued τὸ καθ' ἡμέραν dayly, because the blessed Sacrament is both supersubstantiall and dayly bread, as witnesseth plainly the custome amongst the Apostles and Christians in the primitiue Church, & S. Ambrose giueth the reason wherfore it is called, supersubstantial: (g) *Panem nostrum* (sayth he) *quotidianum da nobis hodie. Memini sermonis mei cùm de Sacramentis tractarem: Dixi vobis, quòd ante verba Christi, quod offertur, panis dicatur: vbi verba Christi deprompta fuerint, iam non panis dicitur, sed corpus appellatur: Quare ergo in oratione Dominica quæ postea sequitur, ait, Panem nostrum? Panem quidem dixit, sed* ἐπιούσιον, *hoc est supersubstantialem. Non iste panis est, qui vadit in corpus: sed ille panis vitæ æternæ, qui animæ nostræ substantiam fulcit, ideo Grecè* ἐπιούσιος *dicitur &c.*

(g) *Lib. 5. de Sacram. cap. 4.*

4. Euen as heer the Ministers haue left their owne Greeke text to mantayne their errour in not translating the Lords prayer as they should haue done, so they haue added to the Lords prayer, *For thyne is the Kingdome, the power, and the glory for euer*. It is manifest, that there be many Greeke new Testaments, that haue not these words, which though they had, it would proue nothing, for (h) Caluin belieueth constantly that the Greek text, now extant, is corrupted. And (i) Beza witnesseth the same: *Itaq; ingenuè profiteor editionem Græcam eo loco mihi videri deprauatam.* Lykewise (k) Caluin granteth that the Greek Euangel of S. Matthew is corrupted, where all the Greek copyes haue (which was spoken by Ieremias the Prophet) yet those words are found in Zachary, and not in Ieremy. Lykewise (l) Caluin leaueth the Hebrew text (as corrupted) of the nynth Chapter of Isay, and the twenty three of Ieremie, and preferreth our Latin Catholik version therunto. And he sayth plainly, (m) That in the seauēth Chapter of the Acts of the Apostles vers. 16. The Greek text is manifestly corrupted, because the word *Abraham* is put for *Iacob*. And vpon the 20. of S. Mathew 16. vers. he sayth that those words, *Many are called, but few are chosen*, are impertinent, and no wyse to the purpose. Lykewise Beza (n) abandoneth in sundry other places

(h) *In 7. act. Apost v. 14.*
(i) *In 46. Gen. v. 17.*
(k) *in c. 27 Matth. v. 9*
(l) *Instit. c. 6 num. 12.*
(m) *Ios 24*
(n) *In c. 10. ad Rom. v. 18. Vide Bell. l. 2. de Verbo Dei c. 2. Iac. Gord. tom. 1. cont. c. 8. Gautier in Dilemmatibus.*

ces the Greek text as corrupted, and followeth the Catholik Latin text, which is called *Vulgata editio*.

5. If the Greek new Testament be falty and erroneous, how can it be the infallible Word of God? For as S. Augustin teacheth very wisely: If the Apostles haue erred in wryting the Euangells but in one place, it followeth, that they had not the infallible assistance of the holy Ghost in that place, and consequently the Reader will euer remaine incertaine, when they had that infallible assistance, and when not: wherof it followeth of necessity, that neither the Greek text of the new Testament, nor the Hebrew text of the old Testament, can be an infallible rule and iudge of Controuersies, because there is no Hebrew, Greek, nor Syriake copy now extant, which doth not containe sundry errours, the originals and autographes which the Apostles writ, not being extant. For this cause S. Hierome sayth wisely: (o) That the Latin copies of the Bible are more correct and true, then the Greek, and the Greek more correct then the Hebrew: *Emendatiora sunt exemplaria Latina, quàm Græca, & Græca quàm Hebræa*. Thus also constantly belieueth S. Augustin (whom Caluin calleth the *Eagle* of the Doctours): (p) *In ipsis autem interpretationibus, Itala cæteris præferatur, nam est verborum tenacior cum perspicuitate sententiæ, & latinis quibuslibet emendandis Græca adhibeantur, in quibus septuaginta interpretum, quoad vetus Testamentum attinet, excellit auctoritas*. And Beza himself the Oracle of the Puritanes, maketh greater account of our Latin Edition, then of the Greek copies that are now extant: (q) *Quin etiam aliquot locis animaduertimus veteris interpretis lectionem, quamuis cum nostris Græcis exemplaribus non conueniat, interdum tamen melius quadrare, nempe quòd emendatius aliquod exemplar sequutus esse videatur*. And a little after, he preferreth our Latin vulgar Edition (which is preferred to all other Editions by the Catholike Church) saying: *Quam ego maxima ex parte amplector, & ceteris omnibus antepono*.

(o) *In præfat. in pentateuc.*

(p) *Lib. 2. de Doct. Christ. c. 15.*

(q) *In præfat. in nouum Testamentum.*

6. Since then, our vulgar Latin edition hath not these words. *For thyne is the Kingdome, the power, and glory &c.* why should the Ministers put them in the Lords prayer?

Aug. l. 2. c. 9. de ser. Domini in monte. Ambro. l. 5. de Sacra. Hierom in c. 6. Matth. Cyril. Cate. Myst. 5. Cypr. tract de orat. Domini. Tertul. de orat. c. 8.

specially since the ancient Greek copies haue them not as may appeare, because S. Augustin, S. Ambrose, S. Hierome, S. Cyril, S. Cyprian, and Tertullian, explicating the Lords prayer, make no mention of those wordes, in whose tyme the Greek copies did not differ herein from the Latin.

7. And it is easie to remark and see in this matter the new-fangled spirits of our Scots Ministers, amongst whom scarsely shall you find three that say the Lords prayer after the same forme: for some say, *Our Father which art in Heauen*, others, *O Our Father*: some, *Hallowed be thy name*, others, *Hallowed and blessed be thy Name*, others, *Hallowed, blessed, and sanctified be thy Name*: some, *Giue vs this day &c.* others, *Giue vs O Lord this day*: some, *But deliuer vs from all euill*, others, *But deliuer vs from that euill one*. And if in so short a prayer ther be such variety amongst Ministers, what marueile is it to see so great variance in matters of Religion, in expounding the Bible? the one suffering banishment for not auowing kneeling, others for receauing kneeling against the solemne Oath and promise inioying their rents and stipends: to the one and the other I will addresse those words of the Bible, for taking out of the Bible the words, *supersubstantial bread*: [r] *If any man shall adde vnto these things, vnto him God shall adde the plagues that are written in this book: and if any man shall diminish &c. God shall take away his parte of the booke of lyfe.*

(r) Reuel. 22. v. 18. 19.

8. The second corruption is in S. Matthew: [s] *And as they did suppe, Iesus took the bread and blessed it, and brake it, and gaue it to his Disciples &c.* in the Greek it is εὐλογήσας, *he blessed*, whereby the Bible shewes that our Sauiour blessed the bread, and by vertue of his blessing and words, turned the bread into his precious Body, for the blessing of Christ is not idle, as when he multiplyed the fyues loaues, and two fishes by his blessing. And notwithstanding that al the Greek Bibles haue the word *Blessed* in S. Matthew: yet the Ministers haue left out the word, *Blessed*, and translated *He gaue thankes*, not making any account of the Greek Bibles in this point, and that only to improue and gainstād the

(s) Matth. 26. v. 26.

Marc. 6. v. 41.

the forme of blessings, which the Catholike Church vseth in administring the Sacraments.

9. The double and peruers dealing of the Ministers in this, is, that the same Greek word εὐλογέω, I blesse, they turne in other parts of the Bible, as it should be turned: as in S. Matthew: (t) *And he looked vp to Heauē, and blessed, and brake &c.* And in S. Luke: (u) *And he lifted vp his hands and blessed them.* And to the Galathians: (x) *In thee shall all Nations be blessed,* and in sundry other places where they turne alwaies the Greek word as it should be, and not in the 26. of Matthew. For the Syriake text maketh plainly for vs: *Nesab Ieschuah lachemo vbarec, Iesus took bread and blessed it.* When the word *blessing* is referred to God, then it may signify to thank God, to praise God; but when it is referred to a creature, as in S. Matthew it is, it cannot be taken for thankesgiuing. But S. Luke say the Ministers, hath only (y) *He took bread, and when he had giuen thanks, he brake it*, not making mention of the word, *Blessing.* I answer that our Sauiour both gaue thanks and blessed the bread, as S. Augustin testifieth, and the two Euangelists, S. Matthew and S. Marke plainly witnesse, vsing the word εὐλογήσας, *He blessed it.* Now it is certaine, that the word blessing, cānot be taken for the word thankesgiuing; as when Iacob desired God to blesse his sonne Ioseph, it cānot be said that he desired God to giue thanks to his sōne Ioseph, & infinite such other places which I omit to be short, only cōtent with those words of S. Paul: (a) *The cuppe of blessing which we blesse, is it not the communion of the Bloud of Christ?* τὸ ποτήριον τῆς εὐλογίας, it cānot be said the cuppe of thankesgiuing which we thanke for. The article ὁ, is the accusatiue case, wherfore the holy Fathers accordingly auowe, that our Sauiour both gaue thankes, and blessed the bread. S. Augustin, *quem citat Beza*: (b) *Non enim omnis panis, sed accipiens benedictionem Christi, fit Corpus Christi.* Shewing plainly that the blessing of Christ, had force to turne the bread into his body, for the blessing & words of Christ are of efficacy and working, not like the words of man, which are idle and without effect sayth S. Ambrose: (c) *Tu fortè dicis, Meus panis est vsitatus: sed panis iste, panis est ante*

(t) Matth. 14. v. 19.
(u) Luc 24 v. 50.
(x) Galat. 3 v. 8.
August. de con Euang c. 49.
Gen. 48. v. 15
(a) 1. Cor. 10. v. 16.
(b) Serm. de verb. Euang.
(c) Ambr. l. 4. de Sacram. c. 4.

 verba

verba Sacramentorum, vbi acceßerit consecratio, de pane fit caro Christi. Hoc igitur astruamus. Quomodo potest, qui panis est, corpus esse Christi? Consecratione. Consecratio igitur quibus verbis est, & cuius sermonibus? Domini Iesu. Nam reliqua omnia quæ dicuntur, Laus Deo defertur: Oratione petitur pro populo, pro Regibus, pro cæteris: vbi venitur vt conficiatur venerabile Sacramentum, iam non suis Sermonibus Sacerdos, sed vtitur Sermonibus Christi. Ergo, sermo Christi hoc conficit Sacramentum. Quis Sermo Christi? Nempe is, quo facta sunt omnia. Iußit Dominus & facta est terra: Iußit Dominus & factum est cælum: Iußit Dominus & facta sunt maria: Iußit Dominus & omnis creatura generata est. Vides ergo quàm operatorius sit Sermo Christi. Can any man speake more plainly, against the Puritanes and Protestants?

10. I doe supercede the prouing of other blasphemous corruptions of the Ministers, referring them to seueral Ages; asking only these three questions of Maister Ramsey. First, to name me any auncient Father, who euer did take the word, *Bleßing*, for *Thankesgiuing*? The secōd, to name me any man of any Nation, who before Caluin corrupted the Bible so blasphemously in this place? The third: Whether the perfect knowledge of the Greek tongue should be rather graunted to the Greek Fathers, (who do read vniuersally the word, *He blessed*, heere) then to our Scottish Ministers, whose ignorance in the Greek tongue is such, that to this day not one of them haue shewed to be skilfull therin (to my knowledge) by any publik testimony.

The

The 3. 4. & 5. Article.

1. That holy Images. 2. The signe of the Crosse. 3. And holy Reliques were with reuerence in vse, amongst the Catholiks, in this first Age.

CHAP. III.

IT is certaine amongst vs Catholikes, that it is not lawfull to pray to Images, to kneele to Images, or to giue that honour to them, which is only due to God; as the Ministers doe teach and deceaue the ignorant people. The vse then of Images in the Catholik Church, is, to vse thē as instrumēts to put vs in memory of the life & passion of Christ, & the glorious actions of his Saintes. For it is certaine that things seene by vs, do moue vs more, then things we heare: specially considering how that the multitude of worldly affaires, the weaknes of the flesh, & tentations of the Diuel, withdrawe vs from thinking on God. Which was the reason wherfore God himself ordayned the vse of Images in the old Law, commanding Moyses to make the Images of Cherubims, which were Angels: (a) *And thou shalt make two Cherubims of Gold &c. at the two ends of the Mercy-seat &c. And the Cherubims shall stretch their wings on high.* Now I aske of the Ministers: Those pictures of the Cherubims eyther they were Images or Idols? If Idols, then God commanded Idolatry, which is a blasphemy: If they were Images, then God commanded the vse of Images, and did neuer recall this Cōmand in any part of the Bible. Yea if those words of Exodus: (b) *Thou shalt not make thee any grauen Image,* were the word of God (as in effect they are not) he had contradicted himself, forbidding

(a) *Exod. 25. v. 18.*

(b) *Exod. 20. v. 4.*

 ding

ding in the 20. Chapter Images, and commanding Images in the 25. of Exodus.

2. Secondly, in the booke of Numbers, the Image of the brasen Serpent is plainly set downe: (c) *God said to Moyses, make thee a fyerie Serpent and set it vp for a signe, that as many as are bitten, may look vpon it and liue.* Where the word of God calleth this fyerie Serpent a *signe*, *Image*, or *Picture*, which signe and Image our Sauiour commendeth greatly, as an Image and figure of himselfe: (d) *And as Moyses lift vp the Serpent in the wildernesse, so must the Sonne of man be lifted vp.* This Image was seen by more then three hundreth thousand Iewes in the wildernesse. Now I aske, Eyther this fyerie Serpẽt was an Image, and figure of Christ, or an Idol? If an Image and figure, then God commanded it, notwithstanding he forsaw that the Iewes after were to abuse this his holy institution, as the Bible witnesseth: If an Idol, then God commandeth Idolatry, which is a horrible blasphemy. And euen as by the viewing and looking vpon the fyerie Serpent, the Iewes receaued health in body and inward comfort; so the Catholiks in viewing deuoutly Images, specially of our Sauiour, receaue sundry times health in body, and comfort in mind. Certes Tertullian calleth this Serpent an Image: (e) *Effigies ænei Serpentis suspensi figuram designauit.* In the Hebrew it is, *Hasé lecha saráph, Make vnto thee a fyerie Serpent*, by reason it was molten by fyre, or made of brasse, which glistereth like fyre, sayth Vatablus, the 70. turne it, a *brasen Serpent*.

(c) *Numb.* 21. *v.* 8.

(d) *Ioan.* 3. *v.* 14.

2. *Kings* 18. *v.* 4.

(e) *Lib. de Idolat.* c. 5.

ὄφιν χαλκοῦν.

3. Thirdly, Salomon (as witnesseth the Bible) did place Images in his Temple and Church, at the command of God: (f) *And within the Oracle he made two Cherubims of Oliue tree, ten cubits high &c.* And againe: *And he put the Cherubims within the inner house.* And againe, the Bible witnesseth, that the Temple of Salomon was wholy of grauen Images, & figures of the Cherubims: (g) *And he carued all the walles of the house round about with grauen figures of Cherubims &c.* Of the which words of the Bible these propositions ensue. 1. *Thou shalt make two Cherubims*, that is, the Images of Cherubims. 2. *Thou shalt make a fyerie Serpent for a signe and Image.*

(f) 1. *Reg.* 6. *v.* 23.

(g) 1. *Reg.* 6. *v.* 29.

3. The

3. *The Temple of Salomon was whole of figures, or Images of the Cherubims &c.* I aske now of the Ministers to giue as plaine words out of the Bible that make against Images, which they shall neuer be able to doe: but rather they will ignorantly rage & boast of their foolish necessary consequences, which are nothing els but their own dreames, inuentions, and plaine heresies. Wherfore let the wise preferre to the Ministers consequences and foolish traditions, the consequences and deductions of the holy Fathers, as the Bible manifestly commandeth vs to do: (h) *Go not from the Doctrine of the elders, for they haue learned it of their Fathers, and of them thou shalt learne vnderstanding, and to make answer in the tyme of need.* Yea we are obliged in conscience, to enquire of the auncient Fathers the true Religion: (i) *Remember* (sayth the Bible) *the auncient dayes, consider the yeares of so many generatiõs, aske thy Father, and he will shew thee, aske thy elders, and they will tell yee.* The Puritanes leauing the waies of their forfathers, shall neuer haue rest in conscience: (k) *Stand in the wayes and behold, and aske for the old way, which is the good way, and walke therin, and you shall find rest for your soules.* Wherunto the Puritanes answere: *We will not walke therin.* For the which cause the Puritanes and Protestants (l) *Haue stumbled from the auncient wayes, to walke in the wayes not troden.* Yea against the expresse words of their owne Bible: (m) *Thou shalt not remoue the ancient bounds, which thy Fathers haue set.* Whereof S. Augustin giueth a very good reason: (n) *Because that which the holy Fathers haue found in the Church, that they haue holden, they haue taught what they haue learned; what they haue receaued from their Fore-fathers, they haue deliuered to vs their posterity.* And specially in matters of Religion, (o) *We should not depart from the first Ecclesiasticall tradition, nor belieue otherwyse, but as the Church of God hath by succession deliuered vnto vs.* Which was euer the practise of the Church of God, as witnesseth Lyrinensis: (p) *If any new question do arise, we doe repaire to the iudgment of the holy Fathers.* Let vs then follow the consequences of the holy Fathers concerning Images, the signe of the Crosse, and holy Reliques.

(h) *Eccl.* 8. *v.* 9.

(i) *Deut.* 32 *v.* 7.

(k) *Ierem.* 6. *v.* 16.

(l) *Ierem.* 18. *v.* 15.

(m) *Prou.* 22. *v.* 28.

(n) *Cont. Pelag.*

(o) *Origen. tract.* 29. *in Matth.*

(p) *Lib. adu. hær.*

Testi-

Testimonyes of the holy Fathers of this first Age, for the vse of Images, the signe of the Crosse, and honouring the Reliques of Saints.

The first Section.

(a) *Ep. ad Phil. ante medium.* τὴν ὁμολογίαν τοῦ σταυροῦ.
(b) *In epist ad Burdegal. c. 8.*

SAint Ignatius Martyr: (a) *Princeps mundi huius gaudet, cùm quis crucem negarit: cognoscit enim crucis confeßionem, suum eße exitium: Id enim trophæum est contra ipsius potentiam, quod vbi viderit, horret, & audiens timet.* The holy Crosse is a banner against the power of the Diuel, who seeing the Crosse abhorreth it, and hearing of it, feareth. S. Martial: (b) *Crucē Domini in quem credidistis, Deum verum & Dei filium, semper in mente, in ore, in signo tenete. Crux enim domini est armatura vestra inuicta contra Satanam.* Haue euer the crosse of God in whō yee haue belieued, in mynd, in mouth, & marke yourselfe therwith &c. And since the signe of the crosse is nothing els but an Image of Christ, this holy Father in commending to vs the signe of the crosse, commendeth likewise the vse of Images.

(c) *Pamphil. Martyr. Innoc. 1. Epist. 18. ad Alexād Episc. Turrian. lib. 1. pro Canon. Apost. c. 25*
(d) *lib. 7. Epist. ep. 109.*
(e) *Orat in Theod.*
(f) *Orat. quod vet & nou. test. vnus sit mediator.*
(g) *7. Syn. act. 2. & 4.*

2. The holy Apostles in that general counsel holden at Antioch say thus: (c) *Ne errent fideles erga Idola, sed exprimant diuinam, humanam, immaculatam, manufactam imaginem veri dei & saluatoris nostri Iesu Christi, ac seruorum eius ex aduerso coram Idolis & Iudæis, neq; amplius errent erga Idola, aut Iudæis similes fiant.* Wherby the Apostles commaunde Christians to vse Images, giuing also the reason wherfore they were first instituted, and shewing a manifest difference betwixt Images and Idols. So that wisely Gregory the great called Images, (d) *the books of the vnlearned.* And accordingly, Gregory Nyssene sayd, (e) *The silent picture speaketh in the wall and profiteth very much.* The reason wherof is, because the view and sight of Images, increaseth in vs faith, the loue of God and of his Saincts, and kindleth in our hartes the coales of deuotion: which S. Chrysostome felt when thus he write, (f) *I loued a picture of melted wax ful of piety.* Gregory Nyssene (g) *was often wont to weep, looking on the Image of Abraham sacrificing*

ficing his sonne Isaac. And Gregory the Great wryting to Secundine Abbot (to whom also he sent the Images of Christ) sayd thus, (h) *I know thou longest for our Sauiours Image, that gazing on it, thou mayst burne the more with the loue of God.* (h) *Lib. 7. ep. 53.*

3. S. Denis Areopagita speaking of the ceremonyes of Baptisme, wherin the signe of the crosse was, and is vsed by the Bishop, who (i) *Inchoans vnctionem trino signaculo, inungendum deinceps Sacerdotibus toto corpore hominem vbi tradidit, ipse ad adoptionis matrem proficiscitur, eiusq; aquam sacris inuocationibus sanctificans, & tribus sanctissimi vnguenti cruciformibus effusionibus illam perficiens.* And a litle after, he sheweth the custome and forme in receauing Monks and religious men to the seruice of God, vsing in such reception the signe of the Crosse, rasure of their heads &c. (k) *Vbi verò omnia hæc, is qui instituitur, promiserit, cruciformi figura consignans eum Sacerdos tondet, trinam diuinæ beatitudinis personam inclamans.* And of Images he sayth thus: (l) *sunt reuera ea quæ videntur, eorum quæ sub aspectum non cadunt certæ claræq; imagines.* (i) *Eccl. Hier. c. 2. p. 2.* (k) *Eccles. Hierarch. c. 6. p. 2.* (l) *Citatur in septima Synodo generali c. 36. Tom. 3. Concil.*

4. Besides the foresaid Doctours, Hermes a most anciẽt and Apostolical wryter of this Age, maketh mention of Reliques, Prayer for the dead, vnwritten traditiõs, of Chrisme, consecration of Monkes, of Altars, places sanctified, & sundry other ceremonyes, of the tonsure of Preists heads, burning incense at the Altar, of merit and iustification of works, of professed chastity in preists, of fasting from certayne meats, of works of supererogation, as witnesseth Hamelinanus a Protestant wryter. Finally we Catholiks cõstãtly do honour the holy Reliques of Saints, not with a diuine honour which is due to God õly, but with a Religious honour, much inferiour to the foresaid, yet aboue a ciuill honour due to the Magistrat; & that we do, & affirme with S. Austin: (m) *Sanctorum corpora & præcipuè beatorum Martyrum reliquias, ac si Christi membra sincerissimè honoranda credimus: si quis contra hanc sententiam venerit, non Christianus, sed Eunomianus & Vigilantianus creditur:* He that doth not belieue that the holy bodies & Reliques of blessed Martyrs should be honored as the members of Christ, he is not a Christian, but a Vigilantian, or Heretik, sayth S. Augustin. *In his book called Pastor.* *Lib. de traditionib. Apostolic.* (m) *De Eccl. dog. c. 73.*

That the Ministers haue corrupted the Bible in sundry places, which proue the vse of Images, of the holy Crosse &c.

The second Section.

SAint Augustine witnesseth, that Faustus Manichæus the Heretike bragged much of the Bible, of the Word of God, of the Scriptures, yet in effect he had nothing but lyes, vanities, and vile superstitions: the lyke is easie to be seene in the Protestants and Puritanes of Scotland, who do vaunt of the Scriptures, of the Bible, yet they cannot proue, yea not one debatable point of their Religion out of the expresse word of the Bible, but rather are forced to giue vs their consequences and foolish illations, for the expresse word of God: wherby they are to be accompted, (a) *Theeues who enter not by the doore* (of the word of God) *but climbe another way to steal, kill, and destroy our soules.* So that by peruerse interpretations of the Ministers, (b) *The Gospell of Christ is made the Gospell of man, or which is worse, the Gospell of the diuell.*

Lib. 5. conf. c. 5. & 6.

(a) *Ioh. 10. v. 2.*

(b) *Hiero. l. 1. in c. 1. ad Galat.*

2. To make Images odious to the commō people, & to stirre vp the Nobility to cast down the Churchs, they haue abhommably corrupted sundry places of the Bible, specially the twenty of Exodus, thus: (c) *Thou shall not make to the selfe any grauen Image &c.* Contrary to the Greeke text, contrary to the Hebrew, *Lo thahhasche leca*, contrary to the Latin, *Non facies tibi Idolum, aut sculptile*, contrary to all the Bibles which haue beene vsed amongst all nations, the space of fiftene hundreth yeares, which all haue in substance, *Thou shall not make vnto thy selfe any Idol.* Wherfore seeing that the Protestans cannot shew any Bible before the comming of Caluin, that hath such blasphemous words, *Thou shall not make to thy selfe any grauen Image*, it followeth, that it is a manifest corruption and nouelty, carying with it selfe many blasphemies.

(c) *Exod. 20. v. 4.* οὐ ποιήσεις ἑαυτῷ εἴδωλον.

3. The first Blasphemy. If God forbad Images, heere it followeth that he contradicted himselfe: for in the 25. of Exodus

Exodus he commandeth the image of the *Cherubims*, & after the Image of the fyrie serpent. 2. If Idol and Image be all one (as the Puritanes say to excuse this their Blasphemous translation) it followeth, that Christ, (d) *who is the Image of the inuisible God*, may be called, *the Idol of God*, and consequently, all those that worshippe Christ, worshippe an Idol. Agayne, If Idol and Image were all one, they must translate thus: (e) *As we haue borne the Idol of the earthlie, so let vs beare the Idol of the heauenly*. And agayne: *We are transformed into the same Idol*, & sundry other such places. 3. That man who is called the Image of God, may be called, *The Idol of God*, which is absurd. 4. It would follow that all the Ministers are makers of Idoles or Images, and consequently are Idolatrous. For the Apostle sayth: (f) *This yee know, that no fornicatour, neyther vncleane person, nor couetous person which is an Idolater, hath any inheritance in the kingdome of Christ, and of God*, they should translate, *nor couetous man, which is a worshipper of Images*, and consequently al the Ministers being couetous, they must needes be all Idolaters. 5. When Idolls are called Gods (to whom the Pagans prayed, and whom they adored) then the Ministers do not translate Images but Idol (though the same Greeke word be alwayes one) knowing well that the Catholikes do not worship Images as Gods. As for example: (g) *And the residue therof he maketh a God, euen his Idoll, he boweth vnto it, and worshipeth, and prayeth vnto it*. And agayne: (h) *Assemble your selues & come, draw neer togeather, the obiect of the Gētils, they haue no knowledge that set vp the wood of their Idol, & pray vnto a God that cannot saue them*: Which two places shewe plainly the malice of the Ministers, and the difference betwixt Catholik Images and the Pagans Idoles. For the Pagans prayed to their Idols, and thought them to be Gods, did put their trust in them, kneeled vnto them &c. 6. The Hebrew Word, *Pesel*, is alwayes translated by the 70. εἴδωλον, and not εἰκών. And the greek word εἰκών euer is turned into *Image*, as the hebrew word *Tselem*, & neuer into Idol. 7. The Ministers shall neuer be able to name me any Grecian wryter of the primitiue

(d) *Coloss.* 1. v. 15. ὅς ἐστιν εἰκὼν τοῦ θεοῦ τοῦ ἀοράτου

(e) 1. *Cor.* 15. v. 49.

(f) *Ephes.* 5. v. 5. *Coloss.* 3. v. 5.

(g) *Esa.* 44. v. 17.

(h) *Esa.* 45 v. 20. *Lephis* lō. i. *his Idol.*

Origen. hom. 8. *in Exod. Theod.* q. 38. *in Exod.*

tiue Church, who confound the word *Idol* with *Image:* for it is certaine that Origene and Theodoret both ancient & learned Grecians, with others holy Fathers of Greece make a manifest distinction betwixt εἰκὼν and εἴδωλον. And all the Latin Fathers without exception make one distinction betwixt *Idol* and *Image*, condemning *Idols* as abhominable, auowing *Images* as commendable. 8. The Ministers themselues breake willingly this Commandement in kneling at the reception of the Supper of the Lord, and that against their owne solemne Oath giuen at their reception, and confirmed and sworne solemnely by the three Estats of Scotland in sundry Parlaments: (i) *Therfore whosoeuer reserueth and worshippeth those Sacraments* (meaning Baptisme, and the Supper of the Lord) *procureth to himselfe damnation*. For since the Ministers belieue, that the Supper of the Lord is but an Image and figure of Christ, in kneeling before such figures, the Commandement of God, according to their translation, is transgressed. As also the second Commandement, *Thou shall not take the name of the Lord thy God in vayne*, is lykewise transgressed by the Ministers, they hauing sworne solemnely not to receaue kneeling vnder the payne of eternall damnation: yet now haue receaued the same against their former Oath, and so haue broken both the first and second Commandement of God, by committing both Idolatry and periury.

(i) *In the confession of Fayth of the Ministers of Scotland.*

The

The 6. & 7. Article.

1. *That the custome of the Catholik Church in this first Age, was to honour the Saints in Heauen.*
2. *And to pray vnto them.*

CHAP. IIII.

SEING by the Law of God, and Nature, Honour is due to Excellency, there must be so many kinds of honour, as there be kinds of excellency, which are three. The first is, of God, which is infinit, for the excellency of God must be infinite. The second excellency is supernaturall, yet created, as that of grace and glorie. The third is, humane, or naturall, consisting in naturall gifts, or worldly dignity. To these three kynds of excellency pertaine three kynds of honour. The first, Diuine, due to God only, which we call, *Latria*. The second belongeth to Saints and holy things, as eleuated by God aboue the course of nature, and this is called, *Dulia*, and *Hyperdulia*. The third is, *Ciuill honour*, due to men according to their naturall qualities. The first is due to God only, the second is due to the Saints in heauen, as to the glorious seruants of God, being now in glory with him. And notwithstanding that the outward actions of kneeling, bowing, kissing, praying &c. be indifferently giuẽ to God, to the Saints, and ciuill men; yet the intention and mind of him who doth those outward actions distinguisheth the same: for kneeling to God is diuine worship: kneling to Saints is an inferiour pious worship or honour; kneeling to a mortall King is ciuill honour. The two last alwayes tending to the honour and glory of God, who will be honou-

λατρεία.
δυλεία.
ὑπερδυλεία.

noured in his Saints & creatures, conforme to that saying of the Scripture, *Gloria hac est omnibus sanctis eius.*

2. This doctrine is confirmed by the holy Fathers, specially by S. Augustine, who sayeth: (a) *We honour Martyrs with that worship of loue and society; wherwith holy men are worshipped in this lyfe, whose heart we perceaue is prepared to like sufferance for the Euangelical verity: But Martyrs more deuoutly, by how much more securely, after all vncertaynties are ouercome, & with how much more confident prayse, we preach them now victorious in a more happy lyfe, then others yet fighting in this life. But with that worship, which in Greeke is called Latria, which in Latin cannot be expressed by one word, we neyther worship, nor teach to be worshipped but one God. And for so much as offering of Sacrifice pertaineth to this worship (wherof they are called idolaters, that offer sacrifice to any idols) we by no meanes offer any such thing, nor teach to be offred, eyther to any Martyr, or blessed Soule, or holy Angell.* May S. Augustine speake more plainly against the Protestants? The same teacheth other Doctours: (b) *Our Lord hath depryued false Gods of the honour they had in Temples, and in place of them, caused his Martyrs to be honored, yet not in the same manner, for we neyther bring hostes nor libaments to Martyrs, but honour thẽ as holy men, and most deare friends of God.*

(a) *Lib. 20 cõt. Faust. c. 21.*

λατρεία.

(b) *Theod. l. 8. ad Græcos. Beda in Luc. 4. ante medium.*

3. To make this mater more plaine, it is to be remarked: that we Catholiks pray not to the Saints in Heauen eyther as Gods to help vs, Redeemers to saue vs, or as the chiefe Authors of any gift or grace bestowed vpon vs. For we acknowledge *only God*, to be the supreme Author and fountaine of all naturall and supernaturall fauours, of grace and glorie. Secondly, we pray not to Saints as *Mediatours of our redemption*, but, *of Intercession only*: for our Mediatour and Aduocat of redemption is only Chryst Iesus, as the Apostle sayth: (c) *If any man sinne, we haue an Aduocate with the Father, Iesus Chryst the Iust; and he is the reconciliation for our sinnes.* And agayne: (d) *There is one God & one Mediator betwixt God and man, which is the man Christ Iesus.* Which place though corrupted by the Ministers, yet speaketh only of *the Mediatour of Redemption*: for the Scripture witnesseth playnly, that Moyses was Mediatour betwixt God and the Iewes:

(c) *1. Ioan. 2. v. 1.*

(d) *1. Tim. 2. v. 5.*

Iewes: (e) *For the Law was ordeyned by Angels in the hand of a Mediatour.* Wherby the Bible auerreth a *Mediatour of intercession*, besides Christ Iesus. And this is the reason wherfore we Catholikes euer addresse all our petitions to Saintes or Angels with this conclusion: *per Dominum nostrum Iesum Christum filium tuum &c.* declaring therby that Chryst is only our Aduocat or Mediator of Redemption, and that the Saints in heauen, are but intercessours besides the holy Trinity for vs; yea when the Minister is desyred to pray for any friend, he is made therby *Mediator of intercession*, though he be a sinfull man, and of little credit with God, yea perhaps of none, in respect of the Saints of Heauen, who are in the estate of glorie, and without spot of sinne.

(e) Galat. 3. v. 19.

4. I conclude then, that the Catholike Church sayth to God only, *haue mercy on vs, saue vs, forgiue vs our sinnes &c.* And to the Saints, *Pray for vs.* And if any Catholike say to any Saint *saue me*, his meaning is, that the Saint saue him by his prayers to God: so we call sometymes the Blessed Virgin Marie our hope, life, refuge, because she brought forth our hope, life, and refuge Christ Iesus. Or because by her intercession she may procure our life and saluation: and in this we follow the practise of the Scripture. For S. Paul calleth the Thessalonians, (f) *his hope, his ioy, his crown of glorie.* And he calleth Timothy, the saluation of others, (g) *This doing thou shal saue thy self & them that heare thee.* And playnly Iob doth pray vnto the Angels according to S. Augustins exposition and meaning, when he sayeth, (h) *Haue pitty vpon me, haue pitie vpon me (o yee my freinds) for the hand of God hath touched me* And in my Iudgemēt S. Augustines opinion alone in this place should be preferred before the new vpstart Ministers dreames and expositions. For the text sheweth that Iob his visible and secret freinds had left him: (i) *All my secret friends abhorred me; & they whome I loued, are turned against me.*

(f) 1. Thess. 2. v. 19.

(g) 1. Tim. 4. v. 16.

(h) Iob. 19. v. 21. S. Augustin in his annotations vpon Iob.

(i) Iob. 19. v. 19.

First then it is manifest by the testimonyes of the Bible, that the Angels and Saints in Heauen praye for vs: (k) *Then the Angell of our Lord answered and said: O Lord of hosts, how long wilt thou be vnmercifull to Ierusalem, and to the*

(k) Zach. 1. v. 12.

Cityes,

Cityes of Iuda, with whome thou hast bene displeased now these threescore and ten yeares. It is certayn lykewise that the Saints in Heauen are equall to the Angels, (l) *For they can do no more, for as much as they are equall to the Angels, and are the sonnes of God, since they are the children of the resurrection,* both then the Angels, and Saints pray for vs.

(l) *Luc. 20. v. 36.*

Secondly, it is lawful to vs to pray to the Angels or Saints in Heauen, according to the example of the holy Patriarch Iacob: (m) *The Angel which hath delyuered me from all euill, blesse the children, and let my name be named vpon them, and the name of my father Abraham & Isaac, that they may grow as fish into a multitude in the midst of the earth.* Cōforme to the which example of Iacob, S. Athanasius (who was thirteene hundreth yeares since) prayeth to the Blessed virgin Marie thus: (n) *Inclyne thy eares to our praiers and forget not thy people. O Lady, Mistres, Queene and Mother of God pray for vs.* And S. Augustine: (o) *O Blessed Marie, receaue our prayers, obtayne our suits, for thou art the speciall hope of sinners.*

(m) *Gen. 48. v. 16.*

(n) *Serm. de deipara.*

(o) *Serm. 18 de sanctis.*

Thirdly, Iob was counselled to pray to the Saints: (p) *Call if there be any who will answere thee, and turne to some of the Saints:* which place the Ministers haue filthily corrupted in translating it, by way of interrogation, *And to which of the Saints wilt thou turne?*

(p) *Iob. 5. v. 1.*

5. Now I would aske of the Ministery to giue me so playne & expresse words of the Bible that make for thē. Secondly, since they abuse the poore people, saying: that they preach nothing, that they belieue nothing but the expresse and playne word of the Bible, in what part of the Bible are these poynts of their faith to be found, *There is no inuocation of Saints? The Saints do not heare our prayers.* And agayne: *It is agaynst the honour of God to pray to Saints.* For their Blasphemous propositiōs are no wise in the expresse word of the Bible. How then shall they proue them out of the Bible? By necessary consequence, say they. But those necessairie consequences are not infallible, but erroneous, and not the word of God, & consequētly we make no such accompt of their foolish and newfangled cōsequences, as of those of the holy Fathers of this first Age. Let vs heare thē.

The

The Testimonyes of the holy Fathers of this first Age, Concerning praying to the Saints in Heauen, and honouring of them.

The first Section.

SAINT Dionysius Areopagita: (a) *Dico autem, oracula sequutus vbiq;, planè vtiles esse in hac vita Sanctorum preces, hoc modo si quis Sanctorum numerum amore incensus, & ad eorum participationem piè affectus tanquam propriæ conscius exiguitatis, quempiam Sanctorum roget sibi fieri adiutorem & comprecatorem, vtilitatem omnino ex eo consequetur omni vtilitate superiorem.* That is: I say, following the holy Scriptures, that the prayers of the Saints are most profitable for vs &c. And in the nynth Chapter of the same booke he witnesseth: That S. Michael the Archangel was giuen by God as a protectour to the Iewes to assist them, and to present their prayers to God: yea the same holy Father auoweth euery particular mā to haue his owne Angell who doth offer our prayers vnto God, and knoweth our necessityes, as witnesseth the holy Angell of Cornelius, who said to him: (b) *Thy prayers and thy almes are come vp into remembrance before God*. Which place sheweth that the Angels, and consequently the Saints in Heauen know our prayers, our necessityes, and good workes. The same holy Father witnesseth, that the prayers of the Saints in heauen help, not only those in this life, but also the faithfull departed out of this life: (c) *Quòd autem & iustorum preces etiam in hac vita, nedum post mortem, ijs duntaxat prosint, qui sacris precibus digni sunt, veræ oraculorum traditiones nos edocent.*

(a) *Eccles. Hierarch. c. 7. parte 3. ante med.*

(b) *Act. 10. v. 4.*

(c) *Loco supra cit.*

2. S. Clement witnesseth the same: (d) *De Martyribus verò præcipimus vobis, vt in omni honore sint apud vos, vt apud nos fuerunt Iacobus Episcopus, & Condiaconus noster Stephanus: hos enim & Deus beatos fecit, & viri sancti honorarunt, & fuerunt puri omnis delicti, & neq; ad peccatum flecti, neq; a virtute detorqueri potuerunt, quorum non sunt dubiæ laudes, de quibus Dauid aiebat, Pretiosa in cōspectu Domini mors sanctorum eius &c.* And a litle after, this holy

(d) *Lib. 5. Const. Apost. c. 8. edit. Turriā. Græc. & c. 7. Latin.*

holy Father inuiteth vs to keep holy the Festiuall dayes of the Saints in heauen, in praying to them, and calling for their help: (e) *In diebus Apostolorum vacent. Magistri enim vestri fuerunt ad docendum vos de Christo, vobisq; Spiritum Sanctum dederunt. In die Stephani Protomartyris item vacent: ac reliquis diebus Sanctorum Martyrum, qui Christum vitæ suæ anteposuerunt.* And in another place he counselleth vs to call vpon, and inuocate the holy Martyrs, (f) *Memoremus Martyres sactos, vt mereamur certaminis eorum participes fieri.*

(e) *Lib. 8. Constit. Apostol. c. 33.*

(f) *Lib. 8. const. Ap. c. 13.*

Martial. ep. ad Burdegal. c. 3.

3. S. Martialis first Bishop of Burdeaux, sent thither by S. Peter the Apostle, witnesseth likewise, that holy Aultars were erected to God in S. Stephens name, where Masse was said to God, and prayers to S. Stephen, to the end he should pray for the Catholike Church: conforme to that which S. Augustine wyselie wryteth: (g) *Iniuria est pro Martyre orare, cuius nos debemus orationibus commendari.*

(g) *Serm. 17. de verb. Apost. prope initium.*

4. S. Peter witnesseth the same in the holy Masse, which he was accustomed to say, and which hath bene famous through all Christendome these sixteene hundreth yeares, where S. Peter prayeth: (h) *Libera nos quæsumus Domine ab omni malo præsēte ac futuro, intercessionibus immaculatæ & gloriosæ Dominæ nostræ Deiparæ, semperq; Virginis Mariæ &c.* That is, Delyuer vs, we pray the O Lord, from all euill present and to come, by the intercession of the Blessed & Immaculate Virgin *Marie &c.* And a litle before, *Be bountifull vnto vs, O Lord, by the intercession of the Blessed virgin Marie, and of all the Saints in heauen.*

(h) *Litur. Pet. ante med.*

5. S. Iames the Apostle witnesseth the same in his Masse, famous specially amongst the Grecians to this day: (i) *Commemorationem agamus sanctissimæ, Immaculatæ, gloriosissimæ, benedictæ Dominæ nostræ Matris dei & semper Virginis Mariæ, atq; omnium Sanctorum & iustorum, vt precibus & intercessionibus eorum omnes misericordiam consequamur.* I pretermit to set down other testimonyes, since the practise of the Catholike Church (to pray to Saints) in this Age, was so vniuersall, that no heretike did call it in doubt, before Vigilantius, who being foure hundreth yeares after Christ, is condemned by the holy Fathers, yea by the Protestants themselues

(i) *In Lit. Iacob. Minor.*

themſelues, as a manifeſt and idolatrous heretike.

That the Miniſters haue corrupted the Bible in ſundry places, which proue the Inuocation of Saints.

The ſecond Section.

THE Catholike Church, and all antiquity readeth to the honour of the holy Apoſtles and Saints in heauen that ſaying of the Prophet Dauid (who as a Prophet did foreſee the honour which the Catholike Church was to giue to the Saints in heauen) (a) *Nimis honorificati ſunt amici tui Deus.* That is; *Thy freinds O God, are become exceeding honorable, Their Princedome is exceedingly ſtrengthned.* Now to make this place obſcure to the Reader and to take away the force of both the Hebrew & Greeke words, the Miniſters haue blaſphemouſlie tranſlated thus: *How deare therfore are thy thoughts vnto me O God, how great is the ſumme of them?* Doth not the Hebrew word make more for vs, and ſignifie, *friends*? Doth not S. Hierome (who alone did vnderſtand better the Hebrew toung, them all the Miniſters together) tranſlate *friends*? Doth not the Greeke text put it out of doubt, ſince it is according to our ancient Latin tranſlation *Thy friends O God*? why do ye hunt after noueltyes and forſake the troden path of antiquity, and paſſe the bounds, which our holy Forefathers haue appoynted, preferring your owne imaginations and new deuyſes, euen there where yee cannot pretend iuſtly eyther the Hebrew or the Greeke, where it is, *their princedome is exceedinglie ſtrengthned,* and not, *how great is the ſumme of them.*

(a) *Pſa* 138 *v.* 16. *al.* 139 *v.* 17.

Regeka,

οἱ φίλοι σου

αἱ ἀρχαὶ αὐτῶν.

2. But this newfangled ſingularity in the blaſphemous tranſlations of our Miniſters ſhall better appeare in their dealing about our Bleſſed Lady, whoſe honour they haue ſoght ſo many wayes to diminiſh, and deface, with their Maiſter Iohn Caluin, who blaſphemouſly and worſe then the Deuils themſelues, ſpeaketh of the Bleſſed virgin: (b) *Videtur Sancta virgo non minus malignè reſtringere Dei potentiam, quàm prius Zacharias.* And a little after: *Neque verò magnopere laborandum eſt, vt eam purgemus ab omni vitio.*

(b) *Cal. in Luc. c.* 1. *v.* 38. *printed by Robert Eſtienne an.* 1568.

3. In

3. In the first Chapter of S. Luke, it is said of the Blessed Virgin Marie: (c) *Hayle Marie full of grace, our Lord is with thee*, in Latine: *Aue gratia plena*; which translation the holy Fathers of the Latin Church haue constantly kept, as Maldonate sheweth. But our Ministers haue found out a new kynd of translation, *Haile thou that art freely beloued*, making the blessed Virgin lesse in fauour with God, then S. Iohn the Baptist, of whom it is said: (d) *And he shall be filled with the holy Ghost*: Inferior to S. Steuen, (e) *who was full of the holy Ghost*. Yet their Mariomastikes will not haue the blessed Virgin Marie, *full of grace*. How can these Ministers be friends to God, who thus disgrace the Mother of God? They are sworne enemyes not only to the Greeke text, but also to the Syriake in this poynt, which the Angell vsed: *Schelom lech, Maleiath taibuthoi*. That is: *Pax tecum, O plena gratia*. *Peace vnto thee, O full of grace*. Will any wyseman more belieue ignorant Ministers, rather then S. Ambrose who calleth the blessed Virgin, (f) *Gratia plena*? Then S. Augustine who prayeth to the blessed Virgin thus: (g) *Aue gratia plena, Dominus tecum: Dominus tecum, sed plusquam mecum &c*. And agayne: *Audite Gabrielem Angelum eam salutantem, Aue gratia plena dominus tecum*? Then S. Hierome who lykewise prayeth and calleth her, *gratia plena*? Then Beda: (h) *Bene gratia plena vocatur, quæ nimirum gratiam, quam nulla meruerat assequitur, vt ipsum videlicet gratia conciperet, & generet auctorem*?

4. As for the Greeke Fathers, they lykewyse called her vniuersally full of grace: (i) S. Athanasius, (k) Epiphanius Theophilactus, and sundry others, whome we should belieue to be more skilfull in the Greeke their naturall tongue, then the Ministers can be, who of malice that they cary to the blessed Virgin, translate other words of the same nature and forme otherwyse, for thy translate: (l) ἡλκωμένος, *Full of sores*, yet they will not translate κεχαριτωμένη, *full of grace*.

5. Secondly, out of their dislike of inherent inward supernaturall grace of God giuen to the blessed Virgin, they translate thus: (m) *Feare not Marie, for thou hast found fauour*

(c) *Luc.* 1. *v.* 28. *In greeke* Χαῖρε κεχαριτωμένη. *Maldonat in primum Lucæ.*
(d) *Luc.* 1. *v.* 15.
(e) *Act.* 7. *v.* 55.
(f) *Lib. de Spir. sanct. cap.* 7.
(g) *Serm.* 18. *de tēp. & l.* 2. *de symb. ad Catech.*
(h) *In c.* 1. *Luc.*
(i) *Athan. hom. de Deipara*, καὶ διὰ τοῦτο κεχαριτωμένη.
(k) *Epiph. hæres.* 78. κατὰ πάντα κεχαριτωμένη.
(l) *Luc.* 16. *v.* 20.
(m) *Serm. de Annūc.*

fauour with God, insteed of translating with all antiquity, *Feare not Marie, for thou hast found grace with God: Ne timeas Maria inuenisti enim gratiam apud Deum*, as S. Bernard sayth: (n) *Ne timeas Maria, inuenisti enim gratiam apud Dominum; quantam gratiã? gratiã plenam, gratiã singularẽ &c.* The Syriake text is playnly for vs, *Schcachethi ger tobutha leuath elebo*: For thou hast found grace before God. Caluin the sworne enemy to God, and the B. Virgin, Beza his beloued Father in Christ, our first Ministers branded Doctour will no wayes suffer the B. Virgin to be called full of grace. For he wryteth of her, that (o) *she doubted in her faith.* Agayne: *That she preferred her selfe to God.* And, *that Christ made no accompt that the B. Virgin was his Mother.* And, *that Christ thought her not worthy to be his Mother.* But let vs leaue these abhominable blasphemyes of Caluin the Capitane of Puritanes, and see rather what S. Augustin sayth of this B. Virgin. (p) *Excepta itaq; sancta virgine* (sayth he) *Mariâ, de qua propter honorem Domini nullam prorsus, cum de peccatis agitur, haberi volo questionẽ. Inde enim scimus, quod ej plus gratiæ collatum fuerit ad vincendum omne peccatum, quia concipere ac parere meruit enim, quem constat nullum habuisse peccatum. Hac ergo virgine excepta, si omnes Sanctos & Sanctas congregare possemus, &c. vna voce clamarent, Si dicimus quia peccatum non habemus, nos ipsos seducimus, & veritas in nobis non est.* Wherunto agreeth ancient and famous Sedulius a Scottish Poet, who was in the same age with S. Augustine; thus sayth he.

(n) *Serm. de Annũt.*

(o) *In c. 2. Luc. v. 35.*

(p) *De nat. & grat. c. 36. vid. S. Thom. 3. part. q. 27. art. 4.*

Et veluti è spinis mollis rosa, surgit acutis,
Nil quod lædat habens, matrêque obscurat honore:
Sic Euæ de stirpe sacra veniente Maria,
Virginis antiquæ facinus noua virgo piaret.

And agayne: (q).

Salue sancta parens enixa puerpera regem,
Qui cælum terramq; tenet per sæcula: Cuius
Numen & æterno complecteus omnia gyro,
Imperium sine fine manet, quæ ventre beato
Gaudia matris habens cum virginitatis honore,
Nec primam similem visa est, nec habere sequentem:
Sola sine exemplo placuisti femina Christo.

(q) *In opere Paschali lib. 3.*

The 8. and 9. Article.

1. *That the Catholike Church in this first Age, beleeued that there was a Purgatory.*
2. *And was accustomed to pray for the soules deteyned in Purgatory.*

CHAP; V.

HAVING maintayned the honour of our noble *Patrones*, the Glorious and triumphant *Saints* in heauen, their *holy Images*, the veneration of their *Reliques:* Now I come to defend the cause of our humble prayers made for the poore afflicted soules in *Purgatory*, which is the place of their punishment. First then we stand not vpon the name, but vpholde the thinge it selfe: that is, We Catholiks constantly belieue that there is a certaine place where some soules of the Faithful after this lyfe are purged & clensed, which place we call *Purgatory*. The Ministers contrary to our beliefe hold these propositions as poynts of faith, necessary to be belieued, *There is no purgatory*; *The prayers for the dead are superfluous*, and such like, which they shall neuer be able to proue by the expresse word of their owne corrupted Bible: but rather being empty and voyd, to proue them against vs Catholiks by the expresse word, they are forced to giue vs, for the expresse word of God, their necessary consequences, which in a word are nothing els but manifest heresies, and playne Idolatry, condemned in Arius a manifest heretike, as S.
Aug. l. 16. Augustine, and Epiphanius witnesse, and some Prote-
de hæres. c. stants themselues auow. True it is, that we Catholiks
35. Epiph. haue not the expresse word for euery poynt of our Reli-
Hæres. 75. gion, and we do not tye our selues to that alone, but rather

to the word of God, together with the consequences and expositions of the holy Church, and Fathers, which hath these sixteene hundreth yeares byn famous amongst all Nations. The Ministers contrary, promise to the poore people *only the expresse word of God*, setting a syde the expositions of the holy Church and Fathers: Yet in effect they giue nothing lesse then he expresse word of God, but rather for the word of God their owne consequences, inuentions, and expositions, not making accompt of the antiquity of the doctrine, of the holynesse of all our Fore-fathers. Can there be any excuse in the day of Iudgment for those men, who willingly & wittingly prefer the expositions of the Ministers, before the constant and vniforme exposition of the holy Fathers? For example S. Augustine (who was aboue twelue hundreth yeares since) proueth *Purgatory* out of these words of the Prophet Malachie, who speaking of the last penall Iudgement, sayth thus: (a) *But who may abide the day of his coming? and who shall endure when he appeareth? for he is lyke a purging fire, and lyke fullers sope. And he shall sit downe to try and fine the siluer: he shall euen fine the sonnes of Leui, and purifie them as gold and siluer*. S. Augustine (I say) hence doth infer Purgatory: (b) *For these words* (sayth he) *cannot signifie a separation only of the polluted from the pure in the last penall Iudgement &c. but must intimate a purgation of the good, who haue need therof*. The same S. Augustine praying to God, vseth these words: (c) *Purge me O Lord, in this lyfe, and make me such a one as shall not neede the amending fire*. And agayne: He proueth Purgatory by a necessary consequence drawen out of those words of the Prophet Isay: (d) *Our Lord shall purge the dregs of the daughters of Sion, and shall wash the bloud of Hierusalem out of the midst therof, in the spirit of Iudgement, and in the spirit of combustion*.

(a) *Malac.* 3. *v.* 2.

(b) *Aug. l.* 20. *de ciuit. Dei c.* 25.

(c) *In Psal.* 37.

(d) *Isa.* 4. *v.* 4.

2. Secondly, S. Luke speaking of Christ, maketh mention of a third place besydes Heauen & Hell: (e) *Whom God hath raised vp, and loosed the sorrowes of death, because it was impossible that he should be holden by it*. Out of which S. Augustin draweth this consequence and exposition: (f) *It is belieued the soule of Christ to haue descended to the place where sinners are punished*

(e) *Act.* 2. *v.* 24.

(f) *Lib.* 12. *de gen. ad lit. c.* 13. *& Epist.* 99. *ad Euod.*

punished, to release them of their torments, whome he in his hidden iustice thought worthy to be released. Otherwise I see not how to expone that text &c. For neyther Abraham, nor the poore man in his bosome, that is in the secret of his quyet rest, was reteyned in sorrowes: auowing, that Purgatory was constantly and vniuersally belieued in his tyme.

(g) 1 Cor. 3 v. 13.

3. Thirdly, S Paul spake plainely of the fire of Purgatory: (g) *Euery mans worke shall be made manifest: for the day shall declare it, because it shalbe reuealed by the fyre: and the fire shall try euery mans worke of what sort it is; if any mans worke that he hath built vpon, abyde, he shall receaue wages; if any mans worke burne, he shall haue losse, but he shall be saued himselfe, neuertheles yet as it were by the fire.* Where three kynds of fire are assigued. 1. The generall fire, which goeth before the day of Doome. *It shalbe reuealed in fire.* The second fire, the tryal of Gods Iudgement, *The worke of euery one of what kynd it is, the fire shall trie.* Thirdly, he cōcludeth of the fire of Purgatory, *he shallbe saued, yet so as by fire.* Which place Origen, S. Cyprian, S. Ambrose, S. Augustine, expound of the fire of Purgatory (with whome all the Greeke and Latin Fathers, after long disputation agree in auowing Purgatory, in the generall Councell of Florēce.) *Why are some said to be saued by fire,* sayth S. Augustine? *because they build vpon the foundation, hay, wood, stubble: but if they would build gold, siluer, and pretious stones, they might be secure from both fyres, not only from that euerlasting, which shall torment the impious eternally, but from that which shall amend them, who shall be saued by fyre &c. Euen so truely, although they be saued by fire, yet that fire will be more paynfull and grieuous, then any thing that can be suffred in this life.* And agayne so plainly, that no vnpassionat man may doubt of S. Augustines Religion in this poynt: (h) *He who hath not happily tilled his field, but hath suffred it to be ouergrowen with thornes, hath in this lyfe the malediction, and curse of the earth in all his works, and after this lyfe he shall haue eyther the fire of Purgatory, or euerlasting payne:* Et post hanc vitam habebit vel ignem purgationis, vel vitam æternam. And before S. Augustine, S. Gregory Nyssene: *Man after sinne in many toylsome labours ought to be exercised, that taught by experience, he might returne to his first happinesse,*

Orig. hom. 6 in c. 15. Exod. Cyp. l. 4. ep. 2. ad Anton. Ambros. in hunc locum. August. in Psal. 37.

(h) *Lib. 2. de Gen. cont. Manich. c. 20.*

happinesse, all vitious affections being purged, eyther in this world by a sober course of lyfe &c. or after our departure hence, by the fornace of Purgatory fire.

4. Caluin the prime Puritan Minister and Apostata, forced by the truth and verity, confesseth that the custome to pray for the soules in Purgatory, was in vse long before S. Augustine, to whose tyme inclusiuè, he auoweth the Church of Rome to haue bene the pure, true, and sincere Church of God: (i) *It is out of Controuersie* (sayth Caluin) *that nothing was changed in the true doctrine of Religion, neyther at Rome, nor in other townes, to the age and tyme of S. Augustine, and other anciẽt doctours.* The very words of Caluin cõcerning the forsaid custome of praying for the dead are: (k) *I deny not but the prayers for the dead were in vse with Chrysostome, Epiphanius, Augustin, and others, who receaued it from their Forfathers.* And agayne: (l) *Thirteene hundreth yeares from hence the custome was to pray for the dead.* And Luther himself, yet euer with the spirit of contradiction: (m) *I belieue strongly, that there is a purgatory, and I am easely persuaded that mention therof is made in the Scripture, as that of S. Mathew, It shall not be forgiuen vnto him neyther in this world, nor in the world to come: meaning therby, that some sinnes are forgiuen in Purgatory. I admit likewise that of the Machabees, It is a holy and healthfull cogitation to pray for the dead that they may be loosed from their sinnes.* Which words the Ministers haue pulled out of the Bible, though Luther receaued them as Canonicall.

(i) *Calu. l. 4. c. 2 Inst. num. 2. & 3. Edit. Gallic.*
(k) *Pag. 1101. Opuscul. edit. Geneu. Gallic. in fol. per Baptistam Pinereul.*
(l) *Lib. 3. Inst. c. 5. num. 10.*
(m) *Tom. 3. edit. VVitemb. ann. 1558. fol. 168.*

5. Besides the foresaid places of the Scripture, I adde these to proue Purgatory, and Prayer for the dead: (n) *Set thy bread and thy wyne vpon the buriall of a Iust man.* Which place though corrupted by the Ministers, declareth the ancient custome to haue bene amongst the Iewes, to giue almes to the poore, and nourish them to pray for the dead. Which custome is yet kept throughout all Christiandome in clothing and feeding the poore, called with vs, *Salies*. S. Chrysostome maketh mentiõ therof, saying: (o) *Why after the death of thy freinds dost thou inuite the poore ones? Why intreatest thou the Preists to pray for them? I know thou wilt answere, To the end, that he who is dead, haue peace and rest.* That the booke of

(n) *Tobie 4. v. 18.*
(o) *Chrys. hom. 32. in c. 9. Matt.*

Tobias is Canonicall, the Councell of Carthage holden anno 419. (besides the tradition of the holy Church) witnesseth playnly, wherof S. Augustine who was present at that Councell giueth this reason: Because we haue no other assurance that the Books of Moyses, the foure Gospells, & other books are the true word of God, but by the Canon and tradition of the Church: for the which cause the same Doctour vttered that famous saying: (p) *That he would not belieue the Gospell, except the authority of the Catholike Church moued him therunto.*

Lib. 2. de Doct. Christ. c. 8

(p) *Cont. Epist. fũd. c. 5.*

6. S. Augustine out of that place of the Bible: (q) *But he that shall speake against the holy Ghost, it shal not be forgiuen him, neyther in this world, nor in the world to come:* And other holy doctours inferre hereupon this consequence: (r) *That some sinnes are remitted in the next life*, and consequently that there is a *Purgatory*. Should not with any reasonable man S. Augustines consequences be preferred to the Ministers dreames and new traditions? Since it shall neuer be possible to the Ministers to proue out of the expresse word of the Bible, that there is no Purgatory; no wyse man will make accompt of their consequences, but rather of the consequences of the holy Fathers of this Age, wherof I will omit the testimonyes of S. Clement, and of S. Martiall, both famous wryters in this first Age, contenting my selfe with S. Denys his testimony.

(q) *Matt. 12. v. 32.*

(r) *De ciu. Dei l. 21. c. 13.*

Greg. l. 4 Dial. c. 39.

The testimonyes of the Fathers of this first Age, prouing Purgatory, and Prayer for the dead.

The first Section.

S. Denis manifestly maketh mention of the custome to pray for the faithfull deceased: (a) *Accedens deinde Diuinus antistes precem sacram super mortuum peragit: precatur oratio illa diuinam bonitatem, vt cuncta dimittat per infirmitatem humanam admissa peccata defuncto, eumq́; in luce statuat & regione viuorum &c.* And a little after, he sheweth that such holy Prayers are only valuable for those that dye in the bosome of the Catholike

(a) *Eccl. Hierar. c. 7. p. 2.* εἶτα προσελθὼν ὁ θεῖος ἱεράρχης εὐχὴν ἱερὰν ἐπὶ τῷ κεκοιμημένῳ ποιεῖται· &c.

Catholike Church: *Quod autem & iustorum preces etiam in hac vita, nedum post mortem, ijs solum prosint, qui digni sunt sacris precibus, Scripturarum nos edocent vera traditiones.* And a litle there after: *De prædicta ante precatione quæ Antistes super defuncto predicatur, quænam ad nos peruenerit à diuinis ducibus nostris traditio, dicere necesse est.* Wherby it is easy to be seene by the testimony of this holy Father Patrone of France, & disciple to S. Paul, that the Prayers for the dead, and the holy ceremonyes which the Catholike Church vseth at burials of the deceased, are Apostolicall tradition, grounded vpon the holy word of God. Secondly that such prayers are profitable to those who dye in the Catholike Church, & in the grace of God.

2. S. Matthew the Euangelist in the holy Masse, which he vsed to say, and which hath bene famous in all Christendome these sixtene hundreth yeares, hath therin the same prayers which we vse this day at the holy seruice: *Memento domine dormientium Principum, Pontificum, Regum, Patriarcharum, Archiepiscoporum, Episcoporum, Sacerdotum, Diaconorum, Parentum nostrorum, & omnium in recta fide quiescentium.* (b) *Extat. tom 6. bibliot. Pat. edit. ann. 1589.*

3. In S. Marke the Euangelist his Masse, which is yet extant in that famous towne of Italie, called Venice, where the very Autograph it selfe is to be seene: (c) *Animabus patrum & fratrum nostrorum, qui antea Christi in fide obdormierunt, dona requiem Domine Deus noster.* That is, *O Lord our God, giue rest to the soules of our parents and brethren, who died in the faith of Chryst.* (c) *Extat. to. 6. bibl. Pat. cit.*

4. In S. Iames the Apostle his Masse yet extant: (d) *Pro requie Patrum & Fratrum nostrorum, qui ante nos dormierunt, dicamus omnes toto amino, domine Miserere.* Finally Caluin the Arch-minister of the Puritanes auoweth playnly, that the custome to pray for the dead was most ancient in the Catholike Church. (d) *Litur. S. Iacob. Minor.*

That the Ministers haue corrupted the Bible in sundry places, which proue Purgatory, or any third place.

The second Section.

IT is to be remarked, that before the coming of Christ, the soules of the Iust did not ascend vnto heauen after their departure, but remayned eyther in the place, called *Limbus Patrum*, or *sinus Abrahæ*, without any paynes or torments; or els in *Purgatory* where transitory torments were: The bad being alwayes condemned to hel where the eternall torments are: (a) *For the way vnto the holyest of all* (sayth S. Paul) *was not yet opened, while as yet the first Tabernacle was standing*. That is, before the coming of Chryst, and during the tyme of the first Tabernacle, the way vnto the holyest of all, that is, to Heauen, was not as yet opened, which after was only opened by the passion of Christ: after the which passion, the soule of Christ went downe to those parts where the soules of the ancient Fathers were detayned, as in *Limbus Patrum*, and *Purgatory*, preaching vnto them their Redemption, conforme to that which the Apostle sayth: (b) *By the which also he went and preached to the spirits, that were in prison*. And conforme to that which we say in our belief, *He descended into hell*. The which name of Hell is giuen, by the holy Scripture and holy Fathers, to the place of the damned, & also to those two places *Abrahās bosome*, and *Purgatory*, which the Apostle calleth the lowest parts: (c) *Now in that he ascended, what is it, but that he had also descended first vnto the lowest parts of the earth?* Yet with this difference, that *Purgatory*, and *Lymbus Patrum*, is called *Hell*, but the place of the damned, is called the *lower Hell*: (d) *Eruisti animam meam ex inferno inferiori*. And the circumstance specified in any place of the Scripture, sheweth whether the word *Hell*, should be taken in the one or the other sense.

(a) *Ad Hebr.* 9. v. 8.

(b) 1. *Pet.* 3. v. 19.

(c) *Eph.* 4. v. 9.

(d) *Psal.* 85. v. 12.

2. The Ministers to blind the poore people, and to take away all memory of *Limbus Patrum*, or *Purgatory*, they haue blotted out of the Bible sundry places, that proue the

the ſame, as, *Thou shall not leaue my ſoule in hell*, which the Prophet Dauid did foretell of Chriſt, to wit, that Chriſts ſoule going down after his Paſſion to the hell of Purgatory and Limbus, ſhould not remayne there. The Miniſters haue tranſlated, (e) *Thou shall not leaue my ſoule in the graue*: declaring therby the ſoule of Chriſt to be mortall and corruptible, and conſequently denying Chriſt to be trew God and man. For whatſoeuer is put in the graue is corruptible in it ſelf. This Blaſphemy is agaynſt the Hebrew text, againſt the Greeke text, againſt all antiquity, wherof all the Miniſters together ſhall not be able to produce one ancient Father who did euer dreame of ſuch a blaſphemous trāſlation. 2. It is agaynſt that of the Creed, *he deſcended vnto hell*, where before it is ſayd, that he was crucified, dead & buried: yea the Proteſtants themſelues do ſing the contrary in their Church of Scotland.

(e) *Act.* 2. v. 27.

ψυχὴν εἰς ᾅδου.

His (f) ſpirit did after this deſcend
Into the lower partes,
To them that long in darkneſſe were,
The true light of their harts.

(f) *The Proteſtāts Creed in meeter at the end of their Pſalmes.*

Heere affirming that the ſoule of Chriſt went to hell and not to the graue.

3. Alſo when Iacob ſayth: (g) *I will go down to my ſonne into hell mourning*, knowing well that Ioſeph his ſonnes ſoule was not in hell of the damned perſons; they haue tranſlated, *I will go down into the graue of my ſonne*: where as Iacob knew not that his ſonne Ioſeph was buried, being perſuaded that (h) *a wicked beaſt had deuoured him, and torne him in peeces*: And as though if Ioſeph had bene in a graue, Iacob would haue gone down to him in the ſame graue. Can there be greater abſurdityes deuyſed? more deſpitfull blaſphemyes inuented? and al to eſchew the force of this place, which maketh for *Purgatory*, conforme to the expoſition of S. Hierome: (i) *Before the comming of Chriſt, Abraham was in hell*, that is, in Limbo, *after his coming the theef was in Paradiſe*. And Tertullian: (k) *I know, that the boſome of Abraham was no heauenly place, but only the higher hell*. Finally S. Auguſtine condemneth this tranſlation of the Proteſtants of manifeſt

(g) *Gen.* 37 v. 35.

(h) *Gen.* 37 v. 33.

(i) *In Epitap. Nepot. c.* 3.

(k) *Lib.* 4 *aduerſ. Marcion.*

heresie saying: (l) *Quis non est derelictus in Inferno? Chistus Iesus, sed in anima sola. Quis resurrectur' in triduo iacuit in sepulchro? Christus Iesus, sed in carna sola.* Agayne: (m) *Quod anima illa in Infernum descenderit, Apostolica doctrina pradicatur. Quandoquidem B. Petrus ad hanc rem testimonium de Psalmis adhibet, vbi de ipso pradictum esse demonstrat, quoniam non derelinques animam meam in Inferno.* I would aske of the Ministers to name me any wryter sacred or profane, who did translate the word ᾅδης for a graue? They shall neuer be able to do it: But rather as they haue cast down Churches, ouerthrowen Abbyes, chāged Princes Estates, taken away Traditions, corrupted the Scriptures, peruerted Sciences, so they will turne vpside down Languages as it pleaseth them.

(l) Tract. 78. in Ioa.

(m) Ep ad Dardanū.

4. Finally, if Christs soule was in the graue, it was vnited with his body, which was lykewyse in the graue, wherin also was his diuinity, & consequently his diuinity, his soule, and his body being in the graue, he behoued to be aliue in the graue the three dayes that he was buryed; which is a horrible blasphemy. To all the foresaid probations that Christs soule went down to *Limbus* and *Purgatory*, I ad this only of a famous Protestāt Maister Bilson, who sayth: (n) *That all the fathers with one consent affirme, that Christ delyuered the soules of the Patriarches, and Prophets out of hell at his comming thither.*

(n) Bilson, in his full Redemptiō of mākind.

5. As the Ministers haue, by translating that Christs soule was put in the graue, denyed the immortality of Chrysts soule, and consequently our Redemption, so they deny the diuinity of Christ, making him *Author of all sinnes*, in saying that God not only giueth vp, casteth off, and withdraweth his grace from man; but also delyuereth thē to the diuel. For these be the very words of the Scotish Catechisme rehersed by the Schollers euery Sonday in Scotland: (o) *God of his infinite mercy doth preserue his faithfull, not suffering the diuell to lead them out of the way, neyther permitting that sinne haue the vpperhand of them: lykewyse he doth not only giue vp, cast off, and withdraw his grace from such as he will punish, but also he delyuereth them to the Diuel, committing them to his tyranny, he stryketh them with blindnes, & giueth them vp to reprobate mynds, vtterly*

(o) The 45 Sunday in the Cathechisme printed in the Psalm-book.

vtterly slaues to sinne, and subiect to all tentations. And to this end they haue corrupted the Bible thus: (p) *Let no man say when he is tempted, I am tempted of God, for God cannot be tempted with euill, neyther tempteth he any man; but euery man is tempted when he is drawen away by his owne concupiscence, and is entysed.* Contrary to the common translation which is, and hath bene these sixtene hundreth years: *Let no man say, that he is tempted of God, for God is no tempter to euill.* And in latin: *Deus enim intentator malorũ est,* they translate *God cannot be tẽpted*, *passiuely,* where the Apostle sayth *actiuely,* that God tempteth no man, as the whole sense and drift of the Apostle sheweth playnly, saying, That euery man is tempted when he is drawen away by his owne concupiscence, and is entysed. The blasphemy was first inuented by Caluin, then followed by Beza, lastly approued by our ministers in their confession of faith, and in their Scottish Catechisme. Caluins words are: (q) *God is cheef author of his owne iust vengeance, and Sathan is but only a Minister therof: That God purposeth, willeth, moueth, loueth, and commandeth the wickednes of sinners, their obstinat blindnes and hardnes of heart.* And Beza: (r) *The Lord leadeth into temptation those, whome he permitteth to Sathans arbitrement, or into whome rather he leadeth or bringeth in Sathan himself, to fill their heart, as Peter speaketh.* The latin words are, *Inducit Dominus in tentationẽ eos, quos Sathanæ arbitrio permittit, aut in quos potiùs Satanam ipsum inducit, vt cor eorum impleat, vt loquitur Petrus.* So by Beza his opinion God brought Satan into Iudas his hart, & so was author of Iudas treason, euen as he was of S. Pauls conuersion. Which impious doctrine, is vniuersally auowed by the Ministry of Scotland, whose words are: (s) *That God is the creator of heauen and earth, that is to say, that the heauen and earth and the contents therof are so in his hands, that there is nothing done without his knowledge, neyther yet against his will* (remarke wel these words Gẽtle reader how that al sins are done by the wil of god) *& so we cõfesse & belieue that neyther the deuils nor yet the wicked of the world haue any power to molest or trouble the chosen childrẽ of God, but in so far as it pleaseth him to vse thẽ as instruments.* Thus our learned Ministers make God to be *causa prima peccati,* & the diuell to be the *instrumentall cause* only.

(p) *Iames* 1 v. 13.

In Greek ἀπείραστος κακῶν.

(q) *Calu. l.* 1. *Inst. c.* 18 §. 1. 2. 3. & *l.* 2. *c.* 4. §. 2. & *l.* 3. *c.* 21. & 23. §. 8.

(r) Annot. *nou. Test.* an. 1556. in 6. *Matt.* v. 13.

(s) *In the Order of Baptisme set down before the Psalmes in the explication of the first article.*

only. How can the Ministers belieue in God, since they hold so impious and diuelish opinions of God? How can the Ministers Religion be acceptable to God, since they belieue constantly that God is the chiefe cause, the diuell the instrumētall cause only of all the abhominations and wickednes of the world? How can there any saluation be for those which dye in the Puritans Religion, since they dye in such abhominable and peruerse doctrine? O Impiety! O Infidelity! For this blasphemous doctrine of Caluin and of the Ministers, our Soueraigne king Iames hath wysely forbidden the reading of so poysoned works of Caluin to the noble Students of his Vniuersityes. Likewise Castalio a learned Puritan familiar with Caluin wryteth, that, by reason of such doctrine, Caluin and the Ministers must needs haue some other God, for their God, then the true God who hath created heauen and earth. (t) *The false God of Caluin is slow to mercy, prone to anger, who hath created the greatest part of the world to destruction, and predestinated them not only to damnation, but also to the cause of damnation. Therfore he hath decreed from all eternity, and he will haue it so, and he doth bring it to passe that they necessarily sinne; so that neyther thefts, nor murthers, nor adulteries, are committed but by his constraint and impulsion, for he suggesteth vnto men euill aud dishonest affections, not only by permission, but effectually (that is, by drawing them to such affections) and doth harden them in such sort, that when they perpetrate euill, they do rather the worke of God, then their owne; he maketh the diuell a lyer, so that now not the diuell, but the God of Caluin is the Father of lyes. But that God which the holy Scriptures teach, is altogeather contrary to thu God of Caluin &c.* And immediatly after: *For the true God came to destroy the worke of that Caluinian God, and those two Gods as they are by nature cōtrary one to another, so they beget & bring forth childrē of contrary dispositions, to wit, that God of Caluin bringeth forth Childrē without mercy, proued, lofty mynded, vncleane, filthy &c.* To whom I adde the censure of Stancarus lykewyse a famous Protestant, who saluteth Caluin & the Ministers, who follow Caluins doctrine set down in the Scots Catechisme, & written first by Caluin in french, thus: (u) *What Diuel O Caluin, hath seduced thee to speake with Arius agaynst the*

(t) *Castalio in lib. ad Calu. de Prædest.*

(u) *Stanc. cont. Calu.*

the sone of God, that thou mightst proclaime him to be depryued of his glory &c. After he concludeth thus: *Beware (O Christian Reader, and specially all yow Ministers) bewar of the books of Caluin, and principally in the articles of the Trinitty, Incarnation, Mediatour, Sacrament of Baptisme, and Predestination, for they conteyne wicked doctrine &c.*

The tenth Article.

That the Sacrament of Confession was vniuersally in practice in this first Age.

CHAP. VI.

I MAY with reason compare the Ministers of Scotland to the Camelion, for as he changeth himselfe into all variety of colours except only white, the most true colour: so our Ministers admit all manner of doctrine, except that which the Catholike Church, whyte without spot, belieueth. And in this present poynt they admit al sort of Confession, except that which is most important to their soules: wherin they chiefly deny, First the power in Priests to absolue from sinnes: Secondly, the necessity we haue to confesse our sinnes to a Priest the lieutenant of God, which notwithstanding I wil deduce and proue out of the words of the Bible.

2. First then it is manifest, that Christ gaue power to his Apostles and their Successours to forgiue sinne: (a) *Then said Iesus to them agayne, peace be vnto yow: as my Father sent me, so send I yow. And when he had said that, he breathed on them and said vnto them: Receaue the holy Ghost, whose sinnes yee remit, they are remitted vnto them; and whose sinnes yee retayne, they are retayned.* Now let vs consider the words of the Bible. Our Sauiour was sent by his Father to forgiue all sinnes, not only by preaching of the word, but also as a Iudge pronoũcing

(a) *Ioan. 20. v. 21.*

cing the sentence of absolution, for so he said to Mary Magdalene without preaching: (b) *Thy sinnes are forgiuen thee*; & to the sick man of the palsie: (c) *Thy sinnes are forgiuen thee*. Where the Euangelist also affirmeth, that he gaue the same power to men: (d) *So when the multitude saw it, they meruailed and glorified God, which had giuen such authority to men.* Now that power which our Sauiour receaued of his Father, he gaue it to his Apostles and to their successours, and that as a great benefite wherof the posterity of man would haue need. Secondly, our Sauiour breathed giuing this authority, declaring therby, that by vertue of the holy Ghost which he breathed in them they might forgiue sinnes, so that when the Priest forgiueth sinnes, it is rather the holy Ghost who forgiueth them, then the Priest, who is only but an instrument. *And Iesus said vnto them, receaue the holy Ghost, whose sinnes yee remit &c.* So that by these wordes, Iurisdiction is giuen to the Preists to forgiue sinnes, as S. Cyrill witnesseth: (e) *It is neyther absurd, nor yet inconuenient that they forgiue sinnes who haue the holy Ghost, for when they pardon or retayne sinnes, the holy Ghost pardoneth or retayneth sinnes by thẽ: and that they do two wayes, by Baptisme first, afterward by Penance:* He sayth not, that by preaching of the word, sinnes are pardoned.

(b) *Luc.* 7. v. 47.
(c) *Matth.* 9. v. 2.
(d) *Matt.* 9. v. 8.
(e) *Lib.* 12. c. 56. *in Io.*

3. Lastly this power granted to Priests was not only to declare by the preaching of the word, the absolution of sinnes, but by a true authority giuen by God to forgiue sins. So S. Athanasius calleth it, (f) *A power giuen by our Sauiour to Priests to loose sinnes.* But specially S. Chrysostome declareth this power to be an inward dignity giuen to Priests by God aboue Kings and Princes. (g) *They that inhabite the earth and conuerse theron, to them commission is giuen to dispense those things that are in heauen. To them that power is giuen, which Almighty God would not communicate eyther to Angell or Archangell: For to them it is not said, Whatsoeuer ye shall bind in earth shalbe bound in heauen &c. Earthly Princes indeed haue also authority to bind, but the bodyes only: but that binding of Preists which I treat of toucheth the very soule it selfe, and reacheth euen to the heauens. In so much as whatsoeuer the Preists performe beneath,*

(f) *Serm. in illa verba, profecti in pagum.*
(g) *Chrys. l.* 3. *de Sacer.*

the very same Almighty God doth aboue: and the sentence of the seruant our Lord doth confirme. And what is this truely els, but that the power of heauenly things is granted by God vnto them? whose sinnes soeuer (sayth he) *ye shall retayne, they are retayned. What power I beseech you can be greater then this? The Father gaue all power vnto the Sonne: But I see the same power delyuered altogether by the Sonne vnto them.* Wherfore as our Sauiour Chryst Iesus had a speciall power to forgiue sinnes, distinct from this power of preaching; so the power he gaue to the Apostles to preach, was distinct from the power giuen to them to forgiue sinnes.

4. This power of *Priests* to forgiue sinnes, being so established, it is easie to declare how confession of our sinnes to a Priest, ensueth necessarly of the forsaid power giuẽ to Preists, and consequently that it is not sufficient to confesse our sinnes to God priuatly, but we must, by the command of God, confesse our sinnes to the Priests, since God hath giuen them power to forgiue vs our sinnes. And in effect that which we confes to the Priest is cõfessed to God himselfe, who hath ordeyned the Priest as an instrument of this holy Sacrament. So sayth S. Augustine: (h) *Let no man deceaue himselfe and say, I do penance secretely, I do it in the sight of God: God who pardoneth me knoweth I do it in my hart. Thẽ without cause was it said: Those things which you loose in earth shalbe loosed in heauen: Then without cause were the keyes giuen to the Church of God. Do we frustrate the Ghospell? do we euacuate the words of Chryst?* Whereby it is euident that sinners are obliged to submit themselues by confession to the Priest: & euen as the commandement which our Sauiour gaue to his Apostles to baptize: (i) *Go teach all Nations baptizing them &c.* This power I say had bene giuen to them in vayne, if all men were not bound to receaue the Sacrament of Baptisme. And as this power of Baptisme & preaching the word, was not only giuen to the Apostles in person, but also to their successours to the end of the world: So the power to forgiue sinnes was not giuen only to the Apostles, but lykewise to their successours. And as the authority to preach which Christ gaue to the Disciples, were in vayne if men

(h) *Aug* 50. *hom.* *ho.* 49.

(i) *Matth.* 28.

men were not obliged therby in conſcience to giue eare to the preached word: ſo idle, and in vayne were the power that Chryſt gaue to his Apoſtles to retayne or forgiue ſins, if all ſorts of men (who haue offended after Baptiſme) were not tyed & obliged to ſubmit their ſinnes vnto the *Prieſts*, who are the Apoſtles ſucceſſours, which ſubmiſſion euery one is obliged to performe for two reaſons.

5. Firſt, becauſe as Boetius ſayth: (k) *If thou deſire the helpe of the Phyſitian, it is requiſite thou diſcouer thy deſeaſe.* Therfore it is neceſſary, that thoſe who are burdened with ſores of many ſinnes, diſcouer the ſame to the ſpiritual Phyſitian appoynted for their cure. Secondly, becauſe Prieſts are made (by the vertue of the commiſſion granted by God to them) not only Phyſitians, but alſo *ſpirituall Iudges*, to vnderſtand the quality of our crymes, to know what medicinable pennance they ſhould apply, to diſcerne what ſinnes are to be remitted, and what are to be retayned. Now I ſay, ſince they are Iudges, they cannot iudge ſufficiently of the quality of ſinnes, and pronounce as Iudges the ſentence of abſolution except that our ſinnes be diſcouered vnto them, conforme to that cōmō ſaying, It is impoſſible for a man to iudge diſcreetly who hath no knowledge of the caſe. And naturall reaſon proueth the ſame manifeſtly, and the cuſtome of all ciuill countries wherin Iudges are cōſtituted ſheweth, that before a Iudge pronounce any ſentence in Iudgement, he muſt needs haue notice and knowledge of the cauſe which he iudgeth. Now there is but two meanes wherby we may giue notice of our ſinnes to the Prieſt, eyther publickly or priuatly. To giue publike notice of ſecret & hidden ſinnes, is againſt the word of God, againſt charity, againſt the law of nature, againſt the obligation we haue to keep our honour and good fame, againſt the obligation we haue to giue good example to our Neighbour. Wherfore it followeth, that we ſhould giue ſecret notice of ſecret ſinnes to the Prieſts, which is by way of *Sacramentall Confeſſion* vſed in the Catholike Church, wherof the ſecrecy is kept ſo ſtrictly among Prieſts that they are obliged vnder the paine of damnation, and by the law of God rather

(k) *De cō-ſolat. proſ.* 4.

ther

therto dy then to reueale the least venial sinne which they heare in confession. Yea the practise and experience which hath bene these sixteene hundreth yeares begun, and yet is amongst all the Kings and Princes of the world, sheweth how faithfull, constant, and honest the Catholike Priests haue bene in this mater of secrecy: & it is very well known to all Scotland, England, and Ireland, how secret and faithfull imprisoned Priests haue byn, not only in maters heard in confession, but likewyse in outward dealing and conuersation.

6. This iudiciall power giuen to the Priests, is playnly collected out of the holy Scriptures by the holy Fathers, whose expositiōs & cōsequences should be preferred before the expositions and consequences of the Ministry. S. Augustine out of those words, (l) *And I saw seates, and they sate vpon them, and iudgement was giuen vnto them*, inferreth this consequence: (m) *This may not be thought to be spoken of the last iudgement, but by the seates are meant the Rulers, thrones of the Church, and the persons themselues by whome they are gouerned. And for the iudgment giuen them, it cannot be better explayned, then in those words; Whatsoeuer yee loose on earth, shalbe loosed in heauen.*

(l) Reuel. 20. v. 4.

(m) Aug. l. 20. de ciuit. Dei c. 9.

7. The other place of the Bible which maketh playnly mention of Confession, is, (n) *Confesse your sinnes one to another:* where the Apostle vnderstādeth confession made to the true pastor & superiour, not to euery particular man: for he giueth an exāple touching the prayer of Elias who was superiour amongst the Iewes, and before he sayth, (o) *Is any sicke amongst you, let him call for the Priests of the Church.* Which two places as making for vs Catholiks, the Ministers haue filthily corrupted, the first thus: *Acknowledge your faultes one to another.* The other: *Let him call for the Elders of the Church.*

(n) Iames 5. v. 16.

(o) Iames 5. v. 14.

8. Wherby it is easie to be seene that those propositions, *Confesse your sinnes one to another: Christ gaue power to men to forgiue sinnes: Christ gaue power to the Apostles to forgiue sinnes*, are in playne termes, and as it were expressely set down in the Bible. Wherfore I aske of the Ministers

nisters to shew me in the expresse words of the Bible, contrary propositions to the foresaid; as, *Men cannot forgiue sinnes; Christ gaue not power to Priests to forgiue sinnes*, and such. But they shall neuer be able to giue any expresse word against Sacramentall Confession: But rather they will bragge and boast of their necessary consequences, which are nothing but their owne inuentions and heresies: Inuentions, I say, against the doctrine of their owne maister, Iohn Caluin, who is of that opinion, that we should confesse our sins to our Pastour, specially when we go to the holy table, & proueth the same by the foresaid saying of S. Iames: (p) *Tametsi Iacobus neminem nominatim aßignando, in cuius sinum nos exoneremus, liberum permittit delictum vt ei confiteamur qui ex Ecclesiæ grege maximè idoneus fuerit visus: quia tamen Pastores præ alijs vt plurimùm iudicare sunt idonei, potißimũ etiam nobis eligendi erunt.* And a litle after: (q) *Quin sistãt se Pastori oues priuata confeßione, quoties sacram cœnam participare volunt, adeo non reclamo, vt maximè velim hoc vbiq; obseruari.*

(p) *Lib. 3. Instit. c. 4. §. 12.*

(q) *§. 13. & 14.*

9. Now, let vs see the necessary consequences, & expositions of the holy Fathers of this first Age, concerning Confession, which necessary consequences any wyse man will preferre to the consequences and expositions of our Scots Ministers, who neyther in learning, pietie, doctrine, or good behauiour can be compared to those holy Fathers.

The Testimonyes of the holy Fathers of this first Age, prouing the vse of Confeßion.

The first Section.

S. Denis wryting to Demophilus, reproueth him for not doing his duty towards a certaine Priest, who was accustomed to heare confessions, and for not doing his duty towards a certaine Catholike who was accustomed to confesse his sinnes vpon his knees, which custome hath bene euer in the Church of God: (a) *Tu verò vt tuæ literæ indicant, (*) procidentem Sacerdoti impium, vt ais peccatorem, nescio quo pacto contra disciplinæ ordinem astans calce abiecisti. Adhuc cùm*

(a) *Dionys. epist. ad Demoph. ante med.* * τῷ προσπίπτοντα τῷ ἱερεῖ.

ille

ille quidem, quod oportuit, fateretur se ad peccatorum remedium querendum venisse; tu non exhorruisti, sed & bonum sacerdotem ausus es lacerare conuitys, miserabilem eum dicens, quòd pœnitentem & impium iustificasset &c. Where this holy Father witnesseth that Sacramentall confession duely made iustifieth the sinner, and giueth consequently remission of sinnes. Secondly he witnesseth that in the primitiue Church the custome was to declare in particular the number of our sinnes in confession, so far as man can remember, for God doth not oblige vs to impossible things. And euen as a souldiour hauing receaued many wounds in warre, it is not sufficient to tell his Physitian in generall only, that he is wounded, but he must shew the seuerall wounds, otherwyse no man will venter to heale and cure him: euen so, it is not sufficient for a Christian wounded in his soule with diuers deadly sins, to complayne and confesse in generall, but he must particularly specify (so far as he can remember) the number and quality of deadly sinnes, that therby the spirituall Phisitian (that is the Priest) may discerne what satisfactory Penance, what good counsell and aduyse he should giue vnto the penitent: which doctrine is of S. Gregory, who sayth: (b) *Euen as in corporall infirmityes there are sundry kindes of medicins according to the diuersity of diseases, so wheras in the disease of the soule there is a great veriety of affections, sundry sorts of medicinable cures ought to be abhibited.* And this is the common doctrine of the Fathers, who do exhort vs very earnestly to make a particuler rehearsal of deadly sins in our confessiõ, to the end the Priest may be fully acquainted with the full estate of our soules, and vnderstand the great variey of our spirituall diseases conforme to that famous saying of S. Hierome: (c) *Then the Bishop or Priest knoweth who is to be bound, and who is to be loosed, when he heareth the variety of sinnes.* And the reason is euident. For except the Priest know distinctly the deadly sinnes of his penitent, he cannot pronounce a iudiciall sentence, for no man can Iudge of things he knoweth not, he cannot apply soueraigne medecins, he cãnot know what to loose or what to retayne; and in a word, he cannot know his commission. And truely if in the old law

(b) *Greg. Nyss. Ep. ad Episcop. Mytil.*

(c) *Super 16. Matth.*

law the Iewes were obliged to manifest in particular their ſinnes vnto the Prieſt of the Leuiticall ſtock, as cōmandeth expreſſely the 5. Chapter of Numbers, and the 5. of Leuit. much more ſhould the Chriſtian Prieſts haue this priuiledge, ſayth S. Chryſoſtome: (d) *The Iewish Prieſts had leaue to iudge, or try ſuch is were purged from corporall leproſy: but to our Prieſts it is granted not to try the purged, but altogether to purge, not the leproſy of the body, but the infection of the ſoule.*

(d) *Lib.* 3. *de Sacerd.*

2. S. Clement in lyke manner wryteth thus of Confeſſion: (e) *Si fortè alicuius ira vel liuor, vel infidelitas, vel aliquod malum ex his quæ ſuperius memorauimus, latenter irrepſerit, non erubeſcat, qui animæ ſuæ curam gerit, confiteri hæc, huic qui præeſt, vt ab ipſo, per verbum Dei & conſilium ſalubre curetur, quò poßit integra fide & operibus bonis pœnas æternæ ignis effugere, & ad perpetuæ vitæ præmia peruenire &c.* By the which words he teacheth three things; firſt that the cuſtome was in this age amongſt the Catholiks to confeſſe their ſinnes priuately to their paſtor. 2. That the abſolution which the Prieſt gaue was grounded in the word of God. 3. That not only by faith, but by faith & good works men did eſchew the paynes of hell, and obtayne heauen.

(e) *Ep.* 1. *ante med.*

That the Miniſters in Scotland haue corrupted the Bible in ſundry places, which make for Sacramentall Confeßion.

The ſecond Section.

THE firſt place is of S. Iames the fifth Chapter: *Confeſſe your ſinnes one to another:* For ſo it is in the Greeke, in the Syriake, and in the Latin: yet the Miniſters haue corrupted it two ſeueral wayes: firſt putting for the word *confeſſe*, the word *acknowledge*, and for the word *ſinnes*, the word *offenſes*, to make the ſentence more obſcure, and to inſinuate their corruption craftily. For the word *Offences* properly ſignifieth outward wronges done to our neigbours; ſo we are accuſtomed to ſay, he hath offended me, which is ſignified by the Greek word προσοχθισμὸς, or πρόσκομμα, but in this place there is the Greeke word παράπτωμα, which ſignifieth properly

ἐξομολογεῖσθε ἀλλήλοις τὰ παραπτώματα. *Hauathun den meden Sacleuathecun.* *Porro cōfitemini alius alij delicta veſtra.* *Confitemini alterutrum peccata veſtra.*

properly a *sinne* done against God; and the Ministers shall neuer be able to name me any wryter or ancient Father, Greeke or Latine, who before *Caluin* did euer insinuate so blasphemous a corruption as the foresaid, wherof *Caluin* was the first inuentour. Truely any wyse man should preferre S. Augustine (who was skillfull in Hebrew, Greeke, and Latin) his iudgement & exposition of this place before any of the Ministry. (a) *In omnibus* (sayth he) *Scripturis diuinis, fratres dilectißimi, vtiliter ac salubriter admonemur, vt peccata nostra debeamus iugiter & humiliter, non solùm deo, sed etiam Sanctis & deum timentibus confiteri. Sic enim per Iacobum Apostolum nos admonet Spiritus sanctus, Confitemini alterutrum peccata vestra, & orate pro inuicem vt saluemini.* And with S. Augustine Irenæus, (b) S. Iohn the Euangelist his disciple, (c) Tertullian, (d) S. Chrysostome, and sundry others manifestly proue, that we are obliged to confesse our sinnes to the Priest. Should not these holy Fathers translations, consequences and illations, be preferred before our new vpstart Ministers illations?

(a) *Lib. 50. Hom. 12. homil.*

(b) *Lib. 1. c. 9.*

(c) *Lib. de Pœnit. c. 8.*

(d) *Hom. 9 in 6. c. ad Roman.*

2. Likewise to make the simple & ignorant people belieue that Ministers and trew Church-men should be maried & haue wyues, they haue corrupted the Bible horribly thus: (e) *Haue we not power to lead about a sister, a wyfe, as the rest of the Apostles*, insteed to translate, as all antiquity hath translated, *Haue we not power to lead about a woman sister?* for our Sauiour himselfe had some holy women, who of charity did furnish necessary things to his sustentation: (f) *And Ioanna the wife of Chusa Herodes steward, and Susanna, and many other, which ministred vnto him of their substance.* To the which custome the holy Apostle alludeth only. And it is certaine that S. Paul was a Virgin and neuer maried, as he witnesseth saying: (g) *For I would that all men were euen as I my selfe.* And not only S. Paul remayned euer a Virgin, but the rest of the Apostles except S. Peter who before his cõuersion being maried, left wife & all he had when he was called to be Christs disciple. (h) *Then answered Peter and said to him, Behold we haue forsaken all, & followed thee,* For the which

(e) *1. Cor. c. 9. v. 5.*

(f) *Luc. 8. v. 3.*

(g) *1. Cor. 7 v. 7.*

(h) *Matt. 19. v. 27.*

cause Tertullian with the rest of the Fathers auow, that all the Apostles except S. Peter were Virgins & vnmaried: (i) *Petrum solum* (sayth he) *inuenio maritum*.

(i) *Lib. de Monogamia ante med.*

3. The Ministers likewise, to persuade the poore people that no good works can be done in this lyfe, they haue corrupted the Bible manifestly thus: (k) *Wherfore Brethren giue rather diligence to make your calling and election sure, for if yee do these things ye shall neuer fall*, where they haue wholly taken out the word *good works*, for so it is in sundry Greeke copyes, and playnly in the vulgar latin. *Wherfore Brethren giue rather diligence that by good works yee make certaine your calling and election. Quopropter fratres magis satagite, vt per bona opera certam vestram vocationem & electionem faciatis*. Doth not the Apostle a little before make mentiō of good works, to wit; to fly the corruption of the world, to ioyne vertue to faith, temperance with patience, and patience with godlynes. concluding afterward, *If yee do these things yee shall neuer fall*, That is; yee shall neuer fall into sinne, but alwayes by the grace of God, keep the Commandements in doing good works?

(k) 2. Pet. 1. v. 10.

The

The 11. and 12. Article.

1. *That man hath Freewill, not only in Naturall and Ciuill Actions.*
2. *But also in Morall and Supernaturall Actions.*

CHAP. VII.

OVR Ministers deny absolutly & without distinction, *Freewill* to be in man, wherin they shew both their folly and ignorance. Which heresy of theirs, they haue forced at sundry Parlaments the three Estats of Scotland to sweare and subscribe publickely, as it is conteyned in their confession of faith thus: (a) *The defence of Christs Church apperteyneth to the Christian Magistrats against all Idolaters and heretiks, as Papists, Anabaptists, with suchlike lymmes of Antichrist, to roote out all doctrine of Deuils and men, as the Masse, Purgatory, lymbus Patrum, prayer to Saintes and for the dead, freewill, distinction of meates, apparell and dayes, vowes of single life, presence at Idol-seruice, mans merits, with such like.* Is it not a great shame to the Nobilite of Scotland, to haue subscrybed, and sworne so blasphemous words, no wayes conteyned in the expresse word of their own corrupted Bible, yea fully against the Bible: to haue subscrybed, I say, that all their Forefathers, all their Kings and Princes, were Heretiks, the space of fifteene hundreth and fifty yeares, were I say, *lymmes* of the diuell, lymmes of *Antichrist*? And yet in the last Parlament to haue sworne the contrary to some of those poynts, as 1. *Distinction of meates*, for lent is straitly cōmanded in Scotland, at the least ciuilly. 2. *Apparell & dayes*, for they haue ordeyned the fiue holy dayes to be kept, & corner cappes and surplises are desired by many. Which

(a) Confessiō of Faith approued by the Church of Scotland and ioyned with the Psalmes.

changing, contradiction, and inconstancy, in so weighty maters of religion, sheweth that the Ministers haue no Religion at all.

2. To vnderstand playnly this point of *Freewill*, we must distinguish as it were foure estates and conditions of man: The first state is of *Innocency*, which Adam had before his fall, in the which Estate the Heretiks both Protestants and Puritanes grant, Adam to haue had freewil. 2. The state of corruption, which Adam and al his posterity incurred by sinne, in the which state some of the Puritans as (b) Caluin, (c) Bucer, with (d) Simon Magus, (e) Marcion, and other Heretiks do deny man to haue any frewill. Others, as (f) Whitaker, (g) Perkins, (h) Whyte, and many English Protestants with Luther, do grant man to haue Freewill in ciuill and naturall things, but not in supernaturall. But this foolish distinction they shall neuer be able to proue out of the expresse word of their owne corrupted Bible, which they will only belieue. 3. The state of vprysing and entring in the grace of God, as when a man not being as yet called to the true Religion, hath some good motions wherunto he cannot freely consent or dissent, say they. 4. The state of Iustification, which is when God giueth some good motions to men now iustified to do good works, to absteyne from euill, to ouercome tentations and such: to the which motions a man cannot freely consent or dissent say the Ministers, and consequently, they say, that man hath no *freewill* to do good works, or to keep Gods Commandements, but rather continually doth transgresse them: (i) *For the flesh euermore rebelleth against the spirit* (say they) *wherby we continually trasgresse the holy Precepts and Commandements*.

(b) *Lib.* 1. *Inst. c.* 16. §. 8. & *l.* 2. *c.* 4. §. 6.
(c) *Lib. de Concord. art. de lib. Arbit.*
(d) *Clemēs l.* 3. *de Recog.*
(e) *Tert. l. de anima c.* 10.
(f) *Lib.* 1. *cont. Dureum p.* 78
(g) *In his reformed Catholik.*
(h) *In the Way to the true Church.*
(i) *In a prayer called the confession of sinnes.*

3. Against this blasphemous heresy the Catholike Church euer hath belieued, that man after the fall of Adam *had and hath freewill*, in matters concerning his saluation, grounded alwayes vpon the expresse word of the Scripture, and word of God, wherin Moyses said vnto the Iewes: (k) *I call this day heauen and earth to witnes, that I haue set before you lyfe and death, benediction and malediction, therfore choose lyfe*

(k) *Deut.* 30. *v.* 19.

lyfe &c. Where moyses putteth in the choyse or freewill of the Iewes, to giue themselus to good or bad things. And a litle before: (l) *I command thee this day, to loue the Lord thy God, to walke in his wayes, to keep his Commandements &c.* How then is it impossible to keep them? In lyke manner God offered a choyse to Salomon: (m) *Aske what I shall giue thee.* Wherby God declareth that Saloman had *freewill*, to choose the one or the other, as Dauid had choyse and free election to take any of the three seuerall punishments which God offered vnto him: (n) *I offer thee three things, choose the which of them I shall do vnto thee.* Which words playnly sheweth the freedome of election of man, the true liberty, not only from constraint, but also from necessity, for it is in our free power to take this or that, one thing or another (as the former examples do witnesse) we are not restrayned necessarily to the one part alone, as the Ministers do impiously teach.

(l) *Vers.* 16
(m) 1. *Reg.* 3. *v.* 5.
(n) 2. *Samuel* 24. *v.* 12.

4. Moreouer the Wyseman sayth: (o) *God hath set before thee water and fire, to which thou wilt stretch footh thy hand. Before man is lyfe and death, good and euill, that which pleaseth him, shallbe giuen vnto him.* Are not these places plainly set downe in the Bible, against the Ministers? are not such words sufficient to conuict them, if they had any conscience or desire to follow the word of God, which obstinatly and impiouslly they deny, in denying, that man hath freewill to do good or euill.

(o) *Eccl.* 15 *v.* 16.

5. The Ministers deceaue the poore people saying, that man hath not *freewill*, but doth things concerning his saluation or condemnation of necessity. Should rather the Ministers, or S. Paul be belieued, who sayth: (p) *He that hath determined in his heart, being setled, not hauing necessity, but hauing power of his owne will, and hath iudged this in his heart to keep his virgin, doth well. So then he that giueth her to mariage doth well, but he that giueth her not to mariage, doth better.* Which place though the Ministers haue corrupted in taking away the word *necessity*, yet it proueth plentifully *freewill*, & that to keep virginity is better then to mary. S. Peter teacheth vs also the same, speaking to Ananias: (q) *Whiles it remayned,*

(p) 1. *Cor.* 7. *v.* 37.
(q) *Act.* 5. *v.* 4.

appertayned it not vnto thee? and after it was sold was it not in thy owne power? Wherupon S. Augustine sayd thus: (r) *That before we vow, it is in our power, but after we haue vowed we ought to performe the same vnder payne not of corporall death, but of euerlasting fire.* And agayne: (s) *In the freewill of man it is, eyther to choose good things, and become a good tree, or euill, and become a bad tree.* What? will not the Ministers belieue the expresse words of the Apostles which I haue cited? will they not belieue the expresse word of Moyses? Of God himselfe to king Salomon, and King Dauid? can there be any saluation for thẽ, who do expone the Bible against the Bible, and who do corrupt the Bible against the Bible, which is a sinne against the holy Ghost?

(r) *Aug. serm 1[illegible]. de Diuers.*
(s) *Aug l. 2. de Act. cum felice Manich. c. 4.*

6. To the foresaid places I wil ad the place where God himselfe in his owne person teacheth Cain to haue freewill, and that Cain should command his lust and appetit, in vertue of his grace, and of naturall reason giuen vnto him to this effect: (t) *If thou do well, shalt thou not receaue againe? and if thou do euill, shall not thy sinne forthwith be present at the dore? but the lust or appetit therof shall be vnder thee, and thou shalt haue dominion ouer it.* Which place the Ministers haue so perniciously adultered, that if there were no other corrupted place in all their Bible but this alone, it were sufficient to condemne their Bible, as not being the word of God, but rather a rapsody of corruptions, inuentiõs, sacriledges, yea plaine heresies of Caluin, and Beza, forged and printed first in Geneua, and from thence brought to Scotland by Iohn Knox that famous Apostata frier, the first planter of this new Religion in Scotland, as witnesseth a Protestant wryter. (u) *Iohn Knox and others his adherents grounding themselues vpon the foresaid opinions, concerning violent reformation, did by priuate motion, without any authority, put in practise a strange maner of reformatiõ in Scotlãd.* The Ministers thẽ haue corrupted the forsaid place after this form. *And thou shall rule ouer him,* that is, ouer Abel, to take away the force of the sẽtẽce which signifieth, that man hath power & freewill, to rule ouer his appetite & lust. Doth not the Greeke Text plainly signify: *And thou shalt rule & maister it?* Doth not the hebrew read thus: *Vnto*

(t) *Gen. 4. v. 7.*

(u) *Sutclif in his answere to a certaine Libel supplicatory pag. 191.*

Vnto thee is the appetite of it, & thou shalt beare rule ouer it. Doth not (x) S. Austine with all the ancient Fathers read, as our Latin translation readeth, which (y) Pererius witnesseth: *Thou shalt beare sway ouer it* (sayth S. Augustine) *What? ouer thy brother? God forbid. Ouer what then but sinne.* The same sayth S. Hierome: (z) *Because thou hast freewill, I warne thee that sinne haue not the soueraignty or Maistership ouer thee, but thou ouer sinne.*

(x) *Aug. l.15. de ciu. Dei c.7.* (y) *Lib. 4. in Gen. c. 4 v 6.* (z) *Hier. quæst. Hebraic in Genesim.*

7. The Catholiks in disputing against the Protestants or Puritans should remember & cal oft to memory, that the Protestants at their first in comming to Scotland, and England, said and preached to the people, and yet do preach, that they were sent extraordinarily to reforme the Church of God. 2. That they would preach nothing, *but the expresse word of God, the playne Scripture, the only word of God:* and vpon this false pretext they haue cast downe our Churches, ouerthrowen our Abbayes, taking away our Priories, casting down to the groũd our anciẽt monumẽts, and Noble mens houses, corrupted the Bible, changed Ecclesiasticall discipline, and made most pernicious, seditious and vngodly Lawes against vs Catholiks, who do now aske of the Protestants, first: *to proue but one debatable poynt of their religion by the expresse word of the Bible,* which they shall neuer be able to doe. 2. *To improue any debatable poynt of our religion by the expresse word of the Bible,* which lykewyse they shall neuer be able to do. 3. *To name vs but one man, who before Luther or Caluin agreeth with them in all essentiall poynts of their Religion,* which likewyse they shall neuer be able to do. 4. *To name vs any Nation vnder the heauens, which maketh accompt of their Scotish, English, or Latin corrupted Bible,* which likewyse they shall neuer be able to do. For it is certaine that there is no Nation now a dayes, nor euer was which did accompt the Latin, English, or Scots Bible now in vse in England, & Scotland, for the word of God: which I obiected at seueral tymes to the Ministers being in prisõ in *Edenburgh*, where without books, pen, paper, inke, or any such cõmodity to passe the tyme, with coales I ouercast the walles with verses, and litle poemes in sundry languages, wherof I heere set down one which was after sent to me out of *Scotland*, it being

being to the prayse of *Scotland*, and commended by friends be placed in this Treatise.

The Priuileges of Scotland.

(1) Fourscore Kings of Scotland al Catholiks.

(2) Scotland the Seminary of many holy and learned men.

(3) VVas neuer vanquished by a foraine Prince.

(4) Al the Kings of Scotland of Scottish bloud.

(5) Scotlād receaued the Catholik Fayth long before England & many other Kingdomes.

(6) Scotlād till the cōming of Caluin and Knox neuer chāged Religion.

QVIS me carcer habet vinctum? quæ septa recludent
Corpora, pro canæ Fidei Regalibus armis
Patrum (1) octodecies longo de stemmate Regum?
Ecce colo sine luce domum, sine iure catenas.
Scotia terra parens, O vbi cælestia (2) dona,
Queis super Imperium sociale excelsior ibas!
Nec (3) Mauors potuit peregrino tradere vestra
Colla iugo, famæ tantum decus Anglia nescit,
Hybernumq; solum: surgit quæ gloria genti,
Quòd Scotos omni reges (4) ex ordine sceptri
Traxerit è patrijs laribus: maius quoq; nomen
Exoritur, quòd sancta Fides (5) radiârit in oris
Scotorum, ante facum multis data semina regnis
Christiadum, signat Donaldi purpura tempus,
(Scotia!) qualis erat terris decor additus, ante
Tempora Caluini? (6) nullis mutata procellis
Religio fidei steterat; pro cuius honoris
Vertice, lectus apex (7) Iacobus nomine Quartus
Protector Fidei titulis celebratur auitis.
Quin memor es (8) Belgis, Alemanno, Angloq; Bataui
Prima dedisse viris primæ sacra germina vitæ.
Nec data (9) Francigenis violasti fædera pacis
Quæ magnis Magnus sanciuit Carolus astris:
Hinc Franco Regi Scotus munimen ahenum est.
Scotia, nonne vides à cælo pignora? testis
Sit mea Morauiæ regio, (a) pulcherrima sedes
Veris, opus floræ, Pomonæ apricior hortus,
Triptolemi Cererisq; lares. (b) Hæc Francia parua
Dicitur, auspicijs Reginæ addicta Stuartæ.
Hanc liquidis vtrinq, fretis duo flumina vallant
Æquoreo lætos cursu lambentia fines.

Speya

(7) The Kings of Scotland called Protectours of the Fayth. (8) To haue conuerted many Nations. (9) Scotland honored by the most auncient Alliance of Europe. (a) The Prayses of Murrayland. (b) Queene Mary the Martyr called Murrayland litle France.

Speya (c) Salmonum nutrix, qua parte recurrit
Solis opus, preceps currit, qua parte caditue,
Nessa fluit; victrix (d) bruinæ, victrixq; rigoris:
Quam placet hæc patriæ species! (*) Ascendere colles
Hic video intonsos, illic descendere valles;
Hic lætas campi segetes agrosq; feraces:
Aspicio glebæ de versicoloribus illic
Pratorum spatijs, Chloris mouet omnia vernæ
Lætitiæ. Hic Lucus Zepherynas sustinet auras,
Illic arboreo fœtu nemus omne grauescit,
Bacciferisq; comis: vitreo cum murmure fontes
Aufugiunt ortus laticum, per prata, per herbas,
Subsiliuntq; vagis lymphis in amore liquorum.
Quot virides scænæ Musis! quot amæna locorum
Castra virent doctæ vatum monimenta coronæ!
Veris amica Domus nulli est reticenda poetæ.
Ast (e) Elgena parens non indonata recedes
Morauiæ vrbs princeps oræ, sanctissima quondam;
Quam diuæ (f) Triados sedes ditabat honore
Balsameo. O vtinam staret domus aurea cæli!
Ægidio (g) sacrata Domus stat tempore nostro
Nobilis ornatus, Diui præsentia firmat
Nutantes animos in religione Parentum.
O quàm multa piæ circum (h) vestigia dantur
Ædis, & vmbra mouet pulchræ sacraria plantæ
Certa virûm qui vota Deo fudere precesq;
Inclusi castis thalamis, castisq; sacellis.
Vna alias inter sedes celeberrima surgit
Condecorans Regis Duffi nomenq; decusq;
Kilflos (i) nomen habet, florum de nomine natum.
Posteritas heu nescit opus florale, pudores
Proh sancti! Duffum (k) regem violârat acerbo
Funere turba virûm, Diuis inimica Danorum,
Furtiuoq; sola laniatum corpore toto
Tradiderat, dum prodit opus iustissima virtus
Flore sato medijs brumis prope pectora Regis
Quo Superi signo niueas monstrare Monarchæ
Exuuias, roseosq; lares Regalis amici

(c) Murrayland betwixt Spey & Nesse.
(d) Nesse frezeth not
(*) The description of Murreyland in general.
(e) Elgin the chief Town in Murreyland
(f) The Trinity, Chaury, or Trinity Church.
(g) S. Giles Church.
(h) Many Abbyes & Monasteries in old tymes in Murrayland.
(i) The Abby of Killos.
(k) Leslæus Boetius & sundry others do make mention of this Miracle of King Duffus.

Virgineæ ſobolis; Iacta te Scotia mater
Muneribus diues Duffi pretioq; coronæ
Angelicæ, qua Duffus habet Capitolia Cæli.

8. The Proteſtants then not being able to proue or improue any debatable poynt by the expreſſe word of God, are forced to proue the ſame (ſay they) by neceſſary conſequences, that is, by their owne expoſitions, ſophiſmes and inuentions: but we reply. 1. That in making theſe conſequences they may erre. 2. That theſe conſequences cannot be infallible, and conſequently cannot be the groũd of any poynt of Religion. 3. That theſe conſequences are manifeſt inuentiõs of their owne head, againſt the expreſſe word of God. 4. That they haue ſworne and ſubſcrybed ſolemnely, that to interprete, expone, or inferre conſequences out of the Bible, doth not apperteyne to any priuate or publick perſon. Heare their owne wordes: (a) *The interpretation* (of the Scripture) *we confeſſe neyther apperteyneth to publick nor priuat perſons, neyther yet to any Church for any preheminency or prerogatiue perſonally or locally, which one hath aboue another, but appertayneth to the Spirit of God &c.* A fooliſh and contradictorious doctrine, for as much, as they ſay the interpretation of the Scripture doth not appertayneth to no publick nor priuate perſon, but to the Spirit of God. For ſome publick or priuate man muſt haue this ſpirit of God, otherwyſe how can we be certayne of the interpretation that it cometh of the ſpirit of God? Truely the Proteſtants do ſhew in this, and in all the poynts of their Religion, that they haue not the ſpirit of God, becauſe they contradict themſelues euery where, as in this Treatiſe the learned Reader may eaſily perceaue.

(a) *In the Confeſsion of their Faith in the actes of Parlamẽt in the year of God 1560. the 17. of Auguſt.*

9. To conclude then, the Miniſters ſhall neuer be able to proue out of the expreſſe words of their Bible theſe poynts of their Religon: *Man after his fall hath not freewil, neyther in ciuill maters nor maters of ſaluation. Man ſinneth neceſſarly: Man continually tranſgreſſeth the Commandements of God, &c.* Nor yet by neceſſary conſequences. Of which conſequeñces or rather hereſies of their owne, a wyſe mã ſhould make no

accompt

accompt, preferring therunto the consequences and expositions of the holy Fathers in this first Age, which I set down heer to the consolation of the Catholike Reader.

The holy Fathers in this first Age, do witnes playnly and plentifully, man to haue Freewill in matters concerning his saluation.

The first Section.

S. Clement: (a) *Si quis sanè audiens sermonem veri Prophetæ, velit recipere aut nolit, & amplecti onus eius, i. mādata vitæ, habet in sua potestate. Liberi enim sumus arbitrij &c. Nunc autem quia liberum est animo, in quam velit partem declinare iudicium suum, & quam probauerit eligere viam, constat euidenter inesse hominibus arbitrij libertatem.* That is: If any man heare the preaching of a true Prophet, it is in his power to make his profit therof, or not, for we haue freewill &c. Now since it is free to man to choose eyther the one or the other way, it is manifest that man hath freewill. And agayne he bringeth in S. Peter the Apostle disputing with Simon Magus, who denyed freewil, against whome S. Peter proueth that if men had not freewill, Lawes would be made in vayne, exhortations and preachings in vayne, admonitions and threatings in vayne. For euer still men might answer: *We haue no freewill to keep those Lawes. We haue no freewill to keep those instructions and preachings*; for what we do, we do it of necessity. (b) *Sed dic, quomodo ergo Deus iudicat secundū veritatem vnumquemq; actibus suis, si agere aliquid in potestate non habuit? hoc si teneatur, conuulsa sunt omnia, frustra erit studium sectandi meliora: sed & Iudices sæculi frustra legibus præsunt, & puniunt eos qui malè agunt. &c.*

(a) S. Clemens Epist. 3. ante medium.

(b) S. Clemens l. 3. recog. non longe ab initio, Vide l. 4. ante medium.

2. S Denis manifestly calleth man αὐτοκράτορα: that is, as hauing free power ouer himselfe, and that God concurreth with man in his actions freely, that is, offereth his grace to man, who may eyther refuse it or accept it. Which if he accept, God concurreth with him, if he accept it not, it is his owne fault. With necessary causes God concurreth necessarily: (c) *Cum liberis liberè, cum contingentibus contingenter*

(c) Lib. de Diuin. nom. c. 4. p. 4.

* καὶ ἄκοντας ἡμᾶς ἐπὶ τὴν ἀρετὴν ἄγειν.

(d) In l. de Diuin. nom. c. 4. lec. 23.

(e) Osee 13. v. 19.

tingenter: *Ideo & vanam multorum non admittemus rationem, qui oportere, aiunt, Prouidentiā etiam(*) inuitos nos ad virtutem ducere, neq; enim est prouidentia violare naturam. Quocirca sicut prouidentia cuiusq; naturæ est conseruatrix, à se mobilibus, vt à se mobilibus prouidet: & vniuersis & singulis iuxta proprietatem totius & vniuscuiusq;, in quantum prouisorum natura suscipit totius ac multifariæ prouidentiæ proportionaliter vnicuiq; attributas prouisiuas bonitates.* The which place (d) S. Thomas exponing plainly sheweth out of this holy Father, that man hath freewill, eyther to accept the grace of God, or to refuse it, to gaynestand good motions sent from God, or to imbrace them, to apply his mind to vertue, or to vice, conforme to the saying of the Prophet: (e) *O Israel thy perdition is of thy self, but thy help and saluation cometh of me.* Which place the Ministers haue corrupted.

(f) Epist. 10. ad Magnesianos.

* φύγωμεν τὸν θάνατον καὶ ἐκλεξώμεθα τὴν ζωήν.

3. S. Ignatius: (f) *Quandoquidem igitur actiones habent præmia, vitaq; ex obedientia proponitur, mors autem ex inobedientia: & singuli qui hoc vel illud elegerunt, in eius quod elegerūt locum habituri sint, (*) fugiamus mortem, & eligamus vitam.* And a little after: *Si quis pietati studeat, dei homo est: si impiè agat, diaboli homo est, non id factus per naturam, sed per suum ipsius arbitrium.* That is: If any study to piety, he is of God; if he do impiously he is a seruant of the Diuell, not by nature, but by his owne freewill. Now whose men shall the Ministers be, who belieue, that continually they transgresse the Commandements, that they are euer in the state of sinne? I omit to set downe other Fathers, the matter being so cleare and manifest in it selfe.

That the Ministers haue falsified the Bible in sundry places, which proue man to haue Freewill in maters of his saluation.

The second Section:

(a) 1. Cor. 15. v. 10.

S. Paul signifieth vnto vs, that he laboured togeather with the grace of God in preaching to the Iewes: (a) *I laboured more abundantly then they all: yet not I, but the grace of God with me.* In the vulgar Latin. *Non ego, sed gratia Dei mecum.* In the Greeke ἡ χάρις τοῦ Θεοῦ ἡ σὺν ἐμοί. Declaring

therby

therby that the grace of God did concurre as the principall agent with al his labours, yet that his freewill wrought (*) withall, as if the Apostle would haue said: *I laboured more abundantly then all they, yet not I alone laboured, but the grace of God which is with me laboured.* That S. Paul laboured it is manifest thus: (b) *They are the Ministers of Christs, I am more, in labours more abundant, &c.* Wherfore he calleth vs, (c) *Gods worke fellowes and helpers*, by reason of the free cooperation of our freewill with the Grace of God. Now the Ministers to ouerthrow this Catholike doctrine haue trāslated thus. *I laboured more abundantly then they all, yet not I, but the grace of God which is with me,* denying therby the cooperation of mans free will with the grace of God, adulterating the text with these two words, *which is,* against the meaning of the Apostle, and against the Greeke text: for the Apostle vnderstandeth, that not only he laboured, but also the grace of God laboured with him. It is a strange matter of our Ministers, that in translating the Bible so ignorantly, they shew that they haue no conscience, no feare of God, nor shame before men, translating so impudently & ignorantly the word of God, to couer their Idolatry and heresies. When I was in prison for the Catholike Religiō in Edenburgh straitly warded and narrowly kept, I offered at seuerall tymes to some Ministers, that for as much as the Bible is diuersly exponed of vs and of them, they neyther being tyed to my interpretation, nor I to theirs; I desired them earnestly to put aside my interpretation, and their owne likewise, referring the mater to the interpretations and Iudgement of the ancient Fathers, of generall Councels, of vniuersall custome, of tymes and places amongst all Nations. M. Andrew Ramsey answered no, we will not referre the mater to the ancient Fathers, rather we will referre it to Caluin, Beza, and such. Whereunto I was content, so he should bring me Caluin and Beza to try thē with the touchstone of the Bible, which he would not performe. Other Ministers at other tymes answered, we will be tryed by the Scriptures only, by the word of God, by the Bible. I replyed, will ye be tryed by the expresse word

*ἐκοπίαζε.

(b) 2. Cor. 11. v. 23.

(c) 1. Cor. 3. v. 9. *Dei adiutores sumus.*

word of God only, or by the word of God interpreted as it pleaseth you? Some of them answered, we haue the spirit of God to interpret the Scripture. I replyed: Thẽ yee will be both party and Iudges; had not the holy Fathers the spirit of God? had no Nation, no kingdome, no Country the spirit of God before the comming of Luther and Caluin? Hath not that bene the brag of all heretiks. Well then (said I) content, we be both tryed by the Scriptures only, by the expresse word therof, because yee will needs haue it so, and consequently I alledged to them the
(d) 1. Machab. 12. v. 44. VVhere they haue fulsy taken away the 46. Verse. booke of Machabees for prayer for the dead: (d) *And if he had not hoped that they which were slayne should ryse agayne, it had bene superfluous and vayne to pray for the dead.* No (said the Ministers) we admit not those for Scripture. Why so? Are not those books approued for Canonicall by the authority of the same Church, of ancient Councels, and Fathers, that the other books are? How do yee know that the Euangell of S. Iohn is Scripture, & the Euangell of S. Bartholmew (for one was put out with his name) is not? if yee reiect the authority of the Church, which giueth not authority to the Scripture as yee calumniat vs, but declareth which is,
(c) 1. Reg. 3. v. 27. and which is not Canonicall Scripture; as (c) Salomon declared the true Mother of the chyld, though she was true Mother before his declaration, but because that was vnknowen to the people, Salomons declaration was fully requisit: So the true Scripture in it selfe hath sufficient authority before all declaration, but for as much as that authority is vn knowen to euery member of the Church, it is fully requisit, there be some supreme power to declare the same, which must be the Church of God. No matter answered the Ministers, we will not admit those books for Canonical because the Iewes admit them not. I replyed, that was to play the Iew and not the Christian, conforme to S. Augustines opinion. Well then, let vs go forward and come to the poynt. Will you allow at least the Iewes Canonicall books of the old Testament, to wit, all that are extant in the Hebrew Bible, and all of the new Testament, without exception? yea that we will. In these books

books then will ye be tryed by the vulgar ancient Latin Bible famous in the Church of God aboue twelf hundreth yeares? No, we care not for your latin Bible said the Ministers. I replyed, will yee be tryed by the Greeke Bible of the Septuaginta interpreters, so authorized in our Sauiours owne speaches? No we will not: how then will ye be tryed? They answered, only by the Hebrew Bible of the old testament, we do thinke it only authenticall & true Scripture. I replyed, why then haue you left the Hebrew text as corrupted, in turning thus: (f) *They pierced my hands & my feet*, for in the Hebrew it is otherwyse if yee be skilfull in the Hebrew toung. For all the Hebrew Bibles read thus, *as a Lion my hands and my feet*. There truely they answered, we wil not follow the Hebrew but the Greeke Text. But that is but one place alone. I replyed, that one corrupted place of the Hebrew Bible is sufficient to take away all infallible authority of the word of God from it, and to hinder it to be the word of God: euen as in a contract band or obligation, if there be but one essentiall fault or falsity, the rest of the contract or band is reiected, and hath no authority, much more in the word of God, wherin all is essentiall & necessary to be belieued vnder the paine of condemnation. For we cannot iudge of the Bible and word of God as of other books, as Virgil, Ouid, William Wallace, and Dauid Lindesay, wherin though there may be some errours, corruptions, and lies, yet there be some truthes and verities, which neuertheles cannot be called infallible verities, but rather fallible. Contrary, the Bible and word of God being ēdyted to the holy wryters as to Moyses, the holy Prophets, Euangelists, and Apostles, by God himselfe, must haue wholly infallible verities, because they were infallibly assisted with the holy Spirit, & that in such sort, that they could not erre in wryting those holy Books: and if we grant that they haue erred but once, yea ōly once, it followeth necessarly that they had not a infallible assistance of the holy Ghost & consequently the reader of such a Bible shall euer be incertayne when they had infallible assistance of God, & when not: which is the reasō

(f) *Psalm. 22. v. 16. Caru. Caari Iadai Sicut Leo manus meæ.*

also wherfore the Scottish & English Bible translated by the Ministers cannot be the infallible word of God. Because the Ministers had not in translating the Bible an infallible assistance of God, but as men, and ignorant men might erre, and erred filthily almost in euery verse.

2. To these discourses of myne, one of the Ministers answered, that it was not a poynt of faith, that the Scottish or English Bible is the infallible word of God, which sundry Ministers of Frãce, speaking of their French Bible, haue affirmed publickly. But we haue recourse said this Minister to the Hebrew text. Wherunto I replyed, all the Hebrew Bibles that are now extant, are corrupted; which verity yee testify your selfe: as for example ye haue translated in your Scottish Bible that of S. Matthew thus. (g) *That it might be fulfilled which was spoken by the Prophet, which was, that he should be called a Nazarite*: Yet there is no Prophet of the old Testament, now extant, that maketh mention of this place, as witnesseth S. (h) Chrisostome, and (i) Theophilact with the rest of the Fathers. Heer then ye haue left all the Hebrew Bibles as corrupted. 2. Ye haue translated that of S. Matthew. (k) *Then was fulfilled that which was spoken by Ieremias the Prophet, saying, And they tooke thirty siluer peeces &c*. Which words are no wyse now in the Hebrew text of Ieremy, but rather in the prophet Zachary; so heer ye haue left the Hebrew Bible as corrupted, and followed our latin translation and the Greeke. 3 (l) Iustinus martyr a famous and ancient author witnesseth, that those words (m) *Regnabit à ligno Deus,* were in the first Hebrew copies and originalls, yet now no Hebrew Bible hath them; for the Iewes (sayth he, togeather with Tertullian) in hatred of the Passion of Christ did scrape them out maliciously. 4. Yee haue trãslated that of S. Paul, (o) *For it is written, cursed is euery one that hangeth on the tree.* Which words S. Paul citeth, as written by Moyses in Hebrew, and yet there is no Hebrew Bible now extant which hath precisely those words. So in this ye haue in lyke mãner left the Hebrew Bible as corrupted, & haue followed our Latin & Greeke Bible. 5. (p) Caluin your Maister & prime Heresiarch acknow-

(g) *Matth.* 2. v. 23.
(h) *Hom.* 9. *in hunc locum.*
(i) *Ibidem.*
(k) Matt. 27. v. 9.
(l) *Apolog.* 2. *pro Christianis*
(m) *Psal.* 95. v. 10.
(n) *Lib. cõtra Iudeos* c. 10.
(o) *Galat.* 3. v. 13. *Deut.* 21. v. 23.
(p) *Lib.* 1. *Instit.* c. 13. §. 9.

knowledgeth thosewords of Ieremy which proue theMessias to be trueGod: (q) *Hoc est nomen quod vocabunt eum, Dominus iustus noster*, to haue bene corrupted by the Iewes, for there is no Hebrew Bible now extant which hath those words, & you lyke Iewes haue followed the Iewes in translating this place against the opinion of your Maister, and against our Latin translation. 6. That place of Zachary: (r) *Tu quoq; in sanguine testamenti tui emisisti vinctos tuos de lacu, in quo non est aqua*, is corrupted in the Hebrew Bible, and referred by the Iewes to the Synagogue, and not to Christ, as it should be. Where your Maister Iohn Caluin playeth the Doctour ignorantly in saying that the Hebrew word *ath*, cannot be but of the feminine gender and referred to the Synagogue. But let him learne this lesson of me, that the word *ath*, without the letter *he* (as it is there) is both the masculine & feminine gēder. Finally yee haue left the Hebrew Bible as corrupted in those words of Ieremy which condemne you all with the Iewes as corrupters of the Bible: (s) *Verè mendacium operatus est stylus mendax scribarum*. Where the Prophet complayneth against the Iewes as hauing corrupted the Hebrew Bible, and ye being guilty of the same cryme haue falsly & obscurely trāslated the same words: *Lo, certainly in vayne made he it, the pen of the scribes is in vayne*. Yea the holy Fathers complayne greately that the Hebrew text is filthily corrupted by the Iewes, and amongst others (t) Galatinus, and (u) Genebrardus witnes the same largely. To these sayings of myne the Ministers (as they are very ignorant in the Hebrew tongue) could not make any answere.

(q) Ierem. 33. v. 16. In Hebrew Adonai, proper only to God.

(r) Zach. 9. v. 11.

See Pagninus in radice Ethe.

(s) Ierem. 8. v. 8.

(t) Gal. l. 1. c. vlt.

(u) In Chronologia ad ann. Dom. 476.

3. As I haue proued all the Hebrew Bible now extant to be corrupted, and far different from the originals which were before Christ and immediatly after Christ, so it shall be easie to proue the Greeke Bible of the Septuagint Translatours (which was of great accōpt amongst the Iewes) to be corrupted; as this place of Ieremy witnesseth: (a) *The sinne of Iudah is written with a pen of Iron, & with the poynt of a diamond*. Which place the Ministers haue translated, & yet it is not in the Greeke Bible, which they haue left as corrup-

(a) Ierem. 17. v. 1.

corrupted. 2. The Ministers haue abandoned the Greeke Bible as corrupted thus: (b) *All flesh come to worship before me, sayth the Lord.* Leauing out these two words, *in Ierusalem,* which are in the Greeke Bible. 3. In the Prophet Ionas: *And Ionas began to enter into the city a dayes iourney, and he cryed and said, Yet fourty dayes, and Niniue shall be ouerthrowne:* In the Greeke text now extant it is, *yet three dayes, and Niniue shalbe ouerthrowne.* So in this place the Ministers haue left the Greeke Bible as corrupted. 4. The holy Fathers proued against the Arrians, that God the Father had a consubstantiall sonne, out of those words of the Prophet Isaias: (d) *Nunquid ego qui alios parere facio, ipse non pariam, dicit Dominus? si ego qui generationem cæteris tribuo, sterilis ero, ait dominus Deus tuus?* in translation of the which place the Ministers haue fully left the Greeke Bible, as corrupted, and haue vitiously translated the same place in their English translation. 5. That place of Leuiticus: (e) *Yee shall not eat the flesh with the bloud,* the Ministers haue fully corrupted. For the two words, *the flesh,* are neither in the Hebrew nor in the Greeke, nor in the Chaldean text. So that eyther those must be corrupted, or els the Ministers must needs be traytors to the word of God. 6. In Isaias: (f) *And cry vnto her, that her warfare is accomplished.* Heer the Ministers leaue the Greeke text as corrupted, wherin it is, *her humility is accomplished.* 7. The Ministers haue translated, that Adam begat Seth being (g) *a hundreth and thirty yeares*, and yet in the Greeke text it is that he begot Seth being two hundreth and thirty yeares. 8. The Ministers follow not the Greek text in these places. (h) *I haue inclyned my hart to keep thy iustificatiõs for reward.* And agayne, *Redeme thy sinnes with almes.* Which places as making for the Catholiks the Ministers haue corrupted, and left the Greeke text. It were superfluous to reckon the multitude of the corruptions either of the Greeke or Hebrew Bibles now extant; wherof it followeth that it is folly to the Ministry in disputing, to betake thẽselues to the Hebrew or Greeke texts, as to incorrupted fountaynes, they not being the infallible word of God.

(b) Isa. 56. v. 2. ἐν Ἱερουσαλήμ.
(c) Iona. 3. v. 4.
(d) Isa. 66. v. 9.
(e) Leuit. 19 v. 26. μὴ ἔσθετε ἐπὶ τῶν ὀρέων, non comedetis in mõtib⁹.
(f) Isa. 40. v. 2. ὅτι ἐπλήσθη ἡ ταπείνωσις αὐτῆς.
(g) Gen. 5. v. 3.
(h) Psal. 119 v. 112.
(i) Dan. 4. v. 24.

4. As for the new Testament in Greeke, sundry ancient

ent Fathers imediatly after the Apostles auow constātly that the Greeke new Testament hath bene corrupted in sundry places. So (k) Irenæus, (l) Tertullian, (m) Origen, (n) Dionysius Bishop of Corinth, and (o) Theodoretus, who witnesseth that in his Bishoprike alone he had found more then two hundreth new Testamēts in Greeke filthily corrupted by the Heretiks, which the Catholiks did not remarke. *Ego inueni* (sayth he) *plusquam ducentos huiusmodi libros qui in honore habebantur in nostris Ecclesijs. Quos cum omnes simul coegissem, deposui, & loco eorum reposui quatuor Euangelistarum Euangelia.* Yea all the ancient Heretiks, as Manicheans, Valentinians, Arians, Macedonians, Nestorians &c. being Grecians by birth, did fully corrupt the Greeke new Testament, setting out copies to fauour their heresies, which S. Hierome himselfe witnesseth, auowing, (p) *Se nouum Testamentum Græcæ fidei reddidisse.* Now it is certayne that the latin new testament of S. Hierome which we vse is different in many places from the Greeke new testament now extant.

(k) *Lib. 1. cōtra Hæres c. 19.* (l) *Lib. 5. cōtra Marcion.* (m) *In vlt. c. Epist. ad Rom. v. 23.* (n) *Apud Euseb. l. 4. Hist. c. 22. & 23.* (o) *Lib 1. de Hæres. c. de Tatiano.* (p) *Lib. de Script. Eccles.*

5. And that the new Testament now extant is corrupted in many places it is manifest: I will only produce two or three, to the end that I be not tedious to the reader. 1. (q) *Behold I shew yow a secret thing, we shall not all sleepe but we shall all be changed.* Which words are manifestly erroneous, and directly against those of the Prophet: (r) *What man liueth and shall not see death?* yea against the same Apostle S. Paul: (s) *It is appoynted vnto men that they shall once die.* Which is the reason wherfore the latin vulgar translation hath rightly *Omnes quidem resurgemus, sed non omnes immutabimur.* 2. In the Reuelation, it is said: (t) *And they ceased not day nor night, saying Holy, Holy, Holy, Lord God Almighty.* Which place as corrupted the Ministers haue not translated, for in the Greeke, the word *Holy* is repeated nyne tymes, and in our latin text but three tymes, which the Ministers haue followed and left the Greeke as corrupted: peraduenture because we Catholiks do repeat the *Aue Maria* nyne or ten tymes togeather, the Ministers would rather leaue the

(q) *1. Cor. 15 v. 51.* (r) *Psalm. 89. v 4.8.* (s) *Hebr. 9. v. 27.* (t) *Reuel. 4. v. 8.*

Greeke text, then approue our holy custome grounded vpon the word of God. 3. The Greeke text is corrupted in those words: (u) *for thyne is the kingdome, power and glory, for euer and euer.* As (a) Erasmus, and (b) Henricus Bullingerus Arch-Ministers testifie themselues, & none of the ancient Fathers readeth so in the Lords prayer. 4. The Greeke new testaments printed at Geneua are in many places filthily corrupted. And to the end the Ministers of Geneua couer the better their corruptions, they haue printed sundry Greeke new Testaments as if they had bene printed in Catholike Townes in France, with these words, *Imprimè a Lyon, Imprimè a Rouen, Imprimè a Paris, Imprimè a Tholouse,* which double-dealing they haue vsed in the printing of sundry of their Hugenot Bibles. 5. Beza a Prime-Minister auoweth the Greeke new Testamēt to be corrupted, as hauing left out those words, which are in our vulgar latin: (c) *Timuit enim ne fortè caperēt eum Iudæi & occiderent, & ipse postea calumniam sustineret, tanquam accepturus pecuniam.* Beza his words are: (d) *Hæc in Græcis exemplaribus non inueni, nec tamen temerè videri possunt addita.* 6. Caluin a hardy companion in his resolutions sayth plainly, that the Greeke new Testament is corrupted, and giueth for example these words: (e) *Then sent Ioseph and caused his Father to be brought, & all his kinred euen threscore and fifteene soules.* Which place sayth Caluin should be corrected as erroneous, and that of Genesis where it is said: (f) *All the soules of the house of Iacob which came into Egypt are seauenty,* should be preferred. 7. Caluin condemneth agayne the Greeke new Testament as corrupted in these words: (g) *Many are called, but few chosen.* Which words he calleth superfluous & no wayes to the purpose. 8. The originals and autographes written by the Prophets and Apostles themselues in Hebrew and Greeke, are no wayes extant, nor can be found: What infallible assurance then can any man haue, that the Hebrew and Greeke copyes now extant are the word of God? wherof this Syllogisme ensueth: The Religiō of the Ministers in England & Scotland cannot be more infallible and certaine then the ground

(u) *Matt.* 6.

(a b) *The one and the other in annot. in* 6. Matth. *Decad.* 5. *Serm.* 5. *in orat. Dominicam.*

(c) *Act.* 23 v. 24.

(d) *In Annot. in hūc locum.*

(e) *Act.* 7. v. 14.

(f) *Genes.* 46. v. 27.

(g) *Matth.* 20. v. 16. *Caluin. in hunc locū.*

ground wherupon it relyeth, which is the Hebrew and Greeke Bible; but that ground is erroneous, fallible, incertayne, and doubtfull as I haue proued. Ergo &c. Likewyse the Proteſtants and Puritans who vnderſtande not the Hebrew & Greeke tongue, can no wayes be infallibly aſſured of their Religion, if it be grounded vpon the Originall Hebrew and Greeke, which they vnderſtand not.

6. But what ſort of Bible amongſt all the reſt is the moſt infallible, and ſhould be moſt preferred? S. Auguſtine anſwereth: (h) *In ipſis autem interpretationibus Itala cæteris præferatur: Nam eſt verborũ tenacior cum perſpicuitate ſentẽtiæ.* This, *Itala interpretatio*, is the ſame which now the holy Church ſpecially vſeth, called the *vulgar* or *latin editiõ*, as witneſſeth playnly S. Gregory, & (k) S. Hierome, who at the Commandemẽt of Pope Damaſus reuewed this Latin and vulgar tranſlation: *Ita*, ſayth he, *calamo temperauimus, vt ijs tantum quæ ſenſum imitare videbantur correctis, reliqua pateremur manere vt fuerant.* And Beza himſelfe maketh great accompt of our vulgar latin, and preferreth the ſame to any other whatſoeuer. Likewyſe the Church of God vniuerſally hath euer had in great honour and reuerence the ſame, as witneſſeth the Councell of (l) Trent, preferring and authorizing it aboue any other whatſoeuer, in eſtabliſhing any poynt of faith and Religion. Which vulgar and latin tranſlation we Catholiks imbrace, as approued ſpecially by the Church of God, which Church muſt be infallible, and infallibly certayne in all her deciſions, following in this the example of S. Auguſtine, who belieued that Bible only to be the true word of God, which by the holy Church was approued. (m) *Ego verò*, ſayth he, *Euangelio non crederem niſi me Eccleſiæ Catholicæ commoueret authoritas*. That is, *I would not belieue the Goſpell, except the authority of the Church did induce me therunto*. And the Apoſtle S. Paul doth aſſure vs: (n) *That the Church of God is the pillar and ground of truth*, wherupon we may rely without feare of falling: which infallible

(h) *Lib.* 2. *de Doct. Chriſt.* c. 15.
(i) *Præfat. in lib. Moral. c.* 5. *ad Leandrũ.*
(k) *Præf. in Pentateuchum.*
(l) *Seſſione* 4. *in Decretis*.
(m) *Cont. Epiſt. Manich.* c. 5.
(n) 1. *Tim.* 3. *v.* 15.

lible ground S. Augustine (with the ancient Fathers) had so deeply printed in his hart, that he gaue commonly this infallible rule to find out the true Religion, touching any Controuersy or question: (o) *Quisquis falli metuit huius obscuritate quæstionis*, *Ecclesiam de ea consulat*. That is, *Whosoeuer feareth to be deceaued by the obscurity of this question*, (which was betwixt S. Augustine and Cresconius the Heretike) *let him go, and aske the Church therof*. Wherfore it is folly to a Protestant, desirous to find the true Religion to trouble himselfe with euery question in particular, but rather he should be carefull, first of all to seeke out diligently what is the Church, which be the marks of the true Church, which be the offices and quality therof; and after that, to be informed of euery Controuersy in particuler: (p) *Ye must not seeke the truth from others, then from those that be in Church, from which Church it is easie to take the same: for so much as the Apostles did most fully place in the same Church, as in a rich treasure house, all things that belong vnto the truth of Christian religion, to the end that euery one that would, might take from thence the drinke of lyfe.*

(o) *Aug. l.3. contra Crescon. c. 33.*

(p) *Iren. l. 3. Hæres. c. 4.*

The

The 13. 14. and 15 Article.

1. *That with the grace of God, men may keep God his Commandements.*
2. *And, that the keeping therof, is meritorious of life euerlasting.*
3. *And, that Faith only doth not iustify, was constantly belieued by the Catholikes in this first age.*

CHAP. VIII.

CALVIN in sundry places doth ignorantly deny, that men though assisted by the grace of God, may keep the commandements: which doctrine our Ministers in Scotland do teach playnly in the maner to examē children before the supper of the Lord, set down in the end of the Scots Catechisme, or Articles of faith, where the Minister asketh of the child thus. *M. Canst thou keep Gods Commandements of thy selfe. C. No verily. M. Who then doth keep and fulfill them in thee?* C. *The holy Ghost. M. When God then giueth thee his holy Ghost, canst thou perfitly obserue them?* C. *No, not so. M. Why, God doth curse and reiect all such as do not in euery point fulfill his Commandements.* C. *It is true.* Of the which impious doctrine these blasphemyes do follow. 1. That a man assisted with the grace of God and holy Ghost, cannot keep perfitly the Commands. 2. That the omnipotency of the holy Ghost (who is God) cannot haue that strength to make a man to keep the Commands. 3. That the power of the diuell in making a man to breake the Cōmāds, is greater then the power of the holy ghost to make a man to keep them. Because a man (say the Mi-

Ministers) cannot keep them perfitly, though assisted by the holy Ghost, yet he breaks them perfitly assisted by the diuell. 4. That the best liuing Protestant or Puritane that is, is euer in the state of the curse and malediction of God: because, say the Ministers, no man can perfitly fulfill the Commands: wheron followeth this Syllogisme. The Ministers are obliged vnder the payne of condemnation to eschew sinne. But the holyest worke which they can do in this world, as to take the supper of the Lord, to pray, to preach, to giue almes, to sing the psalmes, are alwayes conioyned necessarly with deadly sinne. Ergo the Ministers are obliged vnder the payne of condemnation, not to do any
(a) Ioan. 8. v. 34. of those works. The Maior is euident: ([a]) *Whosoeuer committeth sinne, is the seruant of sinne*. And agayne: ([b]) *The wages*
(b) Rom. 6 v. 23. *of sinne is death.* I proue the Minor, because in those actions, of praying, preaching &c. eyther the Ministers keep the Commandements perfitly or not? If not, then that imperfection ioyned with the worke which they do, being a deadly sinne (because they make not a distinction of deadly and veniall sinnes, but al are deadly sinnes with thē) they are obliged vnder the payne of damnation to eschew it, as being against the Commandements of God: If in doing that worke, they keep the Commandements perfitly, then they contradict their owne doctrine, and belye Caluin. Secondly I proue the Minor. The best worke that a Minister can do, as to pray, preach &c. is ioyned with imperfection & sinne. But all the Ministers are obliged to eschew sinne. Ergo &c.

2. I would aske of the Ministers in what part of the Bible is found this distinction of theirs, to keep the Com-
(c) Matt. 19. v. 17. mands *perfectly* or *imperfectly*, since the Bible euer speaketh of that matter without distinction and absolutly, as ([c]) *If thou*
(d) Ioa. 14. v. 21. *wilt enter into life, keep the Commandements*. Agayne: ([d]) *He that hath my Commandements, and keepeth them, is he that loueth me, and he that loueth me, shall be loued of my father, and I will loue him, and will shew my owne selfe to him*. Can there be more playne words against the Ministers impious doctrine?

3. Finally, it followeth of this doctrine, that none

of the Ministers haue true faith in Christ, for they teach in their publick prayer called the Confession of sinnes: (e) *That the flesh euermore rebelleth against the spirit, wherby we continually transgresse thy holy Precepts and Commandements, &c.* And agayne in their Confession of faith sworne publickly they say: (f) *Therfore we feare not to affirme that murtherers, oppressors, cruell persecutours, Adulterers, whoremongers, filthy persons, Idolaters, drunkards, Theeues, and al workers of iniquity, haue neyther true faith &c.* Of which words I argue thus: Those that transgresse the Commandements of God haue not true faith: But all the Ministers continually transgresse the Commandements of God. Ergo &c. The difference betwixt vs Catholiks & the Protestants in this poynt is, that we teach that we may keep the Commandements of God, (being assisted by his grace) according to the rigour of the Law, hauing regard to our weaknes & fragility, yet we cõfesse that sundry tymes we trangresse the Cõmandments, and hauing transgressed them we may ryse from the state of sinne to the state of grace, assisted by the help of God; and thus being assisted by the grace of God, we may do some good works voyde and empty of any deadly sinne. The Protestants do beleue the contrary, that we cannot keep the Cõmandmẽts, though assisted by the grace of God, that cõtinually we transgresse the Cõmandments, that the best worke that a man can do hath sinne necessarly ioyned with it; which doctrines they hold against the expresse word of God, and against all Scripture. So Luther: *Al good actions be sinnes.* Whitaker: (g) *Luther said this, and he said it truely, for in euery action of a man though neuer so excellent, there is some fault, which may wholy marre the action and make it odious to God &c.* Which Blasphemyes are directly against the Bible & word of God; Against S. Paul: (h) *If thou take a wife thou sinnest not.* Against S. Peter: (i) *Doing these things you shall not sinne at any tyme.* Which words the Ministers haue corrupted. Against S. John: (k) *Whosoeuer is borne of God, sinneth not, for his seed remayneth in him, neyther can he sinne, because he is borne of God.* Against S. Matthew: (l) *If then thyne eye be simple, thy whole body shall be light.* Which place the Ministers

(e) *In the prayer called the Confession of sinnes.*

(f) *In the Acts of Parlamẽt holden at Edẽburgh 17. of August. 1560. Artic. 13.*

(g) *In his answer to the 10. reasons of M. Campian.*

(h) 1. Cor. 7. v. 36.

(i) 2. Pet. 1. v. 10.

(k) 1. Ioan. 3. v. 9.

(l) Matth. 21. v. 22.

nisters haue corrupted also. And though these foresaid words of the Apostles be plainly against the Protestans religion, yet effrontedly they say to the people, that they follow the only doctrine of the Apostles.

4. Finally it is against God himselfe who spake of Iob: (m) *In all these things Iob sinned not with his lips, neyther spake he any foolish thing against God.* Which place the Ministers haue corrupted. Do not these foresaid places proue manifestly that sundry actions & good works of men are not sinneful and haue not sinne ioyned with them, which is manifest when a man suffereth martyrdome and sheddeth his blood for the true Religion, what mixture I pray you of sinne can that holy action haue? Truely it can haue none that arryseth from the obiect beloued which is God, not from the will which loueth that obiect; because no feare of excesse, no danger of impurity can possibly flow from the desire to loue God aboue all things, which is then when a man suffereth for God martyrdome. Which excellent action of the loue of God in sundry holy men, is voyd of the mudde of distraction, of the scumme of vayne glory, of the froath of pryde, which imperfections do accōpany very often many of our good actions, yet they are not deadly sinnes, as the Ministers ignorantly do abuse the simple people, but they are veniall sinnes, and take not away the merit and reward of a good worke. As for fleshly motions, rebellious inclinations which sometymes do accompany our actions, they are not sinnes except a man consent therunto, for not in such imaginations or motions, which sometymes cannot be escaped, can there be any sinne, but in the consent therof, because those first imaginations and motions are not in our power, and consequently they cannot be voluntary. (n) *A way away with all excuse* (sayth Seneca, a Pagan) *no man sinneth against his will.* And againe; *It deserueth not prayse not to do, which thou canst not do.* S. Augustine shall decyde this mater betwixt vs and the Ministers, yea and seale vp the mouthes of Protestants Ministers, and quyet the harts of Catholikes, who sometymes in their good actions do remarke many imperfections. Note well his words:

(m) Iob. 1. v. 22.

(n) Seneca l. de moribus.

wordes: (o) *Whatsoeuer cause there be, of the will impelling it to offend, if it cannot be resisted, it is yeilded vnto without sinne; but if it may, let it not be yeilded vnto, and there shalbe no sinne committed. What? doth it perchance deceaue a man vnawares? Let him therfore be circumspect that he be not deceaued. Or is the deceit so great, as it cannot be auoyded? If it be so, the sinnes therfore are none, for who doth sinne in that which can by no meanes be escaped?* Likewyse. *Not in the euill desire it selfe, but in our consent do we sinne.* Moreouer. *In as much as it apperteyneth vnto vs, without sinne we might be alwayes, if this euill of concupiscence were healed, if we should neuer consent vnto it, but in, and for such things, in which if not mortally, yet venially we are ouercome of it, we may daily say, forgiue vs our trespasses,*

(o) *Lib. de Natura & Gratia c. 67. & l. 2. contra Pelagianos.*

5. I aske of the Ministers, those spots, contagions and imperfections of our good works, eyther they are actions distinct from the good works which they defyle, or not distinct. If they be distinct, then they cannot defile the good works, but are to be considered as seuerall sinnes in themselues, as hauing both in nature and quality an obiect different from the obiect of the good worke: If they be not distinct, but rather if the selfe same worke which is good, be spotted with deadly sinne (for there is no distinction of veniall, and mortall sinnes with the Ministry) then all good workes be they neuer so excellent are deadly sinnes and transgressions of the law: (p) *For good aryseth from an enteir cause, euill from euery defect and imperfection, Bonum est ex integra causa, malũ ex singulis defectibus,* say the Doctours. The reason wherof is, because a morall act or action cannot *simul & semel* be good and bad, pure and defiled: for as it inuolueth contradiction, that one and the same assent of our vnderstanding can be at the same tyme both true and false: so it is impossible that one and the same act of our will, should be ioyntly at the same moment good and euil, pleasing and displeasing to God. Wherfore if the best actiõ we can do, hath drosse & spots of sin ioyned with it, it followeth of necessity that all our actions are sins, yea deadly sinnes. True it is, that in materiall substance really distinct, the one substance may be good, and the other bad; the

(p) *Dionys. de diuin. nominibus c. 4. part. 4.*

badnes of the one not hindering the goodnes of the other, as drosse may be mingled with good siluer: But so it is not in morall actiōs, which eyther are fully good or fully bad.

6. Concerning the second poynt that our good workes are meritorious, it is to be remarked, that three things are necessary to make our actions and good workes meritorious, all which three do flow from the merits of Christ and the holy streames of his bloud shed for vs, without the which no worke of man can haue any merit. The first thing requisite is, that no worke of man can truely merit or deserue reward, except being wrought with the help of God, it also prooceed from the inherent grace of God remayning in our soules, wherby our actions are enobled greately in the sight of God. The second thing to be obserued is, that God hath ioyned the seale of his promise & obliged himselfe by his owne word to remunerate our works: for though God be not obliged to ingage himselfe to vs his poore creatures, yet hauing promised and ingaged himselfe to recompense our labours and good workes (to the end he may animate, and stir vs vp therby to do good works) he is obliged to performe his promise: Euen as a king not being obliged to giue some extraordinary aduancement to some poore subiect of his own, yet hauing promised the same, and sealed his promise solemnely, he is obliged to performe the same: so standeth the case betwixt God and vs. The third is, that all meritorious actions be freely and sincerely done; freely from the necessity of compulsion, sincerely from the badnes of sinister intentions. These things presupposed we Catholiks constantly mantayne that good workes are worthy of reward and meritorious of euerlasting life: not that there is an arithmetical equality or proportion betwixt our good works and heauenly felicity, as is betwixt one shilling and another, one crown of Gold and another: for what proportion can be betwixt a finite and infinite thing? But the proportion only is that, which is betwixt grace and glory, as betwixt the seed sowen in the ground, & the statelynes of the tree which cometh of the seed, which is a *vertuall proportion*. For the

the which cause the word of God expressly teacheth vs that our good workes are worthy of God. And specially speaking of the constancy of Catholiks, who do remayne in the midst of heretiks, (q) *Thou hast a few persons names yet in Sardis, which haue not defiled their garments; and they shall walke with me in white, for they are worthy*. And likewyse to the good Catholike who auoweth his Religion before the enemys of God, he sayth thus: (r) *He that ouercometh, shalbe clothed in whyte aray, and I will not put out his name out of the booke of life, but I will confes his name before my father, and before his Angels*: Agayne, (s) *Giuing thanks vnto the Father which hath made vs worthy to be partakers of the inhabitation of the Saincts in light*. Which place the Ministers haue corrupted. And agayne: (t) *Wherefore we pray also alwayes for you, that our God may make you worthy of his calling*. And agayne playnly S. Paul witnesseth, that our good workes do merit before God: (u) *To do good and to distribute, forget not: for with such sacrifices God is promerited: Talibus enim hostijs promeretur Deus*. Which place the Protestants haue corrupted. And agayne: (a) *I am inferior to all thy mercies*, where the Caldeã Paraphrasis readeth, *my Merits are lesse then all thy mercyes which thou hast shewed to thy seruant*. And agayne, the very word *meritum*, is specified: (b) *All mercy shall make a place to euery man according to the merits of his works: Omnis misericordia faciet locum vnicuiq; secundum meritum operum suorum*. Which place the Ministers haue impiously corrupted, as fully making against their wicked doctrine.

(q) Reuel. 3. v. 4.

(r) Reuel. 3. v. 5.

(s) Coloss. 1. v. 12.

(t) 2. Thess. 2. v. 13.

(u) Hebr. 13. v. 16.

(a) Genes. 32. v. 10.

(b) Ecclesi. 16. v. 15.

7. To the former reasons I will adde this only argument: If the best worke a man doth, hath sinne ioyned with it necessarily, then the Protestants are iustified by sin, which is a blasphemy. I proue the consequence, for that act of faith wherby the Protestant is only iustified (for they sweare and subscrybe, (c) *That they receaue remission of their sinnes by fayth only*) must needs be a good worke, or a bad worke: If a good work (cõforme to that of our Sauiour, (d) *This is the worke of God that yee belieue in him whome he hath sent.*) it must needs haue some spot of sinne ioyned with it, and consequently the Protestant is iustified by sinne and sinfull actions.

(c) In their Confession of Faytb.

(d) Ioan. 6. v. 29.

actions. Likewise when the Protestant prayeth thus: *And forgiue vs our sinnes:* eyther this prayer is fully a good worke or els spotted with sinne and iniquity. If spotted with sin, then the Protestants do obteyne remission of their sins, by sins thēselus, & a sinfull petition which is greatly absurd.

8. Last of all I aske of the Protestants in what part of the expresse word of the Bible these propositions are to be found: *The Commandements of God are impossible to be kept. 2. The commandements of God cannot be kept perfectly by the holy Ghost. 3. Our good works are alwayes spotted with sinne. 4. Our good workes proceeding from the grace of God, are not worthy of reward, are not meritorious?* But they shall neuer be able to giue any expresse word of the Bible. As for their erroneous consequences, let vs preferre the consequences of the holy Fathers therunto.

The Testimonyes of the holy Fathers of this first Age, concerning the keeping of Gods Commandements, and the merit of good Works.

The first Section.

SAINT Clement proueth that our Sauiour came to keep the Law and the Commandements, and by his grace to make the Christians to keep them: (a) *Non enim legem soluit, vt opinatur Simon Magus, imò impleuit: Ait*
(a) *Lib. 6. c. 19. const. Apostol.* *enim; Iota vnum aut apex non praeteribit à lege donec omnia fiant: non enim, inquit, veni soluere legem, sed adimplere.* And againe he auoweth that the Catholiks and Christians do fulfill the Law more perfectly then the Iewes, and that they are more obliged therunto. (b) *Qui tunc homidicium interdixit, nunc etiam iram temerè concitatam: Qui tunc adulterium, nunc prauam quoq; cupiditatem, vt tendamus ad amicitiam Cōditoris: amicitia autem efficitur bene viuendo, & voluntati eius obediendo, qua voluntas omnium viuentium lex est.* And againe he teacheth that he, who ioyneth a good life and conuersation with prayer, doth merit much before God: (c) *Audiri autem à deo ita demum merebitur quis, si orationes ipsa bonis moribus & bonis operibus adiuuentur.*

(b) *Lib. 6. Constit. Apost. c. 23. & l. 1. recog.*

(c) *Lib. 3. Const. Apost. c. 12.*

2. S. Ignatius

2. S. Ignatius in his Epistle teacheth manifestly, that the perfection of this life consisteth in true faith and perfect charity, which charity cannot be, sayth he, without the fulfilling of the Law by the grace of God, conforme to that, (d) *He that sayth I know God, and keepeth not his Commandements, is a lyar, and the truth is not in him.* Do not the Ministers playnly say the contrary? *He that sayth that he keepeth Gods Commandement is a lyar?* The same holy Father writing to the Romanes, prayeth them earnestly not to hinder his passion that therby he may merit eternall felicity: (e) *Mihi verò difficile est Deum promereri, si vos mihi non peperceritis pretextu carnalis amicitiæ. Nolo autẽ vos hominibus, sed deo placere, sicut & placetis.* And after. *Ego omnibus Ecclesiis scribo quòd voluntarius morior, si modò vos non prohibueritis: obsecro vos ne intempestiua beneuolentia me complectamini Sinite me ferarum escam fieri, per quas licebit Deum adipisci.* And wryting to a Gentlewoman exhorteth her therby to be constant, and to do good workes: (f) *Præsens namq; labor modicus, (*) multa autem quæ hinc expectatur merces.*

(d) 1. Ioan. 2. v. 4.

(e) Epist. ad Romanos.

(f) In Ep. ad Mariam Cassobolitam.

* τὸ δὲ προσδοκώμενος μισθὸς πολύς.

3. S. Martialis who is of great honour for his holynesse and doctrine in Bourdeaux & Limoges in France to this day, of good workes sayth thus: (g) *Vobis enim Deus est testis, scrutator renum & cordium, in eius obedientia nihil arroganter, nihil superbè, nihil temerè præsumere, sed tanquam pusillus grex Dei, voluntatem eius adimplere studete in verbis sanctis & operibus bonis; etenim frequens & assidua Dei custodia super vos &c.* Could he speake more playnly for good workes, & for the keeping the Commandements?

(g) Epist. ad Thosolanos c. 17.

4. The Merites of good workes S. Dionysius teacheth so playnly, and so manifestly, that no vnpassioned mã cã haue any doubt therof, by reasõ of the Iustice of God, wherby euery man shall receaue, saith he, according to his works good or bad, according to his merits or demerits: (h) *Iustus verò rursum Deus vt omnibus secundum meritum retribuens dicitur, rectamq; mensuram, & pulchritudinem, & ordinem, & dispositionem, & omnes distributiones atq; ordinationes vnicuiq; segregans iuxta definitionem verè iustissimam, & omnibus proprij singulorum operis author existens.* And a little after: *Operepretium*

(h) Ecclef. Hierarch. c. 7. p. 3.

est cognoscere diuinam iustitiam in hoc omnino esse veram iustitiam, quòd omnibus quæ sua sunt distribuit pro singulorum merito, & cuiusq; naturam seruat in suo ordine atq; virtute. And Agayne: *Itaq; vt verum dicam, hoc magis est diuinæ iustitiæ proprium nequaquã emollire ac destruere optimorum virtutem masculam, rerum materialium largitione; neq; si quis id agere conetur, absq; adiutorio linquere, sed illos in præclaro inflexibiliq; statu solidare, & ipsis, quum tales fuerint, reddere secundum meritum*. Can this holy Father speake more playnly? Can he prayse more highly the merits of good Works? can he recommend more earnestly the care of good works? Is not this doctrine far different from that blasphemous doctrine of Caluin who impiously & filthily

(i) *Lib. 2. Instit. c. 17 Sect. 6.* denieth Chryst to haue merited? (i) *Quærere verò an sibi ipse meruerit Christus* (quod faciũt Lõbardus & Scholastici, meaning vs Catholiks) *non minùs stulta est curiositas, quàm temeraria definitio*. Directly against S. Paul, who teacheth that Christ

(k) *Philip. 2. v. 8.* did merit by his death and passion: (k) *To haue a name aboue euery name, he humbled himself: and became obedient vnto the death, euen the death of the Crosse. Wherfore God hath also highly exalted him, and giuen him a name aboue euery name.*

That the Ministers haue falsified the Bible in sundry places, which proue good workes, and the merites therof.

The second Section:

THE holy Catholike Church hath euer taught, that Iustification consisteth in true faith and good works, and not in *only faith*, as the Ministers teach: for this cause the Ministers suppresse the very name & word of *Iustificatiõ* in such places where it signifieth the keeping of the Commandements, or the Law of God; as in that place of S.

(a) *Luc. 1. v. 6.* δικαιώμασι. Luke: (a) *Both were iust before God, and walked in all the Commandements and iustifications of our Lord without reproofe*: *In omnibus iustificationibus*. Where the Ministers haue taken away the word *Iustifications*, to the end that the simple people should not thinke, that our iustification before God consisteth in true Faith, and the keeping of Gods Commandements,

ments, for the which cause they haue put in the word *ordinances*, in place of the word *iustifications*. But I pray you, why translate you *ordinances*, and auoide the word *iustifications*? Signifyeth not the Greeke word, δικαίωμα, *iustification*, δίκαιος, *iustus*? Doth not S. Luke testify that Zacharias and Elizabeth were both iust, because they walked in all the iustifications of our Lord? Lykewise yee haue corrupted that place of S. Paul: (b) *If the vncircumcised keep the iustifications of the law*. Of the which blasphemous corruptions of yours, Beza your prime Minister giueth reason saying: (c) *That he reiected the word Iustification, to auoyde the cauillation of the Papists, which might be made by this word against iustification by faith only*. Is this vpright dealing in translating the word of God, to corrupt it manifestly when it maketh for the Catholiks? Againe, where the Scripture maketh mention of the iustifications or good works of the Saints, as: (d) *for the silke is the iustification of Saints*. The Ministers translate, *the righteousnes of Saints*: they could not say for shame, *ordinance of Saints*, as they said before: they would not say, *iustification of Saints*, with the Catholike Church, but rather, *righteousnes*, though the same Greeke word be in all the former places. But I pray you good Countrymen why turne yee, *they were both iust*, in S. Luke before cited, & not, *they were both righteous*, and yet in this foresaid place yee translate, *the righteousnes of Saints*, though the same Greeke words be, δίκαιος, and δικαίωμα.

(b) Rom. 2. v. 26.

(c) Annot. in 1. c. Luc.

(d) Reuel. 19. v. 8.

2. I intreat the Catholike Reader to consider the double and pernicious dealing of the Ministers, who when the word *Iust* is ioyned with *Faith*, then they vse the word *Iust*, and not *righteous*: as (e) *The iust shal liue by faith*, to make the ignorant beleeue that man *is iustified by faith only*. But when the word *iust* or *vniust* is ioyned with good workes then they vse not the word *iust* but *righteous*, or *righteousnes*, to make the simple people thinke that man is not iustified by good works: as, (f) *For God is not vniust to forget your good workes*, where the Ministers haue translated, *God is not vnrighteous*. Agayne S. Paul to signify that God is obliged (since he hath ingaged himselfe to vs by his promise) of iustice to

(e) Rom. 1. v. 17.

(f) Heb. 6. v. 10. οὐ γὰρ ἄδικος.

giue vs a reward for our good works done by his grace & mercy, sayth: (g) *Henceforth is layed vp for me a crown of Iustice, which our Lord the iust iudge shal giue me at that day:* Where the Ministers haue put in the word *righteous* and *righteousnes*, for *iust* and *Iustice*. For if that place of S. Paul were rightly translated, it would signify, that men are iustly crowned in Heauen for their good works done in this world, and that it is Gods iustice so to do, & that he will do so, because he is *a iust iudge*, as the ancient Fathers (namely the Greeke doctours) do interpret and expone, and that so far, that one of them sayth: (h) *See heere, to suffer for Chryst procureth the kingdome of Heauen according to iust Iudgement*. And yet according to his grace and mercy, conforme to that saying of S. Augustine: (i) *How should God render or repay as a iust Iudge, vnles he had giuen it as a mercifull Father?* Where S. Augustine discouereth the third corruption of the Ministers in the foresaid place not only saying, *righteous Iudge*, for *iust Iudge*, but also putting the word *giue a crown of Iustice*, for *render a crown of Iustice vnto me:* for so it is in the Greeke, (*) he will render or repay, *reddet mihi Dominus in illa die:* that is, a thing due & deserued, which hath relation to works going before. (k) *The Apostle said not* (sayth Theophilact) *he will giue, but he will render or repay, as a certayne debt*.

(g) 2. Tim. 4. v. 8.

(h) Oecum. in 2. Ep. c. 1. ad Thess.

(i) Aug. de Gratia. & lib. Arbit. c. 6.

* ἀποδώσει

(k) Theophil. vpon this place.

3. The other place which they haue corrupted is: (l) *I belieue that the afflictions of this tyme are not equall to the glory which shalbe shewed in vs*, because the afflictions are short, the glory eternall, the afflictions small and few, the glory great & aboue measure. Now the Protestants to perswade the Reader, that there is no worthynes in our good works or afflictions in respect of that heauenly felicity, turne thus in some of their Bibles: (m) *I am certaynly persuaded that the aflictions of this tyme are not worthy of the Glory which shalbe shewed vpon vs.* In the which place there be three notable corruptions. 1. *I am certaynly persuaded*, for, *I suppose, I belieue*. 2. *are not worthy*, for, *are not equall*, as Beza their prime Minister turneth, *Statuo minimè esse paria*, for the Greeke word, sayth he, rightly and properly is spoken of such things, as being weighed, are found of one weight. The third corruption

(l) Rom 8. v. 18.

(m) Bible 1577. λογίζομαι οὐκ ἄξια πρὸς τὴν μέλλουσαν δόξαν, *non sunt condignæ ad futuram gloriam.*

ruption is, *of the glory*, for, *to the glory*. And though our afflictions cannot be comparable or equall to that eternal felicity, as the Apostle sayth heere, yet they may merit and deserue the same: as the afflictions and passions of our Sauiour Christ Iesus were not equall in substance, though in valour, to that eternal glory which he obteyned to his mãhood, and to vs therby; yet did he deserue & merit eternall glory, not only for himselfe, but for all the world: yea by the least affliction he suffered, he did merit and deserue all this. Which is against the doctrine of (n) Caluin, and his fellow minister *Molineus* who impiously speaking of Christs merits sayth: (o) *Errarunt Monachi & Doctores Papistici, vrgentes merita tum incarnationis, tum natiuitatis, tum tentationum & afflictionum Christi; nihil hæc omnia proderant nobis, nihil poterant*. Can there be a greater blasphemy affirmed? 2. The pleasure which a man hath in committing adultery is not comparable nor equall to the eternall torments of hell, yet that action of adultery doth demerit and deserue the same: and shal God be more prone to punish man eternally for a transitory bad action, then to reward him for a good action? 3. The Apostle by making an incomparable difference betwixt the glory to come with the afflictiõs of this life, doth exhort vs Christians more vehemently to suffer all those afflictions couragiously and willingly. But if he had said, as the Ministers do translate, the afflictions are not worthy of heauen, you are neuer the nearer Heauen for them, only belieue; this had not bene a good motiue to exhort them, but rather to discourage them. 4. The Apostle when he will in other places encourage the Christians to suffer patiẽtly all sorts of afflictions and persecutions for their Religion, vseth this argument: That the persecutions though transitory, yet they worke and merit that eternall felicity: (p) *Our tribulation which presently is for a moment and light worketh or causeth aboue measure exceedingly, an eternall weight of glory in vs*. Which place the Ministers haue corrupted. Remarke, I say, the comparison betwixt short afflictions and eternall felicity, and yet the one worketh the other, that is, causeth, purchaseth, meriteth, and deserueth the other:

(n) *Lib. 3. Inst. c. 11. num. 18. 20 & c. 15. n. 2. & 3.*

(o) *Molin. in 51. part. harm. vt refert Feuard Dial. 4. Hæres. 31.*

(p) *2. Cor. 4. v. 17.* κατεργάζεται.

euen as a little seed not being comparable to the great tree, yet causeth it, and bringeth it forth; so our tribulations and good workes otherwayes incomparable to that eternall glory, yet by the vertue of Gods grace working in vs, worketh, causeth, and meriteth the said glory. Yea the very (*) Greeke word which the Ministers turne heer obscurly *Worketh*, in other places (q) they turne playnly *Causeth*. Declaring therby (though against their will) that our tribulations and good workes are cause of that eternall felicity, yet a subalterne cause. 5. That holy and ancient Father S. Cyprian will decyde the whole matter, and declare the meaning of the Apostle, his words be: (r) *O what maner of day shall come* (sayth he) *my brethren, when our Lord shall recount the* (* *merites of euery one, and pay vs the reward or stipend of faith & deuotion*. And a little after: *For that we shall receaue greater things then heere eyther we do, or suffer, the Apostle pronounceth, saying: the passions of this tyme are not condigne, or comparable to the glory to come*. Likewyse S. Augustine: (s) *The exceeding goodnes of God hath prouyded this, that the labours should soone be ended, but the rewardes of the merits should endure without end: The Apostle testifying: The passions of this tyme are not comparable &c. For we shall receaue greater blisse, then are the afflictions of all passions whatsoeuer*. Where these holy Fathers with many others make mention of the very word, *Merit*. Which that prime and branded Minister for the sinne of Sodomy Caluin himself testifieth, saying: (t) *vsi sunt fateor passim vetusti Ecclesiæ scriptores*, meaning the word *Merit*.

* κατεργάζεται.
(q) 2. Cor. 7. v. 10.
(r) Epist. 56
* Singulorum merita.
(s) Serm. 37 de sanctis.
(t) Lib. 3. Instit c. 15. num. 2.

3. Now I would intreat the vnpassionate Reader to remarke diligently how that this poynt of doctrine of good workes with many others which the Catholiks do teach, tendeth fully to the increase of piety, and reformation of manners, to good life and conuersation. Contrary, the Protestants doctrine against good works and merits, against the keeping of the Commandemēts &c. disposeth a man to all sort of wickednes: for the Protestants Gospell and doctrine denyeth a man to haue freewill, to do good, to absteyne from sinne; teacheth the Commandements of God to be impossible to be kept, yea with the grace of God: And

And who will euer assay to do, which he hath not power to will, or possibility to performe? And who can with any courage endeauour to keep that which he knoweth before hand to be impossible to be kept? Likewyse the Ministers hold, that God doth purpose, decree and cooperate to the obstinacy of the wicked, and that whatsoeuer he wil, must of necessity ensue: That God doth creat some and ordeyne them (not hauing any regard to their bad behauiour) to the eternall fyre of hell. Which blasphemy is fully against the tender bowells of his infinite mercy. The Protestants auowe all our good works, euen the best, to be stayned with sinne, and displeasing to God, and therfore do merit damnation: A blasphemy repugnant to the very light of nature, reason, and word of God. In like manner many of the Protestants directly do teach, that a man once iustified cannot loose his iustice whatsoeuer wickednes he doth cōmit. That God doth not impute to the faithfull the vncleanes of their dishonest lyues: Could any Mahometan desire more pleasing dreames to flesh and blood? The Ministers allow no distinction of veniall and mortall sinnes, yea euen the sodayne and inuoluntary motions of the flesh they affirme to be of their owne nature damnable and deadly, yet if they haue faith (that is a forged persuasion of their owne) there is no condemnation to them that are in Christ Iesus, say they. Doth not this doctrine plane the way to all wickednes, to all iniquity, and mischiefe? for that the Protestant who persuadeth himselfe, that no Ambition, Pryde, Pleasure, no wrong done to his Neighbour, can be hurtfull vnto him and procure damnation if he belieue and haue faith: The Protestant I say, who doth belieue the first motions or euill suggestions to be deadly and mortall sinnes, as well as the consent or consummation of them; what stop or barre can such a man haue to absteyne from his violent passions or carnall desyres? For he may reason thus with himself: since I am already drowned in all sort of sinnes, since I continually transgresse the Commandements, since my first motions are deadly sins though I consent not to them, since the best worke I can

VVitaker cont. 2. quaest. 5.

do, is nothing but abhomination before God, what doth it auayle me to striue against the streame? what doth it auayle me to ayme to do what is impossible? All this is confirmed by a Protestãt his owne testimony who sayth thus: (u) *The case thus standeth with vs Protestants, that if any be desirous to see a great rable of knaues, of turbulent persons, deceitfull coosiners, vsurers, let him go to any Citty where the Ghospell is purely preached* (as to *London* or *Edenburgh*) *and he shall find them there by multitudes. It is more manifest then the day light, that there was neuer amongst the Ethniks, Turks, or other infidels more vnbrydled and vnruly personnes, with whome all vertue and honesty is quite extinct, then are amongst the professours of the Ghospell.* These abhominable fruits of this new preached Ghospell be the cause wherfore many of the Protestants and Puritans, specially of the Ministry dye desperatly, which M. Iohn Knox a Prime Minister witnesseth plainly: (a) *True it is* (sayth he) *that this* * *venome of desperation is neuer throughly purged from our harts, so long as we cary this mortall carcasse.*

(u) Andreas *Musculus Dominica 1. Aduent.*

(a) Knox *in the order and doctrine of the generall Fast &c. holden at Edenburgh.* 1565. *id est, poison.

4. Contrary to these blasphemyes, the Catholike doctrine leadeth a man to all sort of vertue; as the doctrine of freedome of will maketh a man carefull to fulfill the law of God. The doctrine of reprobation and damnation, that it proceeds from our selues and not from God, maketh a man carefull to do some good workes & meritorious of heauen. The doctrine, that the fauour of God once gotten may be lost, maketh a man wary and circumspect in his behauiour. The doctrine, that Concupiscence without consent is not sinne, but stoutly resisted is occasion of merit, maketh a man carefull to gaynstand the same. Likewise the Catholike doctrine exhorteth men to the mortification of their passions, denying of themselues, contempt of honours, riches & worldly pleasures. We preach voluntary pennance, chastisement of our bodyes, watching, fasting, contrition, and satisfaction for our sinnes. We incite and stir vp our followers not only to the keeping of Gods Commandements, but also to the imbracing of his Euangelicall Counsels, to religious Pouerty, Chastity, and Obedience: to such vnion with God and

and holynesse of life, that those who imbrace & feruently put in practice the exhortations of our Catholike Church, seeme rather to lead in this mortall flesh angelicall, then humane lyues.

The 16. 17. & 18. Article.

1. That the custome to fast Lent. 2. And some other dayes. 3. And to abstaine sometymes from certaine meates, was vniuersally in vse in this first Age.

CHAP. IX.

HAVING spoken of good workes and the merits therof in generall, it followeth to speake of some good works in particular: as of the keeping of *Lent* &c. Which Caluin with the rest of his fellow Ministers abhorreth greately, as those who haue consecrated their belly to Bacchus, their body to Venus, their Pen to the inuention of prophane noueltyes and contradictions: (a) *Mera stultitia fuit* (sayth Caluin) *ieiunium Quadragesimæ*. And agayne: (b) *Ieiunium per se nullius momenti est.* The contrary Caluin himselfe, alwayes tossed with the spirit of contradiction, as a wyly Fox teacheth, affirming that the Church of God hath power to institute & ordayne fasting, solemne supplications, and such outward ceremonyes. *Reliqua pars disciplinæ, quæ clauium potestate propriè continetur, in eo est, vt pro temporum necessitate plebem exhortentur pastores vel ad ieiunia, vel ad solemnes supplicationes, vel ad alia humilitatis, penitentiæ ac fidei exercitia: quorum nec tempus, nec modus, nec forma præscribitur verbo dei, sed in Ecclesiæ iudicio relinquitur. Huius quoq; partis obseruatio, sicuti est vtilis, ita veteri Ecclesiæ ab ipsis vsq; Apostolus sëper fuit vsitata.* Could Caluin speake more playnly for

(a) *Harm. in Matth.* 4. v. 1. & 2
(b) *Lib. 4. Inst. c. 12. num. 16.*
(c) *Lib. 4. Inst. c. 12. num. 14.*

for the institution of Lent, and other fasting dayes, and sundry other ceremonyes vsed in the Catholike Church? It is certayne that the Bible in diuers places commandeth vs to fast: (d) *Therfore also now the Lord sayth; Turne you vnto me with all your hearts, and with fasting, and with weeping, and with mourning.* Which Commandement being morall, yea naturall, appertayneth as well to the Christian Church, as to the Synagogue of the Iewes, as learnedly (e) S. Leo teacheth, and the Scripture it selfe by the testimony of our Sauiour witnesseth: (f) *But when thou fastest, annoynt thy head, and wash thy face, that thou seeme not vnto men to fast, but vnto thy Father which is in secret: and thy Father which seeth in secret, will reward thee openly.* Which place though the Ministers haue corrupted, yet it sheweth, that since our Sauiour therin maketh mention of some forme and fashion how to fast, much more he commandeth vs to fast, to pray, and to giue almes, as S. Augustine wysely deduceth saying: (g) *I, considering with my selfe the Euangelicall and Apostolicall doctrine of the new Testament, do find, and see that fasting therin is commanded.* If then fasting be commanded vnto vs by the holy Scripture, though the precise fashion, forme, and dayes to fast are not therin prescrybed, it appertayneth to the holy Church (as Caluin himselfe before hath declared) to prescrybe and determine the forme, fashion, and tyme to fast, it being manifest amongst the learned, that *modus præcepti non cadit sub præcepto.*

(d) *Ioel.* 2. *v.* 12.

(e) *Sermo* 4. *de Ieiunio septimi mensis.*

(f) *Matth.* 6. *v.* 17.

(g) *Aug. Ep.* 86. *ad Casulanũ.*

2. S. Paul likewise recommendeth to the Christians earnestly the vse of fasting, with sũdry other good workes, which if they were not in our power to do, & meritorious, in vayne would the Apostle recommend them, in vayne would we performe them: (h) *In al things we exhibit and shew our selues as the Ministers of God, in much patience, in afflictions, in necessities, in distresses, in strypes, in prisons, in tumults, in labour, by watching, by fasting, by chastity, by knowledge. &c.* Which place the Ministers haue corrupted three seuerall wayes.

(h) 2. *Cor.* 6. *v.* 4.

3. M. Iohn Knox an Apostata Fryar or Monke, yea one of the most seditious Ministers which Scotland hath affoarded, in a little Treatise of his concerning publicke

fasting

fasting, as he sheweth intollerable ignorance and horrible lyes, so he taketh vpon him to institute & ordayne publick fastes: (i) *The power,* (sayth he) *that we haue to proclayme this fasting is not of man, but of God &c.* Truely it Knox take vpon him such vsurped power without any warrant of the Bible, which in no place makes mentiõ of any power particularly giuen to him, much more such power should be granted to the Church of God, the holy spouse of Chryst, the authority wherof must needs be infallible. Where I would haue the good Reader to consider, that the Church of God, in this our purpose may be considered two wayes. First, as it is a company of men contayning in it many learned and vertuous men, not considering in it any speciall assistance of Gods spirit, and so doubtles the authority it hath is not infallible, but only is a probable motiue to make a wyse man giue human credit to that which it holdeth. Secondly, it may be considered as it is a company of men assisted infallibly by Gods spirit, sent and appoynted by God, hauing commission to teach others, who are warranted and commanded to heare it, and threatned, if they heare it not to be worthy of eternall damnation: (k) *Who refuseth to heare the Church, let him be to thee, as a Heathen and Publicane.* This second way then, I consider the Church, when I say the authority therof is infallible in instituting any publick fast or such thing. But of this infallibility of the Church I will speake more at length in some other place: This only I say for the present, that all the Ministers togeather shall not be able to improue by the expresse word of their owne corrupted Bible Lent-fasting, nor yet shall they be able to proue their Pharisaicall forme of fasting, in eating of flesh vpon fasting-dayes, in taking two meales those dayes, and such other, by any expresse word of the Bible. As for their consequences drawen out of the Bible, I make no accompt of them, because such consequences of the Ministers are nothing els, but Superstitions and Pharisaicall inuentions, old Heresies condemned in those whome they themselues do acccompt to be Heretiks, and ministeriall traditions preached to the ignorant

(i) *In the order and doctrine of the generall Fast appointed by the generall assembly of the Church of Scotlãd, holden at Edẽburgh the 25. of December 1565.*

(k) Matt. 18. v. 17.

rant sort with a faire shew of words. But let the wyse Reader, who hath care to saue his soule, remarke diligently what the holy Fathers of this age speake of Lent-fasting.

The first Section.

The Testimonies of the holy Fathers of this first Age, concerning the fasting of Lent &c.

S. CLEMENT in his Apostolicall Canons witnesseth, that he who did not kept Lent-fasting, and who did not fast wensday and fryday, should be deposed frō his office, vnles bodily sicknes excused him: (a) *Si quis Episcopus, aut Presbyter, aut Diaconus, aut Hypodiaconus, aut Lector, aut Cantor sanctam Quadragesimam non ieiunat, aut quartam feriam, aut sextam, deponatur, nisi imbecillitas corporis obstet; sin verò laicus sit, excommunicetur*. And agayne, he sheweth, *That Christmas-day was kept in this Age, lykewise Vp-holy day, and the fasting in lent:* (b) *Dies festos agitate fratres, ac primùm quidem diem Natalis, qui vigesimo quinto die mensis noni celebretur: post hunc dies Epiphaniæ in maximo honore sit, in quo Dominus Diuinitatem suam nobis patefecit, is vero dies sit sexto mensis decimi; post quos dies seruandum vobis est ieiunium Quadragesimæ, quod vitæ Christi & legis latæ recordationem continet*. Yea Chemnitius a famous Protestant confesseth playnly that the holy Fathers S. Ambrosius, Maximus, (c) Theophilus, Hieronymus, and others do affirme, the fast of Lent to be an *Apostolicall tradition*. And other Protestants do acknowledge, how that in the primitiue Church Aerius a famous Heretike (for denying the Diuinity of Christ) was specially condemned for denying of Lent-fasting, and of other fasting-dayes; for the which Heresy and others, likewise (d) S. Augustine and (e) S. Epiphanius condemne Aerius as an Heretike. Moreouer as touching the fashion and maner of fasting, the same S. Clement witnesseth the custome to haue bene in his tyme: (f) *To absteyne from flesh on fasting dayes*; affirming further, *the example of S. Peter in that forme of fasting*. (g) Eusebius a famous and ancient history-wryter, witnesseth the same

(a) *Canon. 60. iuxta distinctionem Turriani. extant Tom. 1. Concil.* τὴν ἁγίαν τεσσαρακοστὴν τοῦ πάσχα, ἢ τετράδα ἢ παρασκευὴν μὴ νηστεύσει.
(b) *Lib. 4. Const. c. 12. latinæ editionis, Græc. c. 13.*
(c) *Exam. Concil. Trident. part. 2.*
(d) *S Aug. hæres. 53.*
(e) *Epiph. hæres. 75.*
(f) *Lib. 5. Const. Apost. c. 19. 2. recog. l. 7.*
(g) *Euseb. l. 2. hist. c. 16.*

ſame faſhion to haue bene kept amongſt the Chriſtians from the beginning. Wherby our Proteſtants are conuicted of nouelty in vſing fleſh vpon faſting dayes.

2. S. Auguſtine affirmeth, that in his tyme, he who did faſt vpon the Sonday offended God, faſting againſt the cuſtome of the holy Church: (h) *Quis non Deum offendet, ſi velit cum ſcandalo totius, quæ vbiq; dilatata eſt, Eccleſia, die Dominico ieiunare?* Tertullian: (i) *To faſt on Sonday we eſteeme a ſinne.* And playnly the Councel of Carthage holden in S. Auguſtines tyme, auoweth thoſe not to be Catholiks, who do faſt vpon Sonday, and conſequently condemneth all the Puritans as Heretiks for faſting on the Sonday: (k) *Qui dominico die ſtudioſe ieiunat, non credatur Catholicus.* And (l) S. Epiphanius auoweth, that the *Aerians* were condemned as Heretikes for faſting on the Sonday, and banketting on the fryday & ſaturday, which was alſo the cuſtome of the Manichees, as witneſſeth S. Auguſtine in the foreſaid place. Do not the Proteſtants the ſame now adayes?

3. S. Ignatius: (m) *Diſdayne not the faſt of Lent, for it contayneth the imitation of our Sauiour Ieſus Chriſt. Quadrageſimā ne ſpernatis, imitationem enim continet conuerſationis Domini.* And agayne: *Ne negligatis ieiunare quarta feria & ſexta, ciborum reliquias pauperibus elargientes.* The which holy cuſtome of faſting on fryday was exactly kept in Scotland from our firſt conuerſion, that is, to the yeare of Chriſt 1560. Which cuſtome alſo S. Aidanus a holy Biſhop of Scotland, and Apoſtle of Northumberland brought firſt into England, as witneſſeth (n) Beda. The faſting or abſtinence from fleſh on Wedneſday is yet kept exactly by innumerable Catholiks euery where.

4. The ſame holy Father in the foreſaid epiſtle condemneth of ſinne thoſe, who do faſt on the Sonday: the which to be S. Ignatius true and ſincere Epiſtle ſundry famous Proteſtants do witnes, as (o) *Whitgift*, (p) *Cartwright*, and M. (q) *Hooker*. As for other faſting dayes called *quatuor tempora*, or Ember dayes & vigils, ſundry (r) holy Fathers make mention of them, as being in vſe in the primitiue Church: It being the cuſtome of the ſame holy Church to

(h) *Epiſt. 85. ad Caſulanum.*
(i) *Tertul. de corona militis. c. 3.*
(k) *Concil. 4. Carth. Can. 64.*
(l) *Epiph. hæreſ. 75.*
(m) *Epiſt. ad Philipp. prope finē.*
(n) *Beda l. 3. hiſt. Anglic. c. 5.*
(o) *VVhitgift in his defence p. 102.*
(p) *Alledged ibidē.*
(q) *In his Eccleſiaſt. polic. l. 5. ſect. 72.*
(r) *Leo Magnus ſerm. 2. de ieiun. Pentec. & ſer. 8. de ieiun. ſeptimi menſis. Theophil. in Epiſt. 1. Paſchal.*

absteyne from flesh on these fasting dayes. The which doctrine I conclude with that famous saying of S Augustine, speaking of vnwritten traditions, and in particular of not rebaptizing Heretiks: (f) *The Apostles writings commanded nothing hereof, but that custome which was opposed herein agaynst Cyprian, is to be belieued to proceed from their tradition, as many things be, which the whole Church holdeth, & are therfore wel belieued to be commanded of the Apostles, although they be not writtē.*

(f) *Aug. de Baptis. cōtra Don. l. 5. c. 23. & Epist. 118. ad Ianuar.*

Could S. Augustine speake more playnly in defence of Apostolicall *traditions*, wherof this of fasting is one? yea the chief poynts of the Ministers owne religion is nothing els but manifest traditions, or rather new inuentions of the Ministers, without any warrant of the expresse word of God: as, that fasting should be kept on sūday. 2. kneeling at the communion. 3. the festiuall day of Christmasse and others which they now keep. 4. That there is only two Sacraments. 5. That the Scots Bible is the word of God. 6. Man is only iustified by faith. 7. Ministers may excommunicate. 8. Ministers should haue wyues, and such. Wherof there is no mentiō in the expresse word of the Bible.

That the Ministers haue corrupted the Bible in sundry places which auow Apostolicall Traditions, wherof Fasting is one.

The second Section.

THOVGH the fasting of Lent be not in expresse words in the Bible, as the denyall therof also is not in expresse words: yet it is easie to deduce the same out of the Bible, as before is mentioned: for the which cause it hath bene euer accompted as one of the holy, ancient, and Apostolicall traditions, which are very odious to the Ministers who will no wayes receaue vnwritten traditions, though their religion be no other thing, but a rapsodie of Ministeriall traditions.

2. Remarke Catholike reader, that *Tradition* is no other thing, but a doctrine taught verbally, or by word, and communicated from one to another: for the which

cause

cause the Scripture in seuerall places commandeth vs to follow the holy and Apostolicall traditions of our forfathers. Now the word *Tradition* in the new Testamēt is takē two seuerall wayes: first in a bad sense and meaning. 2. in a good sense and meaning, as when we are commanded to follow traditions. When the word *Tradition* is taken in an euill sense, then the Ministers translate alwayes *Tradition*, to make all Traditions indifferently odious to the ignorant people: as, (a) *Why do yee also transgresse the commandement of God by your tradition?* And agayne: (b) *Thus haue yee made the commandement of God of no authority by your traditiō.* Where our Sauiour condēneth traditiōs which are against the expresse word of God. Here then the Ministers do translate *Traditiō*. But now on the other side whē we are cōmāded to follow & belieue vnwritten traditiōs, thē they turne not the word *tradition*, but rather *ordinances*, preachings, instructions, institutions, to the end the ignorant people should not find the word *tradition* taken in a good sense in the Bible. As, (c) *Therfore brethren stand fast and keep the* * *traditions which ye haue bene taught, eyther by word or by our epistle.* And agayne: (d) *We command you brethren, in the name of our Lord Iesus Chryst, that ye withdraw your selfe from euery brother that walketh inordinatly, and not after the Tradition which he receaued of vs.* And agayne: (e) *Now brethren I command you, that you remember all my things, and keep the traditions as I delyuered them to you.* Heer then the Ministers do neuer translate the word *tradition*, but craftily and deceitfully the word *ordinances*, and *instructions*, or any word els rather then *tradition*, to the end they may make the reader to beleeue that we should not follow traditions. Who would thinke the malice and partiality of the Ministry against traditions, against the word of God, against the Bible to be so great, as to conceale impiously the word tradition, when it is taken in a good sense, and to translate it in other places when it is taken in an euill sense, the Greeke word being one in all those places? Can there be a more impious forme of proceeding? They brag, boast, & preach to the ignorant people and Nobility, that they wil follow nothing but the greeke text, that they will

(a) Matth. 15. v. 3.
(b) Matth. 15. v. 6.
(c) 2. Thess. 2. v. 15.
* κρατεῖτε τὰς παραδόσεις, that is saith Beza on this place, keep diligently, as it is in the Syriak Vecham-senu.
(d) 2. Thessal. 3. v. 6.
(e) 1. Cor. 11. v. 2.
καθὼς παρέδωκα τὰς παραδόσεις κατέχετε.

will translate faithfully the Greeke and Hebrew text: yet in effect they abandon both the one and the other when it pleaseth them. Besides this impious forme of prooceeding in not translating faithfully the Greeke text; in other places, they haue craftely put in their Bibles the word *tradition* when it is not in the Greeke or Syriake, yea in no copy at all of the Greeke and originall text, as: (f) *Why, as though yee liued in the world,* (*) *are ye burthened with traditions?*

(f) *Coloss.* 2. v. 20. * καὶ δογματίζεσθε.

Where they haue put in the word *burthened* & the word *traditions*, which are no wayes in the Greeke nor in the Latin, where it is, *decernitis*. Tell vs playnly: Yee protest to haue skill in the Greeke toung and to translate according to the Greeke text, tell vs then whether this Greeke word, δογμα do signify tradition, and δογματιζεσθαι to be burthened with traditions? Name vs any holy Father, ancient wryter, kingdome or nation who euer before the coming of Caluin so impiously did corrupt the Bible, and translate that place as you do? Iustify your translation if you can, eyther out of Fathers or Lexicons, and be ashamed of your ignorance and malice. Because ye put the word *tradition* where it is not in the Greeke, and would not put it in those places before cited where ye know that it is most euidently in the Greeke. Know ye not that the instructions of Plato, or Aristotle cannot be called Traditions, because Traditions do signify and contayne some antiquity and succession of tyme, some vnwritten doctrine proceeding from one to another? Likewyse are ye not ashamed to translate in S. Peters Epistle, thus: (g) *Knowing that yee were not redeemed with corruptible things, as siluer and gold, from your vayne conuersation, receaued by the traditions of the Fathers?* Yee know that it is not so in the Greeke, but rather thus: *From your vayne conuersation delyuered by the Fathers.* Neuer a word of *tradition.*

(g) 1. *Pet.* 1 v. 18. ἐκ τῆς ματαίας ὑμῶν ἀναστροφῆς πατροπαραδότου.

Can there be any saluation for you, or for those that do follow you, who so impiously do corrupt the Bible? feare yee not that horrible sentence pronounced against you, and against those who allowe, reade, and accompt of your corrupted Bible? (h) *If any man shall adde vnto these things, God shall adde vnto him the plagues that are written in this booke.*

(h) *Reuel.* 22. v. 18
(i) *Prou.* 30 v. 6.
(k) *Deut.* 12. v. 32.

booke. And againe, ([i]) *Put nothing to his words, least he reproue thee, and thou be found a lyar,* And againe: ([k]) *Thou shall put nothing thereto, nor take ought therefrom.* In other places translating the same Greeke word, yee make no mention of Traditions, as in S. Luke 1. Chap. Vers. 2. and els where.

3. If any Minister reply, that our vulgar Latin translation hath here the word *Tradition*, what is that to the purpose? for you professe and protest to translate faithfully the Greeke, and not our vulgar Latin Edition, so great is your partiality and inconstancy to follow the old Latin translation though it differ from the Greeke; and an other tyme you will not follow it though it be all one with the Greeke, as in sundry places before alledged. But all this yee do without shame or conscience, only to frame your translations to your Errours and Heresies, deceauing therby those who are ignorant of the Greeke and Hebrew languages, casting them, in following your translations, into the pit of eternall damnation. Yee protest to them to follow the Greeke and Hebrew; is it the Greeke text that induceth you to translate blasphemously *ordinances* for *traditions*, *traditions* for *decrees*, *Ordinances* for *Iustifications*, *Elder* for *Preist*, *Graue* for *Hell*, *Image* for *Idol*? which abhominable forme of proceeding, proueth you to be manifest heretiks, and sworne enemyes to the true word of God and Scripture.

The

The 19. 20. & 21. Article.

1. *That the custome of the Catholike Church in this first age was, that Church-men and Religgious men should not be marryed.*
2. *But rather lead a single and chast life.*
3. *And that the vowing of chastity, pouerty, and obedience was lawfull, and in vse.*

CHAP. X.

AFTER the treatise of Lent-fasting followeth accordingly to speake a little of single life and vowing of chastity, specially by Church men, which the Protestants do abhorre greately, inuiting the politike Magistrate (a) *To roote out al doctrines of Diuels, vowes of single life &c.* Which abhominable doctrine they learned of Caluin their prime Minister, and of Luther, who as a filthy Epicurean sayth: (b) *As it is not in my power that I be not a man, so it is not in my power to be without a woman.* Vt non est in meis viribus situm, vt vir non sim, tam non est etiam mei iuris, vt absq; muliere sim. And agayne: *Verbum enim hoc quod deus ait, crescite & multiplicamini, non est præceptum, sed plus quàm præceptum; Diuinum puto opus, tam necessarium, quàm vt masculus sim, magisq; necessarium quàm edere, bibere, purgare, mucum emungere, somno & excubijs intentum esse.* Could Epicurus himselfe, or any Turke speake more profanely then this Apostle of the Protestāts, whose common prouerbe was, (c) If the wife will not, let the maide come, *si non vult vxor, veniat ancilla.* The same sayth Caluin in sundry places of his Institutions, contradicting himselfe in his booke of Harmony, where he sayth directly the contrary: (d) *Præclarum donum est virginitas, fateor.* And agayne:

(a) *In the Confession of Fayth of the Protestants of Scotland set out with the Psalme-Book.*

(b) *Luth. Serm. de Matrim. tom. 5. Operum Luther.*

(c) *Luth loco citato.*

(d) *Calu. 1 Cor. c. 7.*

againe: (e) *Summa totius disputationis huc redit, meliorem esse cælibatum coniugio, quia in illo maior sit libertas, vt expeditiùs seruiant homines Deo.* Where he sayth also that ancient holy Fathers made great accompt of single life. But let vs leaue these Epicureans, and come to the point of the matter.

2. The Catholike Church teacheth that neyther in the old or new Law, any man was, or is bound to vow eyther chastity, pouerty, or such: but that it is, and euer was a Counsell & not a Commandement: yet a thing of great deuotion and perfection in the old & new Law, intrinsecally belonging & furthering to the true worship of God: which I proue. In a vow there be two things to be cōsidered: the one is, the good which is vowed, called the materiall part, for example, fasting, praying; the other, the promise it selfe made to God, which is the formall part: the material parts do belōg vnto their seuerall vertues, but the promise and fulfilling of the vow is a substantiall part of the worship of God: the reason is, because by promising and vowing any good thing to God, we acknowledge and professe therby that God is the soueraigne goodnes it selfe, supreme verity and worthy of al sort of holy seruice: in performing also that which we haue vowed, we testify that God is full of Maiesty, Reuerend, and Dreadfull; and consequently, that all promises and vowes made to God righteously are to be accomplished diligently, & without delay, because by those vowes we honour and worship him. By the contrary, they much dishonour God, who breake with him and keep not their vowes. If then all other vertuous seruice done to the glory of God be parts of his true worship, much more vowes are to be thought parts of the true worship of God: wherof it followes necessarily that at all tymes vowes were, and may be vsed; and that they were in practise before the Law of Moyses, it is euident by that vow which Iacob made of setting vp a stone, and of paying the tenthes of all his goods: (f) *Then Iacob vowed a vow, saying, if God will be with me and will keep me in this* (f) Genes. *iourney which I go &c.* Which vow of Iacob was well taken 28. v. 20. by God, was of an indifferent matter, and done freely by

P Iacob

Iacob without any compulsion or Commandement. I aske of the Ministry any expresse text of the Bible, which maketh as playnly against vowing, as this maketh for vowing: which the Ministers shall neuer be able to do. And agayne: (g) *I am the God of Bethell, where thou anoyntedst the pillar, where thou vowedst a vow vnto me*. Where God maketh great accompt of Iacobs vow. Likewise the Prophet Dauid doth inuite vs to vow, & keep our vowes: (h) *Vow and performe vnto the Lord your God all yee that be round about him*. Yea the Prophet Isay foretelleth, that the Christians shall vow vnto God, and therby worship God, ioyning vowes with sacrifice and oblation, which are a speciall part of the worship of God: (i) *And the Lord shallbe knowen of the Egyptians, and the Egyptians shall know the Lord in that day, and do a sacrifice and oblation, and shall vow vowes vnto the Lord, and performe them.* See the Prophets (k) Ionas, (l) Baruch, and (m) Ieremias, who playnly do make mention of vowing and performing therof. Aske of the Ministry as playne words out of the Bible which make against vowes, which discommende and condemne vowes, as they themselues do by word and writ, by life and behauiour.

(g) *Genes.* 31. v. 13.
(h) *Psalm.* 76. v. 21.
(i) *Isay* 19. v. 21.
(k) *Ionas.* 1. v. 16.
(l) *Baruch.* 6. v. 34.
(m) *Ierem.* 44. v. 25.

3. As for the new Teshament and Law of Grace, did not S. Paul make a Vow, worshipping therby God, and that in a very indifferent mater? (n) *After that he had shorne his head in Cenchra, for he had a vow*. Here we haue expresse words out of the Bible for vowing; let the Ministers, if they can, giue me as expresse words against vowing, since they teach that nothing should be belieued but the expresse word of the Bible. (o) *Nihil credendum nisi quod expresso Dei verbo continetur*, sayth Danæus a prime Minister. And Beza: (p) *Nihil aliud quàm purum Verbum scriptum credendum*. The Ministers not being able conforme to their Oath and promise, to giue vs the expresse word of the Bible, do thinke it sufficient to pay vs with their sophisticall consequences, wherunto euery one of vs Catholiks may reply iustly with S. Augustine: (q) *Credo illa quæ in Scripturis sactis leguntur, non credo ea quæ ab hæreticis vanis dicuntur. I beleue that which is read and conteyned in the holy Scripture, I belieue not that which*

(n) *Actes* 18. v. 18.
(o) *Contr.* 3. p. 144.
(p) *Beza contra Heshus.* p. 275.
(q) *Lib. de peccat. Merit.* c. 20.

which by vayne heretiks is affirmed. In the meane tyme let vs follow and preferre the consequences, & faith of the holy, learned, and ancient Fathers of this age.

The Testimonyes of the holy Fathers of this first Age, concerning Chastity, and single life of Religious Men, and Priests.

The first Section.

S. DENIS Areopagita in his Ecclesiasticall Hierarchy, (a) prayseth greatly Religious and solitary life, wherin the vowes of Chastity, Pouerty, & Obedience, are conteyned: he teacheth likewise that the custome of his tyme was, that any man being desirous to leaue the world & become Religious, he was receaued solemnely by some Pastours of the Church, his habit was changed, and he was consecrated by certayne prayers & ceremonyes before the whole assembly, which custome is kept to this day. (a) *Cap. 6. per totum.*

2. S. Ignatius: (b) *Vxores maritis subditæ estote in timore Dei, Virgines Christo in puritate; non abhominantes nuptias, sed id quod præstantius est amplectentes; non in calumniam matrimony, sed in meditãdæ legis gratia.* And a little after, he reckoneth out sundry of the old and new Law, who kept perpetuall Virginity, as Melchisedec, Iosue, Elias, Elisæus, Ieremias, Iohn the Baptist, Iohn the Euãgelist, Timothy, Titus, Euodius, Clemens, with sundry others, as S. Paul, & Christ his disciples (except S. Peter) which is the reason wherfore Caluin himselfe auoweth, that euen from the Apostles the custome was amongst Religious men and Priests to make vowes of Chastity: (c) *Hoc, inquit, ab vltima memoria fuit conseruatum, vt se alligarent continentiæ voto, qui totos se Domino dicare vellent.* And Peter Martyr: (d) *Statim ab Apostolorum temporibus nimium tribui cœptum est cælibatui &c.* (b) *Epist. ad Philadelphenses.* (c) *Inst. l. 4. c. 13. Sect. 17.* (d) *De Cœlibatu & Votis p. 477.*

3. The same holy Father Ignatius witnesseth that many monasteries & colleges of virgins were erected in his tyme: (e) *Saluto Collegium Virginum, & cœtum viduarum.* And agayne he auoweth that Virgins, Widowes, and Preists, who had consecrated themselues by vowing chastity, should be honored: (e) *Ep. ad Philip. in fine.*

nored: (f) *Eas, quæ in Virginitate vitam agunt, honorate, veluti Christi Sacerdotes: Viduas, quæ in sanctimonia, velut altare Dei.* Wherwith agreeth that famous testimony of S. Augustine, who wryting against Manicheus, (who as an heretike, condemned vowes with our Protestants, and taught that there were two Gods, one good and another bad) affirmes that S. Paul did moue a Virgin, fit for mariage, to consecrat her selfe to God in keping her Virginity: (g) *Ipsi iam timeo Apostolo ne dæmoniorum doctrinam intulisse tunc Iconio videatur, cùm puellam oppignoratam iam thalamo, in amorem, sermone suo, perpetuæ virginitatis incendit.* Do not our Countrey-Ministers, with those impious Manichees, call *single lyfe, the doctrine of deuills?*

(f) *Epist. ad Tarsense. prope finē.*

(g) *Contra Faustum Manich. l. 30. c. 4.*

4. Finally S. Martiall witnesseth, (h) that he himselfe did perswade the holy Virgin Valeria to consecrate by a vow, her virginity to God. And (i) S. Matthew the Apostle induced S. Iphigenia to do the same. And (k) S. Paul induced S. Tecla a Gentlewoman well borne. And S. Clement a Romã Lady called Flauia Domitilla: (l) *Quæ* (sayth Beda) *à S. Clemente ob integritatis perseuerantiam fuit consecrata.* In lyke manner the holy virgin S. Pudentiana daughter to S. Pudens a Roman Senatour, and Claudia a Scotish Lady (of both whom S. (m) Paul makes mention) vowed their Virginity vnto God. And (n) S. Mansuetus Bishop of Toul in Lorrayne disciple to S. Peter, a Scottishman borne, perswaded likewise a Gentlewoman of good birth, to vow her Virginity to God.

(h) *Ep. ad Tholos. c. 8*

(i) *Baron. in Martyrol. 21. Septemb.*

(k) *Ambr. l. 2. de Virginib.*

(l) *Beda in Martyrol. 7. Maij.*

(m) *2. Tim. 4. v. 21. Vide Baron. ad 19. Maij.*

(n) *In eius vita in Breuiario Tullensi.*

That the Ministers haue corrupted the Bible in sundry places which proue the authority of Priestood, and of Preists, who alwayes led a single a life.

The second Section.

TO the end that the Gentle Reader may better vnderstand the policy and double dealing of the Ministers against the name of *Priests* (who alwayes led a single life as I shew before) it is to be remarked, that the word *Priest,*

in

in Greeke πρεσβύτερος, in latin *Presbyter*, or *Sacerdos*, signifieth a Church-man who hath receaued the holy Sacramēt of Orders, and consequently power by the imposition of hands, as witnesseth S. Paul saying: (a) *Dispyse not the grace that is in thee, which was giuen thee by Prophecy, with the laying on of the hands of the company of the Preists*. Where the Ministers blasphemously haue translated against all antiquity *Eldership*. Do the Elders of Edenburgh lay on their hands vpon the Ministers when they are chosen? If not, why then do they translate so ignorantly this place? Why haue the Ministers taken out the word (*) *Grace*, translating *gift*, but to signify that sanctifiing Grace is not giuen by the imposition of hands? Shall the Elders make Ministers and Bishops by the imposition of their hands? for certaynly Timothy was a Bishop. Is it not euidēt that the most famous and ancient Ecclesiastical wryters who alwayes haue byn, do take the word *Priesthood*, for the company of Church-men, and not of Laity? So holy Ignatius disciple to the Apostles: *what is* (sayth he) *Priestood, but the holy assembly of Bishops, Confessors &c*. And againe, he calleth it, (c) *The holy priesthood, because Priests are dedicated, by reason of their office, to the administration of the holy Sacraments, and to the preaching of the holy word of God*. The same witnesseth S. (d) Cyprian. S. Hierome calleth the *Priests*, the Senate of the holy Church: (e) *Ecclesia habet Senatum, cœtum Presbyterorum*. Yea that Puritan wryter and Apostata Henricus Stephanus is forced to auow the same, saying: (f) *Quo nomine* (to wit of Priesthood) *existimatur Apostolū significasse cœtum omnium illorum, qui in verbo laborabunt*; remarking lykewise, that when the word Priesthood is found alone, it signifieth the society of Priests, or the power giuen to them.

(a) 1. *Tim*. 4. v. 14.

* *Per gratiam*.

(b) *Ep. ad Trallian*. τί δέ εστι πρεσβυτέριον, ἀλλὰ τὸ σύστημα ἱερὸν συμβουλοι καὶ συνεδρευταὶ τοῦ ἐπισκόπου;

(c) *Ep. ad Antioch*.

(d) *Cypr. l.* 3. *Ep*. 11.

(e) *Ep. ad Rusticum*. *Vide August. de ciuit. Dei l.* 10. c. 10.

(f) *In thesauro linguæ Græcæ*. πρεσβυτέριον.

2. Now the Ministers to take away the holy Sacrifice of the Masse which is alwayes offered by Priests, to take away Altars wheron the holy Masse is said (for those three things, Priest, Sacrifice and Altar, are alwayes conioyned one with another) they haue taken out of the Bible in sundry places the word *Preist* and *Priesthood*, & specially where the word *Priest* is taken in a good sense. As for example,

when there fell out a question in Religion concerning
Circumcision, Paul & Barnabas were sent to the Apostles
(g) *Acts.* and Priests for the resolution therof: (g) *They ordayned that*
15. *v.* 2. *Paul and Barnabas, and certayne other of them should go vp to Ieru-*
* πρεσβυ- *salem, vnto the Apostles, and* (*) *Priests about thu question*. Where
τέρους. the Ministers impiously haue taken away the word *Priests,*
(h) *Acts.* and translated *Elders*. And againe, the very power giuen
14. *v.* 22. to Priests, is signified by the holy Sacrament of Order: (h)
* τοὺς πρεσ- *And when they had ordayned them* (*) *Priests in euery Church, and*
βυτέρους. *prayed and fasted, they commended them vnto our Lord, in whom they*
belieued. Where the Ministers haue committed two euident
Blasphemyes. 1. They haue ioyned to the text, *By election*,
which is not in the Greeke nor Syriake, to signify that the
Priests and Ministers should be chosen by the Laity. 2.
They haue put *Elders*, for *Priests*, to keep the people from
all holy and reuerend cogitations of *Priests:* yet the Ministers shall neuer be able to name me any holy wryter or
nation who turned the word *Elder*, for *Priest*, before Caluin their Prime Sicophant, who was the first Author of
this blasphemous translation. Besides these places, the Ministers haue corrupted sundry other parts where the word
(i) 1. *Tim.* *Priest*, is taken in a good sense, as: (i) *The Priests that rule wel*
5. *v.* 17. *are worthy of double honour, specially they that labour in the word*
and doctrine. Which saying can no wayes be applyed to the
ignorant Elders of Scotland and England who are not ac-
(k) 1. *Tim.* customed to preach. And againe: (k) *Against a Priest receaue*
5. *v.* 19. *no accusation, but vnder two or three witnesses*. And againe: (l)
(l) *Iames* 5. *Is any sick amongst you? let him call for the Priests of the Church, &*
v. 14. *let them pray aboue* (*) *him, and annoynt him with oyle in the name*
* ἐπ' αὐτόν. *of our Lord, and the prayer of faith shall saue the sicke, and our Lord*
(m) *Lib.* 3. *shall rayse him vp: and if he haue committed sinne, it shalbe forgi-*
de Sacerd. *uen him*. Out of which place (m) S. Chrysostome proueth
περὶ ἱερω- the high dignity of Priests in forgiuing sinnes. Do the El-
σύνης. ders of Scotland annoynt the sick? do they giue remission
of sinnes to the sick? do they pray aboue them? Since the
Elders do not these offices, why do they heere vse the
word Elders? Since the Ministers do not practise this poynt
of the Apostles Religion, nor yet belieue the same, how

can

can they with reason say that their Religion is the Religiō of the Apostles ?

3. Now when the word, *Priest*, is taken in a bad sense or meaning, the Ministers translate playnly the word *Priest*, to make it odious to the people, as (n) *And as they spake vnto the people, the Priests, and the captayne of the temple, & the Saduces came vpon them*, and in sundry other places which I do omit, to be short. As for the dignity of Priests and the fashiō kept in ordeyning *Priests*, let the Councell of Carthage (where S. Augustine was present the yeare of God 436.) speake: (o) *A priest when he taketh his Orders, the Bishop blessing him and holding his hand vpon his head, let the Priests also that are present hold their hands by the Bishops hand, & vpon his head.* Which imposition of hands & consequently perpetuall succession of our Bishops and Priests to these our dayes, amongst vs Catholiks, is an euident token that our Catholike Church is the only true Church, according to that worthy saying of S. Augustine: (p) *Tenet me in Ecclesia ab ipsa sede Petri Apostoli, cui pascendas oues suas Dominus commendauit, vsq; ad præsentem Episcopum, successio sacerdotum &c.*

(n) *Acts.* 4. v. 1. οἱ ἱερεῖς.

(o) *Concil. Carthag. Can.* 3.

(p) *Lib. cont. Ep. fund. c.* 4.

4. Besides these corruptions the Ministers haue vsed the like in the word *Kircke*, or *Church*: for the which they haue placed the word *Cōgregatiō*, in the Bibles printed in the yeare 1562. the reason wherof was this. When first that abhominable heresy of Caluin entred in Scotland openly, which was the yeare of Christ 1559. the first day of May, some of the Nobility of Scotland (being peruerted in England) ioyned themselues together, and made open rebellion against the Queene, and resolued to cast down the Churches, ouerthrow the Abbyes, yea & change the Politicall state of the kingdome, vnder pretext of Religion, induced to the same by King Henry the eight, and the English nation. And to the end that the people might take better their doings, they called themselues, *The Lords of the Congregation*, who were the Lord of Glencarne, the Lord Ruthen, Lindesay, Boyde, and some others, whose posterity for the greatest part is already sufficiently punished by God; as for the rest, *respice finem*. Now to the end

that

that the simple people might thinke that the Lords of the Congregation were sent from God, to bring in a new Religion, and change the old of their For-fathers, they made a new Bible to be printed at London (the yeare 1562.) wherin you should neuer haue found, yea not once, the word *Church*, but insteed therof the word *Congregation*, & consequently that of S. Matthew they turned thus: (q) *And vpon this rock will I build my Congregation*. And againe: (r) *If he refuse to heare the Congregation also, let him be vnto thee as a heathen man and a publican*. And agayne: (s) *The congregation of the liuing God is the pillar and ground of truth*. Which impious dealing they vsed, to the end that the people might thinke that the Lords of the *Congregation* were sent from God, since they found thẽ so often named in the Bible. But after they had gotten the vpperhand in Scotland and changed all, then they commanded another Bible to be printed, which euer had the word Church, and not the word *Congregation*. By reason of this impious forme of proceeding, are not the posterity of those Lords vtterly wracked? Is not the hand of God vpon them? are they not remoued from the ancicient lands & possessions of their For-fathers, because they were the first Authors and inbringers of this new deformed Gospell? Let any man consider wysely and he shall easely remarke most ancient and famous houses of noble Lords, Barons, & sundry others in the Prouinces of Fife, Augus, Louthiã, Mernes, Sterling, & euery where almost, wholly changed, ouerthrowen, and no mention thereof, and that by a iust iudgement of God, who hath promised to punish the sinnes of the Fathers, who do bring in a new Religion, to the third and fourth generation.

(q) *Matt.* 16. v. 18.
(r) *Matth.* 18. v. 17.
(s) 1. *Tim.* 3. v. 15.

The

The 22. Article.

That S. Peter his Primacy in the Catholike Church was acknowledged in this first Age vniuersally.

CHAP XI.

SVNDRY Wryters assigne three seuerall maners to gouerne a Common Wealth or Kingdome; wherin if the meaner sort beare sway and command, it is called Democracy: if few of the Nobility command, Aristocracy: if one, Monarchy. The first sort of gouernement is subiect to sundry broyles, by reason of the inconstant multitude: The second is commonly diuyded with dyuers factions of the ambitions Nobility: The third as it is lesse subiect to diuision, so is it most conuenient and fit to guide and keep the subiects in peace and vnity. This is the most diuine and noble forme of gouernement, when one man hath the supreme power in administration, which is easy to be remarked in supernaturall and naturall things: as in the Mistery of the Blessed Trinity, there is the Father, from whome the Sonne, and the holy Ghost proceed, being euery way equall, in proprietyes distinct, in persons three, yet oueruling as one God. In the heauens there is one, by the which the inferiours are moued, called *primum mobile*. One Sũne frõ whom the light of the Moone and Planets is borrowed. Likewyse in man, the little world, there is one heart, from which the vitall spirits; one braine, from which the sinewes; one liuer, from which the veynes haue their head and origine. In euery element ther is one predominant quality. Amongst birds the Eagle, amongst beasts the Lyon, amongst the fishes the Whale do dominier and command. Yea (a) *The very Bees haue their guide* (a) *Cypr. de Idolorum vanitate.*

and captaine whom they follow.

2. Shall not then the Church of Christ militant vpon earth, the holy Citty, kingdome, sheepfold, and the house of God haue one visible pastour, one maister and superiour? whom the Scripture auoweth playnly to be S. Peter and his successours, as our Sauiour witnesseth speaking to S. Peter: (b) *And I say vnto thee, that thou art Peter, and vpon this rocke will I build my Church, and the gates of hell shall not ouercome it: and I will giue vnto thee, the keyes of the kingdome of heauen, and whatsoeuer thou shall bind vpon earth, shall be bound in heauen: and whatsoeuer thou shalt loose on earth, shalbe loosed in heauen.* By the which words our Sauiour promiseth to giue vnto S. Peter supremacy or supereminent dignity aboue the rest of the Apostles, in calling him *a Rock.* (c) *S. Peter is called a rock* (sayth S. Ambrose) *because he, as a rock, or an immoueable stone vpholdeth the full weight and fabrike of the Christian worke.* Because S. Peter is (d) the great foundation, or most solide stone vpon which Christ builded his Church. Which primacy of S. Peter S. Augustine deduceth out of the foresaid words, saying: (e) *Only Peter amongst the Apostles deserued to hear, Thou art Peter, and vpon this rock will I build my Church; worthy truely to be a stone for the foundation of the people, which were to be builded in the house of God, to be a pillar for their stay, a key to open to them the gates of the kingdome of heauen.* Not that S. Augustine thinketh Peter to be the chief and principall foũdatiõ who is Christ: but rather an inferiour, secõdary, or subordinat foũdation: as wysely sayth S. Basill: (f) *God imparteth his dignities, not depryuing himselfe of them, but inioying he bestoweth them. He is the light, and yet he sayth, you are the light of the world. He is a priest, and he anoynteth priests: He is the lambe, and he sayth, behold I send you lyke lambes amõg the midst of wolfes: He is a rock, and he maketh a rock; yea though Peter be a rock, yet he is not a rock as Christ is, for Christ is the true rock imoueable of himselfe, Peter imoueable by Christ the rock.* Which is conforme to that which the Catholiks daily do affirme, saying: That *S. Peter is the head of the Church, but subordinate to Christ Iesus, the chief and independant head.*

(b) *Matth. 16. v. 18.*

(c) *Amb. serm. 7.*

(d) *Orig. Hom. 5. in Exod.*

(e) *Con. 2. in Psal. 30. & in Psal. 69.*

(f) *In Concion. de Poenitent.*

3. Secondly, our Sauiour sayth vnto S. Peter: *To thee I will*

I will giue the keyes of the kingdome of heauen: by which words he giueth to Peter and his successours power to make Lawes, summon, and confirme Councels, appoynt or displace Offices, consecrate or degrade Bishops: in a word, all power & authority which is requisite for the good gouernement and instruction of the Church. Euen as when the keyes of a citty or town are giuē to the King, the whole power & authority of that town is put in the kings hands; and wheras there be two sorts of keyes in the Church of God, *the key of knowledge*, to teach and instruct, called, *Clauis scientiæ*, of which S. Luke speaketh: (g) *yee haue taken away the key of knowledge*. And the key of authority and iurisdictiō to gouerne and rule, wherof S. Iohn: (h) *I haue the keyes of hell and of death*. Againe: (i) *And the key of the house of Dauid will I lay vpon his shoulder*: both those keyes were here giuen to Peter. By the one, he and his successours obteyned infallible assistance and power of God to decyde maters of faith: by the other the scepter of Ecclesiastical gouernement in the mysticall body of Christ.

(g) *Luc.* 11. v. 52.
(h) *Reuel.* 1. v. 18.
(i) *Isa.* 22. v. 22.

4. Thirdly, our Sauiour sayth to Peter: *whatsoeuer thou shalt bind vpon earth &c.* That is, whatsoeuer punishmēt thou shall giue, eyther of excommunication, suspension or such other spirituall censure (for Christ speaketh without restriction) the same shalbe ratified by God himselfe: and whatsoeuer of those thou shall loose, the same shalbe loosed in heauen aboue; wherby power is giuen to S. Peter to loose and bind, to be the foundation of the Church of God, and that by expresse words of the Bible. Let the Ministers if they can giue as playne words against S. Peters supremacy, which they shall neuer be able to do.

5. The Ministers will say, that all the Apostles are called Rockes, & foundatiō of the Church: I answer, they were so in effect, to the end they should plant the faith in euery part of the world: they had all most ample and vniuersall iurisdiction and power ouer others. But S. Peter had ouer them also: they had all the keyes, but with dependance of S. Peter: they were all foundations, but Peter the first after Christ, wherby Peter excelled the rest of

 the

the Apostles in preheminency of power, in preheminency of faith, and of dignity. For the which cause whatsoeuer priuiledge is attributed by the holy Scripture to all the Apostles togeather, the same is imparted agayne to S. Peter alone, in a more peculiar and speciall maner. For as to the Apostles al power was granted to forgiue sinnes: (k) *Whose sinnes yee forgiue, they are forgiuen them: and whose yee retayne, they are retayned;* the same power is giuen to Peter alone, in a more ample forme: (l) *Whatsoeuer thou shalt bind vpon earth, shalbe bound in the Heauens, &c.* For all the Apostles Christ prayed, that they might be constant in faith: (m) *Not for the world do I pray, but for them whom thou hast giuen me.* And the same for Peter alone: (n) *I haue prayed for thee, that thy faith fayle not.* To all the Apostles our Sauiour said: (o) *When the spirit of truth cometh, he shall teach you all truth.* To Peter alone: (p) *Confirme and strengthen thy brethren.* To all the Apostles: (q) *Yee are built vpon the foundation of the Apostles and Prophets.* To Peter alone: (r) *Thou art Peter, & vpon this rock will I build my Church.* To all the Apostles Christ said: (s) *Go yee into all the world and preach the Ghospell to euery creature.* To Peter alone: (t) *feed my sheep.* But what sheep (sayth (u) S. Bernard) *The people of this or that City? Of this or that kingdome? My sheep;* (sayth he) *to whome is it not manifest he designed not some, but assigned all: nothing is excepted, where nothing is distinguished.*

6. The other Argument and Testimony wherby the Bible proueth Peters Supremacy aboue the rest of the Apostles is: (x) *Iesus said to Simon Peter: Simon the sonne of Iona, louest thou me more then these? He said vnto him. Yea Lord, thou knowest that I loue thee: he said vnto him: Feed my lambes.* And againe, *feed my sheep*, & the third tyme, *feed my sheep*. Where our Sauiour vsed the word *feed* three seueral tymes, to confirme more playnly the power which he gaue to Peter aboue the rest, and to put the matter out of doubt: vnderstanding by the word *sheep*, the Pastours and Rectours of the Church, and by the word *lambes*, those of the meaner sort, or the one and the other, as witnesseth Eusebeius: (a) *He committed*, sayth he, *to S. Peter his lambes, and then his sheep, because he made him not only a Pastour, but the Pastour of Pastors. Peter therfore*

(k) Ioa. 20. v. 23.
(l) Matth. 16. v. 19.
(m) Ioan. 17. v. 9.
(n) Luc. 22. v. 32.
(o) Ioan. 16.
(p) Luc. 22 v. 31.
(q) Ephes. 2. v. 20.
(r) Matt. 16 v. 19.
(s) Marc. 16 v. 15.
(t) Ioa. 21. v. 16.
(u) Lib. 2. de consid.
(x) Ioa. 21. v. 15.
(a) Euseb. Emissen. serm. in Natiu. S. Ioa. Euãg.

therfore feedeth the lambes, and also the sheep. He feedeth children and their mothers, he ruleth the people & their Prelats: he is therfore the pastour of all, because besides lambes & sheep, there is nothing in the Church. And what is, *feed my sheep and lambes*, but feed my Church? for all those that are in the Church of God are eyther lambes or sheep. 2. Our Sauiour promised before to build his Church vpon S. Peter, and consequently to giue him power therin: when was, I pray you, this promise performed by Christ, if not in these words, *feed my sheep*? Wherof it followeth necessarly, that S. Peter in vertue of these words receaued a particular power aboue the rest of the Apostles. 3. The Greeke words ποίμαινε τὰ πρόβατα, do put the matter out of doubt. For it is certayn that the word ποιμαίνειν, signifieth to gouerne, to rule as a superiour: (b) *And I will giue you Pastours according to my hart, which shall feed you with knowledge and vnderstanding.* Agayne: (c) *Thus sayth the Lord God of Israel vnto the Pastours that feed my people.* Agayne. (d) *I will feed my sheep and bring them to their rest, sayth the Lord.* Againe. (e) *Out of thee shall come the Gouernour that shall feed my people Israell.* Where alwayes the same Greeke word is which is here, signifiyng alwayes to gouerne, command, and rule. Out of which places, and sundry others I do inferre, that it is all one to haue said, *Peter* feed my *sheep*, my *lambes*, and to haue said, *Peter* gouerne, command, and rule all those that are in my Church, be they sheep or lambes, that is pastors or inferiors. Which meaning is playnly taught by the holy Fathers, who not only do acknowledge in Peter a primacy of grace or calling (as the Ministers, with their sophismes and distinctions, no wayes conteyned in the expresse word of God, which they sweare only to teach and belieue, do dreame and forge) but also a particular primacy of power and authority aboue all others sayth S. Hierome. (f) *Among the twelue one was chosen, that a chiefe or head being appoynted, occasion of dissention might be preuented.* So that Peters Bishoprike which is the sea of Rome is preferred to any other whatsoeuer, (g) *Who knoweth not Peters principality of Apostleship to be preferred before euery bishoprike? but although the grace or preheminence of chaires be different: yet*

(b) *Ierem.* 3 *v.* 15.
(c) *Ierem.* 23. *v.* 2.
(d) *Ezech.* 34. *v.* 15.
(e) *Matth.* 2. *v.* 6. ὅς τις ποιμανεῖ τὸν λαόν.
(f) *Lib.* 1 *in Iouin.*
(g) *Cyprianus.*

yet their glory of martyrdome is one and the same. Which primacy and principality of the seat of Rome, being acknowledge by vs Catholiks doth take away infinite number of heresies schismes and diuersity of religions, which euer shall raigne and do raigne now amongst the Protestants, and Puritanes in England and Scotland, for not acknowledging a supremacy and visible head in matters of religion, (h) *Neq; enim aliunde hæreses obortæ sunt, aut natæ sunt schismata, quàm inde, quòd sacerdoti Dei non obtemperetur, nec vnus in Ecclesia ad tempus sacerdos, & ad tempus Iudex vice Christi cogitatur,* sayth the same holy Father and martyr. Wherof he giueth this good reason: if God who is goodnes it selfe hath so great care of little and small things, and that (i) *one sparrow shall not fall on the ground without him, and that all the haires of our head are numbred;* much more doth it apperteyne to the prouidence & goodnes of God, that in his Church, which is the house of the liuing God, some visible head and superior be placed to iudge in matters of religiō, to the end we be not like Children, (k) *wauering and caryed about with euery wind of doctrine, by the deceit of men, and craftynes.* Which craftynes the Puritanes of Scotland haue deceitfully vsed in promising to preach nothing but *the expresse word of God,* the scripture, the playne words of the *Bible.* Which promise they not being able to performe, no not in one debatable poynt of Religion, will haue vs to take their rotten and stinking consequences, fond distinctions, and new inuented expositions, for the pure glittering gold of the word of God. Let not vs Catholiks make accompt what M. Robert Bruce, M. Robert Rolloke, M. Caluin, and M. Ramsey do say, but what the Bible sayth. (l) *Non audiamus* (sayth S. Augustine) *hæc dico, hæc dicis, sed audiamus hæc dicit Dominus:* who sayth in playne termes to S. Peter, *feed my sheep,* three seuerall tymes: *Peter I will build my Church vpon thee. Peter I will giue thee, the keyes of the kingdome of heauen. Peter whatsoeuer thou loosest in earth &c.* The meaning of the which words shall neyther be taken of the Ministers nor of me, but let the holy Fathers of this first age be iudges therof.

(h) *Cypr. Ep. 55. ad Cornel. Pap.*

(i) Matth. 10.

(k) *Ephes. 4. v. 14.*

(l) *Aug. de vnit. Eccl. c. 3.*

2. But before I enter to produce the sentences of the

the holy Fathers, I would intreat at least the vnpassionate Protestant to consider that notwithstāding this supremacy and superiority in spirituall matters which we Catholiks do acknowledge in S. Peter and his successours, yet we acknowledge likewyse, and constantly belieue, absolute authority, whole power, intier iurisdiction to be in Kings, in temporall matters and their gouernment; yea the want of true religion in kings and superiours cannot bring with it a necessary want of authority in gouernement; for as true faith is not necessary for true iurisdiction, so true authority and iurisdiction is not lost by the losse of true faith, & religiō. Which is the cause wherfore the Catholike Church commandeth vs, (a) *To be subiect of necessity, not only for feare, but also for conscience*; directly against that axiome of the Protestāts, which doth teach, *that the law of kings cannot oblige in conscience*. To the which purpose (b) S. Augustine remarketh, that in his tyme the Catholiks were obedient in tēporal matters to Iulian the Apostata Emperour, when he commanded them in any temporall thing: As to make warre vnder him, to fight against his enemyes; but when he commanded them to do things against their religion and conscience, they would only obey God the king of kings, and Emperour of Emperours. *Iulianus extitit infidelis Imperator*, (sayth S. Augustine) *nonne extitit Apostata? Milites Christiani seruierunt Imperatori Infideli: vbi veniebat ad causam Christi, non agnoscebant, nisi illum qui in cælo erat: quando volebat vt Idola colerent, vt thurificarent, præponebant illi Deum: Quando autem dicebat producite aciem, ite contra illam gentem, statim obtemperabant: distinguebant Dominum eternum à Domino temporali, & tamen subditi erant propter Dominum æternum Domino temporali.* S. Ignatius giueth the reasō of this Catholike doctrine in that Epistle of his ad *Smirnēses* which was writtē fyftene hundreth yeares since. *Because*, sayth he, *as in wordly maters none is aboue the king, nor lyke to him; so in the Church there is none greater then the true Bishop*. As in temporall maters the king hath all soueraignty, so in spirituall some chiefe head must needes be ordeyned, acknowleged, and obeyed. Wherfore if Kings and Princes do persecute vs Catholiks for our

conscience

(a) *Tit.3.*

(b) *Aug. in Psal. 124.*

conscience and religion, we should be both constant and patient; constant in our Religion, remembring that saying of Christ Iesus: (c) *He who denyeth me before men, I shall deny him before my Father in heauen*. Patient, considering that we (d) suffer for well doing, and not as *malefactors*; assuring our selues, that (e) *our tribulation which presently is but mometary & light, will work in vs aboue measure eternall glory*. Let not therfore my deer Countrey-men any grieuance imposed vpon our temporall estates make vs impatient, discontented, or put vs in danger to loose the true religion of our Forsathers, calling to mynd the infinite multititude of Noble men & women who not only haue lost their goods and temporall estates for the Catholike religion, but likewyse haue sealed the same with their blood, hauing won manfully, for transitory things eternall, an infinite riches in heauen; for a momentary calumny and shame of this world, a perpetuall and euerlasting glory before the Angels in heauen; for worldly preferment and fleshly liberty, an eternall preferment and euerlasting liberty in heauen. Finally touching the reuerence & honour which our Catholike religion giueth to Kings and Princes in particular, I say with S. Bernard, the same which at seuerall tymes I sayd, being in Prison, before the Lords of the high Commission: (f) *If all the world should conspire against me, to mooue me for to attempt any thing against the Kings maiesty, yet would I feare God, as not daring to offend the king by him appoynted: for I know it is written, that who resisteth the power, resisteth the ordinance of God, and purchaseth to himselfe damnation.* To conclude then, let vs be euer myndfull of those words of S. Peter, (g) *feare God and honour the King*. And, (h) *To giue to Cæsar, that which is Cæsars, and to God, that which is Gods*.

(c) Matth. 10. v. 33.
(d) 1. Pet. 4. v. 15.
(e) 2. Cor. 4. v. 17.
(f) Bernar. Ep. 221. ad Ludouic. Regem.
(g) 1 Pet. 2 v. 17.
(g) Matt. 22. v. 21.

3. As concerning the reuerence honour and obedience which the Puritans in Scotland, the Hugonots in France, the Lutherans in Germany, and the Anabaptists in Holland, do giue to kings and superiours, conforme to the grounds of their religion; I will set down their owne very words, that the good Reader may giue greater credit to my report. First of all M. Iohn Caluin, the ground and first

Author

Author of this reformed or rather deformed religion, speaking of the authority of kings, who are of a different religion from him, sayth thus: (i) *Earthly Princes do bereaue themselues of authority, when they erect themselues against God; yea they are vnworthy to be accompted in the number of men, and therfore we must rather spit vpon their faces, then obey them.* Which blasphemous doctrine D. Wilkes an English Protestants witnesseth to be Caluins, wryting thus to the seditious Puritanes, Caluins schollers: (k) *They were your teachers* (sayth he) *who accompt those Princes, who are not refined by your spirit, vnworthy to be accompted amongst the number of men, and therfore rather to be spitted vpon, then obeyed; they were your teachers who defend rebellion against princes of a different religion*: which abhominable doctrine of M. Iohn Caluin was put in practise in Geneua it selfe, for as much, (l) *As they of Geneua* (as witnesseth an English Protestant) *did depose their Catholike liege Lord & Prince the Duke of Sauoy, from his temporall right, albeit he was by right of succession the temporall Lord and owner of that Citty and territory.* Hence it was, that M. Iohn Knox an Apostata fryar and the piller of the Scots Deformation, a man trayned vp at Geneua, and whom Caluin calleth, (m) *An excellent man, and his most reuerend brother*, did learne of Caluin that doctrine of Sedition, and brought it into Scotland, to the playne ouerthrow of the authority of kings and of the Nobility, which gaue occasion to an (n) English Protestant to make a booke against the seditious doctrine of Knox, thus intituled: *Of the proceeding of the Scottish Ministers, according to the Geneuian rules of Reformation.*

(i) *Calu. in Daniel. c. 6 v. 22. & 25.*

(k) *In his Book called Odedience or Ecclesiasticall Vnion pag. 60. ante medium.*

(l) *M. Sutcliffe in his answer to a certaine Libell supplicatory pag. 194. & others.*

(m) *Caluin in his Epistle Ep. 305*

(n) *M. Bancroft.*

4. To make this poynt more euident in the confessed doctrine of M. Iohn Knox, Buchanan, and others Scots and English Ministers instructed at Geneua, I wil set down the very words of M. Bancroft an English Protestant, who alledgeth the history of the Church of Scotland set out by M. Iohn Knox, and printed by Vautrouiller. First then he sayth: (o) *That after a certayne sermon of M. Iohn Knox made in S. Andrewes, the houses of the fryars and abbayes of that towne (as after in Striueling, Lithquo and Edenburgh, the Quene being fled thence for feare) were cast downe. 2. Knox & those of that diabolically reformed*

(o) *In his Book intituled Dangerous positiōs, pag. 12. & seq.*

religion kept the feild two moneths, and tooke away to them selues the Coyning-Irons, which is lese-Maiesty. 3. *They gaue the Quene the lye diuers tymes, and vsed her with most despytfull speaches, and renounced their obedience vnto her.* 4. *They depryued her from regiment by a formall act penned by* Knox. 5. (p) M. Sutcliffe another famous Protestant asketh the Puritans, *Whether the reasons alledged by Knox and Willoks, against their gouernour and Prince, were sufficiēt for subiects to depose a Prince or Regēt lawfully appoynted, as they & their fellowes did depose the Quene Regent of Scotland?* 6 What enormityes did the Scots Puritans and Protestants against Blessed Quene Marie, his Highnes dearest Mother, let his Maiesty be witnesse therof. (q) *How they vsed,* sayth his Maiesty, *that poore lady my Mother, is not vnknowen, and with grief I remember it.* 7. Knox (r) in a booke of his to the Communalty sayth: *Reformation of religion* (that is manifest rebelliō) *belongeth to the communalty.* And againe, *That God* (sayth (s) Knox) *hath appointed the Nobility to brydle the inordinate appetites of Princes.* Againe, *That Princes* (sayth (t) Knox) *for iust causes may be deposed.* And againe, *If Princes be Tyrans* (sayth (u) Knox) *against God and his trueth, their subiects are freed from their oath of obedience.* Againe, *The people haue right* (sayth (x) Buchanan a Scots Puritan) *to bestow the crown at their pleasure.* It were tedious and loathsome to set down the abhominable doctrine, diuelish precepts and Idolatrous speaches, which Bucanan setteth down in that booke of his, *de Iure Regni apud Scotos,* which doctrine the Hugenots in Frāce of late did put in practise, giuing therby place to the Prouerb: *That it is as rare to find a whyte Aethiopian, as a faithfull Hugenot.* But let vs come to the consequences of the holy Fathers.

(p) *In his answer to a certaine Libell supplicatory &c. pag. 193.*

(q) *His Maiesties words in the summe of the conference before his Maiesty &c. anno 1604. pag. 81.*

(r) *Fol. 49. 50.*

(s) *Knox in his History of the Church of Scotland pag. 343. and see 372. 373. 500. 502. &c.*

(t) *In his History pag. 372.*

(u) *In a certaine Epistle of his to Englād and Scotland fol. 76*

(x) *Lib. de Iure regni apud Scot. pag. 13.*

The

The Testimonies of the holy Fathers of this first Age, prouing the primacy of S. Peter: And of his successours in the Catholike Church.

The first Section.

S. DENYS S. Paul his disciple conferreth S. Peter with the rest of the Apostles, and calleth him, the chief and head of the rest of the Apostles: (a) τὴν κορυφαίαν καὶ πρεσβυτάτην τῶν θεολόγων ἀκρότητα, *supremum & antiquissimum Theologorum fastigium.* Which verity was so constantly beleued by the holy Fathers of this age, that Origen himselfe doth witnes those of his tyme to haue receaued the foresaid doctrine frō their Forefathers, that is, from those of the first age, which is the cause wherfore he himselfe calleth Peter (b) *Apostolorum principem*, the prince of the Apostles. And againe. (c) *Petrus per promissionem meruit fieri Ecclesiæ fundamentum.*

(a) *Dionys. de diuinis nominibus cap. 3.*

(b) *Hom. 17. in Luc.*

(c) *In Tract. in Matth.*

2. S. Clemens S. Peters owne disciple and successor after Linus in the Apostolicall seat, affirmeth S. Peter to haue bene chosen by Christ as head and Father of the rest: (d) *Simon Petrus, qui veræ fidei merito, & integræ prædicationis obtentu, fundamentum esse Ecclesiæ definitus est: qua de causa etiam Domini ore diuino cognominatus est Petrus, qui fuit primitiæ electionis Domini, Apostolorum primus, cui & primò Deus Pater filium reuelauit; cui & Christus competenter beatitudinem contulit, qui & vocatus est & electus, & conuiua Domini & comes effectus, tanquam bonus & probatissimus discipulus, qui obscuriorem mundi plagam Occidentis (velut omnium potentior) illuminare præceptus est, quiq; & integrè potuit implere præceptum.* And againe he witnesseth that there was not a like equality amongst the Apostles, but one was preferred before the rest. (e) *Nec inter ipsos Apostolos par institutio fuit, sed vnus omnibus præfuit.* And againe he calleth S Peter: (f) *Beatum Apostolum, omnium Apostolorum patrem, qui claues regni cælestis accepit.*

(d) *Clemens Ep. 2.*

(e) *Ibidem post mediū.*

(f) *Ibidem in initio.*

3. S. Ignatius Martyr in an epistle of his to the Romans, commendeth the Roman Church greatly aboue the

the rest as most holy, most famous, and worthy to command others. (g) *Ignatius qui & Theophorus misericordiam consequuta Ecclesiæ sanctificata & illuminata &c. quæ præsidet in loco regionis Romanorum, Deo digna, decore digna, meritò beatissima, digna laude; digna quæ quis potiatur castissima & præcellenti dilectione Christi, ac patris nomen ferens, spiritu plena &c.* Which doctrine was so constantly receaued by the holy Fathers of the ensuing ages that no wyse man may doubt therof. Of the which holy Fathers, some called Peter (h) *Worthy to be preferred before all the Apostles, worthy to be called the Prince of the Apostles:* (i) *The head of the rest,* (k) *the pastor and head of the Church placed by Christ ouer the whole earth:* (l) *The Maister of the whole world; the rock & top of the Catholike Church.* Which authority of Church gouernement affirmed by those & other holy Fathers could not be tyed to the person of S. Peter alone, as to die with him, but was to suruiue and continue in his successours to the worlds end, to procure therby vnity and obedience, and to keep all the Pastours of the world in peace, to conuince heresyes, to settle controuersies of Religion. Truly if God had not set down some head ouer his church, it (m) *should be in a farre worse case, then the meanest Commonwealth, nay almost then a den of theeues, if the Church were left destitute of meanes, eyther to cõuince heresies, or to suppresse them.* And Melancthon another famous Protestant, acknowledged the Popes supremacy descending frõ S. Peter to be wholly necessary in the Church of God. (n) *For as certayne Bishops, sayth he, are president ouer many churches, so the Bishop of Rome is president ouer all Bishops and Canonicall policy, which no wyse man, as I thinke, doth, or ought to disallow &c. for the Monarchy of the Bishop of Rome is, in my opinion, profitable to this end, that consent of doctrine may be retayned: Wherfore an agreement may easily be established in this article of the Popes primacy, if other articles could be agreed vpon.* To whome agreeth M. Iacob an English Protestant, who sayth: (o) *By acknowledging a Catholike visible Church, it followeth necessarily that there is, and ought to be on earth an vniuersall gouernement Ecclesiasticall &c. for if there be properly one visible Church and gouernement Ecclesiasticall throughout the world, then this must be in some one place eminently, for some whither*

(g) *Ep. ad Rom.*

(h) *Optatus apud Fulk in his Retentiue pag. 248.*

(i) *Cyril Hieros. Catech. 2.*

(k) *Cyril. Alexand. l. 12. in Io. c. 64.*

(l) *Chrys. in Ioan hom. 87. & ad Pop. hom. 80. ante medium.*

(m) *M. Couel a Protestant in his examinatiõ &c. pag. 107. paulo post medium.*

(n) *In his Book intituled, Centuria Ep. Theol. Ep. 74.*

(o) *In his reason taken out of Gods Word &c. pag. 24.*

we must go when Christ biddeth vs tell the Church: now there is no place in all the world so likely as Rome, to be the visible and spring head of vniuersall gouernement of the *Catholike Church,*

That the Ministers haue corrupted the Bible in sundry places, which proue S. Peters Primacy, and others poynts of Catholike doctrine.

The second Section.

IT is aboue the expectation of any mã that feareth God, of whatsoeuer Religion he be, to see how impiously the Ministers haue corrupted the Bible to cõfirme their heresies, errours and blasphemyes. And as cõcerning this point of S. Peters primacy they haue corrupted S. Marke thus: (a) *And the first was Simon, and he named Simon Peter.* Where they haue put
in the text these words, *and the first was Simon,* which are no (a) *Marc.*
wyse in the (*) Greeke, nor els in the Syriake, where it is 3. v.16.
only *Veschami leschembhun schema kipho, & nominauit Schemeun* * καὶ ἐπέ-
nomine kipho. Can there be a greater abhomination or sinne θηκε τῷ
before God then willingly & wittingly to put in the vul- Σίμωνι
gar text, which is not in the originall? Can the Ministers ὄνομα Πέ-
beleue in God, who thus do corrupt the word of God? Is τρον.
it not a sinne against the holy Ghost, (b) *which shall not be* (b) *Matt.*
forgiuen to men, to belye the holy Ghost and make him to 12. v.31.
say that, which he did neuer say, and which is not in the originall? to corrupt, bely and speake against the holy Fathers (as the Ministers do) it is a great sinne, (c) *but whosoeuer* (c) *Matth.*
shall speake against the holy Ghost (in corrupting the Originall 12. v. 32.
text of the holy Ghost) *it shall not be forgiuen him neyther in this world, nor in the world to come.* Caluin was the first inuenter of
this corruption, which was confirmed by (*) Beza, who * *In hunc*
granteth that the word *first,* in S. Mathew, is found in all the *locum.*
Greeke copyes: (d) *Now the names of the twelue Apostles are these,* (d) *Matth.*
the first is Simon called Peter: But it hath bene put in, sayth he, 10. v. 2.
by some Papist: *Ab aliquo additum est, qui Petri primatum vellet* πρῶτος
stabilire. But wherfore haue the Ministers put in the text of Σίμων.
S. Marke the word *first,* which is not in the Greeke, since it is playnly in S. Mathew? The reason is, Because in S. Ma-

 thew

thew the Apostles are named conforme to their place, dignity and authority thus: *The first is Simon called Peter.* Not saying after, *the second is Andrew his brother*, but because Peter was first in dignity, he was first named. Nor likewyse by reason of the tyme they were called to Christs seruice, for
(e) Io. 1. v. 40. Peter was called after (e) Andrew, and yet Peter is by all the Euangelistes placed the *first*, by reason he was the chief and the head of the rest, and had primacy aboue the rest. As Iudas Iscariotes is alwayes placed the last by reason of his vnworthynes: So S. Peter is placed the first by reason of his dignity. And because S. Marke maketh mention of the Apostles in order, as their names were changed by Christ, placing first Peter, and then Iames and Iohn &c. and not Andrew, as S. Matthew did, the Ministers haue put in S. Marke the word *first*, to infirme and weaken S. Mathew his fashion of reckoning, by reason of dignity, and to fortifie S. Marks fashiõ of reckoning, which is by reason of the changing of their names; inferring consequently, that both the one and the other in placing S. Peter first, regarded not his Primacy, but because his name was first changed: a crafty and subtile forme of corrupting the word of God, which hardly at the first and simple vew will be perceaued. But why doth S. Paul reckon Peter after Iames?
(f) Galath. 2. v. 9. (f) *And when Iames, and Cephas, and Iohn knew of the grace &c.* By reason of Iames his age wherof he had regard and not of any other thing. Doth not S. Paul in the same chapter declare that Peter had a particular obligatiõ aboue the rest to preach to the circumcised?

2. Another corruption is in the second of the Cronicles, where they haue ioyned to the text many words, which are not in the Greeke, nor yet in the Hebrew. The words are: (g) *Concerning the rest of the acts of*
(g) 2. Chro. 36. v. 8. *Iehoiakim, and his abhominations which he did, and carued Images that were layed to his charge, behold they are written in the booke of the Kings &c.* These words, *carued Images layed to his charge*, are not in the Hebrew text, but impiously put in all the Bibles printed in the yeare 1562. to make the Images odious, and to encourage the people in that yeare to cast

cast down the Churches, and after they had become Maister of all, they tooke those foresaid words out of the Bible printed afterward: which corruptiō I set down heer by reason of the Ministers animosity against the Church of God, wherof S. Peter is head.

3. To make the holy *Processions*, which the Catholike Church doth vse, odious, they haue likewise corrupted the Bible thus: (h) *And when the feast of Bacchus was kept, they were constrayned to go in the procession of Bacchus with garlands of Iuy.* Vsing the word *procession*, which is not in the (*) greeke, and conferring the holy processions of the Catholike Church, where the holy Crosse the Instrument of our redemption is exhibited, to the filthy and abhominable feasts of Bacchus. Is there any Minister so ignorant, that he knoweth not, that πομπεύειν signifieth only, to go in pompe, and not in procession? Doth not their fellow (*) Puritan teach, that πομπεύω is, *cum pompa incedo*? and Ouid, *Cineri materno ducere pompam.* And Budæus πομπικὸν σαλπίζειν. Ignorant Ministers who carry about with them in their pocket the Greeke new Testament for a shew, yet few of them can read it, and very few vnderstand it, wherof I made experience being in Prison in Edenburgh the yeare 1620. The Catholike translation of this place is: *And when the feast of Bacchus was kept, they were compelled to go about crowned with Iuy vnto Bacchus.* Neuer a word of *Processions*.

(h) 2. *Machab* 6. v. 7

* ἠναγκάζοντο κισσοὺς ἔχοντες πομπεύειν.

* *Henricus Stephanus in thesaur. linguæ Græcæ.*

4. To make odious the holy foundations which our forfathers of charity erected for the seruice of God, they haue corrupted filthily the Bible, thus: (i) *And he put down the Chemarims whome the Kings of Iudah had founded, to burne incense in the high places.* In the Hebrew, Greeke, and Latin text it is otherwyse: *And he destroyed the sooth-sayers, which the Kings of Iudah had appoynted to sacrifice in the excelses in the citty of Iuda.* Agayne, to make the great and feruent deuotion of the Catholiks in their prayers odious to the people, they haue corrupted the Bible thus: (k) *For as I passed by, and beheld your deuotions, I found an Altar, wherin was written, Vnto the vnknowen God.* Where without conscience, or any religion at all they

(i) 2 *Reg.* 23. v. 5. *Et deleuit aruspices quos posuerant Reges Iuda.*

(k) *Act.* 17. v. 23. ἀναθεωρῶν τὰ σεβάσματα ὑμῶν.

they haue thrust in the word *deuotion*, which is not in the Greeke, or Syriake text, in the which it is thus, *Passing by, and seeing your Idols, or simulachres*, not, *seing your deuotions*. Could the Diuel himselfe in person inuent greater craft to corrupt the word of God, to deceaue the poore silly soules of the Protestants? What excuse can the Protestants haue in the day of Iudgement, in reading and belieuing such abhominable translations, such malicious corruptions, such detestable Bibles, which are much lesse the word of God, then William Wallace booke, wherin there is no blasphemous nor Idolatrous translation; as is in the Bibles presently read, and preached in Scotland. Remarke the double dealing of the Ministers, who do translate in other places the same Greeke word otherwyse, as that of S. Paul, who speaking of the proude and lofty mynd of the Puritan Minister, or of a Protestant Bishop, sayth: (l) *Who is an aduersary, and exalteth himselfe against all, that is called God, or that is worshipped*. Where the same greeke word is not translated, *deuotion*, but *worshipped*.

(l) 2. Thess. 2. v. 4. ἢ σέβασμα

The

The 23. & 24. Article.

1. That the true Church of God must needs be infallible. 2. And as she hath absolute authority to propone matters of faith, so she cannot erre in proponing such matters to be belieued, as Apostolicall Traditions, which euer haue bene belieued.

CHAP. XII.

THOVGH I haue handled before this matter of the Church, of the markes and propertyes therof, yet I thought good to speake more at length of the infallibility of the true Church of God, and of the absolute authority therof in maters of faith, which once being granted, no difficulty can be found in any other poynt of the Catholike religion; for he who is persuaded that the true Church of God hath sufficient authority to propone maters of faith, & likewyse cannot erre in proponing the same, must needes easily imbrace & belieue whatsoeuer the Church proponeth to be belieued. True it is, that I haue conferred with some Ministers in Scotland, who were certaynly perswaded (as they said) *that the true Church of God could not erre.* That the true Church of God is infallible in proponing matters of faith to be belieued: Others denying the same but ignorantly, of passion rather, then of reason conforme to their custome. But to the end this matter be deduced more playnly I will intreat the Reader to consider.

2. First, that the word *Church*, may be taken foure seuerall wayes. First, for the whole company of Christian professours consisting of sheep and Pastors, that is, of some

who by Gods ordinance and appoyntement, haue office and authority to feed, and teach the right faith and religion; and of others who are taught: and thus the word *Church* is taken when we say, *the Church of God is vniuersal and Catholike: The Church of God hath euer bene and shalbe.* Secondly, the word Church is taken for the more principall part of that company, to wit, the full company of Pastors gathered togeather or dispersed throughout the world. Thirdly for a principal member, to wit, the visible head of this mysticall body, the chief Pastor, Christs vicar, S. Peters successour called the Pope: Not as he is a particular and priuate man, but as eyther alone, or at least assisted with a generall Councel, hath receaued of Christ ful authority to feed the Christian flock, by proponing to them maters of faith. Fourthly, the Church is taken for euery particular Pastour, not as he is a priuate man, but as he is authorized, vnder, and with dependance of the chief pastor to feed that flock particularly, which is committed to his charge: wherby it is euident that those Apostata Priests and Monks, as M. Iohn Knox, Willox, Craig, and such like (nothing els but our dregs, yet the first and chief pillars of the deformed Scots religion) who preached first the Puritans religion, had no ordinary calling to do the same, because they were not authorized by their immediat superiors, nor yet by the chief Pastor, to preach such a new religion. As for extraordinary calling and authority, they had none (though ignorantly they brag of it) by reason as they were not sent extraordinarly and immediatly by God, so they had no marks of extraordinary calling, which are humility, extraordinary good and holy Life and Miracles, as witnesseth the Scripture in Moyses, the Prophets, S. Iohn Baptist, and S. Paul, as learnedly S. (a) Gregory the great teacheth, with sundry others.

(a) *Lib.* 1. *Dial. c.* 1.

3. Secondly, consider that the infallible and absolute authority that I am to proue to be in the Church of God, is with reason called the authority of the Church, specially as the word *Church* is taken in the third signification, as being ordayned to the proffit of the whole Church, and of euery mẽber therof, in regard of the doctrine which

proceedeth

proceedeth, and taketh hold from the authority of the Church: which doctrine as it is in it selfe infallible, so it worketh infallibility in the hart of euery seuerall person, so much, as he groundeth his faith vpon the diuine doctrine reuealed by God to the Church, and proponed to him by the Church. So that God the prime Verity of all doth reueale (conforme to his promise set down in seuerall places of the Bible) to the Church that holy doctrine which we should belieue vnder payne of damnation: for, (b) *He that beleueth not shall be condemned.* And the Church being grounded vpon the word and authority of God, and infallibly assisted by the holy Ghost, doth propone the same doctrine to the Christians to be belieued: wherof it followeth, that we Catholiks do not build our faith and religion vpon the priuat opinion of any one, or some few Doctors or Pastors of the Catholike Church; yea not vpon the priuat opinion of the Pope or chief Pastor, as this priuat opinion is made knowne to vs priuatly, as by a Sermon preached, publick audience, or printed booke: but rather it is necessary that the doctrine of the chief pastour, (to the end it haue infallibility) be delyuered to vs by pastorall authority, as the publick doctrine of the Church, when in matters called in question he defyneth as chief Pastour (specially with a generall Councell) what is to be holden, proponing the same to the whole Church to be belieued, and pronouncing Anathema against those that hold the contrary; or els when the chief pastor expresly signifieth that his intention is with his pastorall authority to oblige the vniuersall Church to hold that which he proponeth as a matter of faith, wherin God hath promised to assist & guide the chief pastour infallibly, saying: (c) *I haue prayed for thee, that thy faith fayle not. Therfore when thou art conuerted, strengthen thy brethren.* Where the word *conuerted,* is to be remarked diligently.

(b) *Marc.* 16. v. 16.

(c) *Luc.* 22 v. 32.

4. Of the which doctrine it followeth, how ignorantly some of the Ministry obiect the lyues of some Popes or of other Pastors, or certayne historyes, & recordes which we beleue not as matters of faith. Likewyse how ignoran-

tly the Ministers do teach, that we beleue whatsoeuer the Church proponeth, as a mater of faith, though it be against the Scripture: for it is impossible that the true Church being infallibly assisted by God (according to his promise) can, or may propone any thing which is against, or besids the Scripture.

5. Fourthly, of the said doctrine it followeth likewayes how ignorantly the Ministers do preach, that we beleue as maters of fayth, all visions and miracles of Saintes &c. Which is a manifest calumny. For as it were temerity, rashnes, & a sort of folly to deny or misbelieue (*fide humana & piè*,) those miracles, which so many wyse, holy and learned Pastours, Kings and Princes, Kingdomes and nations haue constantly auowed; So we believe only those which the Catholike Church (*authoritatiuè*) proponeth to be belieued as maters of faith, which are very few.

6. Fyftly, when I say, the authority of the Church is absolute and infallible, I do not vnderstand, as if it were independant of God or his word, as though the Church might at pleasure pronoũce any doctrine to be *diuine*, without any respect to God or his word. But I accompt the doctrine of the Church to be infallible of it selfe, and the authority to be absolute in respect of vs, in this sense, that we, after the sentence of this or that poynt of faith pronounced by the Church, we (I say) are absolutly bound and obliged to submit our iudgements, and to believe that for infallible truth, which by the Church is defyned for such. The Ministers religion vpon the other side denying the infallible and absolute authority of the Church, can haue nothing but errour, deceit, instability and fallibility for the last ground and resolution therof.

7. First then I proue the Church to haue such absolute authority to propone vnto vs matters of religion to
(d) Heb. 13. v. 7. ἡγουμένων ὑμῶν. be believed vnder the payne of condemnation. I proue it (I say) out of that of S. Paul: (d) *Remember them which haue the ouer sight of you, which haue declared vnto you the word of God, whose faith follow, considering what hath bene the end of their conuersation.*
(e) Heb. 13. v. 17. And againe (e) *Obey your Superiours, and submit your selues, for they*

they watch for your soules, as they that must giue accompt, that they may do it with Ioy, and not with greef, for that is vnproffitable for you. By these words & other places of the Scripture, we are absolutly commanded to obey the Church, our Prelats, and superiours, and to be subiect vnto them, as to men that are to giue accompt for our soules. But absolute obedience and subiection on our syde, supposeth absolute authority to be in them, whom we obey. Ergo, since absolutly we are commanded to obey thē, they must needs haue absolute power to command vs. 2. The reason why we should obey our Superiours, is declared by the Apostle, *because they are to giue accompt for our soules.* Wherof it followeth, that this our obedience (as likewise their authority) extendeth it selfe to all maters perteyning to the saluation of our soules, which are specially matters of faith, without the which there is no saluation: which is the reason wherfore the Bible witnesseth that matters preached vnto vs, haue annexed certayne obediēce, *Wherby those who do preach should be obeyed & belieued:* (f) *But they haue not all obeyed the Ghospell: For Isaias sayth, Lord who hath belieued our report?* Where both the Prophet, and the Apostle testifie, that we are obliged to obey the true Pastours who teach the word of God, to whome consequently absolute authority must needes be granted. 3. The differēce betwixt science and belief, is, that science is grounded immediatly vpon the euidence of things wherof we haue science, and so there may be perfect science though there be no authority at all in the speaker, or in him who maketh a demonstration *à priori*, or *à posteriori*: But so it is not in maters of belief which are grounded immediatly vpon the authority of the speaker, whether the thing be euident or not: yea commonly *diuine* and *humane* faith is, (g) *of things which are not euident or seene*. Which is specially true of *diuine faith*, the reason wherof the Scripture giueth: *Nam quod videt quis, quid credat?* Since therfore we haue not science but belief of *diuine things*, spoken first and immediatly by God to the Prophets and Apostles, spoken immediatly to vs by the Church and the present pastours therof, we cannot expect euidence of those things, but it suffiseth vs to giue credit

(f) Rom. 10 v. 16.

(g) Heb. 11. v. 1.

to the Church and Paſtour therof, for the authority of the ſpeaker: which Church doth, by authority receaued from God, ſpeake and reueale thoſe things to vs. 4. If there were no abſolute authority in the Church, in proponing maters of faith, but rather after the Church hath proponed them, & ſufficiently pronounced ſentence, it were free and lawfull for euery man to examine the proponed doctrine of the Church, with the Scripture, conferring the doctrine therof with ſundry places of the Scripture (as the Miniſters do ignorantly and fooliſhly teach,) ſo that it were lawfull to euery man to admit, reiect or not belieue the doctrine of the Church, becauſe after collation therof with the Scriptures he findeth not the ſaid doctrine, according to his fantaſy, imagination, yea paſſion, well grounded in the Scripture: If this (I ſay) were lawfull to euery man to do, as the Miniſters do teach, there ſhould neuer be an end of examining by the Scripture, ſince this priuat examination hath much more need of a new examination thē the doctrine of the Church, and this other examination, of another, *& ſic in infinitum*. Being in Priſō I asked of M. Andrew Ramſey what certaynty and infallibility he had in preaching the word of God? he anſwered, that in preaching the word he might erre and lye: What certaynty then and infallibility, ſaid I, haue thoſe who do heare you? He replyed, that he deſired them to conferre & examine his doctrine with the Scriptures. I replyed; eyther they may erre in examining your preaching with the Scripture, or not? if they may not erre, then they haue greater certaynty and infallibility then you who are a Miniſter: if they may erre, what auayleth thē to examine your doctrine with the Scripture, ſince after due examination they remayne euer incertayne, and doubtfull of what you haue preached, and what they haue examined; and conſequently neyther can your preaching nor their examination of the Scripture, breed true and diuine faith (which muſt be infallible) in their harts: and this is the reaſon wherfore the laſt reſolution of the Proteſtants faith and religion, is nothing but errour and incertaynty, & conſequently the faith & belief of the Proteſtants cannot

be

be *diuine* but *humane*: for diuine faith, as it is infallible, so the last resolution therof must be in some infallible authority, which cãnot be, except in the authority of the church: which verity gaue occasion to S. Augustine to say, (h) *That he would not, or should not beleue the Ghospell it selfe, if he were not moued therevnto by the authority of the Church.* And thus far concerning the absolute authority of the Church: adding only this, that if a King in his Kingdome had not absolute authority to make lawes, to the good and the proffit of his Kingdome: if a Parliamẽt had not absolute authority to set down things for the good state of the Commõ wealth, but rather if it were permitted to euery particular man, or foure or fiue heady & rebellious cõpanions gathered togeather, to examine the Kings & Parlaments authority in making of the lawes, to examine them (I say) after the sentence of the Parlament duely pronounced; truely neyther could such a King be called a true King, nor such a Parlament, a lawfull Parlament: euen so it is in the Church, in respect of absolute authority.

(h) *Aug. cont. Ep. Fund. c. 5*

8. As concerning the infallibility of the Church, which I promised to proue; it is to be remarked, that I take the word *Church*, as a company of men assisted infallibly by the holy Ghost, the doctrine wherof consequently is called, not meerly *humane*, but rather *diuine*: as proceeding originally and principally from the spirit of God. This being noted, I proue the infallible authority of the church in maters of faith, out of these places of the Bible. First: (i) *And Iesus came and spake vnto them, saying, All power is giuen vnto me in heauen and in earth: Go therfore and teach all nations, baptizing them in the name of the Father, & the Sonne, and the holy Ghost, teaching them to obserue all things, whatsoeuer I haue commãded you; and loe I am with you alway vntill the end of the world.* And againe with this whole power (which he receaued of his Father) he sent the Apostles and their successours: (k) *As my father sent me, so send I you.* And againe, he giueth commission to the Apostles and their successours: (l) *Go ye into al the world and preach the Ghospell to euery creature.* Againe: (m) *He that heareth you, heareth me, and he that dispyseth you, dispyseth me,*

(i) *Matth.* 28. v. 18. 19.

(k) *Ioan.* 20. v. 21.

(l) *Marc.* 16. v. 15.

(m) *Luc.* 10. v. 16.

me, and he that dispyseth me, despyseth him that sent me. Now I say, Chryst our Sauiour (to whome all power was giuen in heauen and earth) had infallible power and authority: euen as he was man, to teach and propone to vs matters of faith, and had power to giue to others the same authority, But what power Christ had in this kynd, he communicated it to his Apostles and to their successours, at least so far as it was necessary for the good of the Church. Ergo, the first proposition is certayne, and as it were, in playne words in the Bible. The Minor I proue: Because Christ sent his Apostles, and their successors with that authority, wherwith his heauenly Father sent him: But that authority was infallible. Ergo the authority of the Apostles and their successours must needs be infallible.

9. Secondly if the authority of the Church, in proponing maters of faith to be belieued, were fallible, or could in such a case erre or deceaue vs, it would follow, that God himselfe could be the author of false belief, by teaching & causing the church to teach false doctrine in maters of faith: but that is impious and abhominable to grant, that God the prime verity can possibly be the author of false belief, causing the Church, or permitting the same to teach false doctrine. That it would follow, God to be the authour of false belief, I prooue it in this sort. What authority the Church hath to propone maters of diuine faith, is grounded wholly in the authority of God, promising infallible assistance to the Church, sending and appoynting the Pastours therof to preach and teach, commanding vs to heare and obey thē, threatning those who will not obey, as the places of the Bible before specified do witnesse. Ergo if the authority of the Church be fallible and may deceaue men, inducing them to belieue that which is false; God himself ordeyning this authority should be iustly esteemed author of this false belief, & men might iustly & with reason say to God in the later day (as learnedly Richardus à Sancto Victore a Scotsman remarketh): (n) *Domine, si decepti sumus, tu decepisti nos: O Lord, if we be deceaued, thou hast deceaued vs,* by reason that God commandeth vs, vnder the payne of damnation, to obey the Church,

(n) *Lib. 11. de Trinit. cap. 2.*

Church, & yet the Church is fallible and erroneous in the Ministers opinion. Thus much concerning the absolute & infallible authority of the Church: Wherof I will speake more amply (God willing) in the following centuryes & ages: only this is to be remarked, that we haue the expresse words of the Bible for vs to proue the absolute and infallible authority of the Church. (o) *The Church is the ground and pillar of truth.* How then can it be fallible? (p) *The ports of hel shall not preuayle against the Church.* What blasphemy then is it to say that they haue preuayled in making the Church to erre? *I shall be with you to the end of the world,* and such other sayings as I haue cited before. I aske now of the Ministers as playne and manifest words of the Bible that proue the cōtrary, which they not being able to do, wil play the sophists & take hold vpon their sophismes & consequēces, which will haue some shew with the sighing sisters & ignorant brethrē, but none at all with vs Catholiks, of whom specially they learne that small portion of Philosophy which they haue; which is euident, by reason that the cheef authors and Philosophers which they read and peruse in their Colledges are Papists and Iesuits, as Cardinall Tolet, Fonseca, Conimbricenses, Ruuius, Zuares, Vasques, Pererius, Zabarella, Balfoureus a Scots man, Mazius and sundry others. For to this day neuer hath a Scots Minister written any thing of accōpt in latin (to my knowledge) of Theologie or Philosophy, or of history to the prayse of his countrey, but little pamphets very fit for the Trone Lords, and the sighing sisters, which cōsequently do not passe the sea, and bringe no great commodity to the printers & bookesellers of Edenburgh. But let vs leaue these sophistical Ministers with their sophismes, foolish consequences & Pamphlets, & see the belefe of the holy Fathers of this age concerning the absolute & infallible authority of the Church in proponing vnwritten traditions to be belieued and receaued.

(o) 1. *Timi* 3. v. 15.

(p) *Matt.* 16.

The Testimonyes of the holy Fathers of this first Age, prouing that the true Church of God must needs be infallible, in proponing maters of faith &c.

The first Section.

S. DENIS renowned and famous in the kingdome of Frāce, witnesseth, how that the holy Apostles (by reason of their absolute and infallible authority) proponed & commanded the Christians to belieue vnwritten traditiōs, making mention of sundry traditions in particular, in that booke of his: (a) *Necessario igitur primi illi nostræ hierarchiæ duces, cùm ex supersubstantiali principio diuino sacri muneris plenitudinem accepissent, & idipsum deinceps propagare à diuina bonitate iussi essent, ipsiq; absq; inuidia cuperent, vtpote deificati, posterorum subiectionem & deificationem, sensibilibus signis supercælestia, varietate & multitudine quod vnicum est collectum, & in humanis diuina, & in materialibus immaterialia, & in ijs quæ nobis sunt familiaria, res supersubstātiales, partim scriptis, partim non scriptis institutionibus suis, iuxta quod sacræ definiunt leges, nobis tradiderūt.* Which doctrine of S. Dennis gaue occasion to S. Chrysostome to say: (b) *The Apostles did not delyuer all things by wryting, but many things without wryting, and those be as worthy of credit as the other.* And Epiphanius: (c) *We must vse traditions, for the Scripture hath not all things, and therfore the Apostles delyuered certayne things by wryting, and certayne by tradition.*

(a) Eccl. Hierarch. c. 1.
(b) In 2. ad Thess. hom. 4.
(c) Epiph. Hær. 61. circa medium.

2. S. Clemens Romanus in his Apostolical Constitutions maketh mention of sundry vnwritten traditions, as the forme and fashion to consecrate Bishops, to receaue publick siners into the church, of the ceremonies of baptisme, of the ceremonyes of the Masse, of the ceremonyes cōcerning holy virgins liuing togeather in monasteries, of holywater, of the Passion weeke, concluding thus: (d) *Omnia secundum mandata Christi nobis tradita faciatis, sciētes quòd qui nos audit, Christum audit, qui verò Christum audit, Deum eius eundemq; patrem audit, cui gloria in sæcula seculorum, Amen.* And againe: (e) *Precationes facite manè, hora tertia, sexta, ac nona, & vespere, atq; ad gallicantum. Manè gratias agentes, quia illuminauit nos nocte sublata & reddito die: tertia, quia ea hora Pilatus iudicium aduersus*

(d) Lib. 8. c. 3. Const. Apost. ver. Turriani c. 4. 5. 6. 7. 8. & 9. &c.
(e) Ibid. c. 34.

aduersus dominum pronunciauit: Sexta, quia ea hora in crucem actus est: Nona, quia tum omnia mota & tremefacta sunt Domino crucifixo, quia horrerent audaciā impiorum Iudaeorum, & contumeliam domini ferre non possent: Vespere, quòd noctem dederit ad requiescendum à diurnis laboribus: ad gallicantum, quòd ea hora nunciet aduentum diei ad facienda opera lucis. Where it is easie to see, that in the very tyme of the Apostles, Catholiks, Papists and religious men were accustomed to pray and sing Mattines, & Euensong in the Church, yea Mattins at midnight: which holy custome was so famous in Scotland, that there were some Monasteryes therof (as that of S. Mongo in Glasco, of S. Brandane in the west Iles, of S. Columbanus in the Ile of Iona, of S. Serf in the Abbey of Culros) which being furnished to the number of six hundreth Religious men, at euery houre of the day and night, foure & twenty were appoynted to sing the prayse of God, one company succeding to another. Which holy custome S. Columbanus erected first in France in the Abbey of Luxouium in Burgundy, called therefore by S. Bernard, *Laus perennis*.

3. S. Martialis (f) in his Epistle to the Christians of Burdeaux testifieth, that the Church of God is constant & firme, and cannot erre, or fall to teach false doctrine. *Inimicus, qui nunc à cordibus vestris proiectus est, venturus est, vt superseminet populo Dei grana errorum. Sed firma Ecclesia Dei & Christi nec cadere, nec disrumpi poterit vnquam*. (f) *Cap.* 11.

4. S. Ignatius witnesseth lykewise in seuerall places the infallible authority of the Church, in proponing vnwritten Apostolicall traditiōs, & maketh mētion of sundry in particular, as witnesseth (g) his owne letter writtē to the Catholiks: and the same affirmeth (h) Eusebius. I omit to set down the testimonyes of other Fathers of this age, the mater in it selfe being so playne and manifest, conforme to all reason and equity. Let vs them see, how abhominably the Ministers haue corrupted the Bible to proue this their Capitall heresy and Idolatry, deceauing thereby the simple people to the eternall perdition of their soules.

(g) *Epist. ad Trallianos paulo ante med.*
(h) *Lib.* 3. *Hist. c.* 30.

That the Ministers haue corrupted the Bible in sundry places, which proue the Churches Authority.

The second Section.

In the Bibles printed anno 1562.
Aug. in Psal. 81.

BEFORE, I did shew how that the Ministers at their first entry and preaching in Scotland, to authorize the Lords of the Congregatiõ in pulling down the Churches and Abbayes, scraped out the word *Kirke*, or *Church*, and placed instead therof the word *cõgregatiõ*, which word may be applyed to an assembly of Iewes, of Turkes, sayth S. Augustine, of Infidels, yea of beastes, considering the word in the original, *congregatio*, though the word *Ecclesia*, church is taken commonly in the holy Scripture, and euer in the new testament, and among the Ecclesiasticall wryters, for the assembly of the faithfull. The Ministers not content with this impious forme of proceeding against the militant Church, they likewyse cast out their blasphemyes against the triumphant Church, wherof this place of S. Paul speaketh manifestly. (a) *Yee are come to the mount Sion, and to the citty of the liuing God, the celestiall Hierusalem, and to the company of innumerable Angels, and to the Church of the first borne which are written in heauen.* Which place the Ministers haue corrupted thus, *and to the cõgregatiõ of the first borne*, taking away therby the force of the Apostles saying, who prayseth the Hebrews made Christians in regard that therby they were ioyned to the *primitiue Church*, or the Church of the first borne; for so readeth S. Chrisostome with vs, *primitiuorum fidelium*. The force of the which word *primitiue Church*, because the Ministers cãnot abide, they haue made the sentence obscure in changing *Church* into *congregation*. So that by this translatiõ of the Ministers there is no more a militant or triumphant Church, but a *Congregation*: and Christ is not the head of the Church, but of the Congregation: and this congregation at the casting down of the Church was in a few Lords whose posterity hath exactly bene punished by God, as all Scotland knoweth.

(a) Heb. 12 v. 22. Accessistis ad Ecclesiam primitiuorũ. καὶ ἐκκλησίᾳ πρωτοτόκων.

2. Lykewise they haue taken out the word *Catholike* in the title of S. Iohns Epistle. *The first Catholike Epistle of S. Iohn:*

Iohn; They haue turned, *The Generall Epistle*: as in the Creed or Beliefe they cannot abide those words, *The holy Catholike Church*, but rather, *the holy Vniuersall Church*: vsing alwayes noueltyes, which is an infallible token of heretiks: neuertheles other Greeke words (which are to their fancy) they keep and vse, as Bishop, Deacon, Baptisme, Eucharist, Psalmes, and such; but the holy Fathers S. Hierome, S. Athanasius, Amphilochius, Nazianzemus, Cyrillus Hierosolymitanus, S. Augustine, and sundry others do call it, *the Catholike and Canonicall Epistle of S. Iohn*. Catholike, because it was written to all Christians, not to particulars, as S. Paul to the Corinthians, Ephesians, &c. Canonicall, because it was belieued as the word of God vniuersally. (b) *Canonica est ista epistola* (sayth S. Augustine) *per omnes gentes recitatur, orbis terræ authoritate retinetur, orbem terrarum ipsa ædificauit*. But neither the Scots nor latin Bible vsed in Scotland, is, or euer shallbe, by any forraine nation acknowledged for the word of God.

(b) *Tract. 7. in 1. Ep. Ioan.*

3. The third place which the Ministers haue corrupted is in the Epistle to the Hebrews, where S. Paul teacheth the infallibility of the faith of the Church of God, though things which we belieue be not euident, for if they were euident, they could not be the obiect of faith. For as, *habitus scientiæ* is euident, so *habitus fidei*, is ineuident, yet infallible. So sayth the Apostle: (c) *Faith is the ground of things which are hoped for, and the conuiction or demonstration of things which are not seene*. Where the Ministers haue turned *the euidece of things*, most ignorantly; since it is certayne that inuisible things which we belieue are infallible, yet not euident as sayth S. Chrysostome: (d) *fides est eorum quæ non sunt manifesta, & eorum quæ non videntur*. And S. Augustine turneth the Greeke word * *conuictionē non apparentiū*, as signifiyng properly conuiction, by reason of the infallibility of the true faith, conforme to that saying of his: (e) *What is faith? to belieue that which thou seest not: the reward of this faith is to see that which is to be belieued*. And againe: (f) *Habet fides oculus suos, quibus quodammodo videt, verum esse quod nondum videt, & quibus certißimè videt, nondū se videre quod credit*: The treachery of the Mini-

(c) *Heb. 11. v. 1.*

(d) *Lib. 2.*

* ελεγχος.

(e) *Aug. serm. 29. de verb. Apostol.*

(f) *Aug. Ep. 58 ad Consent.*

* ἔλεγχος.

*ἔλεγχος. Ministers is to be remarked that in this place they turne the Greeke (*) word, *the euidence* (because it makes for the fallibility of their faith) and not in other places, as in (g) S. Iohn, (h) S. Paul and others, where the same Greeke word is, yet they do neuer turne it *euidence,* but otherwyse and far differently from the word *euidence.*

(g) Ioa. 3. v. 20.
(h) 1. Cor. 14. v. 24.

4. Finally, against the vnity of the Catholike Church the Ministers do translate impiously that saying of Salomō: (i) *Vna est columba mea, My doue is one*; insteed wherof they trāslate *My doue is alone,* to take away the vnity, & to signify their forged inuisibility of their Protestant Church (which they are forced to auow to haue bene *alone* in the wildernes these 1550. yeares) as if it were a like to say: *There is one king in the kingdome,* and, *The king is alone in his kingdome.* Doth not the Hebrew and Greeke word signifie *one,* and not *alone*? Is there not a great difference in the latin tōgue betwixt *vnus,* one, & *solus,* alone. To take away wholy out of the Bible the word Church at the first preaching of their heresy, they changed it in the word Congregation, to the end that the word *Church* should neuer sound in the common peoples eares: then to deface the proprietyes of the Church, as *Catholike,* and *one,* they translate *vniuersall,* & *alone.* To signify that the faith of the Church should not be of ineuident things, eyther to the vnderstanding or to the ey, they translate, *faith is the euidence of things,* meaning therby that we should not belieue the *reall presence,* because that it is not euident to the ey, nor yet to our vnderstanding. O Impiety! O abhomination! to follow the doctrine of these Ministers who are nothing els but (k) *Scripturarum fures & adulteri,* Adulterers of the Scriptures, corrupters of the Ghospell, and false interpreters of the word of God: (l) *whose sinne is written with a pen of Iron, and with the poynt of a diamond, and engrauen vpon the table of their hart,* because they haue so impiously corrupted the word of God, falsified the Bible & defiled the Scripture.

(i) Cant. 6. v. 8.
μία.
(k) Orig. in 2. ad Rom.
(l) Ierem. 17. v. 1.

The Conclusion of this first Century, or hundred yeares.

IT is euident by the forsayd proofs & reasons how that the selfe-same religion which is now presētly professed in France, Spaine, Italy, Poland, Germany, Flanders, in Asia, Africa, Europe, America, publikely; in Scotland England & Irland, though priuatly, was before professed constantly in the Apostles tyme. In the which Apostles tyme it is constantly auowed by the Protestants themselues, that the Ile of great Britany (that is Scotland and the other part thereof which now is called England) was conuerted to the Catholike Apostolike and Roman Fayth: to the selfe same Religion and Faith (I say) wherof I made mention before & which I haue set downe in the twenty foure former Articles: It was preached (I say) to Scotland and England by the Apostles themselues in the first Age, or hundred yeares, as witnesseth Cambdenus, who sayth: (a) *Certum est Britannos in ipsa Ecclesiæ infantia Christianam religionem imbibisse*. In proofe wherof he there alleadgeth sundry ancient authorityes, auowing also that the famous monastery of *Glasterbury* was founded and erected by Ioseph of *Arimathia*, (b) who buryed Christs Body after his Passion; and addeth: *Nec est cur de hac re ambigamus*. M. Harison an English Protestant likewayes affirmeth, that (c) *Ioseph preached in Britany in the Apostles tyme, his sepulcher yet in Glastenbury & Epitaph affixed thereto, is proofe sufficient*. The same is auowed by (d) M. Godwin, & M. Iewel: (e) *The Britans* (sayth he) *being conuerted by* Ioseph of Arimathia *held that fayth at Augustines comming*, And Doctour Fulke: (f) *The Catholike Britans, with whome Christian religion had continued in succession from the Apostles tyme, would not receaue Augustine*. And agayne: (g) *The Britanes before Augustines comming continued in the fayth of Christ euen from the Apostles tyme*. And M. Fox: (h) *The Britanes after the receauing of the fayth, neuer forsooke it for any manner of false preaching, nor for torments*. Finally M. Middleton, a famous Protestand auerreth the same plainly: (i) *The religion* (sayth he) *cleerly taught in the word of God was brought hither first by* Simon Zelotes, *and* Ioseph of Arimathia, S. Paul *the Apostle &c.*

(a) *In his history of Britany p. 401. & 47.*
(b) *Matth. 27. v. 57. 58.*
(c) *In his description of Britany annexed to Holinsheds Chronicle. volum. 1. pag. 23.*
(d) *In his catalogue of Bishops.*
(e) *In his pageant of Popes.*
(f) *Against the Rhems testamēt in 2. cor. c. 12.*
(g) *In his answer to a coūterfait Catholike pag. 49.*
(h) *In his the acts & monuments, printed 1576. pag. 463.*
(i) *In his Papistomactix printed 1606. pag. 202.*

2. If then the selfesame Religion which S. Augustin found in England & Scotland was preached by the Apostles (as particularly of Scotland auoweth (k) Nicephorus, (l) Theodoretus, (m) Tertullian, (n) Origen, (o) S. Chrisostome, (p) Beda & the Protestants, before named:) it followeth of necessity, that the Religion which the

(k) *Nicepho. lib. 2. c. 4.* (l) *Theod. de cur. Græc. affect. l. 9.* (m) *Tertulli in. lib. cōt. Iudæos.* (n) *Origen. in Ezec. hom. 4.* (o) *Chysost. hom. Quòd Christus sit Deus.* (p) *Beda in hist. Eccles. passim.*

the Apostles then preached, is that selfe same religion, for which the Catholikes of Scotland, England & Ireland are now presently persecuted. Because Venerable Bede (the most famous & ancient English history-writer) maketh mention plentifully, that the religion which S. Augustin at his comming found in England & Scotland, was no other, but that which is now professed by the Roman Catholikes, to wit, *the vse of Masse, making of vowes, pilgrimages, inuocation of Saints &c.* as the history of Beda sheweth at large. Moreouer, that this selfe same Religion preached by the Apostles, by Marcus, Dionysius, & Palladius to our Nation of Scotland, by Augustin to England, by S. Patrike to Ireland, hath euer continued as publikely & only professed in al Christendome without any debatable contradiction till the comming of Luther and Caluin, is also manifest; first because no History-wryter, no not one of these three Kingdoms, or of any other Kingdome, before the comming of Luther & Caluin, do make any mention of any change of the Catholike religion in these Kingdomes for the space of 1559. yeares. Secondly the Scots & English history-wryters since Luther & Caluin (yea Protestantes) do make mention of diuers other alterations & changes, which happened either in temporall or Church affayres in these three Kingdoms, yet they make no mention at all, that for the space of 1550. yeares there was any change or mutation in Religion. Haue they not set downe in particular the fundations of many Bishops Seas, Cathedrall Churches, Colledges, Monasteries in Scotland, England and Ireland? yet they speake, no not one word, that euer there was any chãge of religion: Which is an infallible proofe & marke, that the selfe same religion which was taught to vs by the Apostles themselues hath alwaves continued to this our Age. To the wise consideration whereof, as also to the carefull reading of these two former books & parts, I earnestly exhort, & humbly request you, my deere Countrey-men, & that by the respect of your owne saluation, by your Christian zeale to the true religion, by the passion & death of Christ Iesus who suffered for vs all. And so not doubting to preuayle with you in so iust a request, so necessary a petition, & so reasonable a postulation, I will continue my dayly prayers to God for you, that it may please his heauenly maiesty to blesse you with the inward light of the true Religion, with the heauenly gift of the true Catholike Faith & profession, wherin your noble Ancestors, valiant & wise Kings raygned happily, and dyed peaceably.

The end of the second Part, or first Century.

FINIS.

THE GROVND OF THE CATHOLIKE AND ROMAN RELIGION IN THE WORD OF GOD.

With the Antiquity and Continuance therof, throughout all Kingdomes and Ages.

COLLECTED

Out of diuers Conferences, Discourses, and Disputes, which M. *Patricke Anderson* of the Society of IESVS, had at seuerall tymes, with sundry Bishops and Ministers of Scotland, at his last imprisonment in *Edenburgh*, for the Catholike Faith, in the yeares of our Lord 1620. and 1621.

Sent vnto an Honourable Personage, by the Compyler, and Prisoner himselfe.

The third Part, & second Century.

Philip. 1. Vers. 12. & 13.

And I will haue you know, Brethren, that the thinges about me, are come to the more furtherance of the Ghospell: so that my bandes were made manifest in all the Court &c.

Permissu Superiorum, Anno M. DC. XXIII.

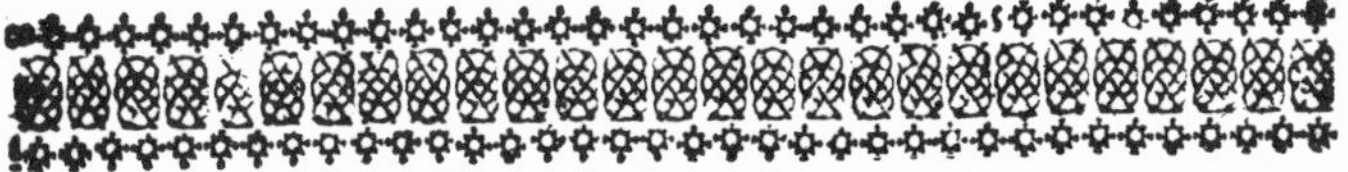

TO THE MOST HONOVRABLE AND CONSTANT CATHOLIKES in Scotland.

WHO doth not see (most dearly Beloued, Worthy and Constant CATHOLIKES) but that this third Part, or Treatise of my Works, doth chiefly, and principally belonge to you that are Cátholiks in Scotland, as hauing receaued the Catholike Religiõ vniuersally in your Country in the second Age, (or at least in the very beginning of the third Age) in the persõ of King *Donald* your first Christian King, and his Nobility, you being most worthy children of so renowned Parents, most honourable Of-spring of so excellent ancestours, most glorious posterity of so famous antiquity, whome future ages will iustly esteeme and extoll aboue many of your predecessours for retaining that in tyme of war which they left to you in tyme of peace, and for defending that by singular constancy in your sufferings, which they both receiued, & left you by quiet Traditiõ.

Which

Which Tradition, or Catholike religion being proued and declared most cleerly in this second age or century; I doe by offering the same vnto you, but present the history of your own Kings of Scotland, the records and Chronicles of your owne families, the pedigree & Genealogy of your owne Forefathers, the antiquity & Nobility of your own progenitors, together with your iust Title & Clayme to their Inheritance, producing iointly for the same the word of God, the Scripture, the Bible, the testimonies of the holy Fathers of this age, yea, the very monuments of your owne Kingdome, which no man but foolish, can deny or call in doubt.

True it is, that by Gods holy prouidence you are borne in this time of warre, tribulation and contradiction, insteed of that large peace and tranquillity which your ancestours enioyed, in the vse and exercise of that religion, for which you striue and suffer now presently in SCOTLAND; which sufferings of yours though for the present they seeme vnpleasāt & distastfull to flesh & bloud, yet assuredly will the houre come when it shall proue a most singular benefit, an eternall blisse, glory & honour in your behalfe; by reason that, (a) *You are become such followers of Christ, and of his Apostles, as receyuing the word of God with ioy of the holy Ghost in great tribulation, you are made an example or spectacle to all other faythfull people in Macedonia and Achaia, by grace of your fayth, which is published euery where throughout the world.*

(a) 1. Thes. 1.

You are of the blessed number of those to whome as the Apostle sayth, (b) *it is granted not only to belieue in God, but also to suffer for God*. Yea, I may say, to my great comfort and consolation, of you as he sayd and gloryed of himselfe, and his fellowes: *Vincula vestra manifesta*

(b) Philip. 1.

manifesta sunt in Christo in omni Pratorio : Your bands & sufferings for Christ are made notorious thoughout all the tribunall seats of Scotland, which God hath visited now of late extraordinarily, by reason of the extraordinary and barbarous proceeding of your enemyes in your behalfe (*Et inimici vestri sunt Iudices*) as your very enemies witnesse the same.

Your Countrey of Scotland hath been exceeding famous and renowned in forraine nations, by reason of antiquity & constācy of the Catholike religion, without any interruption, the space of fourteene hundred yeares, without any marke of heresy or schisme, as (besides many others history-writers) a famous forrayne writer witnesseth saying thus: *Nulla* (a) *gens è Borealibus tamdui perstitit in vnanimi Religionis vnius consensu, vt Scotia*: and by reason of this constancy in religion, Scotland was alwayes free frō the yoake and dominion of forraine Kings, saith the same writer: *Nulla* (b) *gens cujus res vel gracis vel latinis scriptis illustrata, tāto tēpore indigenas habuit reges, vt Scotia*. Your countrey was in such manner ennobled with many holy, learned & famous Bishops, who by reasō of their great zeale & charity did preach the Catholike & Roman religion in diuers forraine Natiōs, specially in Germany, where they were preferred to Ecclesiasticall and politicall dignity by *Charles* the great, and Emperour, before other nations, by reason of their *Holinesse*, *Vertue*, and *Fidelity* sayth Paulus (c) Æmilius: *Honores magistratusq; alienigenis, & imprimis Scotis, mandabat, quorum egregia fide virtuteq; vtebatur*. Your Countrey is in like manner renowned for the great number of holy Catholike Kings, Queenes, and Royall Posterity, famous to this day in diuers Kingdomes of Europe, who all

(a) *Bozius lib. 8. de sig. Eccles. cap. 1.*

(b) *Eodem loco.*

(c) *Lib. 2. de gest. Franc.*

now

now glorious in heauen receaue a particular consolation by your integrity, and constancy in the selfe same Catholike religion, which many of them sealed with their bloud, praying for your perseuerance in that most honourable course & profession.

Which offering of prayers for you, though it be cōmon to all the Saints in heauen, yet particularly that B. Queene and Martyr Q. MARY, our Princes most gracious & holy Grand-mother, doth offer vp her prayers for your perseuerance in the Catholike religion, as hauing experimēted during her mortall life your fidelity in her Seruice, against the calumnies, sedition & rebellion of the Ministers, of whome his Maiesty iustly saith; *Me persecuti sunt à iuuentute mea*.

And as it is a great honour & glory to you to haue had so many Blessed & holy Kings & Queenes, as professours of your owne religion, so it is a great honor & comfort vnto you to haue had, aboue other Christian Kingdoms, the religion for which you do suffer, confirmed & sealed, after fourteen hundred yeares continuance in Scotland, with the holy bloud of a B. Queene; of whom besides others, a forrayne Author saith thus: *Christus hoc magnum laudabilissimumq; bonum septentrioni dedit, vt Scotia haberet martyrem Reginam, Regis filiam, coniugem & Matrem*. Whose holy prayers will be the more effectuall in your behalfe, that be constant in that religion, which she confirmed by the admirable constancy of twenty years Imprisonment, and sealed with her Royal bloud. To the which end I will offer vp likewise my poore prayers to God the Father, as being,

All your most humble Seruant,

P. A.

THE SECOND AGE, OR CENTVRY.

A Table, or Catalogue of some Roman Catholikes, which shew that from the yeare of Christ 100. *vntill* 200. *the Catholike, Apostolike, and Roman Fayth and Religion did successiuely continue, without any interruption.*

CHAP. I.

The yeare of our Lord.	The chiefe Pastours of the Roman Church.	Pastours, Doctours, and Professours of the Roman Fayth.	Kings of Scotland from the yeare of Christ 100. vntill 200.
		Irenæus Bishop of	*Luctacus.* 103.
		Lions and martyr.	*Mogallus.* 136.
		Pius Pope & Mar-	*Conarus.* 148.
	Anacletus.	tyr. *Alexander* Pope	*Ethodius* 1. 162.
103.		and Martyr. *Iusti-*	*Sathrael.* 192.
		nus Philosophus &	*Donaldus* 1. *The first*
		Martyr. *Tertullian*	*Christian and Catho-*
	Euaristus.	who had written	*like King of Scotland,*
112.		before he follow-	*of whom* du Rosiers
		ed *Montanus* many	Tom. 6. stemmat.
		things Catholikly	Lothar. *sayth thus*
121.	*Alexander* 1.	A 2 *Teles-*	*Donal-*

132.	*Sixtus 1.*	*Telesphorus, Polycarpus, Origen, S. Cyprian* and many others. Likewise of	Donaldus 1. Ethodij frater Rex clementissimus, Primus Scotorum re-
142.	*Telesphorus.*	our Scottish Nation sundry holy & learned Bishops,	gum Catholicam & Romanam fidẽ professus;
154.	*Higinius.*	Priests, & Abbots as the Saints Priscus, Amphibalus,	primusque nummos aureos & argenteos, cruce ornatos in
158.	*Pius 1.*	Modocus, Calanus Ferranus, Ambianus, Marnocus, frõ whom *Kilmarnoke*	Scotia cudit. *Of the Conuersion of King* Donald *to the Catholike and Roman*
165.	*Anicetus.*	in *Cuninghame*, called by vs, Culden or *Culdis*, as wor-	*Religiõ sundry foraine Authors do witnesse; as* Baronius, Sãde-
175.	*Soter.*	shipers of the true God, *Cultores dei:* as I haue set down at	rus, Azorius, Gualterus, *& many others which I haue at large*
179.	*Eleutherus.*	large in my booke *Of the famous men of our Scottish Nation*,	*set down in the life of* S. Padie. *To be short, I omit the Kinges of*
194.	*Victor 1.*	intitled, *Menologiũ Sãctorũ regni Scotiæ.*	*England, Ireland, France, Spayne &c.*

The first and second Article.

1. *That the Catholike Romane Church, belieued the Reall Presence of Christs body in the blessed Sacrament, after the wordes of Consecration.*
2. *And that saying of Masse, was vniuersally in vse in this second Age.*

CHAP. II.

AS there is nothing that sheweth more vnto vs the infinite goodnes, the vnspeakable loue, and charity of God, then the institution of the Blessed Sacrament: so there is no mystery of our Faith which the deadly enemy of mankind, the Diuell, aymeth more to ouerthrow, by his familiar instruments the Ministers, then this most blessed, dreadfull, and admirable Sacrament. On the other side, considering with my selfe the voyd, and empty Table of the Ministers, which neyther contayneth the Body, nor Bloud of Christ, it maketh me to remember (a) *Heliogabalus* the Emperour his Table, who inuiting the Romā Princes thereunto, set painted, and artificiall dishes before them, which could neyther please their tast, nor satisfy their hungry appetites: so the Ministers in this holy Banquet, prepared by the hand of our Sauiour, doe forge and deuise figured, and metaphoricall meates, vnworthy of the goodnes of Christ, vnworthy of the Maiesty of God, and no wayes answerable to his promise made vnto vs, nor agreable to the necessities of vs his inuited guests.

(a) *Ælius Lampridius de Ant. Heliogabalo.*

2. Besides those proofes, which I vsed in the first Age or Century, I adde these other drawne out of the expresse wordes of the Bible: (b) *Iesus tooke breade, and blessing brake it, and gaue to them, and sayd, Take eate, This is my body.* Which words

(b) *Marc. 14. v. 22.* καὶ εὐλογήσας ἔκλασε. *Barach.*

wordes (though corrupted by the Ministers) are more playne in the Syriake Language, which our Sauiour spake; in the which word by word it is thus: *This truely is my body, Hithauhi pagri*, or, *Hoc est ipsum corpus meum*: where maliciously *Tremelius* hath left out the affixe *hi*, which hath a great Emphasie. S. Augustine reades these wordes, *This my bloud &c.* in the future tense thus: (c) *This is my bloud of the new Testament, which shalbe shedde for many, in remission of sinnes*. Which translation of his, is alwayes of a great force for vs Catholikes. For eyther the word *Bloud* is taken properly or figuratiuely, for the signe of his bloud. If properly, *S. Paul* is with vs; if figuratiuely, then the true bloud of Christ was not shed on the Crosse for vs, which is a horrible blasphemy. But what *Body* was giuen to the Apostles in the last supper? What bloud was shed for vs in the last supper? *The same Body* (sayth (d) S. Augustine) *in which he endured, & suffered so much.* What bloud? *The same liquor, which flowed from his pierced side.* How then can it be a figure of that liquor? And agayne S. Augustine boldly affirmeth, that, *The same victime, or holy Sacrifice, is dispensed from the Aultar, whereby the hand writing is defaced, which was contrary to vs.* How then can it be a figure? And S. Iohn Chrysostome auoweth, that the selfe same bloud was giuen to his disciples, (e) *Qui ex latere fluxit*, which issued from his side. And the selfe-same body to be in the blessed Sacrament, which was *whipped, imbrued with bloud, wounded with a speare, and which the Sunne seeing crucified, withdrew his beames.* Is it possible for the wit of man to speake more playnely? And a little after, this holy Father cōstantly auerreth that the body of Christ which is in the B. Sacrament, is the selfe same, which was adored by the *Magi*, and put in the cribbe: *Hoc corpus in præsepi reueriti sunt* Magi, *& cum timore, & tremore plurimo adorauerunt: tu verò non in præsepi, sed in Altari, non mulierem quæ in vlnis teneat, sed sacerdotem præsentem, & spiritum superabunde super proposito Sacramento diffusum vides.* And agayne: *Non Angelos, non Archangelos, non cælos, non cælos cælorum, sed ipsum horum omnium Dominum tibi ostendo: neque eum conspicaris tantùm, sed tangis, & comedis; non hominis regium puerum, sed vnigenitum Dei filium accipis.*

But

hi.

(c) *Aug. in exposit. psal. 33 & ibidem in psal. 65.*

(d) *Augu lib. 12. cōt. Faust. cap. 10. l. 3. de Trinitate cap. 10. lib. 6. Conf. c. 13.*

(e) *Hom. 24 in 1. Corinth. c. 11.*

But to take away all ambiguity, and excuse from the Ministers, S. Iohn Damascene speaketh so playnly, and countrepointe, as it were, of set purpose to the Ministers, saying thus: (f) *Christ sayd not this bread is a figure of my body, but this is my body.* The same saith (g) Theophilactus, and (h) Epiphanius.

(f) *Damasc lib. 4. de fide orthodoxa c.* 14.
(g) *in* 26 *Matth*
(h) *in Nic. Synodo* 2. *act.* 6.

3. The other place which proueth the vertue of this Catholike doctrine is the practise of the primitiue Church, which S. Paul remarketh saying: (i) *The chalice of benediction which we doe blesse, is it not the communication of the bloud of Christ? And the bread, which we breake, is it not the participation of the body of our Lord?* Which place (though corrupted by the Ministers) yet sheweth manifestly that the words *blessing*, is referred to the *chalice*, and consequently cannot be turned into *thankes-giuing*; otherwise this absurde translation would insue: *The cup of thankes-giuing, which we thankes-giue.* And commonly when the word *blessing*, is referred to vnreasonable creatures, it is taken properly, and not for *thankes-giuing*, as the blessing of bread in (k) S. Luke: yea our Sauiours blessing euer wrought some admirable effect in the thing which was blessed, which gaue occasion to S. Gregory Nissen to say, that in vertue of Christ his blessing, the (l) *Substance of bread, and wine was turned into the body, and bloud of Christ*. And S. Cyprian therefore also calleth the (m) *Chalice*, consecrated with holy *blessing*. Finally I adde this argument, which I propounded to a Minister when I was very sicke in the Tollbooth of Edenburge. *Our* Sauiour gaue that to his disciples, which was giuen for vs; but Christs true body was giuen for vs; *Ergo*, Christ gaue his true body to his disciples. The *Maior* & the *Minor* are in the Bible. As for the holy Sacrifice of the Masse, S. Luke (who wrote in the greeke tongue) maketh mention that the custome of the primitiue Church, and in the tyme of the Apostles, was to say Masse, which he calleth *Liturgia*: (n) *And as they were ministring to our Lord, and fasting, the holy Ghost sayd* &c. That is; *as they were sacrificing vnto our Lord*, as (o) Erasmus himselfe turneth: *sacrificantibus illis Domino*. Yea (p) Henricus Stephanus (though a Hugenot) affirmeth that λειτουργεῖν, in

(i) 1. *Cor.* 10. *v.* 16. τὸ ποτήριον τῆς εὐλογίας ὃ εὐλογοῦμεν.
(k) *Cap.* 9. *v.* 16.
(l) *Gregor. orat. Catech.*
(m) *Cypr. de cœna Domini.*
(n) *Act. Apost. c.* 13. *v.* 2. λειτουργούντων δὲ αὐτῶν τῷ κυρίῳ.
(o) *In hunc locum.*
(p) *In thesauro linguæ græcæ*

in the Ecclesiasticall History is taken for *offering vp Sacrifice,* which because it is a publik seruice, is called *Liturgia:* which word as it signifieth a publike seruice, so when it is applyed to sacred and holy seruice, is taken for a *Sacrifice:* yea in sundry languages the Sacrifice of the Masse, is called the *Diuine seruice,* as in French, *le Seruice Diuin,* or *le Sainct Seruice*; and in Italian, *il Diuino Seruitio.* The Syriak word signifieth the same more playnely *metthchaschpin*; & our Latin translatour turneth the same Greeke word in other places, *to Sacrifice*; as (q) *Omnis quidem Sacerdos præsto est quotidie ministrans, easdem sæpe offerens hostias.* That is, *And euery Priest appeareth dayly ministring*, where the word (r) *Ministring,* signifieth to *offer vp Sacrifice.* It is well knowne to the learned, that, that which the Latine Church calleth *Missa, Masse,* the Greeke Church calleth to this day *Liturgia*, the soueraygne worship of God; farre different from that Idoll-seruice of the Ministers of Scotland, wherin they bow down their knees before a peece of bread, giuing therby the true worship of God to a pure creature, directly agaynst the first commaundement, and directly agaynst their Oath sworne and subscribed by them in sundry Parlaments.

(q) *Heb.* 10 v. 11.

(r) λειτουργῶν.

4. The 4. place of the Bible is: (s) *He that eateth, and drinketh vnworthily, eateth and drinketh his owne damnation, because he discerneth not our Lords body.* Where the Apostle presupposeth some to take the body of Christ vnworthily. I argue then thus. To receyue the body of Christ worthily, only Fayth is sufficient, say the Ministers, *Ergo,* he who hath not Fayth, cannot receyue at all the body of Christ, neyther worthily nor vnworthily; and consequently none can receyue the body of Christ vnworthily: which is directly against the saying of S. Paul. So that the Ministers doctrine, in receauing Christs body only by Fayth, belyeth manifestly the holy Apostle, seeing that where Faith is, he is worthily receyued, where Fayth is not, he is no way receyued at all; yet the Apostle putteth as an infallible ground, some to receyue Christs body, and that vnworthily; for the which cause, sayth he, (t) *Many are weake, and sicke among you.*

(s) 1. *Corinth.* 11. v. 29.

(t) *Ver.* 30.

5. Of

5. Of the premises I inferre, that we Catholikes haue these manifest places for vs, set downe in the Bible: 1. *This is my body*. 2. *This truly is my body*. 3. *This is my bloud, which is shed for you* 4. *The bread which we breake is the participation of the body of our Lord*. 5. *As they were sacrificing vnto our Lord* (speaking of the Apostles.) 6. *He that eateth the body of Christ vnworthily &c.* I aske now that it might please the Protestants to giue me as playne, and manifest places of the Bible, which make agaynst vs Catholikes, or else to shew this poynt of their Religion in the expresse word of the Bible. 1. *We take the body of Christ by Fayth only, and not really*. 2. *This is a figure of my body*. 3. *This is a figure of my bloud.* Which the Ministers neuer being able to do, will present their dotish consequences for the word of God: but I answere with S. Augustine; That we care not what consequence, this or that Minister makes not set downe in the word of God; but make accoũt what God saith in the expres word of the Bible.

Testimonies of the holy Fathers in this second Age, concerning the Reall Presence, and holy Sacrifice of the Masse.

The first Section.

S. Alexander Pope and Martyr affirmeth the holy Body, and bloud of Christ to be in the holy Sacrifice of the Masse: (a) *In Sacramentorum quoq; oblationibus, quæ inter Missarũ solemnia Domino offeruntur, Passio Domini miscenda est, vt eius cuius corpus & sanguis conficitur, Passio celebretur.* And a little after: *There is nothing so great amongst Sacrifices, as the Body & Bloud of Christ, nor yet any oblation is to be compared with that oblation.*

2. S. Telesphorus: (b) *Nocte vero sancta Natiuitatis Domini Saluatoris Missas celebrent, & hymnum Angelicum in eis solemniter decantent, quoniam & eadem nocte ab Angelo Pastoribus nunciatus est &c. Gloria in excelsis Deo.* Which holy custome to say three Masses on Christmas day hath beene famous, and euer kept to this day in the Catholike Church, signifying therby the threefold generation of Christ: first, from all eternity, as God begotten of the Father. 2. In tyme, being borne of the Blessed Virgin Mary at midnight. 3. His generation

(a) *Alex. Pap mart. ep. 1 ad omnes orthod. extat tomo 1. Conc. & de consec dist. 2. Can. In Sacramentorum.*

(b) *Epist. ad vniuersos. Extat tom. 1. Cõcil.*

ration in euery faythfull soule by his grace, & gifts: wherof speaketh S. Paul: (c) *In Christ Iesus I haue begotten you, through the Ghospell.*

(c) 1. Cor. 4. v. 15.

3. S Higinius Martyr: (d) *Omnes Basilicæ cum Missa debent semper consecrari.*

(d) Tom. 1. Conc.

4. S. Pius Martyr: (e) *Antequam Româ exiisses, soror nostra Euprepia (si bene recordaris) Titulum domus suæ pauperibus assignauit, vbi nunc cum pauperibus nostris commorantes Missas agimus*

(e) In ep. ad Iustum Epis. vien. Extat tom. 1. Concil.

5. S. Soter Martyr commaundeth vniuersally that no Priest should say Masse except he be fasting; which custome was in the Apostles tyme. (f) *Nullus post cibum potumque, siue quodlibet minimum sumptum, Missas facere, nullusque absque patentis molestiæ prouentu Minister vel Sacerdos, cùm cœperit imperfecta officia præsumat omnino relinquere.*

(f) Extat tom 1. Concil.

6. S. Iustinus Martyr one of the most famous, learned, and holy of this age, speaketh playnely of the blessed Sacrament, and the holy Sacrifice of the Masse, saying: that euen as the Incarnation of Christ was made by the omnipotency, and power of the holy Ghost, so the changing of the breade, and wine into the body, and bloud of Christ is made by the same omnipotency: (g) *Non enim vt communem panem neque communem potum ista sumimus: sed quemadmodum per verbum Dei caro factus Iesus Christus Saluator noster, & carnem & sanguinem salutis nostræ causa habuit: Ita alimoniam per precationem verbi ab ipso profecti Eucharistizatam, ex qua sanguis, & caro nostra per mutationem aluntur, incarnati illius Iesu carnem & sanguinem esse edocti sumus.* First, he sayth that it is not *common bread*, as the Protestants bread is. 2. That the flesh, and bloud of Christ Iesus, who became man for vs, is in the blessed Sacrament. 3. And a litle before he auoweth: that after the *Masse* is sayd by the Priest in the presence of the people, the custome was that the *Deacon* distributed the blessed Sacrament to euery one present. And agayne disputing agaynst a Iew called Tryphon he affirmeth, that only Priests did offer vp the Euangelicall Sacrifice much more noble then that of the Iewes: (h) *Neque verò à quoquam Deus hostias accipit, nisi à suis Sacerdotibus. Omnes igitur qui huius nomine sacrificia offerunt*

(g) Apolog 2. ad Anto. Imper.

(h) Dialog. cum Tryphone. post medium.

ferunt quæ Iesus Christus fieri tradidit, hoc est in Eucharistia Panis & calicis, quæ in omni terræ loco à Christianis fiunt.

7. S. Irenæus Bishop of Lions in France, and disciple of S. Iohn the Euangelist: (i) *Quemadmodum qui est à terra panis percipiens vocationem Dei, iam non communis panis est, sed Eucharistia ex duabus rebus constans, terrena & calesti: sic & corpora nostra percipientia Eucharistiam, iam non sunt corruptibilia, spem resurrectionis habentia.* Conforme to the doctrine of this holy Father (who sheweth plainly what Religion was in Frãce in this Centrury, or Age) S. Augustine termeth the holy Eucharist, or Masse, (k) *a most true Sacrifice*, by which true remission of sinnes is purchased; The Sacrifice of our price, or ransome. S. Cyril of Hierusalem calleth the Masse: (l) *an holy and dreadfull Sacrifice profiting the soules of the departed.* And Tertullian to counterpoint the Protestants, calleth it a (m) Sacrifice, *which no woman can be permitted to offer.* With what conscience then can Ministers say that there is no externall Sacrifice except praiers, almes-giuing &c. which are common to men, and women.

(i) Lib. 4. cap. 34. post mediã.

(k) Augu. lib. de ciuitate Dei c. 10 & lib. 9. confes. cap. 12.

(l) Catech. 5.

(m) Tert. lib. de velandis virgin. cap. 9.

8. Tertullian an auncient, and famous writer, maketh plainly mention of the Reall Presence, and holy Sacrifice of the Masse, and of sundry other points of the Catholike Religion, especially before he fell into the errours of *Montanus* the heretike: disputing then agaynst Marcion & the Marcionistes (who with our Puritanes made great account of figures, saying that Christ became not true man, but tooke only the figure, and outward shape of man) proueth that Christ was true man and God, by reason that he left in the Blessed Sacrament, his true body and bloud. (n) *Planè* (sayth Tertullian) *de substantia Christi putant & Marcionitæ suffragari Apostolum sibi, quod phãtasma carnis fuerit in Christo, cum dicit quod in effigie Dei constitutus non rapinam existimauit pariari Deo, sed exhausit semetipsum accepta effigie serui, non veritate* (as sayd the Marcionists) *& in similitudine hominis, non in homine, & figura inuentus, non substantia, idest non carne.* Whereunto Tertullian answereth: *quasi non & figura, similitudo & effigies substantia quoq; accedunt. Bene autem quod & alibi Christũ imaginem Dei inuisibilis appellat: Nunquid ergo & hic quâ in effigie*

(n) Lib. cont. Marcio. cap. 20.

eum Dei collocat? Æquè non erit Deus Christus verè, si nec homo verè fuit in effigie hominis constitutus. Where Tertullian teacheth two sortes of figures, the one which signifieth the thing figured as absent, & not present with the figure; so Manna is called a figure of the Blessed Sacrament, the red Sea a figure of our Baptisme &c. The other sort signifieth the thing figured, and which is present with the figure, as our Sauiour is called (o) *Figura substantia Dei*, the figure of the substance of God the Father; yet the substance of God the Father was really present in Christ. In which sense, and meaning Tertullian here, and S. Augustine in some other place once calleth the B. Sacrament, the figure of Christs body, by reason of the outward shapes of bread, and wine, which in effect are a figure of Christ really there contained, but not a simple figure of a thing absent as the Ministers dreame. As Christ is said to haue taken the forme & figure of man, and yet he was, and is truly, and really man: so it is in this case; though the B. Sacrament be called a figure sometimes, though seldome, yet it is neuer called a figure of Christ absent, but of Christ present, who is signified to vs by the outward shape, and figure of bread, and wine.

(o) *Heb. 1. v. 3. Colos. 1. v. 15.*

9. The same learned, & ancient Father maketh mention that in his time & Age the custome was to offer the Sacrifice of the Masse vpon altars: (p) *Sacrificamus pro salute Imperatoris sed Deo nostro & ipsius.* And againe: (q) *De stationum diebus, non putant pleriq; sacrificiorum orationibus interueniendum, quòd statio soluenda sit accepto corpore Domini. Ergo deuotũ Deo obsequium Eucharistia resoluit, an magis Deo obligat? Nõne solemnior erit statio tua, si & ad aram Dei steteris? Accepto corpore Domini, & reseruato, vtrumq; saluum est, & participatio Sacrificij, & executio officij.*

(p) *Lib. ad Scapulam cap. 2.*
(q) *Lib. de orat. c. 14*

10. Origen a learned Father of this Age putteth the matter out of doubt, and teacheth vs of the Reall Presence, and Sacrifice of the Masse foure things; first, that, that which is receyued in the Blessed Sacrament is incorruptible, and that Christ himselfe intreth into vs: (*) *Quando sanctum cibum illudq; incorruptum accipis epulum, quando vita pane & poculo frueris, manducas & bibis corpus & sanguinem Domini, tunc Dominus sub tectum tuum ingreditur. Et tu ergo humilians temetipsum*

(*) Hom. 5. *in diuers.*

metipsum imitare hunc Centurionē & dicito, Domine non sum dignus vt intres sub tectum meum. 2. He teacheth that the bread *is chāged into the body of Christ*, which change is called, *Transubstantiation*, and that the bread is offered vp in the holy Masse before the change therof: (r) *Nos qui omnium rerum Conditori placere studemus, cum precibus, & gratiarum pro beneficijs acceptis actione oblatos panes edimus, corpus iam per precationem factos sanctum quoddam & sanctificans, vtentes eo cum sano proposito.* 3. He teacheth that the Priests which say Masse should be vnmarryed, and should vow perpetuall chastity: (s) *Certum est, quia impeditur Sacrificium indesinens ijs qui coniugalibus necessitatibus seruiunt. Vnde videtur mihi quod illius est solius offerre Sacrificium indesinens, qui indesinenti & perpetuæ se deuouerit castitati.* 4. That the Priests in saying of Masse, and the Catholikes in receauing the B. Sacrament should be very wary, that nothing of the holy Host perish, or fall to the ground: (a) *Nostis qui diuinis mysterijs interesse consuestis, quomodo cùm suscipitis corpus Domini, cum omni cautela & veneratione seruatis, ne ex eo parum quid decidat, ne consecrati muneris aliquid delabatur. Reos enim vos creditis, & rectè creditis, si quid inde per negligentiam decidit.*

(r) *Lib. 8. contra Celsum.*

(s) *Hom. 23. in Nū.*

(a) *Hom. 13 in Exod.*

11. S. Cyprian that famous, and learned Doctour of Afrike witnesseth lykewise: first, that the bread, and wine is turned into the precious body, and bloud of Christ: (b) *Panis iste communis in carnem & sanguinem mutatus, procurat vitam, & incrementū.* 2. That by the vertue of the wordes pronounced in the person, and authority of Christ, the bread is chāged into his precious body: (c) *quem Dominus discipulis porrigebat, non effigie, sed natura mutatus, omnipotentia Verbi factus est caro; & sicut in persona Christi humanitas videbatur, & latebat Diuinitas, ita Sacramento visibili ineffabiliter diuina se infudit essentia, vt esset religioni circa Sacramenta deuotio, & ad veritatem, cuius corpus & sanguis Sacramenta sint, sincerior pateret accessus, vsq; ad participationem Spiritus.* 3. That the selfe same bloudy Sacrifice, which our Sauiour offered vpon the Crosse, is offered vnbloudily by the Priest at Christs commaundement: (d) *Si Iesus Christus Dominus & Deus noster ipse est summus Sacerdos Dei Patris; & Sacrificium Patri seipsum primus obtulit, & hoc fieri in sui commemorationem præcepit; vtiq; ille Sacerdos vice Christi*

(b) *Serm. de cœna Domini.*

(c) *Eodem serm.*

(d) *Epist. 63. ad Cæcilium post medium.*

sti verè fungitur, qui id, quod Christus fecit, imitatur; & Sacrificium verum, & plenum tunc offert in Ecclesia Deo Patri, si sic incipiat offerre secundum quod ipsum Christum videat obtulisse. 4. That Priests, and Churchmen who offered the holy Sacrifice should not medle thẽselues with worldly things, as to take vpon them to be Tutors, cõdemning therin the fact of one Geminius Victor, for whome (now being departed) S. Cyprian would not suffer, by reason of that fact, the Sacrifice of the Masse to be offered: (e) *Singuli diuino Sacerdotio honorati, & in Clerici ministerio constituti, non nisi Altari & Sacrificijs deseruire, & precibus atque orationibus vacare debent. Scriptum est enim, Nemo militans Deo implicat se molestijs secularibus, vt possit placere ei qui se probauit. Quod Episcopi antecessores nostri religiosè considerantes, censuerunt nequis frater excedens, ad tutelam & curam clericum nominaret; ac si quis hoc fecisset non offerretur pro eo, nec Sacrificiũ pro dormitione eius celebraretur: neq; enim apud altare Dei meretur nominari in Sacerdotum prece, qui ab altari Sacerdotes & Ministros voluit auocare.*

(e) *Epist. ad Clerum & plebem.*

That Ministers haue falsified the Bible in sundry places, which proue the Reall Presence, and holy Sacrifice of the Masse.

The Second Section.

THe holy Scripture maketh mention that Melchisedech King and Priest was a figure of our Sauiour Christ Iesus: (a) *Thou art a Priest for euer according to the order of Melchisedech.* For as Melchisedech was Priest, and King, so was our Sauiour; as Melchisedech offered vp Sacrifice in bread and wine, and then presented both to Abraham, so our Sauiour offered vp a Sacrifice of his body, and bloud vnder the formes of bread, and wine sayth Eusebius: (b) *Euen as he, who was Priest of Nations was neuer seene to offer corporall Sacrifice, but only bread, and wine, when he blessed Abraham: so first our Lord, and Sauiour himselfe, then Priests that came from him, exercising the spiritual office of Priesthood in all nations, after the Ecclesiasticall ordinances, do present the misteries of his body, & healthfull bloud in bread and wyne.* As the Bible it selfe witnesseth in playne

(a) *Psal. 110. v. 4.*

(b) *Euseb. lib. 5. demonst. Euang. c. 3.*

playne termes: (c) *Melchisedech King of Salem, bringing forth bread and wyne, for he was the Priest of God most high, blessed him and sayd &c.* Signifying, that because he was a Priest he offered vp bread, and wine: *for he was the Priest of God.* The Ministers to shew that he offred vp no Sacrifice, do translate agaynst the Hebrew, Chaldean, and Greeke copies thus: *Melchisedech King of Salem brought forth breade, and wyne: & he was a Priest*, not signifying that he offered vp any Sacrifice, though the Hebrew word, (d) *Hotsi, brought forth*, is a word pertayning to sacrifice, and importeth that the bread, and wine was first *offered in Sacrifice*, and then presented to Abraham: and the wordes, *for he was a Priest*, can haue no other sense, but that he did the office of a Priest in offering vp the bread, and wine: and the Greeke word, δὲ, signifieth the cause wherefore he offered; and the Hebrew particle, *ve*, sundry tymes signifieth *causam*, as, (e) *Thou art but dead for the womans sake, which thou hast taken: for she is a mans wife*: according to the Ministers own translation, who here haue translated faythfully this same Hebrew word *ve*, into *for*; though aboue they translated it into *and*, only to fauour their heresy. I demaund of the Ministers; if Christ fulfilled not Melchisedechs figuratiue Sacrifice offered in bread, & wine, in offering vp his owne body, and bloud in his last supper; what other figuratiue Sacrifice of Melchisedech can they find performed by Christ? And when performed he such a Sacrifice? It is not in their power to name any other. 2. Why do the Ministers translate here, *Therefore he blessed him, saying, Blessed art thou Abraham*? Why translate they not the word, *blessing*, into thankes-giuing, as they do in (f) S. Matthew; for they say to *blesse*, and to *giue thankes* is all one: so that Melchisedech in blessing Abraham, gaue thankes to Abraham: can there be greater absurdities imagined?

(c) *Gen.* c. 14. v. 18. *Erat enim Sacerdos Altissimi.*

(d) *Iud.* c. 6. v. 18. 19.

(e) *Gen.* c. 20. v. 4.

(f) *Matth.* c. 26. v. 26.

2. For the better vnderstanding of the second corruption it is to be remarked: that our Sauiour Christ Iesus, as man, was blessed in the first instant of conception; in such sort that his blessed soule was glorified, & saw God *intuitiuè*, face to face euen as now he seeth him in heauen: which is the reason wherefore Christ was on earth both *viator*, and *comprehen-*

comprehensor: & wherefore also Christ being on earth could not walk by Faith: because his blessed soule seeing on earth all things in God, as now he seeth, could not know things by Fayth, which is a great imperfection in respect of the blessed soules in heauen, who haue charity, but not hope or Fayth, as (g) S. Paul teacheth playnly: seeing then our Sauiour had not *Diuine Fayth* in this world, he could not receyue the Sacrament *by Fayth* only, as the Ministers teach, but really, as we say. Now, to signify that our Sauiour receyued not the B. Sacrament neyther by Fayth, nor really, the Hugenots in France haue corrupted that of S. Luke. *Adonc il leur dit*, (h) *I'ay grandement desiré de manger cet Agneau de Pasque auec vous deuant que ie souffre*: Where they haue ioyned to the text the word, *Agneau*, a *Lambe*, which is not in the Greeke; to signify that our Sauiour speaketh not of the last supper, wherein he gaue his precious body, and bloud to his disciples, and to himselfe, as witnesseth the holy Father S. Chrysostome: *Christ drunke his owne bloud, to the end that the Apostles should not be amazed, astonished, and troubled: He did that then himselfe the first, to induce his Apostles to the communication of those holy mysteries, for that cause he drūke his owne bloud*: διὰ τοῦτο καὶ αὐτὸς ἔπιεν αἷμα αὐτοῦ. The same sayth Tertulliā explicating those words: *desiderio desideraui hoc Pascha mãducare vobiscum*: where he saith: (k) *Professus se concupiscentia concupiuisse edere Pascha vt suum; Indignum enim erat quod alienum concupisceret Deus; acceptum panē corpus suum fecit.* And S. Hierome: (l) *nec Moyses dedit nobis panē verum, sed Dominus Iesus ipse conuiua & conuiuiū, ipse comedens & qui comeditur.* (m) Finally S. Augustin is of the same opinion, & it carryeth reason, because our Sauiour sayd; *I haue earnestly desired to eate this Pasch with you before I suffer*; which cannot be vnderstood of the Paschall Lambe, which seuerall tymes he had eaten before with his Apostles. 2. The 14. verse of this same chapter, *And when the houre was come, he sate downe, and the twelue Apostles with him*, sheweth manifestly that those foresayd wordes cannot be referred to the eating of the Paschall Lamb, which behooued to be eaten standing, and not sitting, as witnesseth the 12. of *Exodus* v. 11. as Caluin himselfe auoweth in the 26. of S. *Matthew* v. 20.

(g) 1. Cor. c. 13. v. 13

(h) Cap. 22 v. 15.

Chrysost. Hom. 83. in cap. 26. Matth.

(k) Lib. 4. contra Marcion.

(l) Epist. ad Hedibiam quæst. 2.

(m) in psal. 33.

2o. True is, that some heady Minister would thinke this to be absurd, of whome I would learne, how can he conceiue the selfe same diuine nature, *numero*, to be in three persons distinct really? The one is as hard to be conceyued as the other, yet both must be belieued. Is not the selfe same voice of the Minister, when he preacheth in his owne eare, and in the eare of all those that are in the Church? Wherefore may not the body of Christ be in sundry places together miraculously, seeing the voice of man is in sūdry places naturally, and seing vnto God there is nothing impossible?

3. Now because the Ministers of France auowe that Christ is receyued in the Sacrament onely by Fayth, and since Christ had not diuine Fayth, they corrupt the Bible, by adding vnto it the word *Lambe*, to signify thereby, that those wordes, *I earnestly desired to eate this Pasche*, should be referred to the typicall supper, and not to the mysticall & last supper, wherein he gaue his precious body the night before he suffered; the English Bible doth insinuate the same corruption of the French Bibles, in turning, *I haue earnestly desired to eate this passeouer*, meaning therby the eating of the Paschall Lambe.

4. The third corruption is in the 7. psal. (n) *There shal be an handfull of corne in the earth, euen in the top of mountaynes, & the fruite thereof shall be extolled farre aboue Libanus.* Where the Prophet foretelleth that the Sacrifice of the Masse offred in the formes of bread made of corne, shal be aboue the tops of Mountaynes aboue Libanus, that is, as R. Ionathas expoūdeth: *& erit Sacrificium panis in capite montium Ecclesiæ.* Which prophecy, to deface and disgrace it, the Ministers turne thus: *The fruite thereof shall shake lyke the trees of Libanus.* Doth not the Greeke worde playnely signify *to be extolled*? doth not the Chaldean parap. *Iehi Sabir Lathama, erit substantificus panis*, plainely witnes that the Prophet vnderstandeth the holy bread of the B. Sacrament, which is called *substantificall bread*, by reason that one substance is turned into another? Doth not Rabby (o) Salomon expoūd this of the B. Sacrament, *Ieh pißath bar*, id est, *erit placenta frumenti*, signifying that the bread vsed in the holy Sacrifice, should not be ba-

(n) *Psalm.* 71. v. 16. *alias Psal.* 72. v. 16.

ὑπεραρθήσεται.

(o) *In hunc psalmum.*

 ked

ked in the ouen as prophane bread is, but otherwise: so it is sayd that Christ *brake* the bread, and not *cut it*, because that bread was made after the forme of *wafers*, and not of *loaues*. Doe not the Rabbins expound those wordes of Deutronomy (p) *Missath Nidbath* (where the very word *Missa*, Masse, by reason that it is a voluntary Sacrifice is as it were named) witnes, that in the dayes of the Messias, and in the law of grace there shall be *perpetuum Sacrificium carnis pane inuolutum*, that is, a perpetuall Sacrifice of flesh couered with bread, by reason that the blessed body of Christ is vnder the shapes of bread in the Blessed Sacrament?

(p) Cap. 16. v. 10.

5. The fourth corruption is in S. Marke: (q) and Iesus tooke bread, and blessing brake, & *gaue it to them*. Where the Ministers haue scraped out the word, *blessing* or *blessed*: *And Iesus tooke the bread, and when he had giuen thankes*. If to *blesse*, and *giue thankes* be all one, when the word blessing is referred to creatures, why doe they translate thus: *And without all contradiction the lesser is blessed of the greater?* Were it not more conforme to their sophisticall fashion of translating to say: *And without all contradiction the lesse is thanked of the greater?*

(q) Mark. cap. 14. v. 22.

Heb. 7. v. 7

The 3. 4. and 5. Article.

1. *That holy Images. 2. The signe of the holy Crosse. 3. Holy Reliques were with reuerence in vse among the Catholikes in the second Age.*

CHAP. III.

I Did teach before in the first Age speaking of the Inuocation of Saints, that the holy Scripture maketh mention of three sorts of worshippe, the first due to God only, which is called *adoration*, or *diuine worship*; the second is an inferiour *Religious worship* which is due to the holy Saints in heauen, or holy persons on earth, as also to

their

their holy Reliques, as hauing bene, or being actually in this world the temples of the holy Ghost. This Religious worship was giuen by King Saul to the soule of Samuel: (a) *And Saul vnderstood that it was Samuel, and he bowed himselfe vpon his face on the earth, and adored.* Which place (though corrupted by the Ministers in leauing out the word *adored*) proueth manifestly first, that the worship giuen to the soule of Samuel was not *diuine*, nor yet *ciuill*, Samuel being dead; then it must needs haue *beene religious*. That it was the true soule of Samuell which appeared, S. Augustin witnesseth: (b) *Samuell the Prophet being dead, fortold future things to Kinge Saul yet liuing.* Yea the Scripture it selfe witnesseth the same speaking to the prayse of Samuel: (c) *He slept, and certified the King, and shewed to him the end of his life.* The same is euident by the *religious* honour giuen to the Propet Elias yet aliue by Abdias the chiefe gouernour of the house of Kinge Achab: (d) *And when Abdias was in the way, Elias met him; who when he knew him, fell on his face, and sayd, my Lord art not thou Elias?* This worship of Abdias could not be ciuill, for it were ridiculous to say that so great a Prince should ciuilly worship Elias, farre inferiour in ciuill dignity to Abdias. Likewise Nabuchodonosor adored Daniel, that is, worshipped Daniel religiously; for to say that so great a King should prostrate himself at the feete of his captiue Daniel in respect of his ciuill and secular dignity, were very ridiculous. It was then an holy and *religious* worship, which for the holynes, and sanctity of the lyues of Elias and Daniel, for the excellency of their supernaturall giftes was iustly exhibited vnto them. As Iosue worshipped the Angell not with *a diuine worship*, for he knew him to be an Angell only, not of *a ciuill*, for such is giuen only to ciuill and mortall persons; it followeth then, with *a religious* worship, which the Angell likewise commaunded Iosue to giue to the earth it selfe where he was, in putting of his shoes. This worship of the earth of Iericoa prophane field could not be *ciuill* but rather *religious* in regard of the Angell, for which it challenged righteously a holy, reuerent, and religious honour.

(a) 1. Sam. cap. 28. v. 14.

(b) *Aug. de cura pro mortuis c.* 15.

(c) Eccles. cap. 46.

(d) 1. Reg. cap. 18. v. 7.

Daniel. 2.

Iosue 5.

2. The Arke of the Testament was in such honour among

mong the Iewes that Dauid commaunded them *to adore* it, (for the word *Adore*, is sundry tymes taken in the Scripture for a religious worship) and the Bethsamites curiously beholding the Arke were slayn by God to the nũber of 5000. men. Would God (who is goodnes it selfe) haue so seuerely punished with death such a great number of men' for a meere act of discourtesy, or inciuility? It is folly to thinke, and blasphemy to say it. Wherof I inferre, that the holy Reliques, and Monuments of Saints, may be lawfully worshipped with *religious honour*, or reuerence, without any derogation of *Diuine honour* due to God only. As witnesseth plentifully the auncient and holy Father S. Basil: (a) *The Church by honouring them that are departed, encourageth such as are present.* And S. Gregory playnly witnesseth, that the honour giuen to the holy Martyr S. Theodore is aboue ciuill honour: (b) *To what King is such honour exhibited? What Emperour hath euer bene so famous, and renowned as this poore champion?* S. Paul witnesseth, that *Glory and Honour are due to euery one that doth well.* The Saints in heauen then hauing accomplished so many vertuous acts should be honoured. If to holynes of life honour be due, superiour vnto ciuill as to perfection of supernaturall dignity, the Saints in heauen are so perfectly holy that they are admitted in the company of the *Holy of holyes.* If to wisdom honour be due, they are so wise now in heauen, as they are wise in an higher degree of wisdome, for they see in God whatsoeuer they can wish or desire. If to nobility honour be due, they are enobled to be the children of God, and the inheritours of the kingdome of heauen. If to soueraygne dignity honour be due, they sit with God in that heauenly throne, and haue power ouer nations, and so they are to participate of his honour in an higher degree, as they participate in higher degree of his power and glory. And if the Saints in heauen should be thus honoured, shall not their holy tombes and Reliques be honoured?

(a) *Basil. Hom. de martyr.*

(b) De *Theodoro. Martyre.*

3. I desire to know of the Ministry of Scotland, what honour they giue to the Sacrament of the Lords supper receyued by kneelinge? The Scottish Clergy of the last

Par-

Parlament answereth: (c) *Considering withall that there is no part of diuine worship more heauenly, and spirituall then is the holy receyuing of the blessed body, and bloud of our Lord, and Sauiour Iesu-Christ &c.* Then diuine honour which is onely due to God, is giuen to that action of the receyuing of the supper; which in them is manifest Idolatry, as I proue thus: When diuine honour is giuen to a Creature it is manifest Idolatry, but the action of the receiuing of the Lords supper is a meere Creature. *Ergo*, it is meere Idolatry to giue a diuine honour thereunto. Is not this intollerable ignorance in the clergy, which was present at the Parlament to say, sweare, and subscribe, that *there is no part of diuine worship more heauenly then is the holy receyuing*? Is it not a greater act of heauely worship to adore immediatly God himself, then the figure therof? how can the holy receyuing be diuine honour? How can a creature (as your action of receyuing is) be diuine honour? Diuine honour may be giuen by a creature to God, but that this your outward action of kneeling (which very often is indifferent to diuine, religious, & ciuill honour) in it selfe be diuine honour, is palpable Idolatry, & intollerable ignorance. 2. Eyther the action of kneeling is referred to the bread in the Lords supper, or els to Christ his body in heauen? If to the first, eyther that worship giuen by kneeling is diuine, Ciuil, or Religious. Diuine it cannot be without manifest Idolatry, as I sayd before. Not Ciuill; for what is that, but to prostrate your selues ignorantly to dead, and sensles creatures of bread, and wine, which in that respect haue no preheminence aboue man, who is a reasonable creature of God? If you say that there is some supernatural quality in the bread, & wine, wherũto you prostrate your selues, I aske: either you giue diuine, ciuil, or religious worship to the bread considered with this quality or not? If *Diuine*, conforme to the wordes of the Parlamẽt, it is manifest Idolatry, for this quality though supernaturall, is a creature, and not God? If Ciuill, then you giue Ciuill, worldly, and transitory honour, to a supernaturall thing, which is absurd, and a manifest sacriledge. If yee exhibite religious honour, acknowledge then the same, and remaine not

(c) *In the last Parlament at Edenb the 4 of Aug. 1621. N. 1.*

not still in your palpable ignorance. If this action of kneeling be referred to Christ in heauen, thē yee must acknowledge a horrible blasphemy to be committed in the foresaid words, that *Diuine worship win the receyuing &c.* And since the bread of the Lords supper is a figure, and Image of Christs body (say yow) what is this but to kneele to Images, and before Images, in kneeling before the bread, and wine of the Lords supper? what is sacriledge if this be Religion? What is impiety if this be not, in making the poore people to commit manifest idolatry, at this your Idol-seruice of the Lords supper?

4. Finally the care, which S. Michael the Archangel had to preserue the dead body of *Moyses* from iniury, and dishonour, which the Deuill was to do therunto, proueth manifestly the religious honour due to the body of *Moyses*, as to a holy Relique, and temple of the holy Ghost; the words are: (d) *Yet Michael the Archangel, when he stroue agaynst the deuill, and disputed about the body of Moyses, durst not blame him with cursed speaking, but sayd: The Lord rebuke thee.* Likewise the shadow of S. Peter, much more S. Peters owne person, was an instrument, and holy Relique, whereby God wrought many miracles, as witnesseth the Bible: (e) *So that they did bring forth the sicke into the streetes, and layd them in beds, and couches, that as Peter came his shadow at the least might ouershadow any of them, and they might be deliuered from their infirmities.* Out of the which place S. Augustine proueth both the honour due to Reliques, and S. Peters intercession after his death for vs: (f) *If* (sayth S. Augustin) *the shadow of his body could help, how much more now the fulnes of his power? And if thē a certayne litle wind of him passing by did perfect them that humbly asked, how much more the grace of him now permanent and remayning?* The Scripture also witnesseth the religious honour, which was giuen to S. Pauls napkins by the Catholikes in his tyme. *And God wrought by the hand of Paul miracles not common; so that there were also brought from his body napkins, or handkerchers & laid vpon the sicke, and the diseases departed from them, & the wicked spirits went out.* Which place proueth playnly, as witnesseth (g) *S. Chrysostome*, the honour due to Reliques, by reason

(d) *Iud. c. 1. v. 9.*

(e) *Act. c. 5. v. 15.*

(f) *Ser. 29. de Sanctis.*

Lib. quod Christus sit Deus tom. 1. cōt. Gent.

reason of the infinite miracles, which God worketh dayly, when it pleaseth him, by them, as sundry other most auncient, and holy Fathers witnes. S. Hierome of the miracles of S. Paul the Eremite, and of S. Hylarion: of the miracles of S. Martin, Seuerus Sulpitius: S. Chrysostome in a whole booke to this purpose against the Gentiles, & infidels, who denyed impiously the honour due to Reliques, as our Protestants do: S. Augustine in his bookes *de Ciuitate Dei*, and sundry others, who all did constantly belieue, and say with S. Hierome: (h) *We reuerence, and worship euery where Martyrs sepulchers, and putting the holy ashes to our eyes, and if we may we touch it with our mouth also.* But our Protestāts rather will follow Iulianus the Apostata, and sundry infidels sworne enemies to the holy Reliques of Saints, then the holy Doctours, and Fathers of the Church of God, who are grounded vpon the expresse word of the Bible. Doth not the Ministers Bible (though corrupted) specify in expresse words a miracle wrought by the dead body of Elisæus the Prophet: (i) *So Elisæus died, and they buried him, and certayne bands of the Moabites came into the land that yeare; and as they were burying a man, behold, they saw the souldiers; therefore they cast the man into the sepulcher of Elisæus, & when the man was downe, and touched the bones of Elisæus, he reuiued, and stood vpon his feete.*

(h) *Hiero. ep. 27. c. 5.*

(i) 2. *Reg.* c. 13. v. 20. 21.

5. In the which doctrine it is to be remarked, that we Catholikes belieue not with *Diuine Fayth* euery miracle wrought by God at the holy Reliques, and monuments of Saints, as the Ministers impiously seduce, and teach the simple people; but only we affirme with the Scripture, & holy Fathers, that honour is due to Reliques; and that to misbelieue those miracles, which the holy Church hath confirmed, and auowed, which so many, and diuers nations haue piously, and wisely acknowledged these sixtene hundred yeares, is manifest madnes, and impiety. To conclude then, I aske of the Ministery to giue me as playne places out of their owne Bible, as manifest words, and formall texts, *against the honour due to Reliques, & miracles wrought by them,* as I haue produced to the contrary; which they

not

not being able to doe, must needs in place of the expresse word of the Bible, giue vs their consequences, that is their ministeriall inuentions, traditions, yea abominable superstitions, whereunto the holy doctrine of the Fathers of this second age or Century, and their consequences, and expositions should be preferred by any wise, yea indifferent man.

Testimonies of the Fathers, that holy Images, the signe of the Holy Crosse, and holy Reliques, were in vse with reuerence amongst the Catholikes of this second Age.

The first Section.

S. Pius an holy and famous Martyr, ordayned that whosoeuer should foreswere himselfe vpon an hallowed Crosse (for the custome was then, as now, to sweare by the holy Crosse) should do penance three yeares, and who vpon any other vnhallowed Crosse, should do penance one yeare: (a) *Qui peierat se in manu Episcopi, aut in cruce consecrata, tres annos pœniteat: si verò in cruce non consecrata, annum vnum pœniteat.* And writing to Iustus Bishop of Vienne in France, commaundeth him to be carefull that the holy Relikes of Martyrs (by reason they were the temples & members of God) be honoured: (b) *Cura autem Sanctorum Martyrum corpora, sicut membra Dei, quemadmodum curauerunt Apostoli Stephanum.* Conforme to the which receyued doctrine S. Hierome auoweth, that in his tyme the reuerence, & worship of holy Reliques, was the vniuersall doctrine, *non vnius vrbis, sed totius orbis.*

Extat tom. 1. Concil.

(b) *Pius Pont. ep. 2. ad Iustũ Extat in Biblioth. Pat. tom. 1. & apud Bar. ad an. 166. n. 3.*

(c) *Contra Vigilant.*

2. S. Iustine Martyr, who being famous among the Gentiles for the quicknes of his wit, his learning, his noble extraction, and pedegry, became afterward Catholike, and wrote diuers Apologies for the Catholikes: he then writing agaynst the Gentiles proueth, that the holy tombes and Reliques of the Martyrs worke Miracles: (d) *Quomodo non absurdissimum est hac quidem mutilia habere, ob vtilitatem, quae ex eis capitur?* he meaneth that the Gentiles thought some

(d) *Ad quæst. 28. Gentil.*

some beasts, as fowles, and such, to be cleanly by reason of the vtility they had of them: *Græcos autem detestari Sanctorũ Martyrum corpora, atq; sepulchra, quæ vim habent & tuendi homines à dæmonum insidijs, & curandi morbos qui medicorum arte curari nequeunt?* And a little after this holy Father giueth the reason, wherfore the chiefe Aultars of the Catholike Churches are builded towards the East, and wherefore the Catholiks consequẽtly pray their faces being towards the East. Which doctrine is conforme to that of S. Chrysostome, who writing concerning the holy Relikes of Iuuentius, and Maximus sayth: (c) *Let vs often visite them, let vs adorne their tombes, let vs touch their Reliques with a strong Fayth, that we may receyue some blessing from thence.* And S. Basil. (f) *He who handleth the bones of a Martyr, draweth a certayne touch of sanctification from the grace resident in the body.* S. Ambrose answering to this obiection which the Protestãts make with the infidels against vs: (g) *What dost thou honour in resolued, and decayed flesh? I honour* (sayth he) *in the flesh of the Martyr the wounds or Markes receyued for Christ: I honour the memory of the lyuing by perpetuity of vertue; I honour ashes sacred by the confession of our Lord; I honour in the ashes seeds of eternity; I honour the body, which instructeth me to loue our Lord, which hath taught me for his sake not to be daunted with the horrour of death. And why should not the faythfull worship that body which the very deuills do reuerence?* Could this holy Father chalenge more playnly the impiety of the Protestants, the Antichristian doctrine of the Ministry?

(c) *Chryso. serm. de SS. Iuuent. & Max.*

(f) *Basil. in psal. 115.*

(g) *Ambr. serm. 9. de SS. Naz. & Celso.*

3. Tertullian playnly, and plentifully maketh mention of the custome among the Catholikes to make the signe of the Crosse going out of their houses, going to their worldly busines, at their in-coming, at the table, at diuers exercises, at going to bed, and sundry other occasions: (h) *Ad omnem progressum atq; promotum, ad omnem aditum & exitum, ad vestitum & calceatum, ad lauacra, ad mensas, ad lumina, ad cubilia, ad sedilia, quacumq; nos conuersatio exercet, frontem crucis signaculo terimus. Harum & aliarum eiusmodi disciplinarum si legem expostules Scripturarum, nullam inuenies. Traditio tibi prætendetur auctrix, consuetudo confirmatrix, & fides obseruatrix.* And againe he auoweth, that the Catholikes in his tyme and before

(h) *Lib de coron. mil. c. 3.*

(i) *Apol. c. 6.*

before were called (i) *Crucis religiosos*, that is, Deuotes, or religious worshipers of the holy Crosse. Writing likewise to his wife he testified, that the Catholiks vsed the holy custom, (k) *Repandi in carcerem ad osculanda vincula*, that is: to crepe to the prison, where the holy Martirs were, to kisse their bōds: like to that of S. Hierome, speaking of the wood of the Crosse of our Sauiour: (l) *Will that day once come when it shal be lawfull for vs to enter into our Sauiours denne? and to licke the wood of the Crosse.*

(k) Lib. ad Vxorem n. 26.

(l) Lib. 2. ep. fam. ep. 8.

4. Of the vse of Images Tertullian likewise maketh mention in his booke (m) *De pudicitia*, teaching that the custome was, in his tyme, to engraue or paint vpon the holy chalices, and else where, the picture of our Sauiour carrying a sheepe on his shoulders, conforme to that of the Bible: (n) *And when he had found it, he layeth it on his shoulders with ioy.* Finally he maketh mention of annuall Masses, & oblations offered vp for the faythfull departed, and on the daies wherin the Martyrs shed their bloud for Christ, praysing therby God for their constancy: (o) *Oblationes* (sayth he) *pro defunctis, pro natalitijs annua die facimus.* It is true, that Tertullian a most famous, and learned writer of this age had sundry erroneous opinions, wherof he is accused by the holy Fathers of the ensuing Ages, which errors of his cā no way be preiudicious to the Catholike doctrine, and opinions, which he teacheth to haue beene vniuersally belieued in his tyme and age, and wherof no auncient Father accuseth him as of erroneous doctrine; accusing him neuertheles of sundry particular errours, which as then, so now are agaynst the doctrine of the Catholike Church, whereunto if he submitted his iudgement (as other holy Fathers haue done) in all his bookes, and writings, such doctrine may be called erroneous, though not hereticall.

(m) Lib. de Pudicit. c. 7.

(n) Luke c. 15. v. 5.

(o) Lib. de coron. mil. c. 4. n. 26.

5. Let vs ioyne *Origen* to the foresayd Fathers, who witnesseth, that the deuills feare nothing more, then the signe of the Crosse, knowing well to haue bene vanquished, and ouercome by the holy Crosse. His wordes are: (a) *Quid timent Dæmones? Quid tremunt? sine dubio crucem Christi, in qua triumphati sunt, in qua exuti sunt principatu eorum & potestate.*

(a) Hom. 6 in Exod.

Ti-

Timor ergo & tremor cadent super eos, cùm signum in nobis viderint Crucis fideliter fixũ. 2. (b) He teacheth that the Crosse deuoutly beheld, hath a great force agaynst temptations. (c) That the custom was among the Catholiks before, & in his time to make the signe of the Crosse vpon their forhead. Finally that the holy Crosse was euer in great honour among the Catholikes, (d) *Gaudentes leuemus hoc signum in humeris nostris victoriarum vexilla portemus: Immortale lauacrum portemus in frontibus nostris: cùm dæmones viderint contremiscent. Qui aurata capitolia non timent, crucem timent &c. Exultemus itaq; fratres charissimi, & ad Crucis similitudinem sanctas in cælum leuemus manus: cùm sic nos dæmones armatos viderint, opprimentur.*

(b) *Lib.* 6. *in ep. ad Rom.*

(c) *Hom.* 2 *in psal.* 38.

(d) Hom. 8. *in diuers. Euang. loc.*

6. S. Cyprian is plentifull euery where in this matter especially in his booke *de vnitate Ecclesiæ*, and else where: his words be: (e) *Quòd in hoc dicit Dominus, Transi mediam Ierusalem, & notabis signum super frontes virorum, qui ingemunt, & mærent ob iniquitates, quæ sunt in medio eorum &c.* And agayne, he doth insinuate the custom to mak the signe of the Crosse vpon our forhead: (f) *Frons cum signo Dei pura, Diaboli coronam ferre nõ potuit, coronæ se Domini reseruauit.* Finally cõparing the circũcision of the old law with the signe of the Crosse vsed in the new law, saith, that circumcision was not a remedy instituted for all (as for women) but the signe of the Crosse was instituted for all both for men, and women: (g) *Illud signaculũ feminis non profecit: signo autem Domini omnes signantur.* He auoweth likewise that Moyses holding his hands and armes (making therby the forme of a Crosse) did ouerthrow Amalech: (h) *Hoc signo Crucis & Amalech victus est ab Iesu per Moysem*: which victory the Bible witnesseth: (i) *And when Moyses held vp his hands, Israel preuayled: but when he let his hands downe, Amalech preuayled.* I omit sundry other testimonies of the Fathers of this Age or Century, to be short.

(e) *Lib.* 2. *cont. Iudæos c.* 22

(f) *Serm. de lapsis.*

(g) *Lib.* 1. *contra Iud. cap.* 8.

(h) *Lib.* 2. *cont. Iud. cap.* 22.

(i) *Exod. c.* 17. *v.* 11.

That

That the Ministers haue corrupted the Bible in sundry places, to make Images odious to the people &c.

The second Section.

THe Ministers by their corrupted Bible shew plentifully that they will euer take Antichrists part in denying the honour, and worship due to the Saints in heauen, the true friends of Christ; for the which cause they deny their merites, their good workes, their Reliques, their Images agaynst their owne Bible, which witnesseth that the Saints in heauen (as hauing bene, and being actually the speciall seruants and friends of God) should be honoured, & had in perpetuall memory: (a) *The iust shalbe in eternall memory*, saith Dauid. Agayne, (b) *The memory of the iust shalbe blessed*. To this end then they haue corrupted sundry places of the Bible, to make the Images of the Saints odious, as that of the Acts of the Apostles: (c) *Then the Towne-Clerke, when he had stayed the people, sayd: Yee men of Ephesus, what man is it that knoweth not, how that the City of the Ephesians is a worshipper of the great Goddesse Diana, and of the Image which came downe from Iupiter?* Where the Ministers impiously, and maliciously haue put in the word *Image* which is neyther in the Greeke, nor in the Latin, to discredit therby the vse of holy Images. This forme of proceeding of the Ministers, in adding vnto the text, as it is most abominable before God, so in due tyme it will be punished with eternall damnation, conforme to that of their owne Bible: (d) *If any man shall adde vnto these things, God shall ad vnto him the plagues that are written in this booke*. S. Augustin was farre different in Religion frō the Protestants, who witnesseth that in his tyme the custome was to see at Rome the *Images of S. Peter, and S. Paul* paynted and ioyned together with the Image of Christ: (e) *Credo quod pluribus locis simul eos cum illo pictos viderunt, quia merita Petri, & Pauli etiam propter eundem passionis diem celebriùs, & solemniter Roma commendat*. Declaring therby, that the Saints in heauen are honoured

(a) *Psalm.* 3. v. 7.
(b) *Psal.* 10 v. 7.
(c) Act. c. 19. v. 35. *Quis nesciat Ephesiorum Ciuitatem, cultricem esse magnæ Dianæ Iouisque prolis.* τῆς μεγάλης θεᾶς ἀρτέμιδος καὶ τοῦ διοπετοῦς.
(d) *Reuel.* cap. vlt. v. 18.
(e) *Aug.* lib. 1. de consens. Euang. c. 10.

red in their Images; yea those holy Apostles Peter, and Paul, the Patrons of Rome are there more honoured then euer Romulus the builder of Rome, sayth the same holy Doctour: (f) *Shew me I pray you any Temple of Romulus of such honour at Rome, as I shall there shew the memory of Peter: who is honoured in Peter but Christ, who dyed for all?* (f) Tom. 9. ep. 44.

2. The second corruption is in that place of S. Paul: (g) *And what agreement hath the Temple of God with Idols?* Which place at the first casting down of the Churches in Scotland by the Lords of the Congregation was turned otherwise: (h) *And what agreement hath the temple of God with Images?* If the Ministers had any conscience, any feeling of God, any desire to teach the truth, any zeale to saue soules, and not to blind them lewdly; they would willingly learne, what difference is betweene Images, and Idols of S. Augustine that auncient holy Father, who sayth: (i) *Ipsa simulacra quæ græcè appellantur εἴδωλα, quo nomine iam vtimur pro Latino, oculos habent & non vident, & cætera quæ de his ideo dicuntur, quia omni sensu carent.* If any man would say to my Lord Bishop of S. Andrews: My Lord, you are created to the Idoll of God, and you must ayme to perfit this Idoll of God in you, and to haue a particular care of your children, which are your Idols, insteed of saying: You are created to the Image of God &c. Would not such a man be thought foolish, & doltish? Let vs speake more playnly. Idols, and Images are all one say the Protestants; but the Protestants giue honour to the Kings Images, at the least ciuill honour, *Ergo* the Protestants are Idolaters, seing that no sort of honour can be giuen to Idols: Agayne, euery King in his Kingdome is an Image of God, that is, an Idoll of God, *Ergo*, the Protestants in that they worship, and serue the King, worship and serue Idols: can there be greater absurdities? (g) 2 Corinth. cap. 6. v. 16. (h) *In the Bible* 1562. (i) *In Psal.* 113.

3. The third corruption is in the Epistle to the Romanes: (k) *But what sayth the answere of God to him? I haue reserued vnto my selfe seauen thousand men, which haue not bowed their knee to the Image of Baal.* Beza and sundry Bibles of the Hugenots in France do thus traslate, putting to the text the word *Image*, which is neyther in the Hebrew of the old Testament, (k) Rom. c. 11. v. 14.

stament (whereout this place is taken) nor in the Greeke of the new Testament; yet our gentle Maisters by the internall motion of the holy Ghost may adde, and take away to the written word as it pleaseth them: but the article, τῃ, sayth Beza, sheweth that εἰκόνι should be vnderstood: wherin Beza is a manifest ignorant, for as much as that, rather *Astartes* Iezabel her Goddesse should be vnderstood, as proueth manifestly the first of Kings Chap. 18. 19. 2. Because the word Baal being generall to all Idols, Gods or Goddesses, is now and then of the masculine or feminine gender, as witnesseth (l) *Theodoretus*: And the Hebrew word it selfe *Bahbal*, which signifieth properly to commaund, to gouerne, is diuersly attributed, now to one God or Goddesse, then to another, as (m) *And Israel coupled himselfe vnto Baal-peor*, called so from the hill *Peor*, wheron that false God was honoured. The like is in the second of the (n) Kings where he is called Beelzebub; that is, Lord of the Flyes, by reason of the great multitude of flies, which commonly were vpõ the Gentiles Altars in regard of the beasts there immolated.

In cap. 11. ad Rom.

(l) *Ad cap. 18. Ierem.*

(m) *Num. cap. 25. v. 3.*

(n) *Cap. 1. v. 3.*

4. The Puritans accuse vs Catholikes of Idolatry for the vse of Images; but I intreate the Christian reader to set aside passion, and to consider, how that the doctrine, and Religion of the Puritans, is nothing else but manifest, and abominable Idolatry. For the better vnderstanding hereof it is to be remaked, that the holy (o) Fathers with one consent do auow, that Idolatry then is committed, *when the honour due to God only is giuen to the creatures*, as to the Sunne, to the Moone, to Hercules, to Mercury, and such lyke. Now there be two sorts of this Idolatry, say the same holy Fathers, the *outward*, visible, and materiall Idolatry, which is giuen outwardly to the visible Idols, and Gods; and so the Persians, and Chaldeans adored the Starres for their Gods; the Ægiptians adored sundry beasts, plants, & other pictures; the Græcians their Captaynes, and the foure Elements; the Romanes as they ouercame any nation, or kingdome, they worshipped lykewise the Gods of that kingdome, hauing made, and builded in Rome to such an infinite multitude of Gods a place yet extant, and called *Pantheon*

(o) *Tertul. lib. de Idolol cap. 2. S. Cyprian in exhort. ad Martyres. S Aug. lib. 1. de Trinit. c. 6. & alij passim.*

theon, that is, *to all the Gods*. The other sort of Idolatry is called *spirituall*, inward, and inuisible; which is then, when a man doth imagine with himselfe inwardly, and in his mind a God different from the true God, and defendeth obstinatly erroneous opinions agaynst the true God. The outward Idolatry was in Salomō perhaps without the inward: (p) *For Salomon followed Ashtaroth the God of the Cydoniās, & Milcom the abomination of the Ammonites.* It is very lykly that Salomon after so many blessings, & guiftes of God thought not those Idols truly in his mind to be God. The *inward*, is in all those, who with passion, and obstinacy of mind defend, or follow any opinion agaynst the true Church of God. So the Prophet Samuell called King Saul his transgression, and rebellion agaynst God, *Idolatry*: (q) *For rebellion is as the sinne of witchcraft, and transgression is wickednesse, and Idolatry. Because thou hast cast away the word of the Lord, therfore he hath cast away thee from being King.* For who disobeyeth God or his Lieutenant, or Gods true Pastours (wherefore our Sauiour sayd playnly (r) *He that heareth you heareth me, & he that despiseth you, despiseth me*,) leaueth the Counsell, and Will of God, and honoureth, and adoreth his owne proper iudgement, and fantasie. Conforme to which doctrine S. Hierome sayth of the Iewes: (s) *As the Gentiles adored their corporall Idols, euen so the Iewes do hold for Gods the Idols which they haue made in their soule, and minde, and therefore are Idolaters.* And S. Augustin explicating those wordes of Iosue: (t) *Then put away* (sayth he) *the strange Gods which are among you, and bow your harts vnto the Lord God of Israel*, sayth: (u) *Thinke not that when Ioshua vsed such wordes, that the Iewes had any Pagan Idols among them, since a little before he praysed their obedience: But the Prophet Ioshua then did see that the Iewes had in their harts many erroneous opinions of God, and against Gods Maiesty, which as Idols the Prophet Ioshua commanded to be put away.* Likewise, S. Paul calleth the inward, and sinnefull motions of the minde, Idolatry, (w) *Fornication, vncleannesse, the inordinate affection, euill concupiscence, and couetousnes, which is Idolatry.*

(p) 1. Reg. cap. 11. v. 5.

(q) 1. Sam. cap. 15. v. 23.

(r) Luk. 10. v. 16.

(s) S. Hier. in cap. 8. Hose.

(t) Cap. 24 v. 23.

(u) Lib. 6. qq. in Iosua cap. 29.

(w) Colos. cap. v. 5.

5. The Turkes, and the Iewes in these our dayes haue no outward Idols, yea they belieue God to be Creatour

tour of heauen, and earth: yet by reason that they haue left the true Church, and Religion, forging vnto themselues a God and Religion according to their owne fantasie, are called *true Idolaters*: Conforme to which doctrine S. Hierome, with the rest of the Fathers auowe constantly, that those, who haue left the Catholike & Roman Church forging vnto thēselues new opinions, are Idolaters: (x) *All heretiks haue their Gods, & whatsoeuer they haue forged, they adore the same as sculptile, and conflatile,* (that is) *as a grauen, and molten Idoll.* And agayne he auoweth, *that whatsoeuer is spoken in the Scripture agaynst Idols, or Idolatry, is spoken lykewise against the heretikes as spirituall Idolaters.* For as much as that in denying the authority of the holy Church, the vniuersall consent of the holy Fathers, they tye themselues to the Idoll of their owne fantasie, and iudgement, as the Protestants, and Puritanes do: (y) *Whatsoeuer according to the letter, is spoken against the Idolatry of the Iewes, thou must needs referre all this vnto them, which vnder the name of Christ worship Idols and forging to themselues peruerse opinions, carry the tabernacle of their King the deuill, and the Image of their Idols; for the worship not one Idoll, but for the variety of their doctrine they adore diuers Gods: And he put in very well (which you made vnto your selues) for they receyued them not of God, but forged them of their owne minde.* And speaking of the Idoll of Samaria he sayth: *We alwayes vnderstand Samaria, and the Idoll of Samaria in the person of the heretikes, of whome it is said:* (z) *Woe be vnto them that despise Sion, and trust in the mont of Samaria, for heretikes despise the Church of God, and trust in the falshood of their opinions, erecting themselues agaynst the knowledge of God, and saying, when they haue deuided the people (by schisme) we haue no part in Dauid, nor inheritance in the sonne of Isai.* Which comparison of heresy, and Idolatry, is grounded in good reason: for as Idolatry was the ground, and spring of all vices among the Pagans; so is heresy the sinke of all abominations among the Christians. 2. Idolatry came first in when the world was full of corruption and vice, as of ambition, auarice, ignorance, and pride; euen so the heresies of this our age were planted by Luther, Caluin & Knox in a most corrupted time, & in an age infected with all sort

(x) *Hier. in cap.* 11. *Hosee.*

(y) *Hier. in* 5. *Amos.*

(z) *In* 8 *Amos.*

of vice, and abhomination, especially of pride, and ignorance. 3. Idolatry tooke away the true worship of God vnder pretext of naturall liberty; so the heresies of this our age doe take away the true worship of God vnder the pretext of the Ghospell, and reformation, teaching for iustice, iniustice, for saluation perdition, perfidie vnder the pretext of Fayth, and Antichrist vnder the name of Christ, as wisely sayth S. Augustine: (*) *There is another sort of worshipping Idols much more wicked then this outward, which is then, when men adore their owne fantasies, and call Religion all that which is forged in the fornace of pride, and temerity.* Wherfore the Puritanes leauing the path of the holy Church, not being able to proue, no not one debatable point of Religion by the expresse word of the Bible, refusing the constant, and vniforme doctrine of the holy Fathers, not making account of the Catholike Religion, which hath bene among all nations these sixteene hundreth yeares, and forging to themselues new opinions, new translations of the Bible, new expositions of the word of God, and a new Religion; are conuicted of manifest Idolatry, and of manifest Superstition, wherewith they seduce the poore people, vnder the cloke and pretext of Reformation.

(*) *De vera Relig.* c. 30

The 6. and 7. Article.

That the custome of the Catholike Church in this second Age, was vniuersally to honour the Saintes in heauen, and to pray vnto them.

CHAP. IIII.

HAuing taught before the honour due to God, to the Saints, and to things apertayning to them, it is easy to see that the Protestants in denying the honour due to the Saints the friends of God, deny likewise and refuse the honour due to God himselfe; and consequently doe play the Antichrist, and do agaynst that common and naturall saying among vs in Scotland; *Loue me, and loue mine*, that is, if yee loue me truly, yee must also loue my friends: and we see by experience, when we loue a friend sincerely, we loue for his sake his friends also, yea his seruants, yea his Ring or his Image, and whatsoeuer hath bene deare, and beloued of him. Conforme to which natural light the Catholiks, out of the great loue they carry to God, they loue those who haue bene Gods speciall friends, as the blessed Virgin Mary, the holy Apostles, the holy Martyrs, and such: who as they haue bene speciall and constant friends of God in this world, and do raygne now with him in heauē; so we should loue them specially, and loue those things which doe appertayne vnto them. Wherof I inferre, that the Protestants in denying the honour due to the Saints in heauen, deny in lyke manner the honour due to God himselfe, as is manifest by this example. Put the case, that a particular Gentleman in Scotland

land ſhould profeſſe great loue and honour to his Maieſty, yet could not abide to heare a good word of his glorious mother B. Queene Marie the Martyr; yea would reuile her, miſcall her, vnder the pretext, & colour that he will haue al honour to be giuen to his Maieſty alone, that the honour which is giuen to the mother is taken from the ſonne: put the caſe, that this proud, and lofty-minded Puritane paſſe by my Lords Chauncellour, Preſident, Treaſurer without mouing his cappe, and appeare before his Maieſties honourable Councell, without mouing body, cappe, or knee, & being demanded of this his barbarous forme of proceeding ſhould anſwer: *All honour should be giuen only to his Maiesty, none to his Lieutenants, fauourits, and friends; for that which is giuen to his friends is taken from his Maiesty.* Put the caſe, that whenſoeuer he do find his Maieſties Image he ſhould deface and defile it, vnder the pretext that he giueth all honour to his Maieſties owne perſon, none to any thing that appertayneth to his Maieſty: would you take ſuch a Gentleman to be a loyall ſubiect to his Maieſty? For would you not ſuſpect ſuch loue towards his Maieſty to be nothing elſe, but playne hypocriſy and diſloyalty? So do the Proteſtants in Scotland: they profeſſe all hononr and affection, ſay they, to Chriſt, but they reuile his mother, and will haue no honour giuē vnto her; they beare no reſpect to Chriſts fauorits the Apoſtles, and Martyrs; which is all agaynſt the law of friendſhip, and agaynſt the common Prouerbe, *loue me, and loue my friends.*

2. But the holy cuſtome of the Catholikes hath euer bene to profeſſe mutuall ſociety with the Saints of heauen, mutuall communion, and participation of benefits; in token whereof we ſay in the Creed, *I belieue the Communion of Saints.* We of duty ſhould honour the Saints; they of charity pray for vs; we honour, and prayſe their felicity, they help, and relieue our miſery; we declare vnto them our pouerty, and wants; they ſupply the ſame by their merits. But let vs heare the Bible: (a) *Goe to my ſeruant Iob, and offer vp for your ſelues a burnt-offring, and my ſeruant Iob shall pray for you.* God commaundeth thoſe perſons to addreſſe themſel-

(a) *Iob. c. 42. v. 8.*

ues to Iob, to the end he should pray for them, though Iob was yet liuing in misery, and doth not God much more commaund vs now to pray to Iob, and the Saints raigning in glory? If it was commendable in S. Paul (and no wayes derogating to the mediation of Christ) to desire the Romanes yet lyuing in misery to pray for him: (b) *Also brethren I beseech you for our Lord Iesus Christs sake, and for the loue of the Spirit, that yee would striue with me by prayer to God for me*; shall it not be lawfull to pray to S. Paul now liuing in glory, since they are (c) *beholders of our life and actions*? They see our distresse, & heare the complayntes we make; they know our estate, sayth S. Augustin, by the report of the Angells our faythfull Guardians, who haue dayly intercourse betweene them, and vs. As Cornelius his good Angell witnesseth: (d) *But when he looked on him, he was affrayd, & sayd, who art thou Lord? And he sayd vnto him, thy prayers, and thine Almes, are ascended into remembrance in the sight of God.* Which place is corrupted by the Ministers.

(b) Rom. c. 15. v. 30.

(c) Ambr. l. de viduis.

(d) Act. c. 10. v. 4

3. But how doe the Saints, and Angells in heauen know our prayers, and the present estate wherein we are? Besides the report, and relation of our good Angells, there is other meanes, wherby the Saints in heauen haue certaine knowledge of our outward actions, and inward thoughts, so farre forth as it is needfull for vs, and expedient to them; for as much as that *the Saints do see, and behold our actions, and prayers, in the brightnes of God*, as in a faire resplendent glasse, in which the beames of all creatures, their nature, & perfection more clearly shine, then in themselues, sayth S. Gregory: (e) *What can the Saints be there ignorant of, where they know him who knoweth all things?* The third meanes whereby the Saints in heauen know our prayers, and actions, say (f) S. Gregory, and (g) S. Augustine, is, *by a speciall fauour, & reuelation of God*, who openeth to them, as to our speciall frieds whatsoeuer is behoouefull for them to know. Doth not the Bible witnes, that the holy Angels in heauē know, and reioyce at the conuersiō of a sinner: (h) *There is ioy in the presēce of Angels of God for one sinner that conuerteth?* Doth not the Bible likewise witnesse that the Saints in heauen S. Peter, S. Paul and

(e) Lib. 12. moral. cap. 13. & 15.

(f) Greg. Naz. orat. fun. in sororē Gorg.

(g) S. Au. lib. de cura pro mortuis cap. 15.

(h) Luk. 15. v. 10.

and ſuch, are like vnto the Angells: (i) *In the resurrection they neyther marry wiues, nor wiues are bestowed in marriage, but are as the Angels of God in heauen?* Wherfore then euen as the Angels know the eſtate of their Pupils, know their prayers, and miſeries; ſo do the Saints in heauen know our eſtate, and things belonging vnto vs. If many holy men, euen in this mortall life, either by the guift of prophecy, or by the extraordinary fauour of God haue diſcloſed the hidden thoughts of mens harts, ſundry things to come, and thinges done farre diſtant from them, much more ſhould this priuiledge be graunted to the Saints in heauen, ſince the excellency of that happy eſtate challengeth much more. So Eliſæus, being a mortall man and far diſtant from Giezi, knew of the bribe which Giezi tooke: (k) *Went not mine hart with thee, when the man turned agayn from his chariot to meete with thee? Is this a tyme to take money and receyue garments &c.* Likewiſe S. S. Peter diſcloſed the inward Sacriledge of Ananias, and Saphira: (l) *Then ſayd Peter: Ananias, why hath Satan filled thy hart, that thou shouldſt lie vnto the holy Ghoſt, and keepe away part of the price of the poſſeſsion?* Vpon the which words S. Auguſtine ſayth in commendation of vowing of chaſtity: (m) *If it diſpleaſed God, to withdraw of the money, which they had vowed to God; how is he angry, when chaſtity is vowed, and is not performed &c?* If then S. Peter, yet a mortall man, did know the inward thoughts of Ananias, much more is he able, now being glorified, to know our prayers; which reaſon S. Auguſtin learnedly proſecuteth in Elizæus, and conſequently in S. Peter his fact, ſaying: (n) *If the Prophet Elizæus abſent in body did ſee the bribe, which his ſeruant Giezi receyued of Naaman Syrus; how much more shall the Saints ſee all things when God shall be all in all vnto vs?* I might to the ſame effect produce ſundry other authorityes of the Fathers, which to deny is nothing elſe but an impious, and abominable contumacy of the Proteſtants.

(i) *Matth.* 22. & *Mark.* 12. v. 25.

(k) *Reg.* 2. v. 26.

(l) Act. 5. v. 3. 9.

(m) *Aug. ſerm.* 10. *de diuerſis.*

(n) *Aug. lib.* 21. *de ciuit. c.* 29.

4. I will end with this place of S. Peter exceedingly corrupted by the Miniſters, and whereby S. Peter promiſed to pray after his death for the Catholikes: (o) *And I will do my diligence, you to haue often after my deceaſe alſo, that you may*

(o) 2. Pet. cap. 1. v. 15.

keepe a memory of these thinges. Which wordes seeme to haue bene more playne in the Greeke copies, extant in S. Chrysostome (p) his tyme, who readeth thus: *I will endeauour after my coming to heauen to remember you.* (q) Oecumenius likewise auoweth that sundry holy Fathers proued by this place, that the Saints in heauen after their death did pray for vs mortalls yet in life. Yea S. Leo the Great one of Peters successors in the Apostolike Romayne Sea, often attributeth the good administration thereof to S. Peters prayers: (r) *We are much bound* (sayth he) *to giue thankes to our Lord and Redeemer Iesus-Christ, that hath giuen so great power to him, whome he made the Prince of the whole Church: that if in our tyme also any thing be done well, and be rightly ordered by vs, it is to be imputed to his worke, and his gouernement, to whome it was sayd, And thou being conuerted confirme thy brethren: and to whome our Lord after his resurrection sayd thrise, Feede my sheepe; which now also without doubt the godly Pastour doth execute, confirming vs with his exhortations, and not ceasing to pray for vs, that we be not ouercome with any temptation &c.* Besides these ancient Fathers, sundry learned, & famous doctours of late, proue out of this place the *Inuocatiō of Saints*, as Catherinus, Clarius, Franciscus Suarez, Gregorius de Valentia, Franciscus Turrianus, and others; whose consequences, testimonies, and explications should be preferred by any wise man to the explications, & consequences of the Ministers, who shall neuer be able to proue by the expresse word of their own corrupted Bible, that, *The Saints in heauen do not pray for vs*: that, *we should not pray vnto the Saints*, and such. But with vs Catholikes concerning this poynt of Religion, and all others, (s) *The verity of the Scriptures is holden of vs, when we do that which pleaseth the vniuersall Church, which the authority of the same Scripture commendeth.* Let vs then heare the consequences of the Church of God made manifest vnto vs by the holy Fathers of this second Age, or Century.

(p) Orat. in Princip. Apostol. σπουδάσω μετὰ τὴν ἐμὴν ἄφεσιν τὴν ὑμετέραν μνήμην ποιεῖσθαι.

(q) In 1 Pet. [?] fal. 102.

(r) Serm 3. in aniuers. die assumpt. ad Pontifi.

(s) Augu. lib. 10. contra Crescō cap. 33.

Testi-

Testimonies of the holy Fathers of this second Age, That we should honour the Saints in heauen, and that they pray for vs.

The first Section.

S. Iustine a famous, and holy Martyr, witnesseth that the Catholikes worshipped the true God with Diuine worship only, and worshipped the Angells with a religious worship called *Dulia*: (a) *Quinimò & illum verum Deum, & Filium qui ab eo venit, nosq; hæc docuit, & aliorum sequentium, assimilatorumq; bonorum Angelorum exercitum, & spiritum propheticum colimus & adoramus, verbo, & veritate venerantes; idq; omnibus, qui dicere velint, vt edocti sumus, candidè tradentes.* And agayne he witnesseth that good (b) *Angells* are giuen vs by God to assist vs, help vs, heare our prayer, pray for vs, & defēd vs from dangers of body & soule, & to accompany at our dying day our soule to that eternall felicity, where the Saints in heauen pray for vs. Truly no reason can be giuen why mortall men may be prayed vnto, and not immortall Saints in heauen, whose charity is greater without comparison, then ours heere, sayth S. Bernard: (c) *That blessed coūtry doth not change charity, but augment it.* S. Hierome: (d) *If the Apostles, and Martyrs dwelling in corruptible flesh could pray for others, when they ought to be carefull for themselues; how much more after their crownes, victories, and triumphes?*

(a) *Apol. 2. ad Anto. Pium Imp.*

(b) *Ad quæst 30. Gentil.*

(c) *In vigil SS. Petri & Pauli.*

(d) *Hier. aduers. Vigilantium.*

2. S. Irenæus a holy Martyr, and famous writer of this age could not more playnly auowe the Inuocation of Saints, then calling them *our Aduocats*, and *Intercessours*, which title he giueth in playne termes to the Blessed Virgin mother of Christ: (e) *Sicut Eua seducta est* (sayth he) *vt effugeret Deum, sic Maria suasa est obedire Deo, vti Virginis Eua Virgo Maria fieret Aduocata.* That is, as Eua was seduced to disobey God, so Mary was persuaded to obey God, to the end that of the Virgin Eua, the Virgin Mary might be Aduocate. Which is conforme to that famous saying of S. Bernard: (f) *We need a Mediatour to our Mediatour, and who more profitable then the Blessed Virgin Mary?* Not that we need any me-

(e) *Irenæus lib. 5. c. 19.*

(f) *Bern. serm. de B. Virgine quæ incipit Signū magnum.*

mediatour besides God, in respect of his inhability or litle power, but in respect of our imbecillity, indignity, and base vnworthines: & thus meaned some auncient Fathers saying, that we should not call vpon the Saints in heauen as thinking God not to be sufficient to help vs.

3. Yea it was a common custome in the primitiue Church amongst the Catholikes, to make a couenant in their life tyme, that whether of them went to heauen before the other, he should pray for his fryend yet in life, as witnesseth S. Cypriã who speaketh to the Catholikes thus:
(g) Epist. 57. (g) *Let vs pray mutually one for another, and whether of vs two shall by Gods clemency be first called, let his loue continue, and his prayers not cease for his brethren, and sisters in the world.* And againe this holy Father exhorteth the holy Virgins and Nunnes in his
(h) Lib. de disciplina & habitu Virginum tyme to pray for him after their departure: (h) *Only then haue vs in remembrance, when your virginity shall begin to be honoured:* that is in heauẽ. Conforme to the which custom the Virgin and Martyr (i) Potamiæna promised at the houre of her Martyrdome, that after her death she would procure mercy
(i) Euseb. l. 6. cap. 4. of God for *Basilides*, one of the souldiers that led her to execution: and so she did. (k) S. Augustine lykewise in playne termes desireth to be helped by S. Cyprians prayers. And
(k) Lib 5. de Baptis. cõt. Donat. c. 17. (l) S. Hierome intreateth the holy Matron Paula after her death to pray for him in his old age, affirming that she will the more easily obtayne, the nearer she is now ioyned to
(l) In epita. Paulæ. Christ in heauen. It is well knowne that the receyued custome among the Iewes, before the comming of Christ, was to pray to the Saints deceased, as witnes those wordes
(m) 2. Machab. v. 12. of the Bible: Iudas thought that, (m) *He saw Onias (which had bene the high Priest, a vertuous, and a good man, reuerend in behauiour, and of sober conuersation, well spoken, and one that had bene exercised in all points of godlines from a child holding vp his hãds towards heauen, and praying for the whole people of the Iewes.* Agayne, Onias speaking of Hieremy the Prophet who was
(n) 2. Mac. c. 15. v. 14. dead foure hũdreth yeares before, said thus: (n) *This is a louer of the brethren, who prayeth much for the people and for the holy citty, to wit, Hieremias the Prophet of God* Which place auncient Origen, with other Fathers, citeth to proue the Inuocation

of

of Saints: which holy custome being familiar and vsuall, made the Iewes to thinke that our Sauiour Christ Iesus being on the Crosse did inuocate the Prophet Elias saying, (o) *Eloi, Eloi*, & some of the Iewes when they heard Christ vse those wordes sayd, (p) *This man calleth Elias.* Finally a famous Protestant witnesseth: (q) *That almost all the Bishops, and writers of the Greeke, and Latin Church for the most part were spotted with the doctrine of Free-will, of Merite, of Inuocation of Saints.*

(o) *Matth.* 27. v. 46.
(p) *Matth.* 27. v. 47.
(q) *VVhitgift in his defēce &c.* pag. 473.

4. Origen speaketh playnly, and plentifully of this matter teaching vs first the custome, which was in his time to pray for those in Purgatory, and that those in heauen do pray for vs: (a) *Propterea & memorias Sanctorum facimus, & Parentum nostrorum, vel amicorum in fide morientium deuotè memoriā agimus, tam illorum refrigerio gaudentes, quàm etiam nobis piam consummationem in fide postulantes.* 2. He auoweth that this point of Faith was out of doubt amongst the Catholikes: (b) *Quis enim* (sayth he,) *dubitat, quòd sancti quiq; Patrum, & orationibus nos iuuent, & gestorum suorum confirment, atque hortentur exemplis.* 3. In conformation of this, he citeth the bookes of the Machabees as canonicall, and true Scripture: (c) *Sed & omnes Sancti* (sayth he,) *qui de hac vita decesserunt, habentes adhuc charitatem erga eos qui in hoc mundo sunt; si dicantur curam gerere salutis eorum & iuuare eos precibus suis, atq; interuentu suo apud Deum non erit inconueniens: Scriptum est namq; in Machabæorum libris,* (d) *Hic est Ieremias Propheta Dei, qui semper orat pro populo.* 4. Origen himselfe praieth to the holy Angels after this forme: (e) *Obsecrat te Dominus omnis Angelorum chorus propter me qui pessima consummaui, vt miserearis super ouem, quæ errauit.*

(a) *Lib.* 3. *in Iob.*
(b) *Hom.* 26. *in Nū.*
(c) Hom. 3. *in Cant.*
(d) *Macha.* 15. v. 14.
(e) *In lamento in fine.*

5. Not only he prayeth to the Angels, but also to holy Iob then in heauen saying: (f) *O beate Iob viuens in perpetuum apud Deum, & victor permanens in conspectu Regis Domini, ora pro nobis miseris, vt etiam nos terribilis Dei misericordia protegat in omnibus tribulationibus. &c.* 6. Not only he prayeth to Iob to pray for him, but lykewise to all the Saints in heauen: (g) *Incipiam me genibus prosternere, & deprecare vniuersos Sanctos, vt mihi non audenti petere Deum propter nimietatem peccati, succurrant: O Sancti Dei, vos lachrymis, & fletu pleno dolore deprecor, vt*

(f) Lib. 2. *in Iob.*
(g) *Initio lamenti.*

 proci-

procidatis misericordijs eius pro me misero, and in especial he praieth to S. Abraham thus: *Hei mihi Pater Abraham, deprecare pro me, ne de finibus tuis aliener, quos valde cupiui, nec condignè quidem propter ingens peccatum meum.*

5. S. Cyprian auoweth lykewise the constant, and Catholike beliefe of this Age concerning this point saying, that the holy Innocents, which were put to death by Herod, in heauen pray for vs: (h) *In ordine Sanctorum Protomartyres primum habent locum, & secretorum conscij diuinorum propinquitate familiarissima clementiam Dei pro nostris exorant laboribus, quæ vsq; hodie funestus Herodes prosequitur, quorum sanguine morte Diabolus delectatur*. Agayne, he witnesseth that the dayes of the departure of the holy Martyres, and of others, who dyed in prison for the Catholike Religion were remarked, and in regard therof Sacrifices offered to God in thankesgiuing: (i) *Quanquam Tertullus fidelissimus, & doctissimus frater noster pro cætera solicitudine, & cura sua scripserit, & scribat, ac significet mihi dies quibus in carcere beati fratres nostri ad immortalitatem gloriosæ mortis exitu transeunt, & celebrentur hic à nobis Oblationes, & Sacrificia ob commemorationes eorum, quæ citò vobiscum Domino protegente celebrauimus.* This is then the beliefe & Religiō of our holy, & auncient predecessours of the Church of God through the whole world. Now, (k) *any thing that the whole Church doth practice & obserue throughout the whole world, to dispute therof, as though it were not to be done, is most insolent madnes*, sayth S. Augustine.

(h) *In lib. de stella, Mag●, & Innocentiū nece.*

(i) *In epist. ad Clerum* 37.

(k) *Aug. ep.*118.*c.*5.

That the Ministers haue falsified the Bible in sundry places, which prooue the Inuocation of Saints.

The second Section.

THat place of Iob, where Eliphaz desireth Iob to call vpon some of the holy Angels, proueth manifestly the inuocation of the holy Angells: (a) *Call therfore if there be that will answere thee, and turne to some of the holy Angells.* Where S. Augustine auoweth, that holy Iob did inuocate the Angells: (b) *It seemeth, sayth he, that Iob doth pray the Angells*

(a) *Iob.* 5. *v.* 1.

(b) *In cap.* 5. & 19. *Iob. tom.* 4

gels to pray for him, or else the Saints to pray for him as for a sinner. The wordes of Iob in the three and thirtith chapter witnes this plainly: (c *There shall be an Angell speaking for him, one of the thousands to declare mans equity.* By reason that these two places do make forcibly agaynst the Ministers, they haue corrupted them impiously, turning the first by way of interrogation: *Call now if any will answere thee, and to which of the Saints wilt thou turn?* and taking out the word *Angels,* which is in the Greeke text, as the Caldaicke word *Mikdoschim* sheweth lykewise playnly. It is certayne, that in putting in this interrogation, the sense is fully changed, and the words haue another meaning; for the selfe same sentence made by way of interrogation, & read absolutly, wil haue diuers meanings, as is manifest in many sentences vsed in familiar talke, as also in that sentence of S. Augustin: *He who made thee without thee, shall not saue thee without thee. Qui fecit te sine te, non saluabit te sine te.* Signifying that mans cooperation of freewill is necessary to saluation: which place the Lutherans doe corrupt to signify the plaine contrary, only by reading the same sentence (to proue that man had no free-will concerning his saluation) with an interrogation thus: *He that made thee without thee, shall he not saue thee without thee?* In the second place of Iob, the Ministers haue taken out the word *Angell,* turning thus: (d) *If there be any Messenger with him &c.* putting the word *Messenger,* insteed of *Angell* to make the sentence obscure. After this forme a Iew or Turke may turne all the Bible vpside-down, as that: (e) *Then the Diuell left him, and the Messengers came, and ministred vnto him* Agayne: (f) *The Messengers that goe forth, and seuer the bad from among the Iust* And infinite such places, where it were impiety to turne *Messenger* for *Angell.* Can there be a greater sinne before God, then to corrupt after this forme without conscience, or shame the word of God? Is it marueyle that the Ministers effrontedly corrupt the holy Fathers, since they are not affrayd to do the same to the Bible, the holy Scriptures, the sacred word of God? Is it not the right way to Atheisme to turne for *Angell,* Messenger; *for Church,* Congregation; *for Priest,* Elder; for *Sacrament,* Secret, & for *Hell,* Graue?

(c) Ver. 23.

(d) Iob. c. 33. v. 23.

(e) Matth. 4. v. 11.

(f) Matth. 13. v. 49.

2. The ſecond place corrupted by the Miniſtry, is that ſaying of the Prophet Dauid: *I am partaker of all that feare thee, and that keepe thy commaundements.* Wherby is ſignifyed that all true, and ſincere Catholikes are partakers of all the prayers, good workes, and merites of the whole militant Church, as likewiſe of the prayers of the triũphant Church that is, of the Saints of heauen, which is called in our Creed, *The Communion of Saints.* The Greeke text is directly for vs againſt the Miniſters. The Hebrew, *Chaber*, and the Chaldaick, *Chabera*, ſignify cleerly to any vnpaſſionate man, *I am partaker.* (g) S. Ambroſe, (h) S. Hierome, and (i) S. Auguſtine, and others, turne the ſame place, *I am partaker.* But I pray yow how do our Miniſters diſguiſe, and deface this place? *I am*, ſay they, *companion of all that feare thee, and keepe thy precepts.* And in their merry metre they ſinge: *Companion am I to all them, which feare thee in their hart &c.* Is it a great honour to King Dauid to be Cõpanion to ſome of the Tron-Lords of Edenbrough, who bragge to feare God? How could Dauid accompany, or be Companion to all thoſe that feared God? And ſince none can keepe the commandements, as the Miniſters, ſayth he, how could the holy Prophet be their Companion? Are not the Miniſters in coining ſuch new tranſlations to fauour their new opinions, conuicted by S. Auguſtine to be manifeſt heretiks? for (k) *He is an heretike, ſayth he, who for ſome temporall commodity & eſpecially for his glory, and principality, coyneth, or els followeth falſe or new opinions,* falſe or new tranſlations.

Pſal. 119. v. 63.

(g) Serm. 8. in hunc pſalmum. (h) In Cõment. in hæc verba. (i) Serm. 16 in pſal. 118

(k) De vtil. credendi cap.

3. The third place corrupted by the Miniſters, is this of Ieremias: (i) *If Moyſes, and Samuell ſhall ſtand before me, my ſoule is not towards this people.* Where, as before Chap. 7. 11. 14. God forbad Ieremie to pray for the Iewes, ſo here he ſaith, that though not only Ieremy, but alſo though Moyſes and Samuel, (departed from this world longe before) ſhall pray for this people, yet they ſhall not eſcape the puniſhment for their ſinnes. By neceſſary conſequence whereof it followeth, that Moyſes, and Samuel after their death both could and did ſomtymes pray for the Iewes; otherwiſe the particular mention of theſe Prophets were not to the purpoſe.

(i) Ierem. 15 v. 1. L.

pose if they neuer did, nor could pray for them, as learnedly proue (l) S. Hierome, (m) S. Chrisostome, & (n) S. Gregory the great; and the Prophet Baruch confirmeth the same saying: (o) *O Lord Almighty, the God of Israel heare now the prayers of the dead of Israell, and of their children which haue sinned before thee.* Then the dead of Israell, prayed for the liuing; the Hebrew word *Im rabbamod* in the future tense maketh for vs, and sheweth both the malice, & Ignorance of the Ministry, in turning one tense for another, for they turne thus: *Though Moyses and Samuel stood before me &c.* The Chaldean Paraphrast maketh playnly for vs: *Im Iacum Mosche. &c. If Moyses, and Samuel shall stand before me to pray. &c.* And the Greeke text also maketh for vs agaynst the Ministers, who in corrupting thus the Bible, inuenting Nouelties, & new translations in so waighty a matter, as is the matter of our Saluation, the word of God, and in speakinge peruerse thinges, do shew consequently that they are manifest heretiks.

(l) *In his comment. vpon this place.* (m) *Hom. 1. in 1. Thes. 1.* (n) *Lib. 9. Mor. cap. 11.* (o) *Baruch cap. 3. v. 4.*

4. The fourth place corrupted by the Ministers, is that of S. Peter: (p) *I will do my diligence, you to haue often after my decease also, that you may keepe a memory of these things.* Where S. Peter promiseth to pray after his death for the Christians, hauing promised before in the thirteenth verse to remember them, and to stirre them vp by admonitions, so long as he was in life: and after in the fifteenth verse promiseth consequently to remember them after his death; as with the rest the Greeke, and Latine Fathers playnly witnesseth S. Chrisostom, saying: (q) *Reioyce Peter the Rock of Faith: reioyce Paul the honour of the Church: reioyce Peter the entry of true Religion: reioyce Paul the caire of Churches: reioyce euer in our Lord and offer vp your prayers for vs without interruption; fulfill your promise, for thou O Peter sayst: I will do my diligence, you to haue often after my decease also.* The Ministers to take away the force of this place of the Bible haue first put in the word *alwayes*, in place of the word *often.* 2. They haue taken away all points, to make the sentence obscure. 3. They haue transposed, and changed the words to the same end agaynst the Greeke text, putting the words, *After my departing*, after the

(p) *2. Pet. cap. 1. v. 2.* (q) *In natali beatorum Apost. Petri & Pauli.*

the wordes, *to haue remembrance,* to deceyue therby the reader, and to persuade him, that S. Peter only sayth, that he shall with such diligence exhort the Christians so long as he is in life, that they shall remember him after his death; not that he personally shall remember them after his death; to the which end the Ministers most viciously translate thus: *I will endeauour therfore alwayes that yee also may be able to haue remembrance of these thinges after my departing.* Cã there be a more manifest marke, that the Ministers are heretikes, then thus to corrupt the word of God to proue their owne errours? which while they follow, they seeme to follow the Bible, saith S. Augustin: (r) *All heretikes which receyue the Scriptures, and their authority, will seeme to follow them, whereas indeed they follow their owne errours and are therfore heretikes, not because they condemne them, but because they do not vnderstand them*, or do viciously translate them.

5. The fifth place which the Ministers haue corrupted for the great hatred they haue agaynst the Blessed Virgin Mary, is in S. Luke, where the Blessed Virgin sayth: (s) *Because he hath regarded the humility of his handmayd: for behould from henceforth all generations shall call me blessed.* Which prophecy of the blessed Virgin is dayly fulfilled (by the Catholikes, not by Puritanes, who haue scraped out the word *Generations*, agaynst the force of the Greeke word) when the Church, and the faythfull Christians keeping her festiuall dayes, and saluting her say, *Aue Maria,* and other such holy Anthymes: which place lykewise declareth the great humility of the blessed Virgin, who as she was full of the grace of God; so she was of all vertues, & especially of humility, wherby she pleased God more (say the Doctours) thẽ by her virginity. But the Ministers cãnot suffer her to be praised by reason of her humility, for the which cause they haue thrust out the word *humility*, translating thus: *for he hath looked on the poore degree of his seruant, for behold from henceforth shall all ages call me blessed.* In the Greeke text, the word signifieth *humility*: as the Ministers being better aduised haue trãslated the same Greeke word in other places: (t) *Whosoeuer therfore shall hũble himself as this litle child, the same is the greatst in the kingdom of heauen.*

(s) Luke c. 1. v. 48.

ταπείνωσις.

(t) Matth. cap. 18.

nen. And againe: (u) *God resisteth the proud, & giueth grace to the humble.* The Siriack text likewise is for vs Catholikes, *dechor bemuceco damethbeh &c.* that is, *because he hath regarded the humility &c.* The auncient Fathers both of the Greeke and Latin Church, with one consent, all read, *Because he hath regarded the humility &c.* And not content to haue shewed this litle lyking of the humility of the Blessed Virgin, they seeme willing to dissemble the inward humility of hart, a chiefe vertue in our Sauiour Christ Iesus, the Blessed Virgins sonne, for they haue thus translated that famons sentence of his, (w) *Learne of me,* because *I am meeke and humble of hart,* with leauing out the accustomed word, *humble*: and this newfanglenes in vsing new inuented wordes and prophane noueltyes agaynst the forme of the Catholike Fayth, agaynst the phrase of the old and Apostolyke writers, come to vs by tradition of all ages and Churches, hath beene euer an infallible marke of new Ministers, and heretikes, of whome therefore S. Paul commaundeth vs to beware: (x) *Auoyde prophane nouelties of wordes.* In S. Augustine his daies, when any good thing hapned to Catholikes, or when they entred into any mans house, or met any friend by the way, they vsed alwayes to say, *Deo gratias,* thankes be to God: but the Donatists, and Circumcellians, impious heretiks of that tyme, being alwayes giuen to nouelties of wordes, forsooke the old phrase of the Catholiks, and would alwayes say, *Laus Deo*, praysed be God: from which kind of ordinary salutation (though good yet newly inuented) the Catholikes did so shunne (sayth (y) S. Augustin) that they had as willingly haue met a theefe, as one who would say *Laus Deo*, insteed of *Deo gratias*: so we Catholikes should keep constantly our Forefathers words, so we may the more easily keep our old, and true Fayth receyued of them. Let vs not therefore vse with the new ministry of the Protestants, profane nouelties of wordes, as, *amendment,* for *pennance*; *abstinence*, for *fasting*; *the Lords supper*, for *the Blessed Sacrament*; *Superintendent*, for *Bishop*; *Congregation* for *Church*; *so be it,* for *Amen*; *prayse the Lord*, for *Alleluia*; *Elders,* for *Priests*; *Mystery,* for *Sacrament*; *Idol,* for *Image*; *instruct-*

(u) 1. Petri cap. 5 v. 5. Ioan. cap. 4. v. 9: Rom. 11. v. 16.

(w) Math. c. 11. v. 29.

(x) 1. Tim. c. 6. v. 20.

(y) In psal. 132.

Instructions for *traditions*; and such. Thus if we do, the very wordes will bring vs to the Fayth of our forfathers, & keep vs therin, auoyding alwayes prophane noueltyes of words as S. Paul commaundeth vs to do. Truly those very auncient wordes yet vsed in Scotland, *Candlemasse, Michaelmasse, Andersmasse* shew euidently that the holy *Masse* was in vse in Scotland from the first conuersion thereof to the Catholike Religion, that is, fourteene hundreth yeares since, or rather sixteene hundreth yeares since; for at such festiuall and remarked dayes, the holy *Masse* was sayd with such great solemnity, that sundry gentlemen and commons came from abroad to see the celebration thereof. Do not lykewise the wordes we vse, S. Giles Church, S. Patrickes Church, S. Cuthberts Church, the Lady of Grace, Hallowmasse, and infinite such witnes the honour, and inuocation, which our forefathers vsed towards these Saints? What witnesseth I pray you the wordes, *All soules day*, *holy-Roode day*, *Shirsthursday*, *Palme-sunday*, *Corpus Christi day*; *Imber dayes*, but the antiquity of our Catholike and Romane Religion? Which Religion, as the wordes themselues, did continue without any debatable contradiction vntill the comming of Luther, and Caluin, and yet are in vse; so the Catholike Apostolike, & Roman Religion, did euer continue in England, Ireland, and Scoland without any debatable contradiction vntill the comming of Luther, Caluin, Knox, & Paul Messen a Minister.

6. Their small deuotion vnto the Blessed Virgin Mary, may likewise appeare by their translating those
(a) *Math. c. 1. v. 25.* wordes; (a) *And he knew her not till she brought forth her first born sonne, and called his name Iesus*; with thrusting in the word *he*, thus, *And he called his Name Iesus*, giuing away the honour of the Imposition of the name solely to Ioseph, against the ex-
(b) *Luke c. 1. v. 31.* presse text of the Bible where the Angell sayd vnto her: (b) *For loe thou shalt conceyue in thy wombe and beare a sonne, and shalt call his Name Iesus:* Yea the Ministers considering the matter
(c) *Isa. cap. 7. v. 14.* without passion, turne with vs that of Isay: (c) *Behold the Virgin shall conceyue and beare a sonne, and she shall call his name Emmanuel*, the Hebrew word being of the feminine gender

der, and referred of necessity by the Rabbins to the blessed Virgin. Since then S. Mathew speaketh indifferently without limitation to Ioseph, is it not abuse of Gods word, and partiality agaynst the blessed Virgin, to giue the honour of the imposition of that holy name to Ioseph, only; since both the Prophet Isay, and S. Luke put the matter out of doubt, in giuing it to the blessed Virgin Mary? But let vs Catholikes euer honour the blessed Virgin, as mother of our Sauiour, and speake reuerently of her with the holy Fathers, especially with S. Ephrem (who was thirteene hundreth yeares since.) (d) *O Marie mother of God* (saith he) *vndefiled Queene of all, the hope of all sinners, my lady most glorious, higher then heauenly Spirits, more honourable then the Cherubims, holier then the Seraphims, the hope of the Fathers, the glory of the Prophets, the prayse of the Apostles: by thee we are reconciled to Christ my God, thy sonne: thou art the helper of sinners, thou the hauen for them that are tossed with stormes, the solace of the world, the deliuerer of the imprisoned, the helpe of orphanes, the redemption of captiues, vouchsafe me thy seruant to prayse thee: Hayle Lady Mary full of grace, hayle Virgin most blessed among women.*

Rabby Abraham, Rabbi Dauid, and others.

(d) *Ephrē. Hom. de laudibus B. Virginis.*

7. To disguise the holy virginity of the Blessed Virgin Mary, and to signify that she had not made a vow of virginity, and that she was not Iosephs true wife, before the Angell appeared vnto him and sayd: (e) *Ioseph sonne of Dauid feare not to take Mary thy wife, for that which is borne in her is of the holy Ghost*: The Ministers haue corrupted the forsayd place thus: *Ioseph Sonne of Dauid feare not to take Mary for thy wife*, adding the word, *for*, which is not in the Greeke nor Syriak text, where it is, *Lemariam anthetoc, Mary thy wife*, and not *Mary for thy wife:* which particle, *for*, is added against the holy, and auncient Fathers, who witnesse that the Blessed Virgin *Mary was espoused to Ioseph before* she was found to be with child, and before the Angell appeared to Ioseph. Secondly the Ministers themselues (alwayes addicted to the Spirit of contradiction) shew cleerly that before the Angell appeared to Ioseph, Mary was Ioseps wife: *Then Ioseph her husband.* 3. Ioseph could not haue beene minded to put her away, if she had not bene already marryed. 4. The

(e) *Matth. 1. v. 20.*

Hebrew word, which is in the Prophet Isay (f) *bhalma*, signifieth properly a true Virgin, & hauing with it (as it hath in the Hebrew text of Isay) *be haiedigha*, signifieth a Virgin young in yeares, a pure Virgin in body, minde, and affection, yea a perpetuall Virgin; though without the sayd *be haiedigha*, it signifieth a (g) Virgin also, yet not one, who remayneth perpetually in her virginity, as it doth in Isay, who speaketh only of the Blessed Virgin, whome to haue made a vow to God to keep perpetually her virginity witnes the holy Fathers (h) S. Gregory Nazian. (i) S. Bernard, & others. The which holy exaple of the B. Virgin Mary in vowing perpetuall virginity hath being imitated by an infinite multitude of men, and women of all nations, yea by Kinges, and Princes of diuers Nations. And of our Nation of Scotland, we haue the example of holy King Malcolme the Virgin, of S. Richardis Empresse, S. Fiacre, S. Guthagon, S. Mungo, S. Edmond, S. Fridelinus, S. Mathildis, and many others, of whome I make mention plentifully in my booke intituled *Menologium Sanctorum regni Scotiæ*. But the Ministers drowned in flesh, and blood, and sensuall pleasures, cannot vnderstand such things: no maruayle because, (k) *A sensuall man perceyueth not the things of the Spirit of God, for they are foolishnes vnto him: neyther can he know them, because they are spiritually discerned*: which place the Ministers haue likewise corrupted to hide their turpitude and fleshly sensuality, putting *natural*, for *sensuall*; knowing wel that those wordes, *a naturall man*, are taken in a good part, for any wise, and iudicious man, and not for a sensuall man.

(f) [illegible] 7. [illegible]
(g) Genes [illegible] Exod. Exod. 10. v. 8.
(h) Orat. de natiuit. Domini
(i) Serm. 4. in Missus est.
(k) 1. Cor. cap. 2. v. 14

8. We Catholikes do cal the B. Virgin Mary Queene of heauen with S. Chrysostome, S. Basil, and the holy ancient Fathers, who do pray vnto her after this sort: (l) *Most holy, vndefiled, blessed aboue all, our Queene, our Lady, the mother of God Mary, a Virgin for euer, the sacred Arke of Christs Incarnation, who didst beare thy Creatour: holy mother of vnspeakeable light, we magnify thee with Angelicall hymnes: all things passe vnderstanding, all things are glorious in thee, O mother of God.* The Ministers I say, to dishonour the Blessed Virgin Mary, and to make her

(l) In the Greeke Masses of S. Iames S. Basil and S. Chrysost.

her odious with the common people, haue corrupted impiously that place of Ieremias: (m) *All houses in the toppes whereof they haue sacrificed to all the host of heauen, and haue offered lybaments to strange Gods:* Vnderstanding by the host of heauen, the Moone, and the starres, whereunto impiously the Iewes offered Sacrifice. Now the Ministers insteed of these wordes, *the host of heauen* (which are conforme to the Hebrew, and Greeke) put in their first printed Bibles, but now lately corrected, *Queene of heauen*. Because we Catholikes worthily doe honour, and call the Blessed Virgin Queene of heauen. What is impiety if this be not? And what is hatred agaynst the Mother of God if this be not? Are not the Ministers not only voyde of wit, learning, and common sense in discouering so diuelish a hatred agaynst the Blessed Virgin; but also voyd of shame, and modesty, and more to be blamed then Turkes, and Saracens, who honour greatly the Blessed Virgin Mary?

(m) *Ierem.* cap. 19. v. 13.

The 8. and 9. Article.

1. *That the Catholike Church in this second Age, belieued vniuersally, that there was a Purgatory.*

2. *And that it was accustomed to pray for the soules detayned in Purgatory.*

CHAP. V.

THe most famous writers in this second Age Tertullian, Origen, and S. Cypriā witnesse plentifully not only the Fayth of the Catholik Church concerning *Purgatory*, but also the chiefest, yea almost all the points of Religion, which we Catholiks now a dayes belieue, as (a) the custome to receyue the Blessed Sacrament fasting, (b) Reseruation of the Blessed Sacrament, Sacrifice for the dead, (c) Sacrifice according to the order of Mechisedech, mingling of water with wine in the chalice, (d) Chrisme and Confirmation, & diuers of our Sacramēts, as witnes those words of S. Cyprian speaking of the Sacraments of Baptisme, and Confirmation: *Tunc planè sanctificari & filij Dei esse possunt, si Sacramento vtroq; nascuntur.* And againe (f) Chemnitius witnesseth that S. Ciprian reckoneth vp fiue Sacraments in his sermon *de ablut. pedum.* Lykewise those holy and auncient Fathers do make mention, that ordinary succession of Pastours doth euer accompany the true Church; they do auow also the inferiour orders of Deacons, Subdeacons, Acolites, Exorcists; that (g) Priests might not marry; that neyther Priest, Deacon nor professed widdow might be Bygam; the vow of (h) chastity of Virgines; the religious habite of sacred Virgines; the (i) necessity of Baptisme: (k) vsage of the

(a) *Tertul. apud Centuriatores. Cent.3.Col. 83?.*
(b) *Cypr. serm. 5. Tertul. lib. 2. ad vxo.*
(c) *Cypr. lib. 2. ep. 3.*
(d) *Cypr in serm. de vnctione Chrismatis*
(e) *Lib. 2. epist.*
(f) *Exam. part. 2. pag 58.*
(g) *Cypr. de*

the Crosse in Baptisme; Vnction, and other ceremonies of Baptisme; the vertue of the signe of the Crosse; the erecting of Crosses in priuate houses, and publike places; the necessity of satisfaction and pennance; Confession of sinnes, absolution giuen as now, with imposition of hands. Iustification by good workes; merite of workes; Freewill; the possibility of the commaundements; *Lymbus Patrum*, Prayer for the dead, Purgatory, prayer to Saints, Prayer to Angels, Apostolike and vnwritten Traditions, Fasting-dayes (Sunday euer excepted) Canonicall houres of prayer, prayer towardes the East, and finally the Primacy of S. Peter, and of the *Romane Church*. Which points of Religion the forsayd Fathers constantly auow to haue bene vniuersally in their time, that is, in the second Age (as now in our tyme) belieued by the Catholike Church; and no holy Father did euer reprehend eyther Tertullian, Origen, or S. Cypriã for belieuing the forsayd points of Religiõ, though for other particular errours they were greatly reprehended (especially Origen, and Tertullian) by the holy Fathers; which is an infallible argument that those forsayd points of Religion, were in this second Age vniuersally belieued in the Catholike Church, without any debatable contradiction.

singulare Clericor. (h) *Cypr. l. 1. ep. 9. & 11. Tertul. lib. de velandis virginibus. Cypr. de hab. virginum.* (i) *Cypr. l. 3. ad Quirinum.* (k) *Origen hom. 2.*

2. As concerning *Purgatory* in particular, besides the proofes that I haue set downe in the first Age, this is to be remarked: that two sorts of persons depart this life, the one who hath led a holy life many yeares, and hath fully satisfied for his offences past, grounded alwayes vpon the satisfactions of Christ: another who hath runne a wicked race all his dayes, and committed innumerable sinnes, yet through the mercy of God, repenting in the end is pardoned, in the houre of his death, of his sins, by reason of the great contrition he hath had of them, not hauing leysure to make any satisfaction for them. Now I say, if this second person dying at the same instant with the former, enioy the blisse of heauen as soone as he, me thinkes that it were not conforme to the iustice of God, to reward him equally with the other, who before his death performed great satisfaction,

tisfaction, and therfore he must be delayed for a season of his felicity, vntill the penalty of his sinnes be payed in Pur-
(l) Rom. c. 2. v. 6. gatory, since it is the will, & pleasure of God, (l) *to reward euery one according to his workes.*

3. Suppose then three seuerall sortes of persons departe this world. The one dyeth pure and cleane from all kind of sinne, as the Blessed Virgin Mary; the other guilty of diuers mortall sinnes, and dyeth therein; the third only spotted with some veniall sinnes, as many religious men by a special grace of God: the first without doubt goeth to heauen immediatly; the second to hell; the third goeth not to hell, because he is departed in the fauour of
(m) Apoc. cap. 20. v. 27. God, yet he goeth not to heauen immediatly, because (m) *Thither shall not enter any vndefiled thing.* Of this third sort of persons speaketh S. Augustine, when as he sayth: (n) *It is*
(n) Lib. 21. de Ciuit. Dei cap. 24 *manifest that those who are purged before the day of Iudgement by tēporall paynes are not deliuered to the punishments of eternall fire.* And
(o) Aug. lib. 2. de Gen. cont. Manich. c. 20. agayne: (o) *He who hath not happily tilled his field, but hath suffered it to be ouergrowne with thornes, hath in this life the malediction, and curse of the earth in all his workes, and after this life he shall haue eyther the fire of Purgatory, or euerlasting payne.* The Ministers cite, to disgrace S. Augustines doctrine in this poynt, that place of his, (p) *The third place we are vtterly ignorant of:*
(p) Lib. 5. hypogn. Where S. Augustine denyeth only any third place of euerlastinge Ioy, or euerlastinge payne, agaynst the Pelagians, who graunted to the *vnbaptized infants*, a third place of euerlastinge Ioy. But let vs come to the wordes of the Bible:

4. S. Paul writing to the Corinthians maketh mentiō of the custome then vsed among the Catholikes to afflict themselues for the soules of their departed friends, which affliction the Apostle calleth *Baptisme*; in the which signifi-
(r) Luke 12. v. 50. cation our Sauiour also taketh the word *Baptisme*: (r) *I haue*
(s) Mark 10. v. 38. *a Baptisme to be baptized with.* And, (s) *Can you drinke the Cuppe that I drinke, or be baptized with the Baptisme, wherwith I am bap-*
(t) Cypr. serm. de sæ. Rom. *tized?* meaning his future Passion on the Crosse: yea diuers holy Fathers doe call bodily affliction (t) *Baptisme* of teares, and *Pennance*: S. Paul then alluding to the ancient custome

of

of the Catholikes in his tyme, who did pray, make pilgrimages, afflict their bodyes, giue almes for their departed soules, which they belieued to be in Purgatory, saith: (u) *Otherwise what shall they doe that are baptized for the dead, if the dead rise not agayne at all?* That is; what doth it auayle the Christians, and the Iewes to punish, fast, pray, and afflict themselues for the soules of the departed, if the dead rise not agayne to receyue the fruite, and benefite of their prayers? That the Iewes prayed for the dead, it is manifest by the book of the Machabees cited in the first Age; which booke as the Ministers must needs credit, as much at least as an historiographer, so S. Augustine sayth playnly therof: (a) *The bookes of the Machabees, not the Iewes but the Church of God esteemeth canonicall.* The Ministers seing the force of this place to proue corporall afflictions vndertaken for the departed; haue corrupted it so impiously, that it will be difficile to vnderstand their translation, wherein they haue taken away, to make the sense obscure, two seuerall tymes the greeke article, which is in all the greeke copies; their words be: *Else what shall they do which are baptized for dead &c. Why are they then baptized for dead?* Which impious trāslation hath no more sense or meaning, then if a man should say: *Let vs conuey the dead to buriall.* Is this to translate their Bibles faythfully according to the Greeke copyes? Is not this forme of corrupting the word of God abhomination before him? Is not this a sinne agaynst the holy Ghost, to corrupt thus the Bible, the Sacred Text, the word of God, the holy Scripture?

Greg Naz orat in SS. lumina.
(u) 1. *Cor.* 15. *v.* 29.
(a) *Aug. l.* 18. *de ciuit. cap.* 33.

5. The other place, which proueth Purgatory, is that of the Prophet Baruch, who was scribe to Ieremy the Prophet. This Prophet then in playne termes prayeth for the departed Iewes, saying: (b) *Remember not the iniquities of our Fathers, but remember thy hand, and thy name in this tyme.* And by reason of these manifest words of praying for the departed Iewes, and consequently of Purgatory (whereof the one is so linked with the other, that by the proofe of the former, the latter necessarily ensueth) the Ministers deny this Booke to be canonicall, as lykewise that of the Machabees.

(b) *Baruch* 3. *v.* 5.

bees. But since they cannot shew any authority they haue, by the expresse word of their owne corrupted Bible, to preach and teach, farre lesse haue they authority to make, testify, or declare Canonicall, or Apocriphall bookes. Certes a world of holy and auncient Fathers, besides the Councells of (c) Laodicea, of (d) Florence, and of Trent expresly obserue, that Baruch is Canonical Scripture: and the whole Catholike Church hath euer so belieued. Now (e) *Whatsoeuer the whole Church of God doth practise and obserue throughout the world, to dispute thereof, as though it were not to be done, is most insolent madnes,* sayth S. Augustine.

(c) Canon *vltimo.*
(d) *De vnione Armenorum sessione* 4.
(e) *Epist.* 118. *cap* 5.

6. The third place, is that prayer made by the good theefe to Christ vpon the Crosse, (f) *Remember me when thou shalt come vnto thy Kingdome.* Of the which place sayth S. Augustin (g) *it is manifest, that there be some sinnes, which are forgiuen after this life, as constantly the good theefe belieued, otherwise he would not haue prayed Christ, to haue remembred him after his death.*

(f) *Luke* 23. *v.* 42.
(g) *Aug. l.* 6. *contra Iulianum cap.* 5.

7. The fourth place is that of S. Paul to the Philippians: (h) *At the name of Iesus euery knee shall bow, of those in heauen, of those in earth, and of those vnder the earth.* That is, the Name of Iesus should be honoured by the Angels in heauen, by the Christians on earth, and by those of Purgatory vnder the earth. Conforme to which Apostolike doctrine the Catholikes when they heare the Name of Iesus, do reuerence the same, for the respect and relation which it hath to our Sauiour Iesus-Christ, who is honoured in his name; not that the Catholikes honour the syllables of that name, (as the Ministers slaunderously teach the people) but the thing signified by the name, that is, Christ Iesus. Of the which holy custome S. Augustine maketh mention, witnessing to haue carryed a particular deuotion to the name of Iesus: (i) *This name of my Sauiour* (saith he) *did so piously enter into my hart from my tender age, that whatsoeuer was without this holy name (though true & polished) yet it did not fully delight me.* Since then those wordes *vnder the earth*, cannot be refered to deuils in hel, it must needes be referred to those of *Purgatory*, as the holy Fathers, and late writers (k) witnesse. Yea the Ministers

(h) *Philip cap.* 2. *v.* 10.
(i) *Lib.* 3. *Confes. c.* 4
(k) *In hūc locum.*

ſters forſeeing the force of this place to proue Purgatory, haue corrupted the ſame impiouſly thruſting into the text ſeuerall wordes which are not in the Greeke text, making thereby the ſenſe obſcure, and turning thus: *At the Name of Ieſus should euery knee bow, both of things in heauen, and thinges in earth, and things vnder the earth.* Where thoſe wordes, *both of things*, are no wayes in the Greek. Can things kneele at the Name of Ieſus, or be there any ſenſles things in heauen, in earth, or vnder the earth which kneele at the name of Ieſus?

8. Finally that place of S. Luke, where our Sauiour rayſed from death to life the Prince of the Synaguogue his daughter, proueth a third place different from heauen, and hell: (l) *He holding her hand cryed, ſaying, Mayde ariſe. And her Spirit returned, and she roſe incontinent.* The ſoule of this Mayd as likewiſe the ſoule of Lazarus (who had beene dead foure daies) after the departure, was neyther in heauen, nor in hell, *Ergo*, in ſome third place. Notwithſtanding al theſe forſayd places a ſtubborne Proteſtant will not yield by reaſon of his paſſion and lofty mind, who not being able to giue one place of the Bible, which maketh in expreſſe words agaynſt Purgatory, will bragge, and boaſt of his neceſſary conſequences, leauing therby the expreſſe word of the Bible, and tying himſelfe to his owne expoſitions and cōſequences, alleaging euer that the inward perſuaſion of the holy ſpirit guideth him, or rather blindeth him, But to theſe dreames of his and diabolicall conſequences, let vs preferre the conſequences of the holy Fathers of this ſecond age, or Century.

(l) *Luke c. 8. v. 55.*

Teſtimonies of the holy Fathers of this ſecond Age, in proofe of Purgatory, *and* Prayer for the dead.

The firſt Section.

TErtullian one of the moſt famous and learned writers in this ſecōd Age witneſſeth that the holy Maſſe was in vſe to be ſayd for the departed Chriſtians: (m) *Oblationes*

(m) *Lib. de corona militis. cap. 4.*

(sayth he) *pro defunctis annua die facimus.* And a litle after he teacheth, that this holy custome to say Masse for the dead came by tradition from the Apostles, though there be not expresse wordes in the Bible therefore: (n) *Harum & aliarum eiusmodi disciplinarum, si legem expostules Scripturarum, nullam inuenies; Traditio tibi praetendetur auctrix, consuetudo confirmatrix.* And againe in that booke of Monogamia (where he teacheth how a widdow should behaue her selfe) he exhorteth that she should pray for the soule of her departed husband, otherwise she doth not the duty of a true widdow sayth he: (o) *Enimuero & pro anima eius orat, & refrigerium interim adpostulat ei, & in prima resurrectione consortium; & offert annuis diebus dormitionis eius: Nam haec nisi fecerit, verè repudiauit, quantum in ipsa est.* And his booke *de Resurrectione carnis*, he teacheth accordingly, that, *Martyrs goe directly to heauen, others doe satisfy in the fire of Purgatory.*

(n) Lib. de corona militis cap. 4.

(o) Lib. de Monoga. c. 10.

2. S. Irenæus (p) a holy Father & Martyr witnesseth the same, to wit, that certayne persons, as infants, dying in the grace of Baptisme, & in state of Innocency go directly to heauen without *Purgatory*: *Others there be*, sayth he, *who must needs be cleansed after this life, before they enter into that eternall felicity.* The same holy Father citeth another most ancient writer called Pastor (as witnesseth (q) Eusebius) who maketh mention of the paynes suffered in *Purgatory*: which auncient doctrine of both Pastor, and Irenæus is conforme to that of holy S. Chrysostome, who auoweth that the offering vp of Sacrifice for the dead was enacted by the very Apostles themselues. Heare his wordes: (r) *It was not without good cause enacted by the Apostles, that in the celebration of the reuerend mysteries a commemoration of the dead be made; for they knew that great profit, and much commodity redounded therby vnto them.* Which holy custome of the Catholike Church gaue occasion to (s) Constantine the great (whome our Soueraigne King Iames cleareth from all superstition) Emperour to desire vehemently to be buried in a famous Church, that he might therby partake the benefit of many deuout praiers *after his decease.* Which holy Emperour was imitated by another godly Emperour Theodosius the yonger: who

(p) Lib. 1. cap. 2. & Feuardentius annot. 3. in dictũ librum.

(q) Lib. 5. hist. c. 8.

(r) Hom. 69. ad populum.

(s) Euseb. in vita Constant.

(t) Pro-

(t) *Proſtrated himſelf at the Reliques of S. Chryſoſtom, & made ſupplication for the ſoules of his parents Arcadius & Eudoxia.* The ſame appeareth manifeſtly out of the Greeke Liturgy, or Maſſe extant in the workes of S. Chriſoſtome, where there is expreſly mentioned ſacrifice of praiſe offred for holy Martirs, Prophets, Apoſtles, and Sacrifice offered for others detayned in *Purgatory*. Which S. Auguſtine in lyke manner excellently deſcribeth, ſaying: (u) *Therfore at the table we do not ſo remember Martyrs, as others departed, who reſt in peace, that we may alſo pray for them, but that they may pray for vs.* And againe: (x) *When the Sacrifices of the Altar, or whatſoeuer other Almſedeeds are offered for all the Baptized departed, for thoſe that be perfectly good, they be thankeſgiuings, for ſuch as be not very euill, they be propitiations, for them that be paſsing naught, although they be not any helpes or refreſhments of the dead, yet they be ſome comforts, & conſolations of the liuing.* Declaring therby that the ſelfſame Sacrifice of the Maſſe is a propitiatory, & thankſ-giuing Sacrifice.

(t) Theodoretus hiſt. Eccleſ. lib. 5. cap. 25.

(u) Tract. 84. in Io.

(x) Aug. in Euchr. cap. 110.

3. Finally, the teſtimony of our gratious Soueraigne King Iames putteth the matter out of doubt, ſince his Maieſty freely proteſteth: (y) *That is was a very auncient cuſtome in the publike prayers of the Church, to make commemoration of the deceaſed, and to deſire of God reſt for their ſoules, who dyed in the peace of the Church, few are ignorant.* What? Do not the very auncient monuments of Scotland witnes this holy cuſtome of ſaying Maſſe for the dead? Doe not the very ſtatues of many noble mens houſes, the Immunities, Charters, and decrees of many noble men: ſuch a greate multitude of Deaneries, Chanonries, Monaſteries, Nunneries, Churches, Chappels haue beene erected by our forfathers to no other end then to haue prayers, and Sacrifices offered for their ſoules? To this end the Monaſtery of *Paſly* was erected by the famous and Royall houſe of *Steward*; to this end the Monaſtery of *Newbottel*, the Abbay of *Holy-Rood-houſe*, the Abbay of *Kelſo*, the Abbay of *Lundors*, the Abbay of *Dere*, the Abbay of *Coldingam*, the Abbay of *Killos* in my country of *Murray*: to this end many others haue beene builded in our countrey, whoſe ſumptuous buildings or decayed ruines yet remayning, accuſe the Miniſters of

(y) Caſaubon in the anſwere to the Ep. of Card. de Peron.

horrible Impiety, to haue thus ouerthrowne the most famous, and auncient monuments of their forfathers.

4. Origen giueth sufficient occasion to the Ministers to belieue that there is a Purgatory, since he spake fourteene hundreth yeares agoe so playnly thereof: (a) *Natura peccati similis est materia quæ igni consumitur, quam ædificari Paulus Apostolus à peccatoribus dicitur,* (b) *qui supra fundamentum Christi ædificant ligna, fœnum, stipulam. in quo manifestè ostenditur esse quædam peccata ita leuia, vt stipulæ comparentur, cui vtiq; ignis illatus diu non potest immorari. Alia vero fœno esse similia, quæ ipse non difficulter ignis absumat, verùm aliquanto tardiùs, quàm in stipulis immoretur. Alia verò esse, quæ lignis conferantur, in quibus pro qualitate criminum, diutinum & grande pabulum ignis inueniat. Ita ergo vnumquodq; peccatum pro qualitate, vel quantitate sui pœnarum iusta persoluit.* Likewise explicating those words of S. Paul: (c) *If any mans worke burne, he shall loose, but he shall be safe himselfe neuerthelesse, yet as it were by the fire,* inferreth this consequence of Purgatory: (d) *Idcirco igitur qui saluus fit, per ignem saluus fit; & si quid fortè de specie plumbi habuerit admixtum, id ignis decoquat, & resoluat, vt efficiantur omnes aurum bonum.* And speaking of the space that euery man remayneth in Purgatory, saith very learnedly with the Catholike Church that, that space of tyme is only knowne to God: (e) *Verùm* (saith he) *hæc ipsa purgatio, quæ per pœnam ignis adhibetur, quantis temporibus, quantisue sæculis de peccatoribus exigat cruciatus, solus scire potest ille, cui Pater omne iudicium tradidit.*

(a) *Hom. 14. in Leuiticum.*
(b) 1. *Cor. cap. v. 13.*
(c) 1. *Cor. cap. 3. v. 15*
(d) *Hom. 6. in Exod.*
(f) *Matth. c. 5. v. 27.*

5. S. Cyprian explicating those wordes of S. Matthew: (f) *Thou shalt not goe out from thence till thou repay the last farthing,* inferreth thence *Purgatory,* saying: (g) *Aliud est ad veniam stare, aliud ad gloriam peruenire, aliud missum in carcerem non exire inde donec soluat nouissimum quadrantem, aliud statim fidei, & virtutis accipere mercedem, aliud pro peccatis longo dolore cruciatum, emendari & purgare diu igne, aliud peccata omnia passione purgasse, aliud deniq; pendere in die iudicij ad sententiam Domini, aliud statim à Domino coronari.* He speaketh lykewise largly of Purgatory, & prayer for the dead in his Epistle *ad plebem & clerum Furnitanorum,* which omit to be short.

(g) *In Epist 52. ad Ant.*

6. But what if the Ministers themselues in their Confession

session of Fayth sworne, subscribed, and susteined by the three Estates of Scotland at seuerall tymes, do acknowledg a third place betwixt heauen and hell, where the soules of the elect departed remayne? Heare their wordes: *The elect departed are in peace, and rest from their labours; not that they sleep, and come to a certayne obliuion, as some Phantasickes do affirme, but that they are deliuered from all feare, torment, and temptation, to which we and all God his elect are subiect in this life &c. As contrary the reprobate, and vnfaythfull departed haue anguish, torment, and payne that cannot be expressed; so that neyther are the one, nor the other in such sleepe, that they feele not their torments.* If neyther the elect nor the reprobate are empty, and voyd of torments, it followeth of necessity that the soules of the elect be not in heauen, where there can be no torment at all. If not in heauen then in some third place, which we call Purgatory. 2. In the Ministers opinion the elect do not go immediatly to heauē after their departure, for heare they speak neuer a word of heauen. 3. They cite the text of S. Luke; but let any man read the chapter, and he shall neuer find, no not a word of such abominable blasphemies, or Pharisaicall superstitious doctrine. And this is the Clergy of our Puritane Ministry.

In the Cōfession of fayth ratified by the three Estats of Scotland anno 1560. the 17. of August. n. 17.

That Ministers haue corrupted and falsified the Bible in sundry places which proueth Purgatory, or a third Place.

The second Section.

IT is a wonderfull matter to see how the Ministers haue corrupted the Bible, of hatred they carry to Purgatory, or of any third place betwixt heauen and hell. As in speciall that of the Prophet Hoseas, who fortelling that our Sauiour after his death was to deliuer the soules of the iust who remayned in that third place called *Lymbus Patrum,* and *Purgatory*, conforme to the expresse word of S. Peter, who sayth, that Christ, (a) *Preached to them that were in prison, which had bene incredulous somtyme, when they expected the patience of God in the dayes of Noe.* Of the which words, S. Augustine inferreth

(a) 1. Pet. 3. v. 9. & 20.

(b) Aug. epist 99. reth this consequence, (b) *Therfore who but an infidell will deny that Christ was in hell?* The wordes of Hoseas be: (c) *Out of the hand of death I will deliuer them: from death I will redeeme them. I wilbe thy death, O death; thy bitte will I be, O hell.* which words being vnderstood by the holy Fathers of that third place where the soules of the holy Fathers were detayned, the Ministers haue fully corrupted thus: *I will redeeme them from the power of the graue. I will deliuer thee from death. O death I will be thy death. O graue I will be thy destruction.* Where they haue turned the word *hell* into *graue*, directly agaynst the Hebrew word *Scheol*, and the Greeke word, which the Ministers shamelesly haue turned agaynst the iudgement and vse of all sort of writers. And this they call *Reformed Religion,* to vse words agaynst the meaning and vse all auncient Authors, Fathers, Councels, Nations, & kingdomes.

(c) Hos. 13. v. 14.

ᾅδης

2. The second place which the Ministers haue corrupted, is that of the Prophet Zacharie: (d) *Thou also in the bloud of thy testament hast let forth thy prisonners out of the prison wherin is no water.* Signifiyng thereby, that Christ after his Passion, in vertue of his holy bloud, relieued the soules of the holy Fathers who were in a pit or prison, where there was no water, that is, no tribulation or penalty, as witnesseth S. Paul: (e) *When he ascended vpon high, he led Captiuity captiue.* (f) Tertullian, (g) S. Augustin, and other holy Fathers testify the same: & the Hebrew word *Bor*, as also the Greeke signifieth a prison, as the Ministers themselues do witnesse in Exodus: (h) *Vnto the first borne of the captiue which was in prison.* Where the same Hebrew, and Greeke wordes are. The Ministers to take away the force of this place, not only haue mangled the words, but lykewise haue added three seuerall words *shalt be saued*, which are not in the Hebrew or Greeke, translating thus: *Thou also shalt be saued through the bloud of thy couenant, I haue loosed thy prisoners out of the pit wherin is no water.* Notwithstanding all this impious changing and corrupting of the text, the Ministers do Protest and sweare to the simple people that they haue translated conforme to the Hebrew and Greeke originalls.

(d) Zacha. 9. v. 11.

(e) Ephes. 4. v. 8.

(f) Lib. 2. cont. Mar. cap. 4.

(g) Lib. cōtra Felicianum Arrianum cap. 15

λάκκος.

(h) Exod. 12.

3. The

3. The third place is that of S. Matthew: (i) *As Ionas was three dayes and three nightes in the whales belly: so shall the Sonne of man be three dayes and three nightes in the heart of the earth.* Wherby is signified that our Sauiour after his passion wẽt down to *Lymbus Patrum*, or *Purgatory*, which is in *the hart of the earth.* Conforme to the Greeke and Hebrew, and to the Holy Fathers (k) S. Augustine, (l) S. Ambrose, (m) Tertullian & sundry others. Some Bibles of the Hugenots of France & of the Ministers of Scotland, to signifie that this place is only to be vnderstood of the graue, haue takẽ away the word *heart*, thus: *Ainsi sera le Fils de l'hõme dedãs la terre trois iours & trois nuicts. So shall the sonne of man be three dayes and three nights in the earth.* So great is the hatred they haue agaynst Purgatory, yet they will be thought and called Puritanes, as purged and cleansed from all sinne, not hauing any need of Purgatory.

(i) *Math.* 12. v. 40. ἐν τῇ καρδίᾳ τῆς γῆς

(k) *Epist.* 99. *ad Euodium.*

(l) *De mysterio Paschæ cap.* 4.

(m) *Lib de anima c.* 55

4. The fourth corruption is that of the Acts, where S. Peter declareth that Christs soule after his death was not left in hell, as the Prophet Dauid fortold, (n) *Who forseeing spake of the Resurrection of Christ, for neyther was he left in hell, neyther did his flesh see corruption.* Conforme to the which place S. Hierome saith, that death is the separation of the soule from the body, and that hell is a place wherin the soules are conteyned, eyther tormented with paynes or without paynes conforme to the quality of their merits. His wordes be: (o) *Infernus locus est in quo animæ recluduntur, siue in refrigerio, siue in pœnis, pro qualitate meritorum.* The place without paynes is, *Lymbus Patrum.* See (p) Damascene, and S. Augustin, who teacheth that it is an intollerable impudency to deny that the soules of the departed haue appeared sometymes to those of this world by Gods permission, and he giueth example of Moyses and Elias who (q) appeared vnto Christ. The Ministers haue impiously corrupted the foresayd place, against the Syriake and Greeke text, saying: *He knowing this before, spake of Christ, that his soule should not be left in the graue.* Putting the word *graue* for *hell*, signifying thereby that the soule of Christ, and consequently of all men, is mortall and corruptible, for whatsoeuer is put in the *graue*, must needs be

(n) Act. 2. v. 31.

(o) *In cap.* 13. *Hoseæ.*

(p) *Serm. de defunctis.* Aug. *lib. de cura pro mortuis c:* 15. & 17.

(q) *Math.* 17. v. 3.

εἰς ᾅδου

be corruptible & mortall. The impiety of the Ministry is to be marked in this, that in other places of the Bible (where there is no mention of any third, as of *Lymbus Patrum*, or Purgatory) they translate the same self Greeke word as we do. As that of S. Matthew: (r) *And thou Capharnaũ, which art lifted vp to heauen, shalt be broght downe to hell:* They do not trãslate, *down to the graue.* What great threatning of Christ were it, I pray yow, to say that those Citties or indwellers therof were to be brought downe to the graue, since they were all mortall? The Syriake text of the foresayd Chapter of the Acts condemneth the Ministers of Infidelity, *Eschibebek baschioloph lo pagreh: neyther was his soule left in hell.*

(r) Matth. 11. v. 23.

5. The fifth place is that of S. Paul: (s) *And that he ascended, what is it, but because he descended also first into the inferiour parts of the earth?* Signifying that the same Christ who ascẽded vnto heauen, first descended into the most low parts of the earth, as it is in the Greeke and Syriake, *Lukedam lethacb thuoteh.* Out of the which words (t) S. Irenæus inferreth this consequence; That our Sauiour descended to the inferiour parts of the earth to relieue the soules of the iust who were there: and (u) S. Ambrose likewise out of those words inferreth, Christ to haue relieued the soules of Adam, Abraham, Isaac, and Iacob, and others. Which doctrine was cõstantly belieued by the Church of God sayth S. Augustine: (x) *Hoc habet authoritas Matris Ecclesiæ, hoc fundatus veritatis obtinet canon, contra hoc robur, contra hunc inexpugnabilem murum quisquis arietat, ipse cõfringitur.* The Ministers to take away the strẽgth of the forsayd place in some of their Bibles do turne thus: *Now in that he ascended, what is it, but that he had also descended first, into the low parts of the earth.* Which place in some Bibles is corrected.

(s) Ephes. 4. v. 8.
εἰς τὰ κατώτερα μέρη τῆς γῆς.
(t) Lib. 5. contra hæres.
(u) In hæc verba.
(x) Serm. 14. de verb. Apost.

6. The sixt place is in the Epistle to the Hebrwes where S. Paul teacheth that the Patriarkes and holy fathers were not admitted to heauẽly ioyes in heauẽ, til those of the new Law were associated to thẽ, because the way of euerlasting glory was not as yet opened by the death of Christ, so that all those holy Fathers of the ancient law, (a) *Being approued by the testimony of Fayth, receaued not the promise, God for*

(a) Hebr. 11. v. 39.

vs

vs providing some better thing, that they without vs should not be consummate.; conforme to the Syriake, *Delo belhhadin nete Gamroun.* Which words, notwithstanding their euidency, the Ministers haue obscurely translated thus: *That they without vs, should not be made perfect.* Yet they haue translated with vs the same Greeke word in that of the Reuelation: (b) *Euen the mistery of God shall be finished.*

ἵνα μὴ χωρὶς ἡμῶν τελειωθῶσι

(b) Reuel. 10. v. 7.

7. The seauenth place is that of the Prophet Dauid, where the Prophet speaking in his owne person, or in the person of the auncient Fathers (whome Christ after his death was to relieue out of hell) sayth thus: (c) *Neuertheles God will redeeme my soule out of the hand of hell, where he shall take me.* But how haue the Ministers impiously falsified this place? *God shall deliuer my soule from the power of the graue.* Directly agaynst the Greeke, Hebrew, and Caldaick, which vseth the word *gehenna*, which cannot be taken for the *graue*, as witnesseth playnly (d) S. Matthew. Nor yet heer for the hell of the damned persons, out of which there is no redemption, conforme to that common saying: *Ex inferno nulla est redemptio.*

(c) Psal. 48 v. 15. ἐκ χειρὸς ᾅδου. *Müad scheol naphhebi min gehennā.*

(d) Matth. 5. v. 29. 30.

The eighe place is that of the Machabees, where it is sayd, that Iudas Machabæus a godly and valiant Captayne hauing compassion of his godly souldiours who were slaine in the warres: (e) *Hauing made a gathering, sent twelue thousand drachmes of siluer to Ierusalem for sacrifice, to be offered for the sinnes of the dead. Well and religiously thinking of the Resurrection (for vnlesse he hoped that they that were slayne, should rise agayne, it should seeme superfluous and vayne to pray for the dead) and because he considered that they had taken their sleep with godlynes, had very good grace layed vp for them. It is therefore a holy and healthfull cogitation to pray for the dead, that they may be loosed from sinnes.* The which wordes S. Augustine explicating saith, that a Sacrifice was offered vp heer for the Dead. Let vs heer his wordes: (f) *In Machabæorum libro legimus oblatum pro mortuis Sacrificium &c. Non parua est vniuersæ Ecclesiæ quæ in hac consuetudine claret authoritas, vbi in precibus sacerdotis quæ Domino Deo ad eius altare funduntur, locum suum habet etiam commendatio mortuorū.* The Ministers to disgrace this

(e) 2. Mac. 12. v. 43. 44. 45. & 46. προσαγαγεῖν περὶ ἁμαρτίας. τῶν νεκρῶν θυσίαν.

(f) Lib. de cura pro mortuis. c. 1.

 passage

passage which maketh playnly for vs Catholikes; first they deny the authority of these bookes, wherein S. Augustin and the Church of God contradicteth & belyeth them. 2. They haue scraped out, those wordes, *to be offered for the sins of the dead.* 3. They haue turned and mangled the words in such sort, that it is very hard to a witty and naturall man to vnderstand them. 4. They haue fully taken away the last verse which is the strength & conclusion of the words before. And all this new forme of dealing, of falsifying the Bible, of changing the words thereof, the Ministers do cal *Reformation*, and the *reformed Religion*.

The tenth Article.

That the holy Sacrament of Confession, *was vniuersally in vse, and practise in this second Age.*

CHAP. VI.

IT is not sufficient we disburthen our harts to a lawfull *Priest* by cõfession alone (whereof I spake in the first Age) but we must returne to the fauour of God by contrition & satisfactiõ, which are the parts of sacramentall confession. Cõtritiõ is that, wherby we fully detest the offense cõmitted against God. Absolution is that, wherby actually we receaue remission of our sinnes. And Satisfaction is that, wherby we seeke to recompense the wrong made to God, according to our imbecility, grounding alwaies our satisfaction vpon the satisfactions of Christ. The reason wherfore God will haue vs make some satisfaction for our sinnes is, because two thinges are included in euery mortall sinne (as wisely with the rest of the Catholike Deuines teacheth our famous and learned countryman

(a) Ioannes Duns, called *Scotus* from our countrey, & *Doctor subtilis* for his meruailous wit & subtility) a disloyall *auersion* from Gods goodnes, & an inordinate *conuersion* to the transitory creatures, wherin the sinner taketh delight; to which a double punishment belongeth: to the *auersion* is due the payne or penalty of dammage, that is, the losse of that eternall felicity, which is called *pœna damni*, answering to *malum culpa*. To the *conuersion* is due the paine or punishmẽt *of sense*, that is, the eternall fire of hell, called *pœna sensus*, answering to *malum pœna*. As for the guiltynes of the fault, called *malum culpa*, it is taken away in vertue of Confession and the Priests absolution, which applyeth the force and vertue of the bloud of Christ vnto the penitent sinner. As for the guiltines of the punishmẽt called *malum pœnæ*, though it be vtterly released in respect of the eternall duration, in vertue of Sacramentall absolution: yet oftentimes after the absolution, some temporall punishment remayneth to be suffered, greater or lesse according to the pleasure taken in sinne, as witnesseth the Bible in playne termes: (b) *In as-much as she glorified her selfe, and liued in pleasure, so much giue yee her torment and sorrow.* Which is more cleerly set down in the example of the King and Prophet Dauid, to whome God pardoned his murther and adultery, and pronounced absolution by the mouth of the Prophet Nathan: (c) *Our Lord hath taken away thy sinne, thou shalt not die.* Notwithstanding this absolution, God imposed to Dauid this pennance and satisfaction: (d) *Neuertheles because thou hast made the enemies of our Lord to blaspheme, for this thing the sonne that is born to thee, shal dye*; directly conforme to the former doctrine of the holy Fathers who do teach, that notwithstanding the *absolution* giuen by the *Priest*, we should do pennance and satisfactiõ for our sins: (e) *It is not inough* (sayth S. Augustin) *to change our maners to the better & decline from euills, vnlesse God be also satisfied for those things which we haue done, by the griefe of pennance, by the mourning of humility, by the Sacrifice of a contrite heart, almes-deeds cooperating therto.* And agayne: *By almesdeeds for offenses past God is to be made propitious and fauourable*. And S. Cyprian: (f) *By Good workes God ought to be satisfyed, by merits of mercy*

(a) *In 4. sent. dist. 46. quæst. 4.*

(b) Reuel. 18. v. 7.

(c) Samuel 12. v. 17.

(d) 2. Sam. 12. v. 14.

(e) Aug. in *Enchir. ad Laurent.* c. 71.

(f) Tract. de opere & eleemosina.

(g) Lib. de pœnit. cap. 5. *mercy sinnes should be purged.* And S. Ambrose : (g) *He that doth pennance should not only wash away his offence with teares, but with perfecter workes ought to couer and hyde former faults, that sinne may not be imputed vnto him.* And (h) *Indeed great were Gods iniustice if he would only punish sinnes, and would not receaue good workes and satisfaction for sinne,* sayth S. Hierome.

(h) Lib. 2. cont. Ioui. cap. 2.

2. This being presupposed let vs proue out of the Bible the holy Sacrament of Confession, whereof S. Luke speaketh thus : (i) *And many of them that belieued, came confessing and declaring their deeds : and many of them that had followed curious things, brought togeather their bookes and brunt them before all.* The Greeke and Syriake word importeth, *numbring their sinnes in particular : vmauedim bemodem.* Yea the Greek word *exomologesis* is taken among the Greeke and Latin Fathers, for *sacramentall confession.* Also the word *deeds*, sheweth that they declared in particular their deadly sinnes ; and the Greeke word lykewise sheweth that they confessed their sinnes secretly, as witnesseth S. Basil, who sayth : (k) *Heere the Scripture teacheth that we should confesse our sins, yet not to euery one, but to him who hath receaued power to absolue vs.* Hence it followeth that S. Paul to whom this confessiõ was made caused them who confessed to burne their books. 2. It followeth that in the very tyme of the Apostles *Sacramentall Confession* was in vse, and that S. Paul himself heard confessions, as witnesseth besides the holy Fathers, Gregorius de Valentia, Henricus, Lindanus, à Castro, Hosius, Tapper, Eckius, Petrus Soto, Baronius, Salmeron, and sundry others: and before them, the space of twelfe hundreth yeares since, S. Victor a learned and holy Father writing of the miserable persecution made then by the Vandals agaynst the Catholikes in Afrike, auoweth that the Catholike and common people lamented greately that their Priests being banished by the Arrian heretiks, they could not get the benefit of Confession, weeping and crying : (l) *Who shall baptise those infants ? Who shall Minister pennance vnto vs, and loose vs from the bonds of sinnes.* And therfore (m) S. Cyprian calleth it great cruelty (and such, as Priests shall answere for at the later day) to suffer any man that is penitent of his sins

(i) Act. 19. v. 18 & 19.

ἐξομολογούμενοι.

(k) Basil. 2. reg. ex breuior.

ἐξὸ & ὁμολογίω, that is, to declare inward thoughts outwardly.

(l) Victor. lib. 2. de persec. Vandal.

(m) Ep. 54

to

to depart this life without sacramentall absolution: to whome ioyneth S. Augustin saying: (n) *That it is a pitifull case whē by the absence of Gods Priests men depart this life eyther not regenerated, or fast bound.* That is, not absolued by the Sacrament of Confession, because they are in euident danger of eternall perdition, dying in their sinnes committed against God.

(n) *Ep.* 180 *Aut non regenerati aut ligati.*

3. The second place of the Scripture is that of Leuiticus: (o) *When he hath sinned in any of those things, then he shall cōfesse that he hath sinned therein.* If the Iewes were obliged to confesse in particular their sinnes to sinful men, much more Christians who are vnder the law of grace and of perfection, since that Christ himself sayth: (p) *I came not to break the law or the Prophets, but I came to fulfill the law.* The Ministers do reply. The Priests be men, how can they then forgiue sins? I answere. Euen as Almighty God hath giuen power to men to worke miracles, to rayse the dead, cure the blind &c. so he may also giue, and hath giuen authority to pardon sinnes, saying to the Apostles who were sinfull men: (q) *Whose sinnes yee forgiue, they shalbe forgiuen &c.* Truly if the Protestants could withdraw themselues from the fleshly liberty which their Religion affoardeth, & haue patience to consider a little the manifold fruits and singular commodities which plentifully flow to the Catholikes by reason of *Confession,* they should be forced to auow it to be a most godly and heauenly institution, as dayly experience doth teach vs: and we see lykewise sundry men greately vexed and grieued in their conscience with the combersome load and burthen of sinne, and yet so soone as they haue receaued the benefit of *Absolution,* we see them depart from the Priest so blyth, so gladde, so content, so full of inward comfort, that it is vnspeakeable to man. We haue seene others after many iniuries done to their neighbour, after the Sacrament of Confession, go & reconcile themselues & craue pardō with al humility for the wrōg they had done: we see lykewise dayly proud and lofty men humbled, the dissolute reclaymed, the lasciuious become chast, and such other changes. Whereof we may say with the Prophet Dauid:

(o) *Leuit.* 5. *v.* 5.

(p) *Matth.* 5. *v.* 17.

(q) *Iohn.* 20. *v.* 23.

uid. *This is the mutation of the right hand of God.* Many publike abuses, which neyther by the seuerity of lawes, nor vigilācy of Magistrats can be hyndred, are oftentymes reformed by the help of *Confession*, many wronges satisfied, wicked enterprises stopped, good purposes furthered, much vertue aduanced, and much vice suppressed: (r) *And to this end* (saith S. Augustine) *God exacteth confession to free and release the humble, to this end he condemneth the sinner not confessing, to chastise the proude.* Wherfore since the Protestants will not acknowledge neither the expresse words of their own Bible, which make for Confession, (as I haue declared before) nor yet the infinite commodities which confession frameth, nor yet the ancient custom of the Catholik Church; I addresse vnto them that fearfull and terrible sentence of S. Augustine grounded vpon the wordes of our Sauiour Christ Iesus: (s) *Whosoeuer he be that belieueth not mans sinnes to be remitted in Gods Church, and therefore despiseth the bountifulnes of God in so mighty a worke, if he continue in that obstinat mind till his lyues end; he is guilty of sinne agaynst the holy Ghost.* Let vs see what was the Religion of the holy Fathers of this second Age, cōcerning the Sacrament of Confession.

(r) *In psal.* 66.

(s) *Ep.* 50.

The testimonies of the holy Fathers of this second Age, prouing the vse of Confession.

The first Section.

TErtullian a famous and learned writer in this second Age, hath writen a whole booke of Confession, where he calleth it with the Greeke and Latin Fathers, *Exomologesis*, describing the very particular circumstances of that *Sacrament*: as to kneele in confessing our sinnes before the Priest, to weepe and mourne for our sinnes, to fast and chastise our body therfore, and such lyke. His wordes be: (a) *Itaque Exomologesis prosternendi & humilificandi hominis disciplina est, conuersationem iniungens misericordiæ illicem. De ipso quoque habitu atque victu mandat, sacco & cineri incubare, corpus sordibus*

(a) *Lib. de pœnit. c.* 9

dibus obscurare, animum mœroribus deijcere, illa quæ peccauit tristi tractatione mutare; cæterùm, pastum & potum pura nosse, non ventris scilicet, sed animæ causa: plerumq; vero ieiunijs preces alere, ingemiscere, mugire dies noctesq; ad Dominum tuum, presbyteris aduolui, & charis Dei adgeniculari &c. After he sheweth that there is no other remedy in the Church of God (besides Baptisme) to take away mortall and deadly sinnes, then Confession (b) *Igitur cùm scias, aduersus te gehennam post prima illa intinctionis dominicæ monimẽta, esse adhuc in Exomologesi secunda subsidia, cur salutem tuam deseris? Cur cessas aggredi, quod scias mederi tibi &c.* Lykewise he threatneth those who for shame & worldly respectes, do choose rather to be damned in not confessing then to be saued eternally in cõfessing their sins: (c) *Adeòne existimatio hominum & Dei conscientia comparantur? An melius est damnatum latere quàm palam absolui? Miserum est sic ad Exomologesim peruenire.* He sayth, *palam absolui*, because the custome in the primitiue Church was, and now is, to confesse our sinnes not priuatly in corners and chambers; but publickly in Churches and chappells; vnles the greatnes of persecution, or other lawfull cause doth hinder.

(b) Cap. 12

(c) Cap. 10

2. S. Irenæus speaking of certayne women, who (deceaued and seduced by Marcion, then a famous heretik) reconciled themselues and returned to the holy Church, confessing their sinnes and doing pennance therefore, saith: (d) *Ipsæ sæpenumero cùm ad Ecclesiam Dei redijssent, confessæ sunt.* And a little after he sheweth the very fashion vsed then in the Church at the reception of any heretical person, who was first absolued from excommunication; then after his priuate confession, was absolued from his sinnes; finally pennance beinge enioyned, a notable changement of his life from bad to good was easy to be remarked. *Deinde cùm non sine magno labore fratres eam conuertissent, ipsa omne tempus in Exomologesi consummauit, plangens & lamentans ob hanc, quam ab hoc mago passa est corruptelam.* Calling thereby Marciõ the heretike a Magician & witch, because cõmonly heresy and witchcraft are ioyned together.

(d) Lib. 1. cap. 9.

3. Origen a learned writer of this Age, threatneth bitterly those who receaued the Blessed Sacrament, not hauing

(e) Hom. 2. in Leuit.

uing before confessed their sins to the Priest: (e) *Cùm anima tua ægrotet, & peccatorum langoribus vrgeatur, securus es, contemnis gehennam atq; ignis æterni supplicia despicis & irrides? Iudicium Dei paruipendis, & commonentem te Ecclesiam despicis? Communicare non times corpus Christi, accedens ad Eucharistiam quasi mundus & purus, quasi nihil in te sit indignum, & his omnibus putas quod effugias iudicium Dei? non recordaris illud quod scriptum est, quia propterea in vobis infirmi & ægri, & dormiunt multi: Quare multi infirmi? quoniam non seipsos dyudicant, neq; seipsos examinant, nec intelligunt quid est communicare Ecclesiæ &c.* And agayne he auoweth that we are obliged not only to confesse our sins to God; but lykewise to those who haue receaued power from God to absolue vs. (f) *Si enim reuelauerimus peccata nostra non solùm Deo, sed & his, qui possunt mederi vulneribus nostris atq; peccatis, delebuntur peccata nostra ab eo qui ait:* (g) *Ecce delebo vt nubem iniquitates tuas, & sicut caliginem peccata tua.* Finally he declareth the custom of the primitiue Church which was first to heare the confession of sick persons, & then to giue them the Sacrament of Extreme-Vnction (which he acknowledgeth to be the seauenth Sacrament, or the seauenth way wherby our sinnes are forgiuen vs) in annoynting them with oyle: (h) *Est adhuc & septima, licet dura & laboriosa, per pœnitentiam remissio peccatorum, quum lauat peccator in lachrymis stratum suum, & fiunt ei lachrymæ suæ panes die ac nocte; & cùm non erubescit sacerdoti Domini indicare peccatum suum, & quærere medicinam, secundum eum qui ait: Dixi, pronunciabo aduersum me iniustitiam meam Domino, & tu remisisti impietatem cordis mei. In quo impletur & illud quod Apostolus dicit:* (i) *Si quis autem infirmatur, vocet presbyteros Ecclesiæ, & imponant ei manus, vngentes eum oleo in nomine Domini &c.* Do the Ministers vse this annointing of the sicke as the Apostles did? If not, how can they so shamfully affirme, that their Religion the same with that of the Apostles?

(f) Hom. 17. in Luc.

(g) Isa. 44. v. 22.

(h) Hom. 2. Leuit.

(i) Iames 5. v. 4.

4. S. Cyprian speaketh so playnly of this matter, that his words being read without passion, the Ministers wil see easily the newfangled nesse of their Religion. His wordes be: (k) *Confiteantur singuli, quæso vos fratres, delictum, dum adhuc qui deliquit in seculo est, dum admitti confessio eius potest, dum satisfa-*

(k) Serm. de lapsis.

satisfactio & remissio facta per sacerdotes apud Dominum grata est. And agayne, he setteth down the fashion to make a good Confession: to wit, to confesse with humility of mynd & simplicity of words, with an inward contrition of heart, and not only of deadly sinnes but also of veniall: (l) *Hoc ipsum apud Sacerdotes Dei dolenter & simpliciter confitentur, Exomologesim conscientiæ faciunt, animi sui pondus exponunt, salutarem medelam paruis licet & modicis vulneribus exquirunt, scientes scriptum esse, Deus non deridetur.* Lykewise in a certayne Epistle of his to the holy Martyrs, he testifieth that if a man be in danger of his life, by reason of his corporall infirmities, he should incontinent haue care to confesse his sinnes: (m) *Si premi infirmitate aliqua & periculo cœperint, Exomologesi facta, & manu eis à vobis imposita in pœnitentiam cum pace à martyribus sibi promissa ad Dominum remittantur.* See his tenth Epistle to the clergy, where he setteth downe the very particular circumstances vsed now-adayes in administring the Sacrament of Confession.

(l) *Eodem Sermon.*

(m) *Epist. 11. ad Martyr. confess. & epist. 14. ad Clerum.*

That the Ministers haue falsified sundry places of the Bible which do proue the Sacrament of the Catholike Church, to haue bene in vse vniuersally.

The second Section.

THe Catholik Church teacheth vs, that originall sinne is not a Phisicall quality descending from Adam to vs, but rather a morall spot wherewith the soule of man is defiled so soone as it is vnited with that body, which descendeth from the corrupted stock or root of Adam; wherby, as all those who descend of Adam are corrupted with this originall sinne, so it is wholly taken and washed away by the Sacrament of Baptisme, though some effects, as concupiscence, inclination to sinne, and such (which are not sinne) remayne after Baptisme, as playnly S. Paul teacheth saying: (a) *As by one man sinne entred into the world, and by sinne death, and so vnto all men death did passe, in whome all sinned.* Directly agaynst the Ministers, who do teach, that

(a) *Rom. 5. v. 12.*

Christian mens Children are holy from their Mothers wombe by reason of the parents Fayth, and consequently such children (say they) haue not absolute necessity of the Sacrament of Baptisme (which is called regeneration) a-
(b) Iohn. 3. gaynst the expresse words of the Bible: (b) *Except a man be borne of water and of the spirit, he cannot enter into the kingdome of God.* 2. The Ministers do teach, that originall sinne is not only that forsayd mortal spot, but lykewise that concupiscence and bad inclination without consent of our will, is truly and properly originall sinne, which consequently euer remayneth truly in vs, & is neuer washed away in this life. To the which end they haue falsified the foresayd place of S. Paul, thus: *As by one man sinne entred into the world, and death by sinne, & so death went ouer all men, forasmuch as all men*
ἐφ ᾧ πάντες. *haue sinned.* Putting the word *forasmuch*, for the word *in whom*, (Adam) directly agaynst the Greeke, where it is, *in whome*; directly agaynst the Syriake, *behaidecullethen chatan*, where
(c) Aug. de peccat. merit. & rem. cap. 10. the words *in whom* are referred with (c) S. Augustin to *Adam*. The Pelagian Heretikes, who denyed with our Ministers that baptisme tooke away originall sinne, translated this place to strengthen their heresy, as the Ministers do. Wher-
(d) Lib. 6. cont. Iulia. cap. 12. of (d) S. Augustin bitterly accused the Pelagians in turning *quatenus* into *quantum, forasmuch*, for *that*, in place of *in quo, in whome*, condemning the Pelagians of manifest heresy and
(e) Beza in hunc locũ. of Lese-maiesty diuine, for such impious translations. (e) Beza himself condemneth the Ministers of impiety for turning *in quo, in whom*, referring it to the words before, *as by one man.* Shall the Ministers be able to shew any other place of the Bible, where they haue translated those Greeke words, *in quo, forasmuch*? No truly to my knowledge. Doe they translate those wordes, as we do, in other indifferent
(f) Mark. 11. v. 14. places? That they do, as in S. Marke: (f) *They let downe the bed, wherin the sicke of the palsy lay.* And doth not such double and deceitfull forme of translating shew the Ministers to be
ἐφ ᾧ. infected with the spirit of contradiction, errour and heresy? Now, that baptisme taketh away from the child originall sinne, and that the child cannot be saued without the Sacramẽt of Baptisme, S. Paul auoweth: (g) *Not by the works*

of

of Iustice (he meaneth the workes done before Iustification) *which we did, but according to his mercy he hath saued vs by the lauer of regeneration and renouation of the holy Ghost, whome he hath powred vpon vs aboundantly by Iesus-Christ our Sauiour &c.* Which place the Ministers haue filthily corrupted. And agayne: (h) *Aryse and be baptized, and wash away thy sinnes, inuocating the name of the Lord.* Which place the Ministers haue lykewise falsified. And S. Peter playnly teacheth that we are saued and clensed from our sinnes by the Sacrament of Baptisme: (i) *While the arke was preparing, wherein few, that is, eight soules were saued by water, wherunto baptisme being of the lyke forme, now saueth yow also* But let vs try & examine the very wordes of the Ministers set downe in the articles of their fayth, where they teach plainly that Baptism taketh not away wholy originall sinne (to take away the half therof, is it not follie to thinke?) for in their articles of Fayth rehersed publickely euery sonday in the Churches of Sotland, they affirme, that Baptisme, (k) *Representeth vnto vs the remission of our sins.* They wil not say, that it taketh away originall sin. And agayne the Minister asketh: (l) *Thow meanest not that the water is the washing of our soules? That is, thou meanest not that Baptisme giuen in water, washeth away the sinnes of our soules? C. No, for that belongeth to the bloud of our Sauiour Christ Iesus alone &c.* Finally the ministry concludeth that Baptisme is but a figure wherunto verity is conioyned? What verity is conioyned? what verity I pray yow, if grace and remission of sinnes be not ioyned thereto? The Ministers then to proue and vphold this heresy and blasphemy haue manifestly falsified those wordes of S. Peter thrusting the very word *Figure* into the pure text of the Bible thus: (m) Wherin (to wit, in the Arke) *few, that is eight soules, were saued in the water, to the which also the figure that now saueth vs, Baptisme agreeth &c.* Directly against the Greeke text which auoweth Baptisme *to saue vs,* and cleanse vs of originall sinne, alwayes grounded vpon the bloud of Christ: As the Ministers auow of Fayth which saueth vs, not as a figure but grounded vpon the bloud of Christ. The Ministers take so great delight in figures that I feare they shall get finally heauen in a figure, and hel really.

(h) Act. 22 v. 16.

(i) 1. Pet. 3. v. 20.

(k) 48. sonday.

(l) 94. sonday.

(m) 1. Pet. 3. v. 20.

ἡμᾶς σώζει βάπτισμα

ly. The Syriake text maketh no mention of a figure, but rather sheweth, that euen as Noe with some others were saued truly & not figuratiuely from the deluge of the waters; so Baptisme saueth vs in taking away originall sinne, and not as a figure; as plainly S. Paul witnesseth writing to (n) Titus. But let vs leaue these figuristicall Ministers.

Turphesa græcè ἀντίτυπον.

(n) Tit. 3. v. 5.

2. In the lyke manner the Ministers to take away the effect of Baptisme (which is the clensing of originall sinne) they haue corrupted that of S. Paul: (o) *Husbands loue your wyues, as Christ also loued the Church, and deliuered himselfe for it, that he might sanctify it, cleãsing it by the lauer of water in the word.* Where the words, *lauer of the water*, signify the material parts of this Sacrament, the words, *in the word*, signify the forme of the Sacrament, which is, *I Baptize thee in the name of the Father, &c.* Which being dewly applyed, do sanctify & clense vs, sayth the Apostle, and that in such sort, that after Baptisme, (p) *There remayneth no spot or wrinkle, or any such thing of Originall sinne.* Yea rather we are made by Baptisme *holy and without blame.* The Ministers I say haue falsified the place and do read thus: *That he might sanctify it, and cleanse it by the washing of water through the word.* Signifying therby the preaching of the word to forgiue vs our sinnes, & not Baptisme, directly agaynst the Greeke text, where it is, *in the word*, & not, *through the word.* Yea the Ministers shall neuer be able to name me any holy Father, where the Greeke word is taken for *through:* which corruption was first inuented by Caluin & Beza who do trãslate impiously, *vt eã sanctificaret ab eo purificatam lauacro aquæ per verbum.* Thrusting in three seuerall words, which are not in the Greeke text.

(o) Ephes. 5. v. 25.

(p) Ephes. 5. v. 27.

ἐν ῥήματι.

ἐν.

Beza hic.

3. The Catholik Church teacheth that there be three Sacraments which cannot be reiterated by reason that they leaue after them a certayne signe or character, which perpetually remaineth in him who hath receaued them, which are, Baptisme, Confirmation and Order: as witnesseth S. Paul, speaking of the Sacrament of Confirmation: (q) *And he that confirmeth vs with yow in Christ, and that hath annointed vs, God: who also hath sealed vs, and giuen the pledge of the Spirit in our harts.* Which wordes the Ministers haue falsified, in puting the

(q) 2. Cor. 1. v. 21.

the word *earnest* (which can haue no signification in that place) for the word *pledge*, which signifies the foresayd character. The same verity witnesseth S. Paul to the (r) Ephesians, where in lyke manner they haue falsified the Bible, as the learned Reader may easely perceaue. Finally S. Paul witnesseth this character in the Sacrament of Confirmatiõ, writing thus: (s) *And contristate not the holy Spirit of God, in which you are signed vnto the day of redemptiõ.* As explicateth manifestly (t) S. Basil, (u) S. Cyril Hierosol. (x) S. Chrisostom & sundry other ancient Fathers, accordingly with ancient and famous (a) Prudentius, who twelue hundreth yeares since spake thus of the Sacrament of Confirmation.

(r) Ephes. 1 v. 13. & 14.

(s) Ephes. 4 v. 30.

(t) Hom. de baptism.

(u) Cathec. 3. & 17.

(x) Hom. 2. in ep. ad Ephesios.

(a) in Psycomachia.

Post inscripta oleo fronti signacula, per quæ
Vnguentum regale datum est, & Chrisma perenne.

It were tedious to set downe the infinite multitude of the Ministers corruptions of the Bible concerning the holy Sacraments of Confession, of the Blessed Sacrament (wherof I haue spoken a litle now and then) of the Sacrament of holy Orders: only I wil touch by the way the corruption they vse speaking of the Sacrament of Mariage, wherof S. Paul sayth thus: (b) *For this cause shall man leaue his Father & mother, and shall cleaue to his wife, & they shall be two in one flesh. This is a great Sacrament, but I speake in Christ, and in the Church.* Meaning, that as Christ left, as it were, his Father, exinaniting himselfe by his incarnation, and left the Synagogue his mother, and ioyned himself to the Church; so the maryed must needs forsake Father & mother & cleaue vnto his wife. And as Christ in his incarnation ioyned his Godhead indissolubly with our manhood in one hypostasy (for, *quod semel assumpsit, nunquam dimisit*, say the Doctours) euen so the knot & band of Marryage is indissoluble sayth S. Paul: (c) *Let not the wife depart from her husband. But if she depart, let her remayne vnmarryed, or be reconciled vnto her husband.* Which is the cause that the Apostle sayth: (d) *In Christ, and in the Church.* To signify the double and indissoluble vnion which is in Christ with our manhood, and with the true Church of God.

(b) Ephes. 5. v. 32.

(c) 1. Cor. 7. v. 10. 11.

(d) Ephes. 5. v. 32.

4. The Ministers contrary to this doctrine, to signi-

fy that marriage is not indissoluble, and that it is not a Sacrament, hath with Beza and Caluin filthily corrupted the Bible, thus: *This is a great secret, but I speake concerning Christ and concerning the Church.* Directly against the Greeke word, which (being taken as hath been in vse these sixteene hūdreth yeares among the holy Grecian Fathers, (e) Ignatius, (f) Iustin martir, (g) Clement Alexandrinus, (h) Origen, (i) Athanasins, (k) Basil, (l) Chrysostome and all others learned of that nation.) signifieth manifestly a Sacrament instituted by Christ in the law of grace. Should not the Greeke Fathers be more belieued in the explication of a Greeke word (as the word *mystery* is) then our Ministers, of whom few do vnderstand the Greeke, fewer the Hebrew? S. Augustine amongest the Latine Fathers calleth marriage a Sacrament, saying: (m) *The good of Marriage among the people of God is in the holynesse of a Sacrament.* And agayne. (n) *Huius proculdubio Sacramenti res est, vt mas & femina connubio copulati, quamdiu viuunt, inseparabiliter perseuerent: nec liceat excepta causa fornicationis à coniuge coniugē dirimi; hoc enim custoditur in Christo & Ecclesia, vt viuens cum viuente in æternum nullo diuortio separetur.* And long afore S. Augustin, Tertullian auoweth the same: (o) *Christus vnam habens Ecclesiam sponsam, secundum Adæ & Euæ figuram, quam Apostolus in illud magnum Sacramentum interpretatur in Christum & Ecclesiam competisse, carnali monogamia per spiritalem.* Our sensuall Ministers seeme to commend mariage aboue all things, so farre as it feedeth their concupiscence and fleshly lustes, but to teach that it is a Sacrament hauing grace ānexed therto, to sanctify the parties married, to mak them to liue together in mutual fidelity, binging vp their children in the Fayth and feare of God, they will no wayes do, nor suffer to be done. I aske, in what part of the Bible is the word Sacrament to be found (which the Ministers belieue) if it be not heere? 2. By what Greeke word in vse among the holy Fathers, shall they signify our Latin word, *Sacrament*, if not by the word *mystery*? Is it not abhominable impiety to giue more credit to Caluin and Beza in the explication of these words of the Apostle, then to the ancient and holy Fathers, who proue out of this place

(e) *Epist. ad Philip.*
(f) *Orat. ad Antoniū Pium.*
(g) *Lib. 3. Strom.*
(h) *Hom. 11. Exod.*
(i) *Serm. cont. hæreticos.*
(k) *Lib. de vera virginit. cap. 8.*
(l) *Hom. 20. in cap. 5. ad Ephes.*
(m) *De bono cōiugali cap. 24.*
(n) *Lib. 1. de nup. & concupisc. cap. 10.*
(o) *Lib. de Monogam. c. 5.*

place

place the holy Sacrament of Marriage? Doth not the Syriake word *Arra*, vsed heere signify a Sacrament? If not, what other Syriake word vsed in the Bible, signifieth the same?

5. The second corruptiō of this place is in those words, *But I speake concerning Christ*, to signify that Marriage is dissoluble, conforme to the abhominable practise dayly vsed amongst the Ministers, directly agaynst their owne Bible: (p) *The wyfe is bound by the law, as long as her husband liueth, but if her husband be dead, she is at liberty to marry with whome she will.* Againe, (q) *If while the man liueth, she take another man, she shalbe called an adulteresse.* The Ministers wil not translate, *in Christ*, as it is in all the Greeke copyes, wherby is signified the perpetuall knot of marriage, by the indissoluble vnion of the manhood of Christ with his Godhead, of Christ with the Church, but rather they will translate, *concerning Christ*, directly agaynst the Greeke text. Why do the Ministers translate the same Greeke proposition elswhere otherwayes, as, (r) *Wherefore as by one man sinne entred into the world*, and not *concerning the world*? Yea a thousand such places they translate rightly as we do: why this I pray you? But only to confirme and giue way to their new inuented doctrine, to new ministeriall traditions, in a word, to their manifest & abhominable heresies.

(p) 1. Cor. 7. v. 39.

(q) Rom. 7. v. 3.

(r) Rom. 5. v. 12.

εἰς κόσμον.

6. The other place which the Ministers haue falsified is that of S. Paul: (s) *The women in lyke manner chast, not detracting, sober, faythfull in all things.* Where the Apostle exhorteth that as men, Deacons, and such should *be honest, not double-tounged*, so, *women in lyke manner chast*. The Ministers contrary, to signify that Churchmen should be marryed haue falsified the place, thus: *Lykewise their wyues must be honest, not euill speakers*: Thrusting in the text the word *wyues* for *women*, & all to feed their fleshly liberty, wherby they persuade themselues that none can be fit to be a Churchman, but he, (t) *who seeth his wife haue a great belly, and children wayling at their mothers beasts.* Are not such Ministers chosen to be Bishops? (u) *Whose care is not, how to suck out the marrow of the Scriptures, but how to sooth the peoples eares with florishing declamations.* The Syriake

(s) 1. Tim 3. v. 11.

γυναῖκας ὡσαύτως.

(t) *Hieron. aduers. Vigilant. c. 1.*

(u) *Hiero. ep. 73. ad Ocean. c. 4.*

The Syriake text maketh for vs Catholikes, ***Achano aphe nesche &c. the women in lyke manner chast.***

7. Another of their falsifications is that of S. Paul: (x) *It behoueth therfore a Bishop to be irreprehensible, the husband of one wyfe, sober, wyse, comely, chast, a man of hospitality, a teacher, not giuen to wine &c.* In lyke manner speaking of Deacons he sayth: (y) *Let deacons be the husbands of one wife.* Where the Apostle neyther commendeth, nor counselleth, nor wisheth Bishops or Priests to marry (as the fleshly Ministers do thinke) but that none should be admitted to be a Bishop or Priest, hauing bene twise married, or hauing bene ***Bygamus:*** which exposition as it is agreable to the practise of the holy Church, the definition of ancient Councels, the doctrine of all the Fathers without exception: so I do proue it thus. First, if S. Paul wished by these words, Bishops & Churchmen to marry, he himself would haue contradicted his own command and law. For Timotheus and Titus both Bishops and Priests were neuer marryed, as is manifestly witnessed by the holy Fathers after (a) S. Ignatius, S. Iohn his disciple. 2. S. Paul himselfe both a Bishop and Priest was neuer marryed as he witnesseth of himselfe: (b) *Therefore I say vnto the vnmarryed, and vnto the widdowes, it is good for them if they abide euen as I doe.* How could he then counsell or cōmand Bishops to do that which they could not remarke in himselfe. 3. S. Paul commēdeth the office of a Bishop as a most noble, holy, and sublime office, yet hard and difficile; and in effect (c) *There is nothing in this life, and specially at this tyme, harder, more laborious, or more dangerous then the office of a Bishop, Priest, or Deacon: But before God nothing more blessed, if they be in such sort as our captayne commandeth.* How then could S. Paul, yea thinke only, that it were expedient to a Bishop or Priest to marry? since marriage alone bereaueth a mā wholly of al his wits, by reason of the great burthen, & vnspeakeable cares of marriage, as witnesseth S. Paul speaking to laymen: (d) *If thou takest a wife thou sinnest not, neuertheles such shall haue trouble in the flesh.* Wherby S. Paul witnesseth that diuers marryed persons are a thousand tymes more troubled with fleshly pleasures and tentations, then Virgins

(x) 1. Tim. 3. v. 2.

(y) 1. Tym. 3. v. 12.

(a) Ep. ad Philadelph.

(b) 1. Cor. 7. v. 8.

(c) Aug. ep. 148.

(d) 1. Cor. 7. v. 28.

Virgins or vnmarryed persons, as S. Augustin wysely remarked saying: *Minùs virgo quàm vidua, minùs vidua quàm nupta.* 4. S. Paul sayth: (e) *That the vnmarried woman and virgin careth for the things of our Lord, that she may be holy both in body and spirit. But she that is married careth for the things of the world, how she shal please her husband.* Since then the office of a Bishop requireth, as S. Paul teacheth, so great holynesse in body and spirit, how could he coūsell or cōmand that Bishops should marry? 5. (and this argument is to be remarked) S. Paul declaring after how widdowes should be chosen sayth: (f) *Let a widdow be chosen of no lesse then threescore yeares, which hath bene the wife of one husband.* Meaning thereby that a widdow who hath bene twise marryed should not be chosen at all, for it was neuer the custom amongst the Christians, yea not amongst the Pagans for a widdow to haue two husbands together. Euen so S. Paul speaketh heere of a Bishop, to wit that he who should be chosen to that high office, should not haue bene twise marryed, but rather to haue bene, not to be actually, the husbād of one wife: as witnesseth plainly with all the rest of the Fathers, S. Hierome: (g) *What shall the Church of the East do* (sayth he) *what they of Ægypt, of the Apostolike sea, which take to the clergy eyther virgins or vnmarryed, or such who hauing had wyues cease to be husbands?* The reason of this saying of S. Paul, is because in the tyme of the Apostles the persecutiō was so great & the lacke of Bishops in lyke manner so great, that it was forced to choose to that holy office, not only those who had neuer bene marryed, but lykewise those who had beene once marryed.

(e) 1. Cor. 7. v. 34.

(f) 1. Tym. 3. v. 2.

(g) Contra Vigil. c. 1.

The 11. and 12. Article.

1. *That man hath Freewil, not only in naturall, and ciuill Actions:*

2. *But also in morall, and supernaturall Actions.*

CHAP. VII.

ALbeit the whole decision of this Controuersie may be easily gathered out of the doctrine taught in the first Age, yet I will adde some things in this second Age. The question then betwixt vs and the Ministers, is whether mā couered & burthened with sinne, and before he be iustified, hath any freedome of will to lift vp his heart, and giue assent to Gods heauenly motions, when God of his infinite goodnes doth giue them to him? It is certayne that mans will is much weakned since the fall of Adam, his vnderstanding much diminished, and all the powers of his soule & body made feeble and weake: for the which cause the condition of man is compared with reason to him, who descending from Ierusalem to Ierico (as witnesseth the (a)
(a) *Luc.* 10 *v.* 30. Bible) fell among theeues, who robbed him of his temporall riches, and mayned him in his corporall members: So man by the sinne of his first parents, is spoyled of his supernaturall gifts, wounded in his naturall powers, and left not
(b) *Luc.* 10. *v.* 30. dead, nor wholy alyue, but as the Bible sayth, (b) *half dead. Aliue*, because (as the holy Fathers do say) he had remorse of conscience & liberty of freewill: *dead*, because he lay buried in the sepulcher of sinne, out of which he could neuer haue risen, vnles it had pleased our Sauiour Christ Iesus with his precious bloud to haue healed his wounds, & restored

stored the perishing powers of his soule; so that freewill in man was not vtterly lost (as the Ministers ignorantly do teach) but lesse able to worke; not fully taken away, but mayned; not altogether bound, but vehemently inclined to the corruption of sinne; in a word, (c) *non extinctum, sed extenuatum,* not extinguished but extenuated: yet being moued and strengthned by Christ, it is able to accept his grace or good motions, as it is by nature apt to refuse them, and therefore is free: which I proue by the very wordes of the Bible it selfe.

(c) Conc. Trid. sess. 6. cap. 1.

2. First, I proue it by all those places of the Bible, which inuite and exhorte vs to forsake sinne, to gaynestand sinne, & to repaire to God, (d) *O Israel if thou returne to me, sayth the Lord, and if thou put away thy abhominations out of my sight.* Againe: (e) *O yee disobedient children turne agayne, sayth the Lord.* And agayne: (f) *Whereupon I also haue giuen you dulnes of teeth in all your cityes & lacke of bread in all your places, & yee haue not returned to me saith the Lord.* Againe: (g) *Susana sighed & said, Perplexities are to me on euery side: for if I shall do this, it is death to me, & if I do it not, I shall not escape your hands.* Doth not Susanna testify that she had freewil to choose the one or the other? Somtymes the Bible witnesseth, that God intreateth vs vpon a condition, declaring thereby a Freewill we haue to accept of the condition or not: (h) *If yee consent and obey, sayth God, yee shall eat the good thinges of the land: but if yee refuse and be rebellious, yee shall be deuoured with the sword, for the mouth of the Lord hath spoken it.* Sometymes God seemeth to stay and expect the consent of our freewill, as: (i) *Behold I stand at the doore and knock, if any man heare my voyce and open the doore, I will come to him, and will supp with him, and he with me.* And agayne: (k) *Despysest thou the riches of his bountifulnes and patience, and long sufferinge, not knowing that the bountifulnes of God leadeth thee to repentance?* Sometymes God complayneth of vs that we remayne so long in sinne, declaring thereby the freewill we haue eyther to remayne in sinne or to ryse from sinne, as (l) *Therfore I will iudge yow, O house of Israel, euery one according to his wayes saith the Lord God: returne therfore, and cause others to returne away from all your transgressi-*

(d) Ierem. 4. v. 1.
(e) Ierem. 3. v. 14.
(f) Amos 4. v. 6.
(g) Daniel 13. v. 22.
(h) Isa. 1. v. 19. & 20.
(i) Reuel. 3. v. 20.
(k) Rom. 2. v. 4.
(l) Ezech. 18. v. 30.

greßions: so iniquity shall not be your destruction. Cast away from you all your transgreßions, wherby yee haue transgressed, and make you a new heart, & a new spirit, for why wil yee die, O house of Israel? for I desire not the death of him that dieth, sayth the Lord God: cause therfore others to returne, and liue yee. Should not the Ministers blush to renounce as it were these playne wordes of their owne Bible which make for freewill? should they not be ashamed to impugne that which they call the word of God? What? doth not the very proceeding of the Ministers against vs Catholiks, proue manifestly freewill? for they blame, and seuerely punish all such Catholiks as refuse to subscribe to their assertions and Idolatrous doctrine, & to this purpose they labour to disgrace vs priuatly and publickly: they dayly make seuere lawes against vs, they cast down our houses, confiscate our goods, imprison our persons, and punish vs with all sort of afflictions, and all this they performe to no other end, but to enforce our *freewill* to belieue their Religion: for if we want freedome of will, as they hold, are not their lawes wicked, their conference in vayne, their persuasions foolish to compell vs to that which lyeth not in our power freely to choose, or to do? Sometymes God putteth the full blame of our impenitence to our owne froward and stubborne will, as our Sauiour

(m) *Math.* 23. 37. witnesseth: (m) *Ierusalem, Ierusalem which killest the Prophets & stonest them which are sent to thee, how often would I haue gathered thy childrē togeather as the hen gathereth her chickens vnder his wings and yee would not.* In vayne truly should God exhort vs to returne to him, if we had not *freewill*. In vayne should he expect our consent, or complayne of our delay, if we had not *freewill*. In vayne should he blame vs of obstinacy, if we had not *freewill*. To the which places I will ioyne this

(n) *Iohn* 1. v. 12. of S. Iohn: (n) *As many as receaued him, to them he gaue power to be the sonnes of God, euen to them that belieue in his name.* And ac-

(o) Lib. 50. *Hom. hom* 36. cordingly S. Augustine: (o) *God hath left it in thy owne free choyse, to whome thou wilt prepare a place, to God, or to the Diuell. When thou hast prepared it, he that inhabiteth, shal beare sway therin. Man prepareth his heart, yet not without the aide of God, who toucheth the heart.* To the which purpose is rightly applyed that

that of S. Paul which proueth vs to be freewilled, coadiutors, and collabourers: (p) *I haue laboured more abundantly then all they, yet not I, but the grace of God with me*: which S. Augustine exponeth thus: (q) *Neyther the grace of God alone, nor he alone, but the grace of God with him*. Conforme to that famous saying of the Wiseman, who speaketh of wisdome, thus: (r) *Send her from thy holy heauens, and from the seat of thy greatnes, that she may be with me, and may labour with me, that I may know what is acceptable with thee*, which place the Ministers haue corrupted.

(p) 1 Cor. 15. v. 10.
(q) Augu. lib. de grat. & lib. arb. cap. 15.
(r) The booke of Wisdome cap. 9. v. 10

3. The reason wherfore Freewill must needs be graunted to man, is grounded in the inward nature of vertue and vice, by reason that no action can be morally good or morally bad, except it be voluntary, conforme to that famous saying of S. Augustine. *Sinne is so voluntary, that except it were voluntary, it were not sinne*. Where the word *voluntary*, is taken for that which is freely done, and which was in the liberty of man to do or not to do, directly contrary to that which is done of necessity. So S. Augustine in another place: (s) *Neyther sinne nor well doing can be iustly imputed vnto any man, who of his proper will doth nothing. Therefore both sinne & weldoing is in the free arbitrement of the will*. According to the which saying of S. Augustine, I aske of the Ministers: Eyther it is in the power of man to eschew sinne or not? if it be, he hath freewill and is not bound to sin: if not, he necessarly sinneth, and cannot be charged with the imputatiō of sinne. To the which argument I may ioyne that of our learned coūtreyman Ioannes Duns, who affirmeth that no man should dispute with words against him who denyeth *freewill*, but rather with a good baston beating him, & argumenting after this forme: Eyther I haue freewill to beat thee or I haue it not? if I haue it, then thou auowest freewill; if not, then I beat thee of necessity, and necessarly and consequently I cannot offend in beating thee thus: for (t) *He that is forced by necessity to do any thing, doth not sinne*: And he who doth any thing necessarily, doth it not sinfully.

(s) Lib. 83. qq. 24.
(t) August. cont. Fortunat Manich. disp. 1.

4. I will omit other reasons and proofes, vntil I come

come to the testimonyes of the holy Fathers of this age; content for the present to aske of the Ministers, in what part of the expresse word of their owne Bible are these points of their Religion found, *Man after the fall of Adam hath not freewill?* Is there such a distinction in all the Bible? *Man sinneth of necessity; Man cannot but sinne: Man continually doth transgresse the commandments.* Are such propositions to be found in the expresse word of the Bible? no truly. Shall we then belieue them because the Ministers do teach them without any warrant of the expresse word? No reason. But the Ministers (say the Protestants) will deduce them out of the Bible by necessary consequence. What is that
(u) *Ierem. 14. v. 14.* but their owne inuentions, (u) *A lying vision, and diuination which they prophesy vnto vs?* That is not to preach the Ghospell but to preach their owne heresies, enobled with the name of the Ghospell. Let vs then prefer the consequences of the holy Fathers of this second age or Century concerning *freewill*, to the consequences of the Ministers, who are children without parents, and schollers without Maisters.

The testimonies of the holy Fathers of this second Age, prouing man to haue freewill in maters concerning his Saluation.

The first Section.

S. Irenæus witnesseth plainly, that man hath freewill, by reason of the dayly exhortations, precepts and reprehensions made to euery one of vs: for who maketh lawes to fooles, to mad, men, or little babes by reason they want
(a) *Iren. lib 4. cap. 92.* freewill? his words are: (a) *Id quod semper erat liberum & suæ potestatis in homine semper seruauit Deus & suam exhortationem, vt iustè damnentur qui non obediunt, & qui obedierunt, & credunt ej, honorentur incorruptibilitate* Directly against the Ministers who say that man by the fall of Adam lost freewill: yea this holy Father auoweth that man hath yet frewil, as the Angells

Angels had before their fall. (b) *Posuit autem in homine potestatem electionis, quemadmodum & in Angelis.* To the which purpose he citeth that of our Sauiour: (c) *Ierusalem Ierusalem, how often would I haue gathered thy children togeather &c. and thou wouldst not.* Vpon the which words I frame this argument: *Freewill* hath of it selfe eyther some strength or none at all: if any, then yee grant frewill: if none, then Christ said not true (which is a blasphemy) in saying the Iewes would not cõforme to this holy doctrine of Irenæus, which he plentifully teacheth in the fourth booke & ninth chapter and in sundry other places) S. Augustine wysely auoweth that he who denyeth freewill should be banished out of the company of men: (d) *Vnles the motion, wherby the will is led to and fro, were voluntary, and rested in our owne power, man should neyther be prayse-worthy, turning as it were the hinge of his will to heauenly things: nor worthy of blame, winding it downe to earthly: nor to be admonished at all &c. But whosoeuer thinketh that man is not to be admonished, &c. deserueth to be banished out of the company of men.*

(b) *Lib.* 4. c. 7.

(c) *Matth.* 23. v. 37.

(d) *Lib.* 3 *de libero arbitrio cap.* 1.

2\. Iustinus martyr auoweth likewyse, that if man had not freewill, he would be without blame of vice, or prayse of vertue. (e) *Ac nisi libero arbitrio*, sayth he, *atq; iudicio genus humanum & res turpes fugere potest, & pulchra ac bona sequi, extra causam culpamq; est eorum, qui quoquomodo aguntur. Sed ipsum libero arbitrio, liberaq; voluntate & rectè facere & peccare docemus hoc modo.* The same he teacheth answering the question of the Gentills who denyed *Freewill* with the Protestants; in lykemanner in his booke *de monarchia*, and his dialogues with Triphon he teacheth plentifully freewill.

(e) Apol. 2 ad Antonium Imperatorem.

Quæst. 103.

3\. Tertullian also writeth abundantly of this matter agaynst Marcion the heretike, auowing, that man is called the image of God, specially in regard of his freewill: (f) *Liberum.* sayth he, *& sui arbitrij & suæ potestatis inuenio hominem à Deo institutum, nullam magis imaginem & similitudinem Dei in illo animaduertens, quàm eiusmodi status formam.* The Protestãt replyeth that saying of our Sauiour, *without me yee can do nothing*: agayne, *it is not in him that willeth, nor in him that runneth &c.* I answere to these, and such places of Scripture, that

(f) *Lib.* cõt *Marcion c.* 5.

freewill

freewill of it selfe hath no stength to worke our conuersion without the grace of God, wherwith being inwardly enlightned, confirmed and quickened, it hath force and ability to worke with God, & bring forth the fruit of piety.

(g) 2. Cor. 3. v. 5. Wherfore S. Paul who sayd: (g) *We are not sufficient to thinke any thing of our selues, as of our selues, but our sufficiency is of God.* The same Apostle sayd lykewise: (h) *I can do all things in him*

(h) Philip. 4. v. 13. *that strengthneth me.* As the eye in darknes cannot see, yet with the benefit of the light it can see; so the earth of it self bringeth foorth no corne, yet tilled, watered with raine, and quickned with seed, and the sunne, it bringeth foorth corne. To the better vnderstanding wherof the doctours of diuinity do teach a threefold grace, wherby the freewill of man is greatly helped, confirmed and quickned.

4. The first is called *a preuenting grace,* that is, *gratia praeueniens,* wherof the Bible speaketh: (i) *His mercy shall go before*

(i) Psal. 59. v. 10. *me.* And S. Paul, (k) *It is not in him that willeth, nor in him that*

(k) Rom. 9. v. 16. *runneth, but in God that sheweth mercy.* Secondly it is necessary that God assist & help our freewil to imbrace his holy inspirations, & this is called *concomitant grace*, that is, *gratia con-*

(l) Psal. 70 v. 1. *comitans,* wherby God accompanieth and cooperateth with vs. The which grace King Dauid asked of God: (l) *Incline vnto my help, O God, O Lord make hast to help me.* And S. Paul:

(m) Rom. 8. v. 28. (m) *To them that loue God all things cooperate vnto God.* The one and the other grace is fitly explayned by those wordes of

(n) Reuel. 3. v. 20. the Bible: (n) *I stand at the doore and knocke, if any shall heare my voyce and open the gate, I will enter in vnto him, & will sup with him, and he with me.* To stand and knock at the doore of our freewill, is the office of Gods preuenting grace; to open the doore of our freewill to God, is both the worke of man and the worke of God: it is mans worke, in giuing his free consent to opē the doore of his heart; it is Gods, in that he worketh and helpeth man, to open his heart, with his cooperating grace: for the which cause the self same actions

(o) Psal. 51. v. 10. which in way of our conuersion, are giuen to God by the Bible, are lykewise giuen to man. As to God King Dauid

(p) Ezech. 18. v. 31. prayed: (o) *Create a cleane heart in me, O God.* To man Ezechiel witnesseth: (p) *Make to your selfe a new heart, and a new spirit.*

spirit. Of God S. Paul testifyeth, that he doth work all in all things of man: (r) *worke your saluation with feare and trembling.* Which place the Ministers haue falsified thus: *so make an end of your saluation* The third grace, distinct from the former, giuen to man by God, is called *a subsequent grace*, that is, *gratia subsequens.* Wherby God giueth oportunity to execute the good which we intended before: the first grace God is sayd to worke *in vs without vs*, that is, without our free consent. The second *in vs with vs*, because God worketh therby with vs. The third *in vs by vs*, that is, putting, by vs, our holy purposes in execution.

(r) Philip. 2. v. 12.

5. This holsome and Catholike doctrine witnesseth Tertullian, who sayth that man (notwithstanding the fall of Adam) hath freewill: (s) *Eumdem hominem, eamdem substantiam animæ, eumdem Adæ statum, eadem arbitrij libertas & potestas victorem efficit hodie de eodem diabolo, quum secundum obsequium legum eius Dei administratur.* And agayne: (t) *Oportebat igitur imaginem & similitudinem Dei, liberi arbitrij & suæ potestatis institui, in qua hoc ipsum imago & similitudo Dei deputaretur, arbitrij scilicet libertas & potestas: in quam rem ea substantia homini accommodata est, quæ huius status esset afflatus, vtiq; liberi, & suæ potestatis.* It were superfluous to cite more places of Tertullian who is so ample, so playne and pithy in all his works concerning *freewill*, that no reasonable mã can doubt of Tertullians opinion and Religion in this matter.

(s) Lib. 2. 8. contra Marcionẽ.

(t) Lib. 2. cap. 6.

6. Origen speaketh in the lyke manner so playnly agaynst the Ministers, that the attentiue reading of his words will giue great comfort to the constant Catholike: first thẽ wryting on those wordes of the Scripture: (u) *And now Israel what doth the Lord thy God require of thee, but to feare the Lord thy God, to walke in all his wayes*, he saith thus: (x) *Erubescant illi ad hæc verba, qui negant in homine liberum esse arbitrium: Quomodo posceret ab homine Deus, nisi haberet homo in sua potestate, quod poscenti Deo deberet offerre?* And agayne: (y) *Sui arbitrij est anima, & in quam voluerit partem est ei liberum declinare: & ideo iustum Dei iudicium est, quia sponte sua siue bonis siue pessimis monitoribus paret.* 2. He witnesseth, that a man may be the cause (vnder God) of his owne saluation, and lykewise the

(u) Deut. 10. v. 12.

(x) Hom. 12. in Num.

(y) Hom. 20. in Num

(a) Hom. in Ezech.

cause of his eternall perdition by reason of his *freewill*, (a) *Tu verò homo quare non vis arbitrio tuo te derelictum? Quare ægrè fers nisi, laborare, contendere, & per bona opera teipsum causam tuæ fieri salutis? An magis te delectabit dormientem & in otio constitutum æterna prosperitate requiescere?* 3. He witnesseth that freewill (not only as it is opposed to constraint and force, as Caluin dreameth, but also as it is opposed to necessity) was constantly belieued in the Catholike Church in his tyme: (b) *Est & illud definitum in Ecclesiastica prædicatione, omnem animã rationabilem esse liberi arbitrij & voluntatis.* Finally writing agaynst a famous Pagan and Epicurean of his tyme, called Celsus, who denied *freewill* with the Protestants, teaching that al things were done by necessity good or bad, by reason of the forsight or forknowledge of God, framing his argument with our Protestants after this forme: (c) *Whatsoeuer a man doth good or euill, is forseene by God. Ergo, it must needs be done of necessity, otherwise Gods forsight and prescience would be inconstãt and changeable.* Wherunto Origen answereth learnedly with vs Catholikes, that man doth not this or that good or euill action, because God forsaw it (as if the forsight of God were the necessary cause of mans actiõs) but rather God doth forsee our actions, because we out of our freedom shal do them, so that our actions are, as it were, the cause of Gods forsight or forknowledge, & not Gods forsight the cause of our actions: Euen as a man is not reprobate or condemned eternally to hell, because God forsaw him to become reprobate, but because he will euer remayne in sinne, and in a false religion for worldly respectes, God doth forsee, that he is to be eternally in the number of the reprobate. Origẽs wordes are: (c) *Videamus quid dicat postea. Hæc, inquit, cùm Deus esset prædixit, & omnino oportebat fieri quod prædixerat Deus: Ergo, suos discipulos & Prophetas, cum quibus cibum & potum sumebat, eò necessitatis adduxit, vt contra ius ac pietatem facerent, &c. Respondebimus & ad hæc, quando iubes vt ne ista quidem argumenta prætercam, quæ mihi videntur friuola. Celsus putat, quòd aliquis præscius prædixit ideo fieri quia prædictum est. Nos verò hoc modo non concedentes, aimus non prædictorem causam esse futuri, sed futurum illud, quod omnino euenturum erat, etiam nemine prædicente, præcognitori*

(b) In præfat. lib. 1. de principijs.

(c) Lib. 2. cont. Cels.

cognitori

cognitori causam prædicendi præbuisse. Which is conforme to that of the Bible: (d) *Thy perdition, O Israel, is of thee, in me only is thy help.* Which wordes as prouing freewill, the Ministers haue falsified impiously.

(d) *Hosea 13. v. 9.*

7. S. Cyprian auoweth the same doctrine of freewil saying: (e) *Conuersus ad Apostolos suos dixit, numquid & vos vultis ire? seruās scilicet legem qua homo libertati suæ relictus & in arbitrio proprio constitutus, sibimet ipse vel mortem appetit vel salutem.* And agayne: (f) *Credendi vel non credendi libertatem in arbitrio positam in Deuteronomio legimus:* (g) *Ecce dedi ante faciem tuam, vitam & mortem, bonum & malum; elige vitam & viues. Item apud Isaiam:* (h) *Si volueritis & audieritis me, bona terræ edetis: si autem nolueritis & non audieritis me, gladius vos consumet: Os enim Domini locutum est ista.* I omit to cite other holy fathers who all are playne and plentifull in this matter, and consequently do condemne the Ministers of manifest heresy, Idolatry and infidelity.

(e) *Epist. ad Cornel.*

(f) *Lib. 3. ad Quirin. cap. 52.*

(g) *Deut. 30. v. 19.*

That the Ministers haue falsified the Bible in sundry places, wherby Freewill is proued.

The second Section.

I Being in Edinburgh in prison, and conferring there with two Ministers (as I did at seuerall tymes with sundry, though destitute of all sorts of bookes) and seing the Greeke new testament in the hand of one, I asked of him. Be you content to be tried by the Greeke new Testament? Yea sayd he. By what Greeke new Testament, said I, for there be sundry copyes? By all Greeke copyes of the new testament answered the Minister. Will yow then, said I, allow that Greeke copy which speaketh to the prayse of good works, thus: (a) *Wherfore Brethren labour the more that by good workes you may make sure your vocation and election.* For sundry Greeke copyes haue those words as witnesseth (b) Beza, and all the Latin copyes without exception. The Minister answered, no: I appeale to that Greeke copy, which hath not those words, *by good works.* Well said I, if

(a) *Pet. 2. 10.* διὰ τῶν καλῶν ἔργων.

(b) *in hunc locum.*

you wil haue it so, take your pleasure, wil yee then be tryed by this Greeke new testament which is in your hand? cõtent sayth the Minister. Let vs see then that of S. Luke who
(c) Act.7. v.14. ἑβδομήκοντα πέντε. sayth, that all the kinred of Ioseph were, (c) *Threescore and fifteene soules*: yet Moyses in the booke of Genesis sayth that they were not so many in number, to wit: (d) *All the soules*
(d) Genes. 46. v. 26. *that came with Iacob into Egypt, &c. were in the whole threescore and six soules*. Here appeareth as it were a contradiction, the one place saying, *threescore & fifteene soules*, as all the Greeke Bibles do witnesse, the other, *threescore & six soules*; you say that Ministers haue the particular spirit to interprete the Scripture, let vs see, if this particular spirit may make yow to agree these two places. Which of the two places is more to be belieued? that of Genesis, said the Minister, for that of the Acts to be false witnesseth learnedly Beza, whose
(e) Beza in this place printed anno 1560. words are. (e) *Itaq; ingenuè profiteor editionem Græcam eo loco videri mihi deprauatam*. I replyed, then the Greeke new Testament which ye haue in your hand cannot be the word of God: for granting one errour therin, the authority of the word of God (who cannot lye nor erre, no not once) is taken from it: as if one errour or lye be foũd in a Charter or contract, it looseth the force of a true contract, though the rest be true. Truely a learned man, said I, might make a greater volume without comparison then your Bible is, concerning your falsifications, Blasphemyes, shiftes and turnings therof, all to couer and vphold your palpable errous and heresies.

(f) Rom.2. v.27. 2. The other place which they haue corrupted is that of S. Paul: (f) *Shall not vncircumcision, which is by nature, fulfilling the law, iudge thee who by the letter and circumcision art a preuaricator of the law?* Declaring therby that the Gentil & vncircumcised keeping the law, by the grace of God and light of nature, as holy Iob did, is to be preferred before a circũcised Iew, who keepeth not the law, confirming that
(g) Rom.2. v.13. which he had said before: (g) *Not the hearers of the law are iust with God, but the doers of the law shallbe iustified*. Wherof he giueth the reason in the verse following. Now the Ministers to insinuate craftily to the reader that neyther Gentil, Iew,

nor Christian can keep the law, they haue corrupted the text, thus: *Shall not vncircumcision which is by nature (if it keep the law) iudge thee, which by the letter and vncircumcision &c.* Where the Ministers of an absolute proposition of S. Paul do make a conditionall, thrusting into the text the word, *if*, which changeth wholy the force of the Apostles saying, and which is not in any Greeke copy, yea the most corrupted Greeke copyes printed at Geneua haue not the particle *si*, which is in the verse before, but not in this, speaking first conditionally and then absolutly, and declaring by the first that we may keep Gods commandements; by the second, that in effect some of the Gentils, much more of the Iewes and Christians haue (being assisted by Gods grace) kept Gods commaundements: as vpon this place learnedly (h) S. Chrysostome teacheth with the rest of the Fathers, of whom S. Augustine directly counterpoynts the Ministers heresy in this, saying: (i) *Non igitur Deus impossibilia iubet, sed iubendo admonet* &c. The Syriake text lykewise readeth absolutly, without the word *in*, which signifieth *if*. Could the Apostle speake more plainly in the praysе of good works then to say, (k) *God will reward euery man according to his works*? Yet the Ministers will not giue eare to those expresse words: they will not submit their iudgment to the holy doctrine of the Catholike Church, but will alwayes be contentious, rendring themselues therby inexcusable in the day of iudgement, as the Apostle sayth: (l) *vnto them that are contentious, and disobey the truth, and obey vnrighteousnes shall be indignation and wrath.* The second corruption in this place is that they haue translated, *and vncircumcision*, manifestly against the Greeke text, where it is, *and circumcision*.

τὸν νόμον τελοῦσα.

(h) *Hom.* 6. *in* 2. *ad Romanos.*

(i) *De nat. & gra. c.* 43.

(k) Rom. 2. v. 6.

(l) Rom. 2. v. 8.

3\. The third place is that of S. Paul to the Romans: (m) *For why did Christ, when we as yet were weake, according to the tyme, dye for the impious?* Declaring that mankind by the originall sinne of Adam, became weake and wounded in his vnderstanding, will, and memory, as in the treatise of *freewill* I declared at large before. The Ministers to persuade the ignorant and simple people, that man though baptized and

(m) Rom. 5. v. 6.

ὄντων ἡμῶν ἀσθενῶν.

and regenerate, hath no *freewil*, nor strength to good, conforme to that common saying of theirs: *So that in vs there is no goodnesse, for the flesh euermore rebelleth agaynst the spirit, wherby we continually transgresse thy holy precepts and commaundements:* They haue turned, I say, thus: *for Christ when we were yet of no strength.* Directly agaynst all the Greeke texts printed at Geneua which haue no negatiue at all, as the Ministers thẽselues auow in turning the same Greeke word in other places, as we doe, as: (n) *I haue shewed you all things, how that so labouring, yee ought to support the weake.* Agayne: (o) *To the weake I become as weake, that I may winne the weake.* And in sundry other places. Can there be greater impiety vsed agaynst God, then thus so willingly and wittingly to corrupt the true word of his heauenly Maiesty? Had not our gratious and most learned Soueraygne iust occasion to say in the summe of the Conference before his Maiesty, &c. *That the Geneua translation of the Bible, wherunto the English Bibles are conforme, is the worst of all, and that in the Marginall notes annexed to the Geneua translation, some are very partiall, vntrue and seditious?* Doth not a famous English Minister called M. Carliel say of all the English and Scots Bibles and translatours: (q) *They haue depraued the sense, obscured the truth, & deceyued the ignorant, and in many places they do detort the Scripture from the right sense, they shew themselues to loue darknes more then light, falshood more then truth?* How can then such Bibles be the ground of saluation? How can they be the word of God? And how can they beget true diuine fayth in the harts of the Readers, since they are wholy full of errours, corruptions, sacriledges and blasphemies? As for their psalmes which they sing so sweetly in their Churches, and so merryly in their houses, how can God take any pleasure in such singing, since they themselues do speake thus of thẽ: (r) *Our translation of the Psalmes comprised in our booke of common prayer, doth in addition, substraction, and alteration differ from the truth of the Hebrew in two hundreth places at least: in so much, that we do therfore professe to rest doubtfull, whether a man with safe conscience may subscribe therto.* Which innumerable multitude of errours & sacriledges conteyned in the English Bible gaue occa-

(n) Acts. 20. v. 35. ἀσθενούντων.

(q) *In his booke that Christ descended not into hel. p. 116. & 118.*

(r) *In the Treatise intituled a petition directed to her most excellent Maiesty, pag. 76. & 71.*

occasion to our gratious soueraygne to say, that, (s) *He could neuer yet see a Bible well translated into English.* As for the vulgar edition of the Bible, which the Catholike Church vseth, *Inimici nostri sint iudices, let our enemies be iudges thereof:* Specially Beza: (t) *The old Interpreter seemeth to haue interpreted the holy bookes with meruailous sincerity and Religion.* And Molinæus a learned Hugenot: (u) *I can very hardly depart from the vulgar accustomed reading, which also I am accustomed earnestly to defend.* And D. Couell: (x) *The vulgar Latin edition was vsed in the Church a thousand three hundreth yeares ago, & I prefer that translation before others.*

(s) *In the summe of the confere[n]ce before his Maiesty*
(t) *Beza in annot. in cap. 1. Lucæ.*
(u) *In nouum Testam. part.* 30.
(x) *In his answere to M. Iohn Bourges pag.* 94.

The 13. 14. and 15. Article.

1. *That man with the grace of God, may keep his Commaundements.* 2. *And that the keeping therof is meritorious of euerlasting life.* 3. *And that Fayth only doth not iustify, was constantly belieued in this second Age.*

CHAP. VIII.

Hauing spoken sufficiently in the former age of keeping of Gods commandemēts, & of the merits of good works, it resteth to speak of Fayth. To the better vnderstanding wherof it is to be remarked, that the Ministers do make two sorts of Fayth (besides their historicall Faith, whereof there is no mention in the Bible) to wit, a Fayth whereby they belieue generally that God will faythfully accomplish all his promisses, will giue remission of sinnes to all true belieuers: & a particular and *speciall Fayth*, wherby euery Protestant persuadeth and assureth himself (as an essentiall point of his Faith

10

to be belieued vnder the payne of eternall dānation) that his sins are forgiuen him, inferring consequently that this only Fayth doth iustify him. And in this solifidian, foolish, & childish persuasion the Protestants do place their *iustifying Fayth*, agaynst the which I make this argument. The Protestant who by this *Fayth* is iustified, may after fall into fornication and other damnable sinnes, or not? That he can not fall, no man will say, by reason that they continually transgresse the commandements: if he may fall, I aske, whether falling into those horrible sins he loose that particular Fayth or retayne it stil? To graunt that he looseth it, is to make all sinners Atheists and Infidels, for he who is bereft of Fayth must needes be infected with atheisme and infidelity: if he still retayne his true Fayth, notwithstanding the infinite multitude of such sinnes, is to hold, that he abydeth still in the estate of saluation, and may enioy the kingdom of heauen dying in such a miserable estate, which is directly agaynst the Bible: (a) *Do not erre, neyther fornicators nor seruers of Idols, nor adulterers, nor the effeminate &c. shall possesse the kingdome of God.*

(a) 1. Cor. 6. v. 9. & 10.

2. The second argument agaynst the *iustifying Faith* of the Protestants may be taken out of S. Iames who saith: (b) *What shall it proffit, my brethren, if a man say he hath Fayth, but hath not workes? Shall Fayth be able to saue him?* Agayne: (c) *So Fayth also if it haue not workes, is dead in it self.* Agayne, (d) *But wilt thou know, O vayne man, that Fayth without workes, is idle? Abraham our Father was he not iustified by workes, offring Isaac his sonne vpon the Altar?* Agayne. (e) *Yee see then how that by workes a man is iustified, and not by Fayth only.* Which words shew playnly that Fayth alone cannot iustify. 2. That the Apostle speaketh of true Fayth, presupposing that true fayth (though not liuely Fayth called by the Doctors *Fides formata*) may be without good workes, which good works the Apostle opposeth as it were, to Abraham his Fayth, which was a true Fayth, as the Scripture witnesseth. 3. The Apostle prayseth in a certayne forme that Faith which may be without good workes, saying: (f) *Thou belieuest that there is a God, thou doest well, the diuells also belieue it, and tremble.*

(b) Iames 2. v. 14.
(c) Iames 2. v. 17.
(d) Iames 2. v. 20. & 21.
(e) Iames 2. v. 24.
(f) Iames 2. v. 19.

How

How could he haue answered, *thou doest well*, if such were not *a true Fayth*, though not liuely; as when a tree in winter is bereft of her blossomes and fruit, yet is a true tree, though without fruit: in lyke manner the sunne ouerclouded giueth not his naturall beames vnto vs, yet remayneth alwaies the sunne: the fire couered with ashes, is truly fyre: euen so Faith wherof the Apostle speaketh heer, is *truly Fayth* though not liuely. The Ministers will say, that S. Iames speaketh heere of Fayth outwardly professed only, not of inward Fayth, wherby we are iustified in the sight of God. I answere, that to be false, because he speaketh of the Faith wherby we belieue in God which is inward Fayth. 2. He speaketh of Abrahams Fayth, which was a true and inward iustifying Fayth. If yow say in lyke manner that, that testimony of Saint Paul, maketh for the Ministers iustifying Fayth: (g) *Know that a man is not iustified by the works of the law, but by the Fayth of Iesus-Christ.* I answere that the Apostle saith only, that man is iustifyed *by the workes of the law*, that is, by the ceremonies of the law of Moyses, which is most true. Some Fathers do say sometymes, that man is not iustifyed by workes absolutely, meaning the workes of nature, of morall vertues without the grace & knowledge of Christ, or els workes done in the state of sinne before iustification, but neuer say the Fathers, that workes proceeding from a liuely fayth, and done in the grace of God, do not iustify.

(g) *Galath.* 2. *v.* 16.

3. The third argument, when a Protestant persuadeth himselfe or belieueth infallibly his sinnes to be forgiuen him, by this his particular and iustifying Faith; eyther he hath his sinnes by that Fayth remitted to him before, or after he thus belieues: if after, then his persuasion is false & deceitfull, belieuing the remission of his sinnes which was not when he made that act of Fayth: if before that act of Fayth his sinnes were remitted, it followeth that iustification was before his beliefe, which cannot be, for without Fayth it is impossible to please God. If the Minister say, that his beliefe causeth immediatly the remission of his sinnes which he belieueth, it is lykewise false; for after that

forme, the Ministers beliefe were omnipotent, in making the obiect which it knoweth, the mystery it belieueth. As if a man by belieuing himselfe to be a great Doctor in Phisik, should consequently be a perfect Doctor by reason of his beliefe, directly agaynst that famous saying of S. Augustine: (h) *That no knowledge or beliefe can be, vnles things knowen & belieued precede, and be before.* Because as our knowledge is true or false, by reason the obiect which we know is true or false; so our beliefe is certayne & true, because the thing is infallible which we belieue. As by example, God is omnipotent, not because I belieue him to be omnipotēt, but because he is omnipotent in himself, I belieue him to be so, the obiect of Faith alwaies being before the act of Faith, as the obiect of science is alwaies before the habite of sciēce. Plaine contrary to this, the Ministers in belieuing infallibly, & as a point of Fayth their sins to be forgiuen them, do make the obiect of their Faith in belieuing, which is a manifest absurdity. 2. The Ministers in belieuing infallibly their sinnes to be forgiuen thē, do keep in that the command of God, or breake the command of God. If the first, eyther they keep it perfectly (in that act of Fayth) or imperfectly, & with blemish? If perfectly, it followeth that a man may sometymes and in some things perfectly keep the commaunds, which they will not grāūt. If imperfectly, that imperfection being a deadly sin (for al are deadly sinnes in the Ministers opinion) it followeth of necessity that the Protestants are iustified by a deadly sinne, which is a palpable absurdity.

(h) *Lib. 4. Gen. ad lit. cap. 32.*

4. The fourth argument is framed out of those wordes of the Bible: (i) *He that shall belieue and be baptized, shall be saued, but he that will not belieue, shall be damned.* Whereof followeth that infants being baptized are iustified before God, yet not by an act of the speciall Fayth of the Ministers, because they can haue none such, being infants, but rather they are iustifyed by the habituall qualityes or inward habits of Faith, hope, & Charity and consequently all others are iustifyed by the lyke habit, and not by the speciall Faith of the Ministers, which is no other thing but a diuelish Idoll inuented by Caluin, and adored by the Protestants.

(i) *Mark. 16. v. 16.*

5. The

5. The fifth argument. This proposition of the Ministers, (k) *We receaue free remission of sinnes, and that by fayth only &c.* sworne and subscribed at seuerall tymes by the three estats of Sotland, is directly against those wordes of the Bible: (l) *Yee see then how that by workes a man is iustifyed, and not by fayth only.* Finally there is no part of the Scripture which maketh mention of this presumptuous Fayth of the Ministers, no not when it speaketh of the Fayth of Abel, Noe, Abraham, whose Fayth was not an infallible persuasion of their sinnes, but an assent and credit they gaue to the reuelations which God made to them, as lykewise in those wordes wherin S. Iohn doth place our saluation, saying: (m) *These things are written that yee might belieue that Iesus is Christ the sonne of God,* there is neuer a word of this particular Faith of the Ministers. And in that of S. Paul: (n) *This is the word of Faith which we preach, for if thou shalt confesse with thy Lord Iesus, and shalt belieue in thy heart, that God raysed him vp from the dead, thou shalt be saued:* heere I say is neuer a word of the Ministers presumptuous Fayth.

(k) *In the Confession of Fayth printed at Geneua & approued by the Church of Scotland*

(l) *Iames 2. v. 24.*

(m) *Iohn. 20 v. 31.*

(n) *Rom. 10 v. 8. & 9.*

6. I being in prison, a certayne Minister affirmed, that true Fayth wherby we are iustifyed is that which alwayes hath charity and good works ioyned therto. I replied thus, how is charity inseparable from true Fayth? Or is it separable as the fruit of the tree is separable from the tree, which remayneth a true & perfect tree without the fruit, or is charity an accidentall quality, or inseparable passion which floweth from Fayth, as the power of laughing from the nature of man? If so, it would follow, that charity could not be in heauen without Fayth which is false. Or is charity an essential forme which is required to the integrity of this iustifying Fayth? If so, then Fayth alone doth not iustify, which is directly agaynst your confession of Faith. If Faith together with charity iustify, as that Fayth is imperfect and mingled with deadly sinne, so is that charity; and consequently it followeth that we are iustifyed by Fayth and charity which conteyne in themselues deadly sinnes.

7. Of this forsayd discourse I inferre, that our iustification cōsisteth in the habit of charity, that is, in Faith & cha-

rity linked together. So that Fayth is the entry as it were to iustification, Hope the progresse, & Charity the consumation of this happy vnion with God, wherof the Bible saith thus: (o) *He that abydeth in Charity, abydeth in God, and God in him.* Which is the reason wherfore when the Scripture speaketh of our iustificatiō, it attributeth the same now to Faith, now to charity, not to fayth alone, not to charity alone, but to Fayth and charity ioyned together. Of Faith it saith: (p) *The iust lyueth of Fayth.* Of charity it sayth the lyke: (q) *We know that we are translated from death to lyfe, because we loue the Brethren: he that loueth not his brother, abydeth in death.* Of Fayth it sayth: (r) *Euery one that belieueth is iustified.* Of charity it sayth the same: (s) *He that hath my commandements and keepeth them, is he that loueth me: and he that loueth me, shalbe loued of my Father, and I will loue him.* Of Fayth we read: (t) *Without it, it is impossible to please God.* Of charity: (u) *If I had all Fayth, so that I could remoue moūtaines, & had not charity, I were nothing.* Which gaue occasion to S. Augustine to say: (x) *Nothing but charity maketh Fayth it selfe auaylable, for Fayth may be without charity, but it profyteth not without charity.* Finally S. Paul himself sayth: (y) *In Christ Iesus neyther circumcision auayleth ought, nor prepuce, but it that worketh by charity.* Wherfore if Fayth by reason of these testimonies be not the fruit but the true cause of our iustification, say the Ministers, why should not charity lykewise be the cause of our iustification, and not the fruit only, since it hath the authority of the Bible for it? Yea with greater priuiledge then Fayth, since S. Paul playnly preferred Charity before Fayth, saying: (z) *Now there remayneth Fayth, hope, and charity, these three, but the greater of these is charity.* Where it is to be remarked, that the Ministers haue corrupted the Bible almost in all those foresayd places in putting the word *loue* for *charity*, to make the sentence more obscure to the disprayse of charity, and that maliciously. For the word *loue* is taken in a good or euill sense, but the word *charity* is alwayes taken in a good sense. Now the reason wherfore charity is more perfect then Fayth, is because the loue of supernaturall things, which exceedeth the compas of our nature heere, is more perfect then the knowledge

(o) *Iohn* 4. *v.* 16.
(p) *Rom.* 1. *v.* 17.
(q) 1. *Iohn.* 3. *v.* 4.
(r) *Act* 1. *v.* 39.
(s) *Iohn* 14. *v.* 21.
(t) *Heb.* 11. *v.* 6.
(u) 1. Cor. 13. *v.* 2.
(x) *Lib.* 15. *de Trinit. cap.* 18.
(y) *Galat.* 5. *v.* 6.
(z) 1. Cor. 13. *v.* 13.

of them which is by Fayth. For we know them only answerable to the proportion of restrayned formes, which represent thē to vs; but we loue them according to the ful sea of goodnes, which is included in them: which gaue occasiō to the Philosopher to say: *To speculate diuine things, doth purify the soule, but to loue thē doth deify the soule, or turne the same as it were into God.* But let vs com to the testimonies of the Fathers.

The Testimonies of the holy Fathers of this second Age, prouing that with the grace of God, we may keep Gods Commandements; and that the keeping therof is meritorious &c.

The first Section.

ORigen teacheth playnly that our iustification cōsisteth in Faith and keeping the commands of God; that is, in Faith & charity together, and not in Fayth only: (a) *Regnum calorum assimilatur virginibus decem, et si quidem in ijs qui rectè credunt & viuunt, & ideo iustè assimilatur quinque prudentibus: qui autem profitentur quidem fidem in Iesu, non autem præparant se bonis operibus ad salutem, reliquis quinque assimilantur virginibus fatuis.* (a) *Tract. 30. in Mat.*

2. He auoweth, that true Fayth may be without charity (which before he called *fides in Iesu*) and that God is to render to euery man according to his workes, presupposing alwaies that true Faith in Christ may be without good workes, directly agaynst the Ministers opinion: (b) *Nunc requiramus de iusto iudicio Dei, in quo reddet vnicuiq; secundum opera sua. Et primò quidem excludantur hæretici, qui dicunt animarum naturas bonas vel malas, & audiant, quia non pro natura vnicuiq; Deus, sed pro operibus suis reddit: secundo in loco ædificentur fideles, ne putent sibi hoc solùm sufficere posse, quod credunt, sed sciant iustum iudicium Dei reddere vnicuiq; secundum opera sua.* And finally cōcludeth, true Fayth without good works is not accompted of before God, & true workes without a liuely Fayth likewise is not accompted of: (c) *Alterum namq; sine altero reprobatur, quia & fides sine operibus mortua dicitur, & ex operibus sine fide nemo apud Deum iustificatur.* (b) *In lib. 2. in cap. 2. ad Rom.* (c) *Sub finem eiusdē libri.*

2. S. Cyprian sayth lykewise, good workes & the keeping of Gods cōmandments are easy by the grace of God &

(d) *Lib. de opere & eleemosyna.* & in our power, speaking specially of almes-giuing, which is conforme to the command of God: (d) *Praeclara & diuina res, Fratres charissimi, salutaris operatio, solatium grande credentium, securitatis nostrae salubre praesidium, munimentum spei, tutela fidei, medela peccati, & res posita in potestate facientis, res grandis & facilis &c.* 2. He auoweth that good workes are meritorious of eternall lyfe, writing to the holy Martyrs who were in prison for the Catholike Religion, and suffred many things therfore: (e) *An ego possum tacere & vocem meam silentio premere, cùm de charissimis meis tam multa & gloriosa cognoscam, quibus vos diuina dignatio honorauit; vt ex vobis pars iam martyrij sui consummatione praecesserit, tormentorum suorum coronam de Domino receptura: pars adhuc in carcerum claustris, siue in metallis & vinculis demoretur: exhibens per ipsas suppliciorum moras corroborandis fratribus & armandis maiora documenta; ad meritorum titulos ampliores tormentorum tarditate proficiens, habitura tot mercedes in caelestibus praemijs, quot nunc dies numerantur in poenis: quae quidem vobis fortissimi ac beatissimi fratres, pro merito religionis ac fidei vestrae accidisse non miror, vt vos sic Dominus ad gloriarum sublime fastigium clarificationis suae, honore prouexerit, qui semper in Ecclesia eius custodito fidei tenore vigilastis, conseruãtes firmiter Dominica mandata.* Yet the Ministers do teach that no man hath euer kept, nor can keep the commandements.

(e) *Epist. ad Mmesianum.*

3. S. Iustin martyr auoweth that those persons only are acceptable to God who imitate him in goodnesse, iustice, humanity and other vertues, declaring therby that our iustification consisteth not in only Fayth, but in Fayth & good workes togeather, which do merit greatly before God: (f) *Deum illos tantum charos habere docuimus, nobisq; persuasimus & credimus, qui ea, quae in eo insunt imitantur temperantiã iustitiam & humanitatem, atq; omnia quae Dei sunt propria.* And agayne: (g) *Homines, qui dignos se eius voluntate & consilio, operibus praestiterunt, cũ eo victuros esse meritis suis accepimus ac regnaturos: sic vt ab omni interitu perturbationeq; sint liberi. Vt enim eos cùm non essent principio, effecit: sic fore speramus, vt ex eo quod sponte secuti erunt ea quae illi, probantur eos & immortalitate, & consuetudine dignetur.* And a litle there after: *Censemus vnumquemq; salutem consecuturum pro operum dignitate.* Which is conforme to that of

(f) Apol. 2. ad Anton. Pium.

(g) *Apol. 2. ad Ant.*

S.

S. Chrysostome who speaketh of Fayth thus: (h) *What profit will Fayth affoard vs, if our life be not sincere and pure?* And S. Basil: (i) *Fayth alone is not sufficient, vnlesse there be added conuersation of lyfe agreable therto.*

(h) *Lib. 1. contra vituper. monast. vitæ*

(i) *In psalterio psal. 110.*

4. S. Irenæus in lyke manner auerreth, that God maketh great accompt of our good workes and rewardeth vs therfore, not by reason of our Faith only, but by reason of our Fayth & good Workes togeather: (k) *Sicut Salomon, ait,* (l) *qui miseretur pauperi fœneratur Deo. Qui eum nullius indigens est Deus in se assumit bonas operationes nostras, ad hoc, vt præstet nobis retributionem bonorum suorum. Sicut Dominus noster ait,* (m) *Venite benedicti Patris mei, percipite vobis præparatum regnum. Esuriui enim & dedistis mihi manducare &c.*

(k) Lib. 4. *cap. 34.*

(l) *Prou. 19 v. 17.*

(m) *Math. 25. v. 34.*

5. Tertullian teacheth vs manifestly, that Fayth only doth not iustify, and that our good workes do merit before God: Let vs heare his wordes: (n) *Si enim sicut in Adam omnes moriuntur, ita & in Christo viuificabuntur; Carne viuificabuntur in Christo, sicut in Adam carne moriuntur. Vnusquisq; autem in suo ordine scilicet quia & in suo corpore: Ordo enim non aliud quàm meritorum dispositor. Merita autem cùm corpori quoq; adscribantur, ordo quoq; corporum disponatur necesse est, vt possit esse meritorum.* And agayne: (o) *Tunc restituetur omne humanum genus ad expungendum quod in isto æuo boni seu mali meruit, exinde pendendum immensam æternitatis perpetuitatem.* It were tedious to me to cite all the places (they being so many in number) whereby Tertullian proueth that true Fayth may be without good workes, and that Fayth only is not sufficient to saluation: in like manner that good workes grounded vpon the grace of God are meritorious of saluation. I will adde this only place to the forsayd: (p) *Quomodo multæ mansiones apud patrem, si non pro varietate meritorum? Quomodo & stella à stella distabit in gloria, nisi pro diuersitate radiorum?* Are not all these renowned and ancient Fathers sufficient to persuade the Protestants that they wander out of the trodē path of so many our holy and learned predecessours, and do fellow rather the crooked turnings of Caluin & Luther manifest Apostata's, who bring them to the labyrinth of eternall perdition?

(n) *De Resurrect. carnis cap. 48*

(o) *In Apo. cap. 48.*

(p) *In Scorp aduersus Gnosticos cap. 6.*

The

That the Ministers haue falsified the Bible in sundry places, which do proue, that Fayth only doth not iustify &c.

The second Section :

BEza one of the most famous amongst the Puritans hath set out long since a Bible in Latin, which as it is full of blasphemies, corruptions and sacriledges; so Castalio, a learned Puritan lykewise, hath written a booke agaynst Beza, whose Bible our Scots or English Bible followeth commonly, leauing the trodden path of all antiquity and of other nations. Beza then to make his reader belieue that man iustifyed by Fayth only, turneth that of S. Paul: (a) *The iust shall lyue by Fayth.* Beza I say hath translated: *qui verò ex fide iustus est, viuet*; he that is iust by Fayth, *shall lyue.* Directly agaynst the Greeke, directly agaynst the Syriake, where the word *ha,* which signifyeth *is*, is not at all; directly likewise against the Caldaike text, where it is, *Vetsadikaia bhal kuschetebun.* Directly agaynst S. Augustin who explicating this place sayth: (b) *Of what Fayth speaketh heere the Apostle? Of the Catholyk Fayth, which maketh a iust man, & distinguisheth between the iust and the vniust, for it is not a reprobate Fayth that we speake of, but that which worketh by Charity.* In the Hebrew text likwise it is, *the iust shal liue by Fayth.* To the which purpose learnedly S. Augustin, doth explicate those words of the Bible: (c) *We accompt a man to be iustifyed by Fayth without the workes of the law.* (d) *Non hoc agit Apostolus*, sayth he, *vt percepta ac professa fide opera iustitiæ contemnantur, sed vt sciat se quisque posse per fidem iustificari, etiamsi legis opera non præcesserint; sequuntur enim iustificatum, non præcedunt iustificandum &c.* That is: *The Apostle meaneth not by the workes of the law, those which follow iustification, but those which goe before iustification.* Should not S. Augustin his exposition, and consequence drawen out of this, be preferred before the Ministers consequences for their *solifidian* iustification, which by all antiquity hath bene to this day esteemed as a manifest heresy and poynt of

Idolatry

(a) *Rom.* 1. v. 17. *Beza his new Testa. printed anno* 1598. ὁ δὲ δίκαιος ἐκ πίστεως ζήσεται. Habakuk 2. v. 4.

(b) *Lib.* 3. *cont.* 2. *ep. Pelag.*

(c) Rom. 2. v. 28.

(d) *Aug. lib. de fide & operibus cap.* 14.

Idolatry, directly against the expresse words of sundry places of the Bible: (e) *If yee do not forgiue men their trespasses, no more will your Father forgiue you your trespasses.* Then Faith only is not sufficiẽt. Truly since there be so many deadly hatreds amongst the Puritanes and Protestants, very few of them can obteyne remission of sinnes, or haue true fayth: since they remaine in perpetuall hatred one against another. 2. (f) *If yee know these things, blessed are yee if yee do them.* Fayth alone then is not sufficient. 3. (g) *Yee are my friends if yee do whatsoeuer I command you,* he sayth not, *If yee belieue only in me.*

(e) Matth. 6. v. 15.
(f) Iohn. 13. v. 17.
(g) Iohn. 15. v. 14.

2. The second corruption is that of S. Paul to the Romanes: (h) *The wrath of God from heauen is reuealed vpon all impiety & iniustice of those men, that deteyne the verity of God in iniustice.* Where the Apostle condemneth men of impiety, specially those who do deteyne the verity of God in iniustice, not absolutly all men. Yet the Ministers to insinuat to the reader that all sorts of men are condemned heere by the Apostle; & that all sorts of men do euer remaine in impiety & iniustice, as (i) Beza playnly teacheth, and consequently that no man can keep the commandements, they haue trãslated thus: *For the wrath of God is reuealed from heauen, agaynst all vngodlynes and vnrighteousnes of men, which withold the truth in vnrighteousnes:* making the Apostle to speake absolutly. Was not S. Paul a faithfull and godly man, & consequently not conteyned vnder this his owne saying: for he speaketh of himselfe thus: (k) *I am not guilty in conscience of any thing, but I am not iustifyed therin?* Yet the Protestants are assured, say they, that they are iustifyed, though their conscience do accuse them of all impiety, of all sort of vices, and sins. But how, I pray you, do the Ministers translate this last place of S. Paul, *I know nothing by my selfe?* Is it then all one to say, *I am not guilty in conscience of any thing*, and to say, *I know nothing by my selfe?* May not the most sinfull Minister say with truth, that he knoweth nothing by himselfe, but by the assistance of God; yet may he say, *I am not guilty in conscience of any thing?* Can there be greater impiety committed? Can there be a more heynous sinne in the sight of God then to translate after this forme the holy Bible? making by such diuelish and abhominable translations, God to be the author

(h) Rom. 1. v. 18.
(i) In hunc locum. & in 1. Ioan. cap. 5.
(k) 1. Cor. 4. v. 4.
οὐδὲν γὰρ ἐμαυτῷ σύνοιδα.

thor, teacher, and sayer of all their abhominations, and sacriledges ?

3. The third falsification of the Ministers is that of S. Paul to the Corinthians : (l) *I chastice my body, and bring it into seruitude, least perhaps, when I haue preached to others, my self become reprobate.* Where the Apostle teacheth vs, to worke our saluation with feare & trembling, as he himselfe witnesseth, saying: (m) *Therefore my dearest &c. with feare and trēbling worke your saluation.* Which place as it playnely impugneth the Protestants presumptuous and solifidian Iustification, and certitude of their predestination ; so by them it is impiously corrupted thus : *Make an end of your owne saluation with feare and trembling.* Directly agaynst the force of the Greeke word, which in other places they translate as we do, *labour*, or *work*: as (n) *We labour working with our owne hands.* And agayne: (o) *For it is God which worketh in you.* Is this to translate the Bible faythfully according to their oath and conscience, or rather impiously to fortify their heresies and belye God himselfe in falsifying his word ? Let vs returne to the disproofe of the former third falsification, which is thus: *I beat down my body and bring it into subiection, least by any meanes, after that I haue preached to others, I my selfe should be reproued.* Hath not this sacrilegious translation wholy another sense, specially read by the common people? The first falsification heere is in putting, *I beat downe*, for, *I chastize.* The second in putting, *least by any meanes*, for, *least perhaps*, the third in putting, *I my selfe should be reproued*, for, *my selfe should become reprobate*. Remarke the Ministers treachery & craft to eternall perditiō. For in other places, which make no wayes agaynst them by reason that they are indifferent places, they turne as we do the word *reprobate*, and not *reproued*. As that of S. Paul : (p) *Know yee not your selues, how that Iesus-Christ is in you, except yee be reprobates ?* Agayne : (q) *Men of corrupt minds, reprobate concerning the Fayth.* The Syriak word, *Esthele*, signifieth a reprobate, *à radice Sela*, which signifieth to reprobate : doth not the Apostle himselfe in other places manifestly cōdemne the Protestants of this their infallible assurance of their predestination and saluation,

when

(l) 1. *Cor.* 9. *v.* 27

(m) *Philip* 2. *v.* 12.

μετὰ φόβου καὶ τρόμου τὴν ἑαυτῶν σωτηρίαν κατεργάζεσθε.

(n) 1. *Cor.* 4 *v.* 12.

(o) *Philip.* 2. *v.* 13.

ὑπωπιάζω *castigo*, μήπως, *ne forte*, ἀδόκιμος *reprobus.*

(p) 2. *Cor.* 13. *v.* 5. ἀδόκιμοί ἐστε.

(q) 2. *Tim.* 3. *v.* 8.

when he writeth: (r) *Thou standest by Fayth, be not high-minded but feare.* Where playnly S. Paul teacheth, that a man may fall from the true Faith, and consequently he cannot be infallibly sure that he is predestinat and is to be saued. Againe S. Paul as it were forwarned the Protestants of the great danger of this their opinion and Religion: (s) *Therfore,* saith he, *he that thinketh himselfe to stand, let him take heed least he fall.* What excuse shall the Protestants pretend in the day of iudgement, since so many euident places of their Bible do cōdemne that presumptuous security of theirs cōcerning their saluation? How can the Protestants be infallibly sure that they are predestinate, since predestination dependeth on the will of God, & the will of God cannot be infallibly knowē to vs in particular, without a particular reuelation? 2. Our Sauiour saith: (t) *He that shall perseuere to the end, shall be saued.* But no Protestant can be infallibly sure that he is to perseuere to the end. *Ergo, &c.* See we not euery day now presently in France many Ministers and Gentlemen of worth abandon the Hugenots Religion and become Catholikes? what infallible assurance then could they haue had being Hugenots to perseuere in their Religion? And what greater then they, can any other haue? 3. Sundry Protestants who haue become Catholikes and dyed Catholikes, eyther were predestinat being Protestāts or not? If they were how then could they become, and dye Catholikes? If not, what abhominable doctrine is that to make them to belieue as a poynt of Religion that they were predestinat? We Catholikes belieue, that by the grace of God we may haue a morall certitude and assurance, that we are his children, shal perseuere vnto the end, be saued; but we can not be infallibly certain, nor so certain that we may not still feare the successe of our weaknes. The which doctrine the Bible teacheth vs: (u) *Looke to your selues, that yee loose not the things which yow haue wrought, but that yow may receaue a full reward.* If they could haue lost them, truly they could not be infallibly sure of them. Agayne, (x) *Hold that which thou hast, that no man take thy crowne.* And (y) *Serue our Lord in feare and reioyce in trembling.* Agayne: (a) *Blessed is the man that feareth alwayes: but he that har-*

(r) Rom. 11. v. 6.

(s) 1. Cor. 10. v. 12.

(t) Matth. 24. v. 13.

(u) 2. Iohn v. 8.

(x) Reuel. 3. v. 11.

(y) Psal. 2. v. 11.

(a) Prou. 28. v. 14.

hardneth his heart shall fall into euill. Do not the Protestants in this poynt, and in all harden their hart agaynst the Bible, agaynst reason, agaynst all antiquity, agaynst the holy Fathers, and agaynst the very light of naturall reason?

The 16. 17. and 18. Article.

1. *The custome to fast Lent*. 2. *And some other dayes*. 3. *And to abstayne some tymes from certayne meates, was vniuersally in vse in this second Age*.

CHAP. IX.

AFter the first iustification, which is performed by charity wherof I spake in the former verity; followeth, as it were, a second iustification, that is, the increase and augmentation of the first by good works, in which holy men dayly walk and go forward by the grace of God, as
(a) Prou. the wyseman teacheth in his prouerbs: (a) *The way of the iust*
4. v. 18. *shyneth as the light, and shineth more and more vnto the perfect day*. That is, as the dawning appeareth brighter & brighter, vntill it come to Noone, or to the fulnes of the day; so the iust man increaseth by good workes, going alwayes forward
(b) Reuel. in the way of perfection, till he come to the full state ther-
22. v. 11. of, conforme to that of the Bible: (b) *He that is iust, let him*
ὁ δίκαιος δι- *be iustified yet*. Which is more plainly signifyed in the Greeke
καιοσύνην text, thus: *He that is iust let him do iustice yet*. Signifying ther-
ποιησάτω by the increase of iustice by good works; which place the
ἔτι. Ministers haue falsified, to signify that there is no increase of iustice by good worke, translating thus: *And he that is righteous, let him by righteous still*. Moreouer they who proceed in outward good workes of iustice, increase therein, and become

come more gratious vnto God: euen as when they were ſubiect to ſinne, by often and continuall ſinning they augmẽted their wickedneſſe, and became more odious to God: ſo the Godly by good workes increaſe in iuſtice, ſayth S. Paul: (c) *As you haue exhibited your members to ſerue vncleanes and iniquity, vnto iniquity: ſo now exhibit your members to ſerue iuſtice, vnto ſanctification.* As the ſame Apoſtle ſpeaketh yet more playnly exhorting the Coloſſians: (d) *That they might walke worthy of our Lord and pleaſe him in all thinges, fructifying in all good workes, and increaſing in the knowledge of God.* Which wordes S. Auguſtine fitly explicateth ſaying: (e) *That we are iuſtified, and that iuſtice it ſelfe increaſeth, when we proffit and go forward in all good workes.* Meaning an inward, inherent and true iuſtice, not that imputatiue and outward iuſtice of the Miniſters, which the Bible condẽneth as impious, ſince it may remayne with all ſort of inward abhomination. And accordingly the holy Apoſtle S. Iohn ſpeaking of that iuſtice wherby we are iuſt, meaneth an inward and inherent iuſtice, not a imputatiue or outward. The words of the Apoſtle are: (f) *He that doth iuſtice is iuſt, euen as he alſo is iuſt.* But he, to wit Chriſt, is truely iuſt before God by an inward and inherent iuſtice, worthy of heauen, therfore he that doth iuſtice is alſo iuſt before God, by the lyke inherent iuſtice, or elſe the ſimilitude of S. Iohn maketh not to the purpoſe: yea the Apoſtle warneth vs to beware of the Miniſters who teach this their iuſtice, for the faſhion only, ſaying: (g) *Little children, let no mã ſeduce you.*

(c) *Rom.* 6. *v.* 19.

(d) *Coloſſ.* 1. *v.* 10.

(e) *Augu. ſerm.* 16. *de verb. Apo.*

(f) 1. *Iohn* 3. *v.* 7.

(g) 1. *Iohn* 3. *v.* 7.

2. The faſting in holy Lent and abſtinency from certayne meates is one of thoſe good workes, wherby a man increaſeth in iuſtice, wherof I haue ſpoken in the former age more at length, deſirous, ſpecially in this age, to proue by the holy Scipture that the Catholike Church may ordayne certayne faſting-dayes to the ſpirituall proffit of the Catholiks, which I proue firſt by the example of *Heſter* & *Mardochæus*, whereof the word of God ſayth, that: (h) *To confirme thoſe dayes of Purim according to their ſeaſons, as Mardochæus the Iew and Heſter the Queene had appoynted them, and as they had promiſed for themſelues, & for their ſeed, with faſting & prayer.*

(g) *Heſter.* 9. *v.* 31.

If Hester & Mardochæus might institute particular fasting
(i) Iohn 14 v. 26. dayes, much more the Church of God, which is infallibly
assisted by the holy Ghost for euer, as the Scripture sayth: (i)
But the Cōforter, which is the holy Ghost, whome the Father will send in my name, he shall teach you all things to your remembrance which I haue told yow. Of the which power receaued from God, the Catholike Church gaue a manifest proofe in that generall Councell and Assembly made in the tyme of the Apostles, where that which was ordeyned by that Councell (which represented the Church) is sayd to haue bene ordeyned by God himselfe as the Scripture testifyeth: (k) *For it seemed good*
(k) Act. 15. v. 28. *to the holy Ghost, & to vs, to lay no more burthen vpon you, then these necessary things, that is, that yee abstayne from things offred to Idols and bloud, and that which is strangled.* The Catholike Church then ordeyned that we should absteyne from bloud and strangled: and shall not the true Church now haue power to command to absteyne from certayne meates, to the end we may serue God the better?

3. S. Paul maketh mention of fasting then vsed in his tyme in the Church of God, saying: (l) *So when much tyme*
(l) Act. 27 v. 9. *was spent &c. because also the fast was now passed, Paul exhorted them:* And shall not the same Church of God vse much fasting, and command to her subiects the vse thereof? Of the which doctrine I inferre, how ignorantly Whitaker a prime English Puritan chargeth Pope Calixtus to haue bene (m) *The first that ordayned ieiunium quatuor temporum.* By reason
(m) Cont. Duræum lib. 7. that Whitaker alledgeth no ancient writer, who chargeth thus Calixtus, it is only an inuētion of Whitaker his own. Besides that I haue shewed in the former age the institutiō of such a fast to haue beene long before Victor, much more before Calixtus, yea to haue proceeded, *from the doctrine of the holy Ghost*, as witnesseth S. Leo, saying: (n) *Ecclesiastica*
(n) Serm. 8. *ieiunia ex doctrina Sancti Spiritus, ita per totius anni circulum di-*
(o) Tim. 4. v. 1. & 3. *stributa sunt.* As for that of S. Paul: (o) *In the later tymes some shall depart from the Fayth &c. forbidding to marry, to absteyne frō meates which God created, to receaue with thanksgiuing for the faithfull.* Where the Ministers haue corrupted the Bible, putting in the word *commanding*, which is not in the Greeke text: &

where

where the Apostle speaketh not of the fasting of the Catholike Church, but rather agaynst the Manichees, Encratites, Marcionists, and such heretikes, who affirmed that marriage was of Sathan, and the act of Matrimony was instituted by an euill God. Lykewise they taught that men might not eat of certayne sorts of meats, by reason that they were not made (sayd they) by the good God, but by the euill, as witnesseth the ancient Fathers vpon this place, (p) Irenæus, (q) Chrysostomus, (r) Ambrosius, (s) Augustinus and others. Yea M. *Hooker* an English Protestant witnesseth the same: (t) *Agaynst those Heretikes which haue vrged perpetuall abstinence from certayne meates, as being in their very nature vncleane, the Church hath still bent her self as an enemy, S. Paul giuing charge to take head of them &c.* Doth not the foresayd place of S. Paul speake playnly agaynst the Ministers? For they are come in the later tymes; they haue departed from the Fayth which was in vse before their comming: They forbid to marry lawfully, when they teach that Mariage is not a Sacrament; when they teach that once marryed persons may marry to others, their partie yet being alyue; when they teach that the Fayth and promise giuen in Mariage cannot be kept, because, say they, no man can keep the commaundements of God. The Ministers command to absteyne from meats on the sunday from morning til night, which none but heretikes were accustomed to do. Finally hauing confirmed the holy custom of fasting by sundry passages of the Bible, by the exemples of Hester, of the Rechabites, as witnesseth the (u) Prophet Ieremy, (x) of the Nazarites, (y) of the Nininites, (z) of Moyses, (a) of S. Iohn Baptist, (b) and of Christ himselfe; I aske and challenge the Ministers to cite as manifest testimonyes agaynst fasting, which they not being able to do by the expresse word of God, let them giue glory to God, and confesse plainly that they teach nothing lesse thē the word of God, thē the Scripture giuing in place therof their owne inuentions, traditions, superstitions and foolish consequences, wherunto let vs Catholikes preferre the consequences of the holy Fathers of this Age.

(p) *Lib.* 1. *cap.* 22.
(q) *Hom.* 12. *in* 1. *ad Tim.*
(r) *In hunc locum.*
(s) *Hæres. Manich.* 46.
(t) *In his Ecclesiasticall policy. lib.* 5. *sect.* 72.
(u) *Ierem.* 35.
(x) *Numb.* 6.
(y) *Ionæ* 3.
(z) *Exod.* 34.
(a) *Matth.* 3.
(b) *Matth.* 4.

The

The holy Fathers of this second Age, do witnesse that the custome was vniuersally in the Church of God, to keep the fast of Lent, and to absteyne sometymes from certayne meates &c.

The first Section.

TErtullian writing to his bed-fellow witnesseth, that it is a great hindrance to a Catholik, married with one of another Religion, to keep the fasting dayes of the Catholike Church, by reason that a Catholike gentlewoman being marryed with such a one: (a) *Domino certè* (sayth he) *non potest pro disciplina satisfacere, habens in latere diaboli seruum, procuratorem Domini sui ad impedienda fidelium studia & officia. Vt si statio facienda est, maritus de die conducat ad balneas; si ieiunia obseruanda sunt, maritus eadem die conuiuium exerceat; si procedēdum erit, nunquam magis familiæ occupatio adueniat.* 2. He auoweth that the fast before Pasche, which we cal the fast of Lēt, and which he calleth (b) *Paschatis ieiunium*, was in vse in his tyme. 3. He setteth down the forme & fashion, which was kept in fasting, to wit, to absteyne from flesh, saying: (c) *Xenophagias obseruamus, siccantes cibum ab omni carne &c.* Which yet more playnly he signifieth by these wordes: (d) *Sublato, diminuto, demorato cibo.* Signifying by the first and second word, that fasting consisteth in abstinēce from flesh, & taking one meale in the day: which last circumstance he signifyeth, by the word *diminuto*, as by the third *demorato*, he signifyeth, that it is lawfull to change the tyme of taking of that one meale for a iust cause.

(a) *Lib. 2. ad Vxorem cap. 4.*

(b) *Lib. de ieiunijs c. 2. & 13.*

(c) *Eod. libro cap. 1.*

(d) *De eodem libro cap. 2.*

2. Origen speaketh plentifully to the prayse of fasting in diuers homilies, and in particular maketh mētion of the fast of Lent, & of wednesday and fryday, his words be: (e) *Nec hoc tamen ideo dicimus, vt abstinentiæ Christianæ fræna laxemus. Habemus enim quadragesimæ dies ieiunijs consecratos, habemus quartam & sextam septimanæ dies, quibus solemniter ieiunamus.* 2. He affirmeth that it was lawfull to euery man to fast priuatly according to his deuotion, & that fasting was instituted, to chastize

(e) *Hom. 10. in Leuit.*

chastize our body and to make vs therby more fit to prayer and deuotion: (f) *Est certè* (sayth he) *libertas Christiano per omne tempus ieiunandi, non obseruantia superstitione, sed virtute continentiæ. Nam quomodo apud eos castitas incorrupta seruatur, nisi arctioribus continentiæ fulta subsidijs? quomodo scripturis operam dabunt? Quomodo scientiæ & sapientiæ studebunt? Nonne per continentiam ventris & gutturis?* The care of wyfe & children maketh the Ministers ignorant in their calling, greedy and auaricious in their doings, lewd in their conuersation, carelesse in preaching, and couetous in their neighbours possessions. (f) *Ibidem.*

3. S. Cyprian in lyke mãner auerreth that no man hath euer attained to the perfectiõ of vertue without fasting: (g) *Quotquot* (sayth he) *viros virtutum vidimus, sine ieiunio non legimus ascendiße, nec aliquid magnum moliti sunt, nisi prius abstinentia praceßisset. Quoties aliquid à Deo obtinere conati sunt, ieiunijs incubuere & lachrymis, & pernoctantes in orationibus, cilicijs carni harentibus supplices beneficia postularunt.* 2. He auoweth (h) that the custome to fast fourty dayes of Lent came from the example of our Sauiour who fasted lykewyse fourty dayes. (g) *Tract. de ieiunio & tentat. Christi.* (h) *Ibidem.*

4. S. Irenæus (i) in a certayne letter of his written to S. Victor Pope and Martir, witnesseth playnly and plentifully the ancient custome of the Catholikes to fast Lent and other dayes, according to the command of the holy and Catholike Church. (i) *Extat. apud Euse. lib. 5 histo. cap. 24.*

5. S. Telesphorus (k) in lyke maner maketh mention in a letter of his directed to the Catholiks, how that the custome was to keep exactly the fasting of Lent, specially in absteyning from flesh. But of this controuersy I will speake more at length God willing in the Centuryes following. (k) *Extat tom. 1. Cõcil.*

That the Ministers haue falsified the Bible in sundry places which do approoue good workes, and the reward thereof, wherof Fastinge is one.

The second Section.

THe first is that of S. Peter who speaking of the holy &
(a) 2. Pet. 2 v. 7. 8. iust Lot, sayth: ([a]) *God deliuered iust Lot oppressed by the iniury and luxurious conuersation of the abhominable men. For in sight and hearing he was iust: dwelling with them who from day to day vexed the iust soule with vniust works.* Signifying therby that Lot was iust in sight and hearing, keeping his sight from filthy and vncleane obiects, & his hearing from vnclean speaches, & consequently keeping therby God his commandements. 2. S. Peter calleth Lot his Soule iust, to signify vnto vs the inherent iustice, which enobleth the vpright Catholike soule before God; condemning therby the imputatiue iustice of the Protestants, who to disgrace this place of the Bible haue first changed the wordes agaynst the order of all
βλέμματι γὰρ καὶ ἀκοῇ ὁ δίκαιος. the Greeke copyes, thus: *For he being righteous, and dwelling among them, in seeing and hearing, vexed his righteous soule from day to day with their vnlawfull deedes.* 2. The Protestants to signify their imputatiue iustice, they haue turned *Righteous soule*, which word *Righteous* they put alwayes commonly in place of the word *Iust*, to signify that no man, though assisted by Gods grace can be truly iust, and without spot of deadly sins, but only to the outward shew of man, directly against the expresse words of their owne Bible, which
(b) Luk. 1. v. 6. speaking of Zacharias & Elizabeth saith: ([b]) *They were both iust before God, and walked in all the commandements and ordinances of the Lord without reproofe.* Where the Euangelist teacheth vs three things agaynst the Protestants. 1. That iust and holy men do keep all Gods commandments assisted by his grace. That man is not iustifyed by Fayth alone, but by walking in the commandements. 3. That the keeping of the commandements proceding of a liuely Fayth is our iustificatiō.

The

The Ministers in turning *righteous* for *iust*, to take away all inherent and inward iustice, giue way to the Iewes to deny that our Sauiour is the true Messias, by reason that he is called by those same Greeke and Syriake words *Iust*, wherwith others are thus called, as: (c) *Haue nothing to do with that Iust man.* Agayne: (d) *Truly this man was iust*, and many such, where alwayes the same Greeke word is, which word if it signify only an outward and imputatiue iustice, by no place of the Scripture can we proue our Sauiour to haue had a true inherent and inward Iustice: which is a horrible blasphemy, seing his iustice and goodnesse, is the ground of all our Iustice and merits.

(c) Matth. 27. v. 19. (d) *Luk.* 23 v. 47. δίκαιος.

2. The second corrupted place is that of Esdras: (e) *And we fasted and besought our God hereby: and it fell out prosperously vnto vs.* Where fasting is accompted to be a good and meritorious worke: because it fell out properously to the Iewes by reason of their fasting. The Ministers, to signify the contrary, & that fasting is no meritorious good work, peruert the place thus: *So we fasted and besought our God for this: and he was intreated of vs.* The French Hugenots adde boldly three wordes, *par nos prieres*, which are not in the text. The Hebrew is manifest: *Waiahhather lanu; & exorabilis fuit nobis.*

(e) *Esdras* 8. v. 23.

3. The third falsifyed place is that of the Prophet Dauid, who applyed his mynd to keepe Gods commandements (which are called Iustifications, because the keeping of them do iustify vs) for a reward eternally in heauen. Declaring therby that good workes are meritorious of lyfe euerlasting, & that they haue their reward besides God. The Prophets words be: (f) *I haue inclyned my hart to do thy iustifycations for euer for reward.* Remarke how the Protestants haue falsifyed this place craftily to take away all hope that our good workes do merit or haue any reward, they turn thus. *I haue applied my hart to fulfill thy statutes alwaies euen vnto the end.* Taking wholly away the word *reward*, which is in the Greeke, and which they haue turned with vs in other places, as: (g) *In keeping of them there is great reward.* The same Hebrew word being euery where *hhekeb*. For in effect the king-

(f) *Psalm.* 119 v. 112. *propter retributionē.* δι᾽ ἀνταμειψιν. (g) *Psal.* 18. v. 11.

kingdome of heauen is a reward due to our good workes grounded vpon the merits of Christ, by reason of the promise wherby God hath obliged himselfe to vs; yet all is his mercy and grace, by reason that he hath obliged himselfe to vs; and yet all is without any merit or obligation of ours going before; so heauen is giuen both of mercy, and as a reward. Thus S. Augustin: (h) *Quando facis bonum opus, propter vitam æternam fac: si ideo facis, securus facis, hoc enim mandauit Deus.*

(h) *In psal.* 120.

4. The fourth place falsifyed by the Ministry is that of Daniel the Prophet, who speaking to King Darius affirmeth, that God had so preuēted him with his grace, that he was found iust and innocent before God of any sinne, yea and before man: declaring therby, that a man by the grace of God may keep Gods commandements. His wordes be: (i) *My God hath sent his Angell, and hath shut vp the mouthes of the lyons, and they haue not hurt me: because before him Iustice hath bene foūd in me: yea & before thee, O King, I haue done no offence.* How do the Ministers deface and disgrace this place to proue their heresie of imputatiue Iustice, & that the commands are impossible to be kept? *My Iustice,* say they, *was found out before him, and vnto thee, O King, I haue done no hurt.* Who seeth not a great difference betwixt these translations? What wise man can thinke the Ministers to haue any conscience, seeing so boldly they corrupt thus the word of God? Is it meruayle they deny the authority of the holy Fathers, of ancient Councels, of sacred doctours, seeing thus they falsify agaynst all antiquity the Scripture, the holy word of God, the Bible it selfe?

(i) *Daniel.* 6. *v.* 22.

5. The fifth corruption is that in S. Luke, where it is sayd, that our Sauiour was sent into this world to preach the Ghospell to the poore, to heale the broken harted, to preach deliuerance to the captiues: (k) *To preach the acceptable yeare of the Lord, and the day of retribution.* By the last wordes, *the day of retribution,* is signifyed, that in the law of grace, the good workes of the Catholikes, grounded vpon the merits of Christ, should haue great rewardes, and merits appoynted for them, which the holy Father (l) S. Ambrose, and others

(k) *Luk.* 4. *v.* 19.

(l) *Lib.* 4. *in Lucam.*

thers do proue by this place. The Ministers cannot abyde the word *merit*, or the word *retribution*, as due of Iustice. For the which cause they haue blotted out of their Bible these last wordes, *and the day of retribution*, translating thus: *And that I should preach the acceptable yeare of the Lord.* Notwithstanding that in all the Hebrew copyes those wordes are found sayth Beza himselfe: (m) *Quæ verba in Hæbrais quidem habentur & in multis Græcis codicibus.* Can there be a greater Impiety before God then thus to falsify the word of God? (n) *O yee heauens be astonished at this: be affrayd and vtterly confounded.* For the Ministers haue committed two euills, *they haue forsaken the fountayne of lyuing waters, to digge them pits, euen broken pits, that can hold no water*: That is, they haue forsaken the fountayne of the Hebrew and Greeke tongues in their translations, forsaken the translations and expositions of all the holy, learned, and auncient Fathers, to digge to themselues pits, in following their owne fansies and inuentions, agaynst the cleare water of the word of God and sacred antiquity. Remarke heere the spirit of contradiction (which is familiar to all Heretikes) of Beza who in the first edition of his commentaries vpon this place printed the yeare of Christ 1556. sayth: *Quæ verba in Hæbrais quidem habentur, & in multis Græcis codicibus.* Yet he sayth wholy the contrary in the same commentaryes printed 1598. *Quæ verba*, sayth he, *in Hæbrais quidem habentur, sed in nullis Græcis codicibus à me reperta sunt.* The which fashion of proceeding of the Ministers sheweth it self, forasmuch as the same Greeke word which signifieth heere *reward*, they haue translated in other places of the Bible; condemning therby themselues, who deny that our good workes can merit, or haue any reward. As that to the Colossians: (o) *Knowing that of the Lord, yee shal receaue the reward of inheritance.* And S. Paul speaking of Moyses: (p) *For he had respect vnto the recompence of the reward.*

καὶ ἡμέραν ἀνταποδόσεως.

(m) *Annot. in hūc locum printed the yeare 1556.*

(n) *Ierem. 11. v. 12.*

(o) *Coloss. 3. v. 24.* τὴν ἀνταπόδοσιν.

(p) *Hebr. 11. v. 26.*

6. The sixt corruption is that of S. Iohn, where it is sayd, *that one of the Ministers gaue a blow to our Sauiour Christ Iesus*: (q) *When he had sayd those things, one of the Ministers standing by, gaue Iesus a blow:* which wicked fact of those Ministers, was a figure of the Ministers doing in this our age: wher-

(q) *Iohn. 18. v. 22.* εἷς τῶν ὑπηρετῶν ἔδωκε ῥάπισμα.

wherin they haue giuen such a blow to the Church of God to the Saints in heauen, to the Sacraments, to the Scriptures; that the first they haue cut in pieces, to they second they refuse religious honor, of seauen Sacraments the haue made but two, the Scriptures they haue wholly mangled, corrupted, peruerted, and cut asunder, calling that Apocrypha, which all nations euer did accompt as Canonicall. Now to couer this detestable fact of theirs against our Sauiour, they haue translated thus: *one of the officers which stood by, smote Iesus with his rod.* Putting the word *Officers*, for the word *Ministers*, directly agaynst the Greeke word, which in other places of the Bible, when it is to their prayse and auantage they translate the very word *Minister*, as: (r) *I haue appeared vnto thee for this purpose, to appoynt thee a Minister &c.* Why doe yee translate the word *Minister* in the one, and not in the other? is not the same Greeke word in both places? Is this the fidelity which yee promise to follow the Greeke text precisely?

Vnus Ministrorum dedit alapā Iesu.

(r) Act. 26. v. 16.

ὑπηρέτην.

The

The 19. 20. and 21. Article.

1. *That the custome of the Catholik Church in this second Age was, that Churchmen should not be marryed.* 2. *But rather lead a single & chast lyfe.* 3. *And that the vowing of chastity, pouerty, and obedience was lawfull, and in vse.*

CHAP. X.

BY reason that I haue spokē of this matter at length in the first Age, & that many of the chiefest noble men & Protestants in Scotland and England auow openly, that the Ministers and Bishops should lead a single lyfe, I wilbe short, touching heere only this particular, that many of the Iewes (as testifyeth Iosephus) were much giuen to lead a single and chast lyfe: (a) *The righteousnes*, sayth he, *of the Essenes, is meruailous, they enioy their riches in common, and in this course aboue foure thousand men do lyue, hauing neyther wyues, nor seruants.* And elswhere he affirmeth: (b) *They are Iewes by nation, and do obserue continency, auoyde marriage, are contemners of riches, and enioy things in common, none being richer then other.* And Philo a famous writer who liueth in the Apostles tyme maketh mention of those Iewes, who being conuerted to the Catholike Religion, and (c) *Forsaking their goods, did dwell without the walles, louing solitarines.* He maketh mention lykewise of their *Monasteries*, where being solitary, they studyed the Mysteryes of holy lyfe, specially of their *wonderfull great fasting from flesh.* And to omit sundry other proofes which I might alledge, besides that of Isay, whome the Protestants acknowledge to fortell vowes which were to be performed in the law of grace, and in the Catho-

(a) *Ioseph. antiq. Iudaic. lib. 18. cap. 2.*

(b) *De bello Iudaico lib. 2. cap. 7.*

(c) *De vita contemp.*

(d) Isa. 19. v. 21.

Catholike Roman Church: (d) *In that day they shall do sacrifice and oblation, and shall vow vowes vnto our Lord, and performe them.* I will set downe only the testimonyes of two Protestant writers. First M. Hooker, who acknowledgeth, (e) *Ananias to haue made a solemne vow vnto God, which strictly bound him to the giuing of his possessions to the Churches vse.* Lykewise M. Fenton auoweth the same: (f) *Albeyt we had liberty* (sayth he) *before to vse Ecclesiasticall liuings, as meere temporals; yet after those vowes, our case is the very same with that of Ananias.* Yea the very wordes of S. Peter spoken to Ananias witnesseth the same: (g) *Thou hast not lyed vnto men, but vnto God.* Wherupon S. Augustin writeth thus: (h) *If it displeaseth God to withdraw of the money which they had vowed to God, how is he angry, when chastity is vowed, and is not performed? For to such may be sayd that which S. Peter sayd of the money: Thy virginity remayning, did it no remayne vnto thee? and before thou didst vow, was it not in thy own power? For whosoeuer haue vowed such thinges and haue not payed them, let them not thinke to be condemned to corporall death, but to euerlasting fyre.*

(e) In his Ecclesiastical policy lib 2.
(f) In a sermon of his of Simony, printed 1604. pag. 46.
(g) Acts 5. v. 4.
(h) Serm. 10. de diuersis.

2. The other place of the new Testament which signifyeth the vowing of chastity to haue bene in vse in the Apostles tyme, is that of S. Paul to Timothie, who speaking of widdowes who had brokē their vowes, saith thus: (i) *But refuse the yonger widdowes, for when they haue begun to wax wanton agaynst Christ, they will marry, hauing damnation, because they haue broken their first Fayth.* Where the promise and vow of chastity is called *Fayth*, because as the promise made betwixt marryed persons, is called *Fayth*, so the promise to keep chastity to God, is likewise called here *the first Fayth*, in respect of the later promise, which breakers of vowes make to them with whome they pretend to marry, as sayth S. Augustine: (k) *What is it to breake their first Fayth they vowed and performed not?* And agayne: (l) *They breake their first Fayth, that stand not to that, which they vowed.* Which is yet more playnly set downe by the Fathers in the Councell of Carthage where S. Augustin was present with two hundreth and fifteene Fathers. *If any widdowes, how young soeuer they were left of their husbands deceased, haue vowed themselues to God, left*

(i) 1. Tim. 5. v. 11. & 12.
(k) In psal. 75. prope
(l) Lib. de sancta virgin. c. 33.

of their laycall habit, and vnder the testimony of the Bishop & Church haue appeared in religious weed, and afterward go any more to secular marriages, according to the Apostles sentence, they shall be damned, because they were so bold to make voyde the Fayth or promise of chastity, which they vowed to our Lord. Finally all the auncient Fathers that euer wrote cōmentaryes vpon this Epistle, Greeke and Latin Fathers do expone the forsayd wordes of the Apostle, of the vow of chastity or continence.

3. Out of the foresayd discourse I inferre, that we Catholikes haue the playne words of the Bible for making of vowes of chastity, pouerty and obedience. 1. *Vow yee & render your vowes vnto God.* 2. *Whosoeuer voweth a vow vnto the Lord &c. He shall not breake his promise, but shall do according to all which proceedeth from his mouth.* 3. *When thou shalt vow a vow vnto the Lord thy God, thou shalt not be slacke to pay it, for the Lord thy God will surely require it of thee.* 4. *When thou hast vowed a vow vnto God deferre not to pay it &c. It is better that thou shouldest not vow, then that thou shouldest vow, and not pay it.* Now I aske of the Ministers to giue as playne and manifest words agaynst the making of vowes. For we Catholikes will euer prefer the expresse word of God and the consequences of the holy Fathers drawne out of the same, to the Ministers manifest heresies. Let vs heare then the consequences of the Fathers of this second Age.

The Testimonies of the holy Fathers of this second Age, prouing that Churchmen should not be marryed, but rather lead a single, and chast lyfe.

The first Section.

TErtullian hath written a whole booke *de velandis Virginibus*, where he condemneth of sacriledge those who violate sacred Virgins: (a) *O sacrilegæ manus, quæ dicatum Deo habitū detrahere potuerunt? Quid peius aliquis persecutor fecisset, si hoc à virgine electum cognouisset? Denudasti puellam à capite &c.* What would Tertullian, I pray yow, haue sayd, if he had seen so many Nunnes and Nunryes sacrilegiously violated

(a) *In Lib. de velandis virginibus. cap. 3.*

 lated

lated at the casting down of the Churches in Scotland? 2. He teacheth that marriage is good, but to keepe chastity is better. : (b) *Prohiberi* (sayth he) *nuptias nusquam omnino legimus, vt bonum scilicet: Quod tamen bono isto melius sit accepimus* (c) *ab Apostolo, permittente quidem nubere, sed abstinentiam praeferente; illud propter insidias tentationum, hoc propter angustias temporum.* 3. He witnesseth that in his tyme sundry did vow chastity to God from the very instant of Baptisme, which many in the primitiue Church receaued being of good Age: and others (though marryed) did keep chastity and virginity in the very bond of Marriage, by mutual consent of the parties; which is, and hath bene practised in the Catholike Church by Kings and Emperours, as is well knowne to those who haue read the Ecclesiasticall history: (d) *Quotquot enim sunt* (sayth Tertullian) *qui statim à lauacro carnem suam obsignant; quot enim qui consensu pari inter se matrimonij debitum tollunt? Voluntarijs spadonibus pro cupiditate caelesti saluo matrimonio abstinentia toleratur, quanto magis adempto.* 4. He answereth the lecherous Nicolaits, heretikes who with our Protestāts giuen to fleshly pleasures, calumniated Catholikes as forbidding Marriage, by reason of vowed chastity & virginity performed by many millions of Virgins. He answereth also to Marcion the heretike who condemned Marriage : (e) *Sine dubio ex damnatione coniugij institutio ista* (Marcionis) *constabit. Videamus an iusta, non quasi destructuri felicitatem sanctitatis vt aliqui* (f) *Nicolaitae assertores libidinis atq; luxuriae, sed qui sanctitatem sine nuptiarum damnatione nouerimus, & sectemur & praeferamus, non vt malo bonum, sed vt bono melius. Non enim proijcimus sed deponimus nuptias, nec praescribimus sed suademus, sanctitatem seruantes, & bonum & melius, pro viribus cuiusq; sectando.* He meaneth by the word *sanctitatem*, virginity and chastity. Finally he affirmeth that a vow being made obligeth the maker to performe the same: (g) *Votum cum à Deo acceptum est, legem in posterum facit per authoritatem acceptoris: exinde enim faciendum mandauit, qui factum comprobauit.*

2. S. Iustinus Martyr in his Apologie for the Catholikes witnesseth great multitudes of those that vowed virginity to haue bene in his time: (h) *Ac pleriq; & pleraq; sexagima*

(b) *In lib. 2. ad Vxor, cap. 3.*
(c) *1. Cor. 7. v. 38.*
(d) *In lib. ad Vxorem cap. 6.*
(e) *Lib. 1. cont. Marcion. cap. 29. & lib. 5. cap. 15.*
(f) *Reuel. 2. v. 6. & 15.* See Pamelius and Rhenanus *in hunc locum.*
(g) *In lib. de ieiunijs cap. 11.*
(h) *In Apol. ad Anton. piũ Imper.*

aginta & septuaginta annos nati, qui à puero in Christi se disciplinam tradiderunt, incorrupti permanent: & glorior quòd in omni hominum genere tales monstrare possim.

3. S. Pius a holy martir sayth concerning holy virgins: (i) *Vigines non velentur ante viginti quinque annos ætatis, nisi fortè necessitate periclitantis pudicitia virginalis.*

(i) *Extat tom. 1 concil. & 20. quæst. 1. can. virgines nõ velentur.*

4. Athenagoras in his Apologie agaynst the gentils for the Catholiks, in lyke manner witnesseth great multitudes of those who had vowed virginity to haue bene in his tyme: (k) *Inuenias*, sayth he, *multos ex nostris & viros & fæminas, qui in cælibatu consenescant, quòd Deo coniunctiores se futuros sperent. Quod si perseuerantia in virginitate & in Eunuchismo magis Deo conciliat, cogitatio verò & concupiscentia abducit; certè illa quorum cogitationes fugimus, multo priùs, ne ipso perpetremus facinore, cauebimus.*

(k) *In Apolog. pro Christianis.*

5 Origen affirmeth the vowing of virginity to be a worke of supererogation, that is, a worke counselled and not commanded: (l) *Cæterum*, sayth he, *apud Christianos non propter humanos honores, non propter mercedes pecuniarias, non propter gloriolas viget virginitatis studium, &c.* And agayne: (m) *Ea verò quæ supra debitum facimus, non facimus ex præceptis: verbi gratia, virginitas non ex debito soluitur; neq; enim per præceptum expeditur sed supra debitum offertur. Audi deniq; Paulum dicentem:* (n) *De virginibus autem præceptum Domini non habeo.* 2. He affirmeth the custome to haue bene in his time amongst Priests to vow perpetuall virginity or continency: (o) *Certum est*, sayth he, *quia impeditur Sacrificium indesinẽs ijs, qui coniugalibus necessitatibus seruiant, vnde videtur mihi quòd illius est solius offerre Sacrificium indesinens, qui indesinenti & perpetuæ se deuouerit castitati.*

(l) *Lib. 7. contra Celsum*

(m) *in lib. 10. in Epist. ad Romanos.*

(n) 1. *Cor. 7. v. 25.*

(o) *Hom. 23. in num.*

6. S. Cyprian writeth plentifully in his booke intituled *de disciplina & habitu virginum*, exhorting the Nunnes and religious women in his tyme, and speaking thus to the prayse of virginity: (p) *Nunc*, sayth he, *nobis ad virgines sermo est, quarum quo sublimior gloria, maior & cura est. Flos est ille Ecclesiastici germinis, decus atq; ornamentum gratiæ spiritualis, læta indoles, laudis & honoris opus integrum atq; incorruptum, Dei imago respondens ad sanctimoniam Domini, illustrior portio gregis Christi.*

(p) *In lib. de disciplina & habitu virgin.*

 2. He

2. He auoweth though marriage be good and expedient for many, yet virginity is better, and more fit for others: (q) *Quia etsi bona sunt, & à Deo instituta coniugia, melior tamen est continentia & virginitas excellentior, quam non cogit necessitas aut mandatum, sed perfectionis suadet consilium.* 3. He witnesseth the custome to haue bene lykewise in his tyme to make vowes of pouerty, in leauing all they had, as the Apostles did, and after the Apostles many: (r) *Vt Apostoli,* sayth he, *& sub Apostolis multi, & nonulli sæpe fecerant, qui & rebus suis & parentibus derelictis, indiuiduis Christo nexibus adhæseruut.* To be short, I omit many other testimonies, the matter being so playne and manifest it selfe, and grounded vpon the word of God.

(q) *In tractatu de natiuitate Christi.*

(r) *Sermo. de lapsis.*

That the Ministers haue falsified the Bible in sundry places, which do make for good workes, wherof the vowing of Chastity is one.

The second Section.

CAluin that prime Puritan Minister and Apostata Priest, in his articles of the Faith made in Geneua, and rehearsed euery sonday in the Churches of Scotlād (a Treatise ful of blasphemies, sacriledges, and abhominable opinions) speaking of good workes auoweth, first that by good workes, or merits thereof, (a) *We do not prouoke God to loue vs, but much rather we therby do stir him to be more and more angry against vs.* 2. He teacheth, *that although our workes make a fayre shew to mans sight, yet they be wicked before God.* 3. He auoweth, that good workes haue no part in our iustification: *Therfore I say, that without any consideration of our owne workes God doth receaue vs into his fauour.* 4. He teacheth that there is no worthines in our good works though proceeding of the fauour & grace of God: (b) *How is it* (asketh the Minister) *that they be not worthy of thēselues to be accepted, since they proceed of the holy Ghost? C. Because there is mixed some filth through the infirmity of the flesh wherby they are defiled.* Where I would aske of crafty Caluin

(a) *In the 19. Sunday*

(b) *In the 20. Sunday*

uin who euer playeth the Sophist, If Fayth be not *mingled with some filth*, seeing it proceedeth of a sinfull man borne in sinne and iniquity: if it be, then it cannot iustify vs. The Ministers to vphold this blasphemous doctrine of Caluin haue corrupted the Bible in sundry places, as in that to the Romans: (c) *That the iustification of the law might be fulfilled in vs, who walke not according to the flesh but according to the spirit.* Wher (c) *Rom. 8. v. 4.* the Apostle teacheth first, that the law, that is Gods commandements, may be kept and *fulfilled* by the grace of God. 2. That such keeping of the law is *iustification*, and consequently that our iustification consisteth in keeping of the law, which euer presupposed a true and liuely Fayth. The Ministers to insinuate the contrary to the reader of their Bibles haue translated thus: *That the righteousnes of the law might be fulfilled in vs.* Taking away fully the word *iustification*, which is plainly set down in the Greeke, playnly set down ἵνα τὸ δικαίωμα τοῦ νόμου. in the Syriake, *decinutho donomuso*, turned by Tremellius thus, *quo iustificatio legis,* remarke the Ministers crafty, double and vnfaythful dealing in so weghty a matter: for the same Greeke word, which in this place they turne *righteousnes*, in other places which do not make so playnly against them, they turne *iustification*, as that of S. Paul: (d) *But the gift is of* (d) Rom. 5. v. 16. & 18 εἰς δικαίωμα. *many offenses to iustification.* In the which verse the Ministers haue added at least fyue senerall wordes which are not, no not in one Greeke copy. And againe where the same Greek word is, and doth signify our iustification by good workes playnely, as that, *for the sick is the iustification of Saints*, they haue turned, (e) *for the fine linnen is the righteousnes of Saints.* Being ashamed of the sacriledges they committed in tearing (e) Reuel. 19. v. 8. the silks, and consecrated vestements to the seruice of God, they thrust in the Bible, the words *fine linnen.* Doth crafty Caluin the sophist proue his forsayd catechisticall doctrine by Scripture? No verily: Yea the holy Bible plainly sheweth Caluin to be a Sicophant and ignorant, auowing in playne wordes that man is iustified by good workes: (f) (f) *Iames 2. v. 21.* ἐξ ἔργων. *Abraham our Father, was he not iustifyed by workes, offering Isaac his sonne vpon the altar?* Which place the Ministers haue falsified putting the word *through*, for *by*, to make the sentence obſcure. And agayne: (g) *Yee ſee then how that a man is iuſtifyed by workes, and not by Fayth only.* Where the Miniſters to take away the force of the ſentence, do put *of*, for *by*, yet elſwhere the ſame Greeke word they tranſlate *by*, as, *The iuſt shall lyue by Fayth.*

(g) *Iames* 2. *v.* 24. (h) *Galath.* 3. *v.* 11. ἐκ πίστεως

2. The ſecond place which the Miniſters haue corrupted, is that of S. Paul: (i) *Therfore as we haue borne the image of the earthly, let vs beare alſo the image of the heauenly.* That is, as we haue borne the image of the earthly Adam in following the pleaſures of the fleſh, ſo let vs beare the image of the heauenly, that is, of Chriſt in confirming our lyfe to his, to our poſſibility. The Marcioniſts ancient Heretikes in Tertullians tyme fourteene hundreth yeares ſince, preached that our Sauiour tooke not our mortall nature vpon him, but rather ſome heauenly and celeſtiall matter, & that our bodies after the reſurrection would not be of fleſh & bloud but of ſome heauēly matter: to vphold this their hereſy the ſayd Marcioniſts corrupted this place, tranſlating thus: *As we haue borne the image of the earthly, ſo shall we beare the image of the heauenly.* Tranſlating in the future, and not in the Imperatiue, conforme to the Greeke, of the which corruption of Marcion, Tertullian maketh mention after this forme: (k) *Et ideò iam ad exhortationem ſpei cæleſtis ſicut portauimus, inquit, imaginem terreni, portemus & imaginem cæleſtis, non ad ſubſtantiam vllam referens reſurrectionis, ſed ad præſentis temporis diſciplinam. Portemus enim inquit, non portabimus, præceptiuè, non permiſsiuè &c.* (l) Irenæus readeth with vs agaynſt the Proteſtants and Marcioniſts, together with (m) S. Chryſoſtome. Now the Miniſters haue playnly tranſlated this place as the Marcioniſts did, *And as we haue borne the image of the earthly, ſo shall we beare the image of the heauenly.* Referring the matter to the life to come, and ſignifying that no man poſſibly can in this life beare the image, and conforme himſelfe to the life of Chriſt Ieſus.

(i) 1. Cor. 15. *v.* 49. φορέσωμεν καὶ τὴν εἰκόνα.

(k) *Lib.* 5. *aduerſus Marcion c* 10. (l) Lib. 5. *aduerſ. hæreſ. cap.* 9. (m) *In hūc locum.*

3. The third place falſifyed by the Miniſters is that of S. Paul to the Corinthians: (n) *I dye dayly for your glory, brethren, which I haue in Chriſt Ieſus our Lord.* Signifying that he ſuffereth willingly bodily afflictions and mortifications in

(n) 1. Cor. 15. *v.* 24.

ſatisfaction

satisfaction for the Corinthians sinnes & iniquityes, which being abolished, their glory in heauen may increase and be augmented; which the Apostle teacheth more playnely writing to the Colossians thus: (o) *Now I reioyce in my sufferings for you, and fulfill the things which want of the afflictions of Christ in my flesh, for his body, which is the Church.* Where the passions & afflictions of euery member of the Church, are called the passions of Christ, by reason of the vnion which is betwixt the head and the members. Which gaue occasion to Christ to say to S. Paul, who did not persecute Christ in person: (p) *Saul, Saul, why persecutest thou me?* Of the like satisfactions and afflictions suffered for the Corinthians he speaketh: (q) *And I will most gladly bestow, and wilbe bestowed for your soules.* Yet more playnly: (r) *I suffer all things for the elect, that they also may obtayne the saluation.* Which mutual sufferings one for another is grounded lykewise in those wordes of the Creed, *The Communion of Saints.* And is the ground of Indulgēces & pardons which the Church of God dayly dispenseth. Of the which ancient custome in distributing pardons and Indulgences (s) S. Cyprian maketh mention fourteene hūdreth yeares since, with (t) Tertullian & (u) Origen. Yea S. Paul vseth the very word Pardon, saying: (x) *Whome you haue pardoned any thing, I also: for my selfe also that which I pardoned any thing, for you in the person of Christ.* which place though impiously corrupted by the Ministers, the holy Fathers S. Ambrose, S. Chrysostome, S. Thomas, S. Anselme, Primasius, (y) Baronius, and sundry others with the Councel of Nice *can. 11. & 12.* do vse, to proue the antiquity of Pardons and Indulgences. But how haue the Protestants translated the former place of S. Paul? Thus they: *By our reioycing, which I haue in Christ Iesus our Lord, I dye dayly.* Putting *our reioycing*, for *your glory*, directly agaynst the Greek and Syriake word *Beschube harechun*, that is, *your glory*: As S. Ambrose, S. Hierome and S. Augustin do read, and therby condemne the Ministers of sacriledge and perfidy.

(o) Coloss. 1. v. 24. ἀνταναπληρῶ τὰ ὑστερήματα *quæ desunt passionum Christi.*
(p) Acts 9. v. 4.
(q) 2. Cor. 12. v. 15.
(r) 2. Tim. 2. v. 10.
(s) *Epist.* 11 21. & 22.
(t) Ad martyr. cap. 1.
(u) *Lib. 7. cont. Celsum.*
(x) 2. Cor. 2. v. 10.
(y) Tom. 1. pag. 592.
ὑμετέραν καύχησιν.

That

The 22. Article.

That S. Peter his Primacy in the Catholike Church was acknowledged in this second Age vniuersally.

CHAP XI.

HAuing before in the first age demonstrated S. Peters superiority and supremacy aboue the rest of the Apostles and Christians: it resteth to shew how this same power and supremacy was communicated to S. Peters successours in the Roman sea, which I proue, first by the ex-
(a) Matth. 16. v. 18. presse words of Christ to Peter: (a) *Thou art Peter and vpon this rock will I build my Church, and the gates of hel shall not preuayle agaynst it.* Christ sayth, *my Church*, generally, not a part or portion of his Church, not that part only, which flourished in Peters dayes, but all his whole Church which euer was since Christ, or euer shalbe to the end of the world. For this priuiledge granted by Christ to Peter, could not be grãted only to Peter in his owne person, he being a mortall man. Therfore it must needes be graunted to others in-
John. 21. steed of Peter, that is, to Peters successours. 2. When Christ sayd to Peter, *Feed my sheepe*; Did he not command him to feed all his sheep, seeing he speaketh generally, without any restriction? Did he not lay, and charge vpon Peter which he should neuer forgo? And seeing the office of a Pastour is a perpetuall office during as long as there be any sheep to feed, which because Peter in his own person could not perform these many hundreth yeares past, there must needs be some other Pastour to execute the same in Peters roome, in respect of whome S. Peter may be sayd still to accom-

accomplish his duty, and feed the sheepe committed to his charge, sayth S. Leo speaking of Peter: (b) *In whome the care of all Pastours, with the custody of the sheep committed vnto him still perseuereth, and whose worthy dignity in his vnworthy successours fayleth not.* Wherby it is euident that the pastorall priuiledge granted to S. Peter was not restrayned to him, but extended to others, not giuen him as a priuate, but as a publike person, and consequently to continue with them that succeed. Euen as a King, being a publike person, still continueth, and the authority giuen to him still remayneth with his successours. For the which cause it is sayd in the law, *The King neuer dyeth.* The same is also seene in prerogatiues of honour, in priuiledges of power imparted to Kings, cittyes or publike Magistrates, which neuer fayle: as the worthy title of *Protectour of the Fayth*, was giuen to King Iames the fourth King of Scotland, by Pope Iulius, and descended to King Iames the fifth, and now presently in our most dreadfull soueraygne King Iames the sixt. So was the primacy communicated to S. Peter, not personall, but publike; not proper to him, but common to his successours, in whom (c) *Blessed Peter liueth and gouerneth, in his own proper seat, deliuereth the verity of Fayth to them that seeke it*, sayth Chrysologus.

(b) *Leo sermon.* 2.

(c) *In Ep. ad Eutych.*

2. The reasons which moued our Blessed Sauiour to make some head of the Church, were all tending to the benefite of the same Chhurch, as to preuent schismes and diuisions, to appease dissentions, and heresies, to set all the Church in peace, to indow her with a most perfect forme of gouernement, which is Monarchicall, as the Protestant Melanchton witnesseth saying: (d) *The Bishop of Rome is President ouer all Bishops, & this Canonicall policy no wiseman doth or ought to disallow &c* The same sayth Cartwright: (e) *This poynt of keeping peace in the Church is one of those, which requireth as well a Pope ouer all Archbishops, as one Archbishop ouer all Bishops in a realme.* By experience we see many stryfes and contentions in matters of Religion dayly fall out amongst the Christians, who shall appease them? The Bishops. What if there aryse contentions amongst the Bishops themselues? The Primats

(d) *In Cẽ. Epistolar. Theolog. epist.* 471

(e) *In his second Reply part.*

and Patriarches. What if variance be amongst these also, to whome shall we then repayre? To a generall Councell. But who shall summon and order this Assembly, who shall cōpose the dissentions in the Councell, vnlesse one be appoynted by the prouidence of God, whose decree is inuiolable, & whose infallible censure ought to be obeyed? Cōforme to that of the Bible: (f) *There shalbe made one fold, & one Pastour*.

(f) Iohn. 10 v. 16.

3. The Synagogue of the Iewes long triumphed in the lyneall succession of the high Priest, whose primacy first giuen to Aaron, did continue in Aaron his successours, as in Eleazarus, in Phinees, and in others after him vnto the end and abrogation of the Mosaicall law: And is it not more then reason that the Church of Christ should haue a lyke, if not greater priuiledge, established in better promises, planted by Christ, and not by Moyses, hauing greater necessity then euer the Sinagogue of the Iewes, seeing it was to imbrace all nations and Kingdomes (amōgst the which commonly there is no great vnion?) Which doctrine is cleerly confirmed by the testimonyes of the holy Fathers; of S. Chrysostome, who sayth: (g) *Why did our Lord shed his bloud? Truly to redeeme those sheep, the care of which he committed both to Peter, and also to his successours.* Of S. Hierom writing to Damasius the Pope of Rome: (h) *With the successor of the fisherman, and with the disciple of the Crosse I speake: I following none chiefe but Christ, hold the fellowship of Communion with your Holynesse, that is, with Peters chayre. Vpon that rocke I know the Church to be builded. Whosoeuer shall eat the Paschall Lambe out of that house, is a prophane person.* Of S. Augustin who adresseth these words to our Puritanes: (i) *Number the Priests euen from Peters seat and see who succeeded one another in that row of Fathers; that is the rocke which the proud gates of hell do not ouercom.* And agayne: (k) *The principality of the Apostolicall chayre, alwaies flourished in the Roman Church.* Finally he sayth: (l) *The Bishops of that sea haue the preheminence of higher roome in the Pastorall Watchtower, which is common to all Bishops.*

(g) Lib. 2. de sacerd. (h) Epist. ad Damas. (i) In psal. cont. part. Donat. de vtilitate cred. c. 17. (k) Lib. 1. cont. 2. ep. pelag. cap. 1 (l) ibidem.

4. Besides these authorityes, the continuall practise and consent of al nations approue the supremacy in spirituall

all matters of the Pope of Rome, and therfore to him appeales haue bene made frō al parts of the world. In like mãner to the ſame as to the Oracle of truth, the Chriſtiãs were wont to direct the ſumme of their beliefe, their bookes and writings; yea famous Councells, their Canons and decrees. So Iuſtinian the Emperour ſent the profeſſion of his Fayth to Agapetus the Pope: (m) S. Auguſtin ſent his workes to be examined and amended to Pope Boniface: (n) S. Hierome, ſent his workes to Pope Damaſus with this petition, *If any thing be heere vnaduiſedly ſet forth, we intreat that it may be amended by thee, who holdeſt the Fayth and ſeat of Peter.* The Councell of Chalcedon ſent their Canons and decrees to Pope Leo.

(m) *Cont. 2. epiſt. Pelag. lib. 1. cap. 1.*

(n) *In explicat. ſymbol ad Damaſum.*

5. To be ſhort, the Popes of Rome haue alwayes had their legats, as preſidents in all Oecumenicall Councells, as Hoſius in the firſt Councell of Nice, S. Cyryll in the Councell of Epheſus. The ſame I may ſay of ſundry others. In lyke manner the Biſhops of France, of Spaine, of Grece, of Germany, of Scotland, England and Ireland receaued their Archiepiſcopall Palls from the Popes of Rome. Kings and Emperours haue receaued ſundry fauours and titles of honour, as the honorable ſtyle of *moſt Chriſtian* in France, *Catholyke* in Spayne, *Protector of the Fayth* in the Kings of Scotland, *Defender of the Fayth* in the Kings of England. Moreouer the Popes of Rome did preſcribe the faſhion of crowning of ſūdry Kings, which is to this day obſerued: for example the King of France is conſecrated and annointed by the Arch-biſhop of *Rhemes*, acccording to the ordinance of *Hormiſda* Pope. The King of England by the Arch-biſhop of Canterbury, by the ordinance of Pope Hadrian the third. The King of *Scotland* by the Arch-biſſhop of *S. Andrewes* by the preſcription of Pope *Vrban* the ſecond. Yea long before Pope (o) *Hadrian, S. Columba* or *Columbanus* a holy mã in the Ile of *Iona*, twelue hundreth yeares ſince was cōmanded by the Angell of God to annoynt and conſecrate holy Aidanus King of *Scotland*, in the which miraculous conſecration the Kings of *Scotland* are no wayes inferior to the Kings of France. The King of *Germany* is conſecrated by

(o) *Apud Henricum Caniſium tom. 5. antiq. lectionum in vita S. Colūba.*

by the Arch-bishop of Mentz. The King of *Bohemia* by the Arch-bishop of *Praga*, which sheweth manifestly the supreme power, in spirituall maters, of the Roman Church.

6. But the Protestants do say that some Kings and Princes hath resisted and deposed the Pope. I answere, that inferiours may resist and persecute their superiours in spirituall matters; but wrongfully. True it is, that Emperours might call sometymes generall Councells, as Aduocats and helpers of the Church, by reason of their temporall power and authority, not as hauing spirituall authority to do the same. True it is lykewise that Gregory the great writing against Iohn the proud Patriarch of Constantinople (who presumptuously called himself Vniuersall Bishop) sayth, that the name of Vniuersall Bishop is a prophane, proud and sacrilegious title: & so it is indeed, as that Patriarch vsurped it, to wit, to be such an absolute and vniuersall Patriarch and Bishop, as to derogate from all others their Patriarchall dignity, desirous that no other should be called Bishop, but he himselfe, which was in effect a prophane nouelty; but the Pope vseth not thus the name of Vniuersal. Moreouer it is reason that the Pope of Rome should rather inherite (as S. Peters successour) that prerogatiue, then the Bishop of Antioch where Peter first did sit, or the Bishop of Ierusalem where our Sauiour dyed, wherof S. Paul

(p) *Heb. 7. v. 12.* giueth this reason: (p) *If the Priesthood be changed, then of necessity must there be a change of the law,* yea and of the chiefe place, from whence the law proceedeth. And Christ foretold

(q) *Math. 21. v. 43.* and sayd to the Iewes: (q) *The Kingdome of God shall be taken from you, and giuen to a nation yielding the fruits thereof.* And S.

(r) *Act. 13. v. 46.* Paul: (r) *To you it behoueth vs first the speake the word of God, but because yow repel it, and iudge your selus vnworthy of eternall lyfe, behold we turne to the Gentills.* But wherfore at Rome? (s) *To the*

(s) *Serm. 1 de Natiuit. Apost. Pet. & Pau.* *end* (sayth Leo) *that the head City of superstition might be made the chiefe seat of Religion.* In a word, because so it pleaseth God, whose prouidence hath bene so great towards the Romane Seat in speciall, that notwithstanding many cruel Tyrants haue bent their full power to disturbe the Popes from Rome, as Clemens Pope was disturbed by Traiane, Cornelius

nelius by Decius, Liberius by Constantius. Yea notwithstanding three & thirty Popes, who haue bene put to the sword one after another; notwithstãding I say their remouing for a tyme to Viterbo, Auinion, Rauena; yet the Popes haue still returned and placed their seat at Rome. All other Patriarchall seates haue bene rent in peeces; but the seat of Rome, no death, no banishment, no Tyranny of men, nor malice of Satan could euer ouercome. No the diuision amongst themselues, the manifold difficultyes & dangers in their elections, not the great vices which haue bene noted in some of their persons. Which is an euident demõstration of Gods prouidence in preseruing the Apostolike seat of his Vicar Generall in that holy place, & not at Antioch, nor at Ierusalem, where the succession of the Apostles hath bene interrupted by Schisme, infected by heresies, and ouerthrowen by Turkes and Infidels.

7. To conclude, it is a most certayne Tradition that the Pope succeedeth to Peter, and that Peter translated his chayre to the citty of Rome, and there continued Bishop the space of twenty fiue yeares, there ended his lyfe with a glorious martyrdom: and whosoeuer denyeth this, gainsayth all histories, chronicles, and records of holy Fathers, giuing way to deny in lyke manner effrontedly the succession of the Kings of Spayne, of England, France, Scotland, which we know only by historyes. Finally we Catholikes haue the expresse words of the Bible for vs concerning S. Peters Primacy. *Thou art Peter and vpon this rock I will build my Church.* 2. *The Gates of hell shall not ouercome the Church.* 3. *Feed my sheepe.* 4. *Other sheepe I haue also which are not of this fold: them also must I bring, and they shall heare my voyce, and there shalbe one fold and one Pastour.* I aske of the Ministers as playne and expresse wordes of the Bible which make agaynst S. Peters supremacy or speciall authority; or otherwise I aske of them expresse Scripture for these articles of their Religion: *S. Peter is not head of the Church.* 2. *S. Peter was neuer in Rome.* 3. *The Popes do not succeed to S. Peter. I will admit nothing but the expresse word of God. I will giue place to nothinge except the expresse wordes of the Bible &c.* If the Protestants aske of

vs Catholikes for euery article of our Religion the expresse words of the Bible, I answere 1. That there is no place in the Bible forbidding vs to belieue things which are not cōteined in the expresse word therof. 2. I answere that the Ministers haue obliged thēselues (t) and not we Catholiks before God and the world, by solemne oath set downe in the confession of their Faith, in the acts of Parlament, to belieue nothing, but that which is conteyned in the expresse and playne word of God, and consequently are obliged to keep this their oath. Remarke their words speaking of Generall Councels. (u) *So far then as the Councell proueth the determination and commandement that it giues, by the playne word of God, so soone do we reuerence and imbrace the same.* 3. I answere with S. Augustin, that: (x) *The verity of the Scriptures is holden of vs, when we do that, which pleaseth the vniuersall Church, which the authority of the same Scripture commendeth vnto vs.* And by reason that we may be deceaued by diuers crafty, and subtile Protestants expositions of the Bible, we aduisedly do follow the counsel of that same holy Father, who sayth: (y) *Because the holy Scriptures cannot deceaue, whosoeuer feareth to be deceaued in the obscurity of any question, let him therof aske counsell at that Church which the holy Scripture without any ambiguity pointeth vnto.* The which Church, yea the light of Nature, doth oblige vs to preferre the consequences of the holy Fathers of this second Age, to sophisticall consequences and superstitious opinions, and noueltyes of the Ministers of Scotland.

(t) *Lib. 1. cont. Maxim. Arian. Epist.*

(u) *In the Acts of parlament holden the* 17. of Aug. 1568.

(x) Augu. *cont. Crescon. lib. 10. cap. 33.*

(y) *Ibidem.*

8. But before I set downe in particular the consequences of the holy Fathers, I will briefly aduertise the vnpassionat Reader, that notwithstanding this spiritual authority which is in Peters successours, they cannot therfore do things according to their fansie, agaynst Princes and Kings, by reason that their authority was giuen, (a) *In aedificationem, & non in destructionem, to edification and not to destruction. For since God is he,* (b) *By whome Kings do raygne:* and since (c) *All power is from God*; it followeth that the temporall power granted by God to Kings is in them absolute and independant, and no man whosoeuer can haue power at his pleasure to crosse and ouerthrow the same. And this is that holy

(a) 2. *Cor.* 13. v. 10.

(b) *Prou.* 8. v. 15.

(c) *Rom.* 13. v. 1.

ly doctrine which our holy mother the Catholike Church doth teach, saying to euery one of vs in particular: (d) *My sonne feare the Lord, and the King, and meedle not with them that be seditious.* And as God himselfe commanded the Israelites during their captiuity in Babylon, to pray for the citty where they were captiues, saying: (e) *Seeke you the prosperity of that citty, whither I haue caused you to be carried away captiue, and pray to the Lord for it, for in the peace therof you shall haue peace.* In lyke manner God commanded them, (f) to pray for the lyfe of King Nabuchodonosor, though an infidel, and for the lyfe of Baltazar his sonne, *that their dayes might be on earth as the dayes of heauen &c.* Much more doth God command vs Catholikes (though greatly persecuted) to continue our humble prayers for our afflicted countreys of Scotlād, Englād, and Ireland, and specially for our Christian soueraygne & and King, for our Princely and hopefull Baltazar, for all the Royall issue, for the Councell of Scotland and Englād, that lykewise *their dayes may be on earth lyke the dayes of heauen, and that we may long do them seruice and find fauour in their sight.* Which God of his infinite goodnesse grant vnto vs. Amen.

(d) *Prou.* 24. *v.* 21.

(e) *Ierem.* 29. *v.* 7.

(f) *Baruch.* 1. *v.* 11. & 12.

9. As concerning the disobedience of Puritans and Protestants to their Kings, Princes and Superiours, besides the example of the late rebellion of the Hugenots in Frāce, for the which their owne brethren do confesse, that *it is as difficile to find a loyal subiect of the Hugenots & Puritans Religion, as it is to find a white Moore*, experience doth teach vs, that whereuer this new and reformed Religion of the Puritanes and Protestants hath entred and taken hold, it hath bene by manifest rebellion and sedition, as in Holland, Germany, Scotland, England, France, and Sueden. To the proofe wherof I will set down the very words of the Protestant wryters. Sleydan a Protestant wryter in Germany sayth of the Emperour thus: (g) *Considering that Cæsar doth intend destruction of Religion, he giueth occasion wherby we may resist him with good conscience: for in this case it is lawfull to resist &c.* And Zuinglius a prime Puritane: (h) *When Princes* (sayth he) *do any thing agaynst the true Religion, they may be deposed. Possunt haud dubie*

(g) *Sleydan in the* 18. *booke of his history & lib.* 8. *ante med.*

(h) *Tom.* 2. *in explan. artic.* 42. *fol.* 84.

hic deponi. To proceed next with Caluin the Prime Puritan Minister of France, of whome and of his fellow Ministers, M. Bancroft a Protestant Arch-bishop of Canterbury sayth thus: (i) *That the doctrine of Caluin and certayne other Ministers residing at Geneua, teacheth that it is lawfull for subiects to reforme Religion when Princes will not, yea rather then it fayle, euen by force of armes.* Of the which Ministers, Knox our Country Minister was one, as witnesseth Beza writing to him thus: (k) *Ioanni Knoxo, Euangelij Dei apud Scotos instauratori, Fratri & Symmistæ obseruando.* Lykewise Caluin writyng to a prime English seditious Minister called *Goodman* (in effect a bad man for England) called him: (l) *An excellent and reuerend brother, and most faythfull adiutor to Knox.* Which seditious doctrine of Knox is partly touched in Holinsheads great Chronicle in the history of Scotland the last edition to my knowledge: and by M Bancroft in his booke intituled, *Dangerous positions &c.* who in lyke manner do report that abhominable doctrine of Buchanan, who in his booke *De iure regni apud Scotos,* writeth: (m) *That it were good that rewards were appoynted by the people for such as should kill Tyrants* (O abhominable doctrine of a Scots Puritan!) *as commmonly there is for those that haue killed wolues.* And, *That the people may araygne their Princes and Kings.* And in speciall Goodman an English Prime Minister in a book of his intituled *Obedience*, as witnesseth M. Bancroft, and M. Sutcliffe before cited, speaking of Queene Marie of England, sayth, (n) *That it is lawfull to kill wicked Kings and Tyrants, and that both by Gods law and mans law Queene Marie ought to be put to death as being a Tirãt, a monster, and a cruel beast.* And that: (o) *By the word of God in such a defection, a priuate man hauing some speciall inward motion may kill a Tyrant.* I intreat the vnpassionat Reader to peruse Holinsheads great Chronicle, volume 3. pag. 1104. and Stow his Annales printed 1592. pag. 1058. both Protestant writers, and he shall see manifestly the seditious conspiracy of Protestants agaynst their soueraygne. Wel inough is knowen to the world that seditions and diuelish doctrine of the Waldenses, Wicklefistes and Hussits (whom our Protestants do call their forfathers) concerning abhominable sedition

(i) *In his Surney of the pretended holy discipline pag.* 12.

(k) *Beza in epist Theol. epist.* 74.

(l) *Caluin epist.* 306. *Christophoro Goodmano.*

(m) *Buchanan de iure regni apud Scotos. See M. Doue in his defẽce of the Churches gouernement.*

(n) *In his booke intituled Obedience pag.* 99. & 103.

(o) *In his Obedience pag.* 100.

dition agaynst their naturall princes in Morauia: of Luther *Zuinglius* and *Carolostadius* in Germany: of *Caluin* and *Beza* in France: of *Knox*, *Buchanan*, and of the Earle of *Gauiy* in Scotland: of *Goodman*, *Gibby*, *Whittingham* in England, & of others of the lyke sort in Sueden, Denmarke, Poland, Zeland, and Holland. The fruits and effects of whose rebellion agaynst their naturall Princes vnder the pretext of reformation of Religion, are two much apparent in these our dayes.

10. To what end should I produce history-writers since the very grounds of the Puritans Religion do lead the high way to all sort of sedition. Is not this one of the chiefest principles of their Religion preached publickly at the baptizing of euery child in Scotlãd: (p) *There is no other but he* (Christ) *in heauen, nor earth that hath iust authority and power to make lawes, to bind the consciences of men?* To what end then are oathes of fidelity made to Princes, if there be no obligation in conscience to keep them? O abhominable doctrine! O seditious & detestable Religiõ! The second principle is set down in the Ministers confession of Fayth thus: (q) *Besides this Ecclesiasticall discipline, I acknowledge to belong to this Church a politicall magistrate who ministreth to euery mã iustice, defending the good and punishing the euill, to whome we must render honour and obedience in all things which are not contrary to the word of God:* That is, contrary to the Ministers fansies and superstitious doctrine, and to the Ministers newfangled Religion: which former words are confirmed by an act of Parlament, thus: (r) *We confesse and acknowledge not to disobey or resist any that God hath placed in authority, whiles they passe not ouer the bounds of their office.* The Hugenots of France (whose pryde God hath daunted now lately) do testify the same in expresse words: (s) *Nous tenons* (say they) *qu'il faut obeir aux Loix des Roys, payer tributs, Imposts & autres debuoirs, & porter le ioug de subiection d'vne bonne & franche volonté, moyennant* (remarke these words) *que l'Empire du Soueraigne demeure en son entiere &c.* 3. The Ministers do teach, that it is impossible to keep Gods commandements, whereof these be two of the chiefest: (t) *Feare God, Honour the King*. Agayne, (u) *Submit your selues to all manner of*

(p) *In the order of Baptisme.*

(q) *In the Confession of Fayth of the Ministers.*

(r) *In the Acts of Parlimẽt 500. the 17. of August. arti. 4.*

(s) *Confess. de foy art. 40.*

(t) 1. *Pet.* 2. v. 17.

(u) 1. *Pet.* 2. v. 13.

of ordinance of man, for the Lords sake &c. And such others set down in the expresse word of God. But if it be impossible to keepe those commandements, how can the Puritanes be faythfull and obedient to their Kings and Princes? 4. The Ministers do excommunicat Kings and Princes and the Politicall Magistrate, & consequently do teach that they haue power aboue them: remarke their words: (x) *Therefore in the name and authority of the eternal God, and of his sonne Iesus-Christ, I excommunicate from this table, all blasphemers of God, all Idolaters, all Murtherers, all Adulterers, and all that be in malice & enuy, all disobedient persons to Father and Mother, Princes or Magistrates, Pastors or Preachers, all theeues and deceauers of their neighbour &c. charging them as they will answere in the presence of him who is the righteous Iudge, that they presume not to prophane this most holy table.* Is it not more dangerous for a King or prince to be subiect to the excommunicatiō of euery light-headed Minister of his owne kingdome, then to the excommunication of a stranger and forayner? What place of the Bible giueth Ministers power to excommunicate? Their commission is none. Their authority is null. Happy is he who is excommunicat by the instruments of the Diuell and Antichrist; happy is he who is at the diuels horne; happy is he who is put out of the Synagogue of the wicked.

(x) *In the manner of giuing the Lords Supper.*

That man is blest, that hath not bent
To such men tyed his eare,
Nor led his lyfe, as Ministers teach,
Nor sit in Puritans chayre.

5. Can there be a more dangerous, yea diuelish opinion agaynst Kings and Princes then to belieue constantly, that whatsoeuer wicked rebellion is stirred vp agaynst a King is by the will of God? Remarke their own words: (y) *We do cōfesse that God is Creator of heauen & earth, that is to say that heauē & earth & the contents therof are so in his hand, that there is nothing done without his knowledge, neyther yet agaynst his will.* So that no rebelliō, no diuelish enterprise of a Minister against his King shalbe agaynst the will of God, but rather conforme to his wil, for that which is not against the wil of God, must needs be cōforme to his will. 6. How can the Hugenots of Frāce be

(y) *In the order of Baptisme in the explication of the first article.*

be faythful to their King, & the Puritans to their Princes & Superiours in Germany, since they belieue that all Kings and Princes, that are of a diuers Religion from them, are lymmes of the Diuell and of Antichrist? Which thing they belieue as a point of Religion set down in their confession of fayth in these wordes: (a) *The defence of Chrišts Church apperteineth to the Christian Magistrat agaynst all Idolaters and heretikes, as Papists, Anabaptists, with such lyke lymmes of Antichrist &c.* 7. It is a ground of the Puritanes Religion, whatsoeuer rebellious course any seditious-dealing-wicked persons (yea the Diuells) take in hand, that it is the will of God, who compelleth them (say they) therunto. And what I pray you is more excellēt then to do the wil of God: which we aske dayly to be done, saying: *Thy willbe done in earth as it is in heauen.* Remarke the Ministers own wordes: (b) *What sayest thou,* (the Minister asketh) *touching the Diuells and wicked persons, be they also subiect to him?* (The child answeres thus) *Albeyt that God doth not guyde thē with his holy spirit, yet he doth bridle them in such sort, that they be not able to stirre or mooue without his permission or appoyntment. Yea and moreouer* (remarke the words) *he doth compell them to execute his will, although it be agaynst their intent and purpose.* Euery seditious enterprise then, shall it be the will of God? So it is indeed in the Puritanes Religion, who do conclude thus: *The knowledge hereof doth wōderfully comfort vs; for we might think our selues in a miserable case, if the Diuells and the wicked had power to do any thing contrary to the will of God.*

(a) In the confession of Faith receaued and approued by the Church of Scotland.

(b) In the articles of Fayth the 4. Sunday.

11. Behold O Scotland my deare Countrey, to what impious, seditious, and Idolatrous doctrine the Ministers haue induced thee? Why didst thou leaue that Religion, wherin fourscore wyse, valiant, and godly Kings of thy owne Nation happily gouerned and commanded? Why didst thou forsak that Religiō wherby thou wast honored abroad by the most famous Kings & Princes of Christendome? wherby thou was blessed by God at home with peace, wealth and grace? Wheron doest thou now rely and ground thy Religion? Not vpon the Bible, the expresse word of God, the playne text of Scripture, as I haue before

proued: but vpon the new fangled expoſitions, ſuperſtitious ſophiſmes and explications of the Miniſters, which being in themſelues nothing els but inuentions of men; of men, I ſay, without authority & commiſſion, are in effect againſt all holy Fathers, Councels, Antiquity, and common Conſent of all nations of the world, and of all ages before the comming of Luther and Caluin. Is it not intollerable pryde, for thee to preferre the new fangled expoſitions of thy Miniſters (whoſe lyfe and conuerſation thou ſeeſt to be bad, whoſe commiſſion and authority thou knoweſt to be none) to the expoſitions of all the holy and learned, who haue bene theſe ſixtene hundreth yeares? (c) *For theſe things, O Lord, I weep; myne eye, euen myne eye caſteth out water, becauſe thy enemyes do proſper:* and becauſe (O Scotland) thou doeſt follow the ſtinking puddle, and filthy doctrine of the Proteſtant, and Puritan-Miniſters, thy ſworne enemies.

(c) *Ierem.* 1. *v.* 16 & 5.

The Teſtimonyes of the holy Fathers of this Age concerning the primacy of S. Peter, and his Succeſſours in the Catholike Church.

The first Section.

S. Irenæus Biſhop of Lyons in France auoweth firſt, S. Peter & Paul to haue preached the Ghoſpell at Rome: (a) *Petrum & Paulum Romæ euangelizaſſe & fundaſſe Eccleſiam*. 2. Writing againſt the Heretiks called *Gnoſtici*, proueth the Primacy, infallibility, & perpetuall ſucceſſion of the Roman Church, refuting thoſe heretiks therby after this forme: (b) *Sed quoniam valde longum eſt, in hoc tali volumine omnium Eccleſiarum enumerare ſucceſſiones, maximæ & antiquiſſimæ & omnibus cognitæ à glorioſiſſimis Apoſtolis Petro & Paulo Romæ fundatæ & conſtitutæ Eccleſiæ, eam quam habet ab Apoſtolis traditionem, & annunciatam hominibus fidem, per ſucceſſiones Epiſcoporum peruenientem vſque ad nos, iudicantes, confundimus omnes eos, qui quoquo modo vel per ſui placentiam malam, vel vanam gloriam, vel per cæcitatem & malam ſententiam, præterquam oportet, colligunt. Ad hanc enim Eccleſiam, hoc eſt eos qui ſunt vndique fideles, in qua ſemper ab his, qui ſunt*

(a) *Iren. l. aduerſ. hæreſ. cap.* 1.

(b) *Lib.* 3.

sunt vndiq3, conseruata est ea quæ est ab Apostolis Traditio. Fundantes igitur & instruentes beati Apostoli Ecclesiam, Lino Episcopatũ administrandæ Ecclesiæ tradiderunt.(c)*Huius Lini Paulus in ijs quæ sunt ad Timotheum Epistolis meminit. Succedit autem ei Anacletus, post eum tertio loco ab Apostolis Episcopatum sortitur Clemens, qui & vidit ipsos Apostolos, & contulit cum ijs, cùm adhuc insonantem prædicationem Apostolorum & traditionem ante oculos haberet. Non solus enim, adhuc multi supererant tunc ab Apostolis docti. Sub hoc igitur Clemente dissensione nõ modica inter eos qui Corinthi essent fratres facta, scripsit quæ est Romæ Ecclesiá potentissimas literas Corinthijs, ad pacem eos congregans, & reparans fidem eorum, & annuncians quam in recenti ab Apostolis receperunt traditionem.*

(c) 2. Tim. 4. v. 21.

2. S. Victor Pope and Martyr; to whome King *Donald* of Scotland sent that learned and worthy Abbot *Paschasius* the yeare of Christ 200. to receaue of his Holynes Doctors to plant publickly the Catholike and Romane religion in Scotland, to the which end two famous & learned were sent, *Marcus* and *Dionisius*, who conuerted King *Donald*, and the rest of the Nobility the yeare of Christ 203. as witnesseth (d) Genebrardus, (e) Baronius, (f) Boetius, (g) Lesleus, (h) Gualterius, and sundry others: This pope I say in a certayne (i) letter of his to Theophilus Bishop of *Alexandria* witnesseth playnly, and plentifully S. Peters primacy, and supremacy aboue the rest of the Churches.

3. S. Sixtus Martyr in a decree of his, witnesseth the same, and sayth: (k) *Si quis verò vestrum pulsatus fuerit in aliqua aduersitate, licenter hanc sanctam & Apostolicam appellet Sedem, & ad eam, quasi ad caput, suffugium habeat, ne innocens damnetur, aut Ecclesia sua detrimentum patiatur.*

4. S. Pius Martyr in a certayne epistle of his directed to the Catholiks, affirmeth that Christ Iesus gaue Primacy to S. Peter and his successours: (l) *qui & hanc sanctã sedem Apostolicam* (sayth he, speaking of Rome) *omnium Ecclesiarum caput esse præcepit, ipso dicente Principi Apostolorum, Tu es Petrus, & super hanc petram ædificabo Ecclesiam meam &c. & tibi dabo claues regni cælorum.*

5. S. Anacletus plentifully testifieth the primacy of the Roman Church to haue bene giuen to S. Peter, and

(d) *In Victore in Chronologia.*
(e) *Ad annum 429.*
(f) *Lib. 6.*
(g) *Passim.*
(h) *In Chronologia seculo tertio.*
(i) *Extat tom. 1. cõc.*
(k) *Extat tom. 1. concil.*
(l) *Epist. sua ad vniuersos. extat tom. 1. concil.*

to haue continued in *Linus*, *Cletus*, *Clemens*, (m) *nostro* (sayth he) *sancto prædecessore & Martyre*. 2. He auoweth that this primacy was giuen by Christ himselfe to the Roman Church: (n) *Hæc verò* (sayth he) *sacrosancta Romana & Apostolica Ecclesia, non ab Apostolis sed ab ipso Domino Saluatore nostro primatum obtinuit, & eminentiam potestatis super vniuersas Ecclesias, ac totum Christiani populi gregem assecuta est, sic, vt ipse Beato Petro Apostolo dixit: Tu es Petrus, & super hanc petram ædificabo Ecclesiam meam*.

(m) Epist. 3.

(n) Ibidem.

6. Tertullian in his booke *de Monogamia*, auoweth the Church to haue bene builded vpon S. Peter, and as it were maryed with him as the Head therof, wherof the one and only Mariage of S. Peter (amongst the rest of the Apostles) was a figure. (o) *Petrum* (sayth he) *solum inuenio maritum, per socrum: Monoganum præsumo, per Ecclesiam, quæ super illum ædificata, omnem gradum ordinis sui de Monogamis erat collocatura. Ceteros cùm maritos non inuenio, aut spadones intelligamus necesse est, aut continentes*. 2. He also doth testifie Primacy to haue bene giuen to Peters successours by the Catholike Church, by whome then the Pope was tearmed (p) *Pontifex maximus, Episcopus Episcoporum, bonus Pastor, Benedictus, Papa Apostolicus*. 3. He prayseth the Church of Rome, by reason that S. Peter & Paul did preach & shed their bloud there: (q) *Felix Ecclesia, cui totam doctrinam Apostolicam suo sanguine profuderunt*. 4. He affirmeth *Marcion* and *Valentin* to be Heretiks, for as much as they being first Romã Catholiks, were thrust out of the Roman church by reason of their heresies. (r) *Marcionem* (sayth he) *& Valentinum Catholicam primò doctrinam credidisse apud Ecclesiam Romanensem, donec sub Episcopatu Eleutherij benedicti, ob inquietam semper eorum curiositatem, qua fratres quoq; vitiabant, semel & iterum eiecti*.

(o) Lib. de Monog. cap. 8.

(p) Lib. de pudicitia cap. 1. 13. & 21.

(q) Lib. de præscrip. cap. 36.

(r) Lib. de præscrip. c. 30.

7. Origen giueth an infallible Rule wherby we may discerne the true doctrine and Religion from the false, to wit, that to be only true which hath the perpetuall succession of Bishops and Pastors. His words be: (s) *Cùm multi sint qui se putent sentire quæ Christi sunt, & nonnulli eorum diuersa à prioribus sentiant, seruetur verò Ecclesiastica prædicatio per successionis ordinem ab Apostolis tradita, & vsq; ad præsens in Ecclesiis permanens*

(s) In proœmio lib. de principijs.

mens; illa sola credenda est veritas, quæ in nullo discordat ab Ecclesiastica traditione. 2. He teacheth vs, that Peter was the Apostle, vpon whome the Church was builded. (t) *Petrus* (sayth he) *super quem ædificata est Christi Ecclesia contra quam inferorum porta non prævalebunt*. 3. He witnesseth that when pope *Zepherinus* gouerned the Romã Church as head therof he himselfe went to Rome, as to the head, and most ancient Church: (u) *Romanam Ecclesiam gubernantis Zephyrini tẽporibus Romam iter suscepisse, quòd ecclesiam Romanam antiquißimã videre exoptaret*.

(t) *Lib. 5. in Euang. Ioannis.*

(u) *Apud Euseb. lib. 6. hist cap. 11.*

8. S. Cyprian first most learnedly & wysely teacheth vs, that heresies, schismes, and diuersity of Religion do fall out, by reason that one head of the Church is not acknowledged: (x) *Neq; enim aliunde hæreses obortæ sunt, aut natæ sunt schismata, quàm inde quòd sacerdoti Dei non obtemperatur; nec vnus in Ecclesia ad tempus Sacerdos, & ad tempus Iudex vice Christi cogitatur: cui si secundum magisteria diuina obtemperaret fraternitas vniuersa, nemo aduersum sacerdotum collegium quicquam moueret; nemo sibi placens ac tumens seorsum foras hæresim nouam conderet*. 2. He teacheth, that God hath a particular care of the Priests, Bishops, and specially of the head of the Church, not suffering him to erre, when he doth propone to all the Catholiks things to be belieued, as matters of faith. For if God hath care of little things, much more will he haue care of the gouernement of his Church: (y) *Cum Dominus* (sayth he) *in Euangelio suo dicat*; (a) *Nonne duo passeres asse veneunt, & neuter eorum cadit in terram sine patris voluntate? Cùm illa nec minima fieri sine voluntate dei dicat, existimat aliquis summa & magna, aut non sciente, aut non permittente Deo, in Ecclesia fieri, & sacerdotes, id est, dispensatores eius, non de eius sententia ordinari*. 3. He sayth that primacy of the Church was giuen to S. Peter: (b) *Primatus Petro datur, vt vna Christi Ecclesia, & cathedra vna monstretur*. 4. He calleth the Roman Church, (c) *Matricem & radicem Ecclesiæ Catholicæ*. I conclude then, that this holy Father with al those of this second age belieued constantly this poynt & matter of religion.

(x) *Epist. 55. ad Cornelium Papam.*

(y) *Ibidem.*

(a) *Matth. 10. v. 29.*

(b) *Lib. de vnitate Ecclesiæ.*

(c) *Epest. 45 ad Corn.*

That

That the Ministers haue falsified diuers places of the Bible, concerning the Blessed Trinity, and the Person of Christ, who gaue infallible power to S. Peter aboue the rest of the Apostles, and consequently gaue infallible power to the Church of God.

The second Section.

IT were tedious to me, and to the Reader, to set down at length the infinite multitude of Blasphemyes & Idolatrous opiniõs which Caluin the Sophist teacheth against the Blessed Trinity, against the Person of Christ in his Institutions, wherof the first word is in french *Tout*, all, and the last, *Iniquitè*, iniquity; signifying therby to vs, that all which is cõteyned in those foure books of his Institutions, is nothing els, *but playne and manifest iniquity, Idolatry & blasphemy*. Conforme to Caluin his Institutions, *the Confession of faith of the Puritanes of Scotland*, was framed in *Geneua*, brought to *Scotland* by *Knox* the Apostata Fryar, and after sworne and subscrybed at seuerall Parlaments. In the which confession it is easie to remarke in like maner dyuers blasphemyes against God: As that in the very frontispice and begining, (a) *There was no meanes to bring vs from that yoke of sinne and damnation, but only Iesus Christ our Lord.* O horrible blasphemy against the Omnipotency of God, who had infinite other meanes to redeme mãkynd, but he thought the sending of Christ the fittest, to draw, and allure the loue of man vnto him, as Christ himself witnesseth, saying: (b) *And I, when I shalbe exalted from the earth, will draw all men vnto me.* Lykewise can there be a greater Blasphemy inuented then to say, that not only Christ suffered on the Crosse, but also that for a season he suffered the very wrath of God, and torments of the Reprobate, in soule & body? Their words be: (c) *Christ suffered not only the cruell death of the crosse, but also he suffred for a season the wrath of his Father which sinnes had deserued: But yet we auow, that he remayned the only well-beloued and blessed Sonne of his Father, euen in the midst of his anguish and torment*

(a) *In the Confession of Fayth vsed in the English cõgregation at Geneua receaued & aproued by the Church of Scotlãd.*
(b) *Iohn.* 12. v. 32.
(c) *In the Acts of Parlament holden at Edenburgh 17. of August.* 1568.

ment which he suffered in body and soule. Was there euer any Heretike, Turke, or Iew who said Christ to haue suffered in his soule, which was glorified, and saw God face to face (as it doth now) from the first instant of the creation therof? Read in the articles of the Ministers faith from the nynth Sonday to the eleauenth, and yee shall see concerning this poynt horrible blasphemyes against Christ, of whome amongst others, they say thus: *That very payne which Christ susteyned for a tyme, the wicked must indure continually*. O abhomination! O diuelish doctrine! O Idolatrous religion! what can we iudge of the pittyfull estate of all those Puritanes and Protestants, who haue dyed in Scotland within these fifty yeares past in this abhominable belief & Religiõ?

2. The first place then which the Ministers haue falsified is that of S. Matthew, where Christ sayth: (d) *All things are delyuered me of my Father*. Wherby the ancient and holy Doctours proued against *Arius* and *Sabellius* heretiks, that Christ was God of God the Father, called therfore the sonne of God the Father; for though the outward actions, as Creation, Conseruation &c. which are called *actiones ad extra*, are common to God the Father, God the Sonne, and God the Holy Ghost; yet the inward actions called *actiones ad intra* are peculiar and proper to euery person; as the *action of generation* is proper to God the Father only; the *action of procession* to God the Father, & God the sonne only: *Caluin* and the Ministers to ouerthrow this holy doctrine, and to deny that Christ is the Sonne of God the Father, as hauing receaued his essence from all eternity of God the Father, as he witnesseth heer, saying: *all things are delyuered me of my Father*: The Hugonots I say, and Caluin haue corrupted the Bible filthily, and most abhominably, ioyning two seuerall wordes which are not in the Greeke copy; *All thinges are giuen me in hand by my Father*: Their wordes be, *Toute chose m'ont esté donné en main de par mon Pere*: Thrusting in the text the two wordes, *en main*, *in hand*, to signify with the Arrians, (who were in the same heresy with Caluin and Knox) that Christ speaketh not heer of the inward generation of God the Father, wherby he

(d) *Matth. 11. v. 27.*

πάντα μοι παρεδόθη ὑπὸ τοῦ πατρός.

he receaued all of his Father, but only of the outward go-uernement. Let vs heare Caluins blasphemous words: (e) *Quicõque dit que le fils de Dieu soit essentié du Pere, il nie qu'il ayt estre propre de soy.* That is. *Whosoeuer sayth that the sonne of God hath receaued his essence frõ God the Father, denyeth him to haue a proper being of himselfe. De-Saincts* a Catholike Doctour, & *Stancarus* a Protestãt haue written whole bookes against the impiety and Atheismes of Caluin the sophist. Some English Bibles had the former corruption, but now they haue corrected them, as they haue done many others, wherby it is easie to see that the English Bibles are far different from the Bibles of the Hugenots in France, and from the Lutherans in Germany. In the Blessed Trinity there be three persons, yet not different, but distinguished, not three Gods but one God: the essence of one person is the essence of another, none before other in tyme, nor by nature, *sed ordine*; none the originall cause of the other, which is directly against that Blasphemy set down in the articles of the Ministers faith of Scotland: (f) *Because* (say they) *that in the substance or nature of God, we haue to consider the father as the fountayne, beginning and originall cause.* For God the Father cannot be the originall cause of God the sonne. And if the Ministers vnderstand that God the Father is the originall cause alone of all creatures, it is alwayes a blasphemy, for he is not alone the originall cause of such, by reason that *Actiones ad extra, sunt communes toti Trinitati*. Finally the Doctours do remarke these notions wherby we may distinguish the three persons, *Innascibility, Paternity, Filiation, Spiration actiue*, and *Spiration passiue*: how many of the Ministers will vnderstãd this doctrine?

(e) *Lib.* 1. *de instit. c.* 13. *num.* 23.

(f) *In the Articles of the Fayth Sunday* 3.

3. Remarke secondly in the same Articles of the Ministers, another blasphemy against the omnipotency of God: (g) *What meanest thou* (sayth the Minister) *by that thou callest him Almighty?* C *I meane not that he hath a power, which he doth not exercise.* May not God create ten thousand worldes, worke infinite miracles, and punish sensibly the Ministers for such blasphemyes? and because he doth not exercise such a power, shall we say that he hath not power

(g) *In the Artilces of Fayth Sunday* 3.

to do it? Remarke thirdly, what good doctrine the Ministers do giue concerning the lawes of Kings and Princes, as touching the oath of Allegiance, or any other such; Remarke diligently I say, their words which are: (h) *There is no other but he* (Christ) *in heauen nor earth that hath iust authority to make lawes to bind the cōsciences of men.* What auayle then the Protestants oathes, since they belieue constantly, that they are not obliged in conscience to keep them? What auayleth it his Maiesty to take the oathes of Allegiance and Supremacy of the Protestants, seing they belieue constātly, as a poynt of faith, that no law of Man man bind and oblige them in conscience?

(h) *In the order of Baptisme in the explication of that article* Borne of the Virgin Marie.

4. The second place which the Ministers haue falsified is that of S. Paul: (i) *There is one God, one also mediatour, God and man, which is the man Christ Iesus, who gaue himselfe a Redemption for all men*: Signifying therby that we haue but one *mediatour of Redemption*, though there may be diuers *mediatours of Intercession*, as I proued before. In the which few words the Ministers haue made at least three impious falsifications. First in some of their Bibles they haue put the word *only*, or *alone*, saying, *there is one alone mediatour*, which words they haue also in their Confession of faith, and in the French Bibles, *vn seul moyenneur entre Dieu & les hommes*. wherin the frēch Bibles do differ from our last printed English Bibles. 2. They haue put into the text these two words, (*which is*) which words are neyther in the Greek nor Syriake. 3. They haue taken away the word *redemption*, by reason that we make a distiction betwixt *Mediator of Redēption*, and *mediatour of Intercession*, grounded specially vpon this place, & they haue put the word *ransome* insteed therof translating thus: *Who gaue himselfe a ransome for all men*; notwithstāding that in other places they haue turned the same Greeke word *in redemption*, as we do heere; as in that to the Hebrews, (k) *and obteyned eternall redemption for vs*: which place likewyse they haue corrupted, putting those two words *for vs*, which are not in the Greeke. Agayne: (l) *That death which was for the redemption*, and in sundry other places. Can there be a greater impiety then to with-hold

(i) 1. Tim. 2. v. 5. εἷς καὶ μεσίτης θεοῦ καὶ ἀνθρώπων.

λύτρωσιν ἀπολύτρωσιν.

(k) Heb. 9. v. 12.

(l) Heb. 12. v. 15.

from the common people the true translation of the Bible? Can there be any sinne compared to this sinne of the Ministers? Is not (m) *the wrath of God reuealed from heauen against all vngodlines & vnrighteousnes of such men, who withhold the truth in vnrighteousnes*? Is it not a sin against the holy ghost to permit, yea to command the simple and ignorant people to read at dinner & supper, & els where such falsified Bibles, corrupted translations, and venemous doctrine?

(m) *Rom.* 1. v. 8.

5. The third place falsified by the Ministers is that of the Prophet Dauid, who speaking of, and to the prayse of Christ Iesus, sayth: (n) *Thou hast made him a little lower then the Angels; with glory and honour thou hast crowned him.* The Greeke and Hebrew text hath the same, *Me hat Meeloim:* the same hath also the Chaldæan Paraphrase, and the Syriake in the Epistle to the Hebrews, with al the Fathers without exception. The Ministers accustomed euer to follow the doctrine of Caluin the Sycophant, and Knox the Apostata who do teach in sundry places, that Christ is not God, do translate this place thus: *for thou hast made him a little lower thē God*, turning the Hebrew word *Elohim* God, which as in sundry places, so heer cannot be translated, without blasphemy, except in *Angels*. Not one of the Iewish Rabbins, no not one of the holy Fathers and learned wryters did euer take the word *Elohim*, in this place, otherwyse then for *Angels*, as witnesseth Genebrard. And since the words, *thou hast made him*, cannot be referred, but to the person of Christ in Caluins opinion, and since the person of Christ includeth both God and man, it cannot be said without a manifest blasphemy, *that Christ was made a little lower then God*. It cannot be said, that to the shew, during his life tyme heer, that *he was a little lower then God*. By reason that to the outward shew he was infinitly lower then God. But if we say that Christ, though God & man, to the outward shew was made lower then the Angels, though as man he was aboue all Angels, such a doctrine is Catholike, most true & cōform to the meaning of the holy Fathers, & as S. Paul manifestly witnesseth, & the Ministers thēselues now do translate with vs after this forme: (o) *Thou madest him*

(n) *Psal.* 8. v. 5. παρ' ἀγγέλους.

Geneb. in hunc locū.

(o) *Heb.* 2. v. 7.

him a little inferior to the Angels. I thought good to set down heer the selfe same doctrine of Caluin the author of the deformed religion of Scotland, cõcerning the sonne of God our Sauyour Christ Iesus, but because it is nothing els but a heape of blasphemyes against God, I thinke it expedient to cite his owne french language and proper words, to the end that the Scots or English Reader should not be harmed therewith.

6. The first blasphemy of Caluin against Christ the Sonne of God the Father is, *that he denyeth him to be properly Creatour of heauen and earth*. Heare his words: (p) *Certes nous confessons d'vn consentement, que Christ est improprement appellé Createur du Ciel & de la terre*. 2. He denyeth the generation of God the sonne to be naturall and eternall: (q) *Il a engendré son filz, seulement, pour ce qu'il a voulu*. 3. He fauoureth greately the Arrians who denyed the sonne of God to be of the same substance with God the Father: against whom the holy Fathers produced that of S. Iohn, (r) *I and the father are one*, signifying vnity of substance. Caluin sayth with the Arrians, that it signifyeth only *vnity of will*: And the Ministers to insinuat this horrible Blasphemy of Caluin haue corrupted the text, ioyning therunto the word *my*, which is not, no not in their owne falsified Greeke copyes, translating thus: *I and my Father are one*. 4. Caluin teacheth, that the sonne of God is God of himselfe, (s) *de par soy mesme, & n'est point essentié du Pere*. This blasphemy is so euident, that as it maketh many Gods, so in making many it ouerthroweth all God-head. 5. Caluin teacheth that the name of *God*, is giuen specially and by way of prerogatiue to God the Father, & not to God the sonne: (t) *Nous auons franchement dict, que par prerogatiue le nom de Dieu est attribué au Pere*. Which doctrine is the cause wherfore the Ministers do neuer, neyther, in the Article of their faith, neyther in their seuerall confessions of faith, call or name God the sonne, Creator of heauen and earth: Yea rather they do acknowledge him to be a creature with Arius and not the Creator. Heare their owne words rehearsed euery sõday in the Church of Scotlãd, wher the Minister maketh the chyld to say: (u) *Because that*

(p) *Lib. cõt. Valent. Gẽtil. pag.* 1924.

(q) *Ibidem* 1930.

(r) *Iohn.* 10 *v.* 30.

ἐγὼ καὶ ὁ πατὴρ ἕν ἐσμεν.

(s) *Contra Valent. Gent. pag.* 1924. & *lib.* 1. *instit. cap.* 13. *n.* 26.

(t) *Eodem libro cont. Valent. Gentil.*

(u) *In the Articles of Fayth Sunday* 3.

that in the substance or nature of God, we haue to consider the father as the fountayne, beginning & originall cause of all things &c. For if God the Father be the cause of God the sonne, he behoued to be before God the sonne, for, *omnis causa est prior suo effectu, saltem natura.* 6. Caluin teacheth that the feare of dānation did greatly trouble Christ: (x) *L'abysme & confusion horrible de damnation l'a viuemēt & rudement tourmentè de crainte & angoisse.* And a little after: *Il a estè saisi d'vne frayeur & espouuentement de la malediction de Dieu.* This is the selfe same doctrine of the Ministers, who do say in the articles of their fayth: (y) *Because he presented himselfe before the iudgement-seat of God to satisfy for sinnes, it was necessary that he should feele this horrible torment of conscience, as if God had vtterly forsaken him, yea as though God had bene his extreme enemy.* To this blasphemy they ioyne another, that Christ indured the very paynes and torments of the reprobate in hell. Heare their owne words: *That very payne which Christ susteyned for a tyme the wicked must indure continually.* Making no difference betwixt the torments, which Christ suffered, say they, after his death (for the Ministers do speake of Christ his descent into hel, which was performed after his death) and in his soule, & the torments which the reprobat in hell do susteyne, except in duration; and consequently the Ministers must needs auow that the passion of Christ vpon the Crosse was not sufficient for our redemption, but that it was likewyse necessary to suffer those torments after his death. Which blasphemy as it is against the holy word of God, against the person of Christ, against all reason and ancient Fathers, so it is the very way to all Atheisme and Infidelity.

(x) *En son harmon. in* 26. *Matth.*

(y) *In the articles of Fayth* 10. *Sunday.*

7. The Ministers to fortify this their former blasphemy haue impiously (conforme to their custome) falsifyed these words of S. Paul: (a) *Who in the dayes of his flesh with a strong cry and teares, offering prayers & supplications to him, who could saue him from death, was heard for his reuerence.* Wherby the Apostle witnesseth that our Sauiour as man, was euer heard in his prayers, by reason of the great reuerence, respect, and honour he caryed to God the Father: Which saying the Ministers haue corrupted thus; *Which in the*

(a) *Heb.* 5. *v.* 7.

the dayes of his flesh did offer vp prayers and supplications, with strong crying and teares vnto him that was able to saue him from death, and was also heard in that which he feared. Putting in the word *feared* to fortify their blasphemy, that Christ feared the damnation of the wicked; or wrath of his Father, sayth Caluin: (b) *Diros in anima cruciatus damnati & perditi hominis pertulit.* He sayth the same explicating this place. Remarke the Sycophancy or impious dealing of the Ministers, who haue trāslated well and with vs the same Greeke word in other places: as, (c) *And there were dwelling at Hierusalem Iewes, deuout men of euery nation.* Beza: *viri religiosi ex omni natione.* It is wel knowen that the Greeke word signifyeth a Religious and reuerentiall respect, which our Sauiour caryed to God the Father, conforme to the true translation of the former place, which is, *He was heard for his reuerence.* I will not defyle Christian eares with the rest of Caluins blasphemies agaynst God the sonne, which are without number: neyther will I be more tedious to the reader in setting downe the corruptiōs, falsifications and blasphemies of the English or Scots Bible, which are in such number, without number, that if my dayly infirmityes and weaknes did not hinder me, great and many volumes and bookes might be set out of such falsifications and corruptions.

(b) *Instit. lib.* 2 c. 16. *num.* 10. ἀπὸ τῆς εὐλαβείας.

(c) *Act.* 2. v. 5. εὐλαβεῖς.

The

The 23. & 24. Article.

That the true Church of God must needes be infallible: and as she hath absolute authority to propone matters of Fayth; so she cannot erre in proponing such matters to be belieued, as Apostolike Traditions, which euer haue bene belieued.

CHAP XII.

BEing in prison in *Edenburgh* I was forced to enter dispute with a Minister (as I did with many others) without books or any other such necessary helpes, cōcerning the authority and visibility of the true Church, wherof I made this argument. *That is the true Church of Christ which he commanded vs to obey, and threatned vs if we obey not. But he cannot command vs to obey an inuisible Church, nor punish vs if we obey it not. Therfore and iuuisible Church cannot be the true Church of Christ*. The Minister was incertayne what to deny in this argument; so remayning amazed, another Minister answered, and denyed the *Minor*, which I proued in this manner. God cannot commād vs to do a thing impossible, for that is against the very naturall wit of man, who will not command to his seruants impossible things. But it is impossible to heare, & so impossible to obey an inuisible Church. *Ergo*. The other Minister knew not what to answer to this argument, but went out of the prison in passion promising neuertheles to come back agayne, which he performed not. But his fellow Protestants being ashamed of this their ouerthrow, did bring in a few dayes after another Ministers nister, agaynst whome I made this argument. The true Church of Christ hath alwayes perseuered: But the Protestants Church hath not alwayes perseuered; Therefore it is not the true Church of Christ. He denyed the *Minor* which I proued after this forme. If your Church was extant in any age from the Apostles dayes to the comming of Luther, Caluin, and Knox, the space of a thousand fiue hūdreth and fifty yeares, eyther it was visible or inuisible. But neyther can be sayd: Therfore it was not extant at all. The Minister answered, that their Church is, and had bene visible, as witnesseth (sayth he) M. Foxes Cronicle. Wherunto I replyed thus. No manifest and knowne heretikes cā constitute the Church of Christ: but all your false Martyrs and pseudoconfessors whome Fox nameth, were knowne heretikes. *Ergo*, they could not constitute the Church of Christ. I proue the *Minor*. Fox nameth Waldenses, Albigenses, Wicklifists & others; but all these were known heretiks. *Ergo*. I proue the *Minor* againe. Waldenses & Albigēses &c. Hold many articles of Fayth, which yow condemne as heresies, and M. Iewell a Prime-Minister, sayth thus of them: (a) *They be none of ours*: and Osiander: (b) *The opinion of Waldenses, Albigenses &c. were absurde, wicked, and heretical.* To this argument the Ministers could neuer answere, or if they can, let them aduise and answere now.

(a) *In his defence of Apology pag. 84.* (b) *Centur. 15.*

2. The Reasons (besides the former) which perswade that the Church is infallible, are these following most forcible For what could moue any Infidel, Pagan, or Puritane to forsake his errours, and come to the true Church, if she might also beguyle him with errour and fallibility? What meanes could the true Church haue to condemne an heretike if she could erre in disprouing his errours? How should we know where to rest, whom to consult in doubts of Fayth, if the true Church the highest Iudge might iudge amisse. What assurance can the Protestants haue of their beliefe, Religion, Scripture, Sacraments, Preaching, yea of Christ himselfe, if the Church, which teacheth these particles to them, may erre in teaching? The tradition or testimony of the Romane Church, of whome the Prote-

stants haue receaued the Scriptures, of what accōpt can they make it, if it be fallible and subiect to errour? The Fayth which they gather out of the Scriptures, the Religiō which they ground vpon such Scriptures must lykewise be fallible & vncertaine. For the truth gleaned frō the Scriptures cānot be more sure, then the Scriptures themselues from which it is gathered. If they then be fallible, the Scriptures must needes be fallible (in the Protestāts opinion) by reason that the true Church, who hath deliuered the Scriptures to vs, is infallible, say they. And wheras neither Religiō nor Church can without supernatural Fayth, nor supernatural Faith be attained without infallible certainty of the things belieued; if then the Protestant Preachers & Ministers be fallible, the articles they belieue haue not that infallibility which is required to the nature of Fayth; *Which hath nothing* (sayth S. Bernard) *ambiguous our doubtful, yea, if it hath any thing ambiguous it cannot be Fayth.* Which is the reason wherfore S. Paul witnesseth that God placed in his Church: (c) *Some Apostles, some Prophets, and other some Euangelists, and other some Pastors and Doctours &c.* Behold heere foure things. 1. Whome he appoynted: *Apostles, Prophets, Euangelists, Pastors, Doctours.* 2. To what function did he imploy them: *To the consummation of Saincts, to the worke of the Ministery, to the edifying of the body of Christ.* 3. How long was it to continue: *Vntill we meete all into the vnity of Fayth and knowledge of the sonne of God.* 4. To what end was this: *That now we be not children wauering and caryed about with euery wind of doctrine, in the wickednes of men, in craftinesse to the circumuention of errour.* If this be the end and drift of God, specifyed in the Protestants owne Bible, is not God frustrate of his intent? Pastours spoyled of their assurāce? Doctours incertayne of their doctrine, if the true Church may erre and be fallible? I ioyne to this that infallible warrant of Christ speaking of the true Church: (d) *He that heareth you, heareth me, and he that despiseth you, despiseth me.* But it were not all one to heare Christ, & to heare his Church, to despise Christ, & to despise his Church, vnlesse the Church and the Pastours thereof were infallibly inspired by God to deliuer all things with such certaynty and infallibility, as is

(c) *Ephes. 4. v. 11. 12.*

(d) *Luk. 10 v. 16.*

is requisite. Lykewise seeing Christ cōmandeth vs to heare the Church and our true Pastours as himselfe, he who saith that the Church may erre, must needes lykewyse inferre that Christ himself may erre, which is a horible blasphemy.

3. Moreouer the Prophet Isay speaketh in the person of God to the Church, thus: (e) *My spirit that is in thee, and my wordes that I haue put in thy mouth, shall not depart out of thy mouth, and out of the mouth of thy seed, and out of the mouth of thy seedes seed, sayth our Lord, from this present and for euer.* What spirit was there in this Prophet, but the spirit of God? What words in his mouth, but the words of truth? Therfore the spirit of God and wordes of truth shall neuer depart from the Church of God, or the true Pastors therof. Can any thing be written more effectually? can any thing be spokē more pithily? Conforme to the which doctrine Christ cōmanded vs to follow the doctrine of the Church, as infallible doctrine, & that vnder the payne of condemnation & excommunication: (f) *If he will not heare the Church* (sayth Christ) *let him be to thee as the heathen and Publican.* How could God threaten vs vnder the curse of damnation to heare and obey his Church, if she could erre, and be infallible? To say, that the Church cannot erre so long as she followeth the word of God, is folly: for if the Church may depart from the word of God she cannot but erre: since then she cannot depart from the word of God, she cannot erre. 2. What priuilege I pray you, can that be aboue any hereticall assēbly? for no heretike, Infidell, Iew, or Turke, yea not the Diuel himselfe can erre as long as he speaketh conforme to Gods word. A certayne Minister replyed to this saying of myne, distinguishing two kinds of errour, one curable, and another incurable; one to probation and another to damnatiō confessing lykewyse that the Church might fall into curable errours, but not into incurable. Is this distinction in the expresse word of the Bible? where? in what place? Against which foolish distinction I frame this argument: Whosoeuer heareth the Church, followeth the commandement of God. *Ergo*, no error curable or incurable can we incurre by hearing the Church. I proue the *Minor* thus:

(e) *Isa.* 59. v. 21.

(f) *Matth.* 18. v. 17.

No offence against God can we incurre in following his commandements: but euery error curable or incurable (specially in maters of fayth) is an offence against God. *Ergo*, no errour curable or incurable, can we incurre by following Gods commandements. I would aske of the Ministers what be those errourrs; be they fundamentall and such as cannot stand with the integrity of faith; or be they sleight and indifferent things which do not harme the integrity of faith? If they be sleight and indifferent, we need not to be cured of them, we may without losse of Gods fauour remayne and die in them. The new Gospell then of the Protestants was needles, their reformation, in indifferent errours, superfluous, their breach detestable in making so great a schisme for slēder matter not necessary to saluatiō. Why do they persecute vs & trouble vs for so sleight maters? Fundamental and incurable they cannot be, vnlesse yee graunt that the Church is fallible, and may erre in fundamentall poynts, which I haue refuted before, and which is directly against the doctrine of the holy Fathers. Irenæus who speaketh thus of the infallibility of the Church: (g) *The Apostles haue layed vp in the Church, as in a rich treasure, all truth, that he that will, may from thence draw the water of life.* And againe. (h) *She keepeth with most sincere diligence the Apostles faith & preaching.* S. Hierome: (i) *In the Church is the rule or square of truth.* S. Cypryan: (k) *The Church neuer departeth from that, which she once hath knowne.* S. Augustine explicating those words of S. Mathew: (l) *In the chaire of Moyses the Scrybes and Pharisees, sit: all therefore whatsoeuer they bid you obserue, that obserue and do, but after their works do not, for they say, and do not.* Conforme to which place S. Augustine sayth learnedly and wysely: (m) *That, God maketh vs secure of euill gouernours of the Church, least for their cause the chayre of holseome doctrine should be forsaken, in which euen the euill are constrayned to deliuer true things, for they are not their owne things which they delyuer, but Gods, who hath placed the doctrine of verity in the chaire of Vnity.* To conclude then, the true Church of God was, is, and shall be infallible, as the Scriptures and reasons do conuince. And seeing the Puritanes do confesse that their Church may erre, is fallible & erro-

(g) *Lib.* 3. *cap.* 4. & 40.
(h) *Lib.* 1. *cap.* 3.
(i) *Lib.* 3. *aduersus Ruffinum. cap.* 8.
(k) *Epist.* 55. *ad Corn.*
(l) Math. 23. v. 2.
(m) *Epist.* 166.

erroneous: we must needs conclude, that their Church is not the spouse of Christ, wherof the Prophet fortold in the persō of Christ. (n) *I will despouse thee to me for euer*, but rather the harlot of Sathan, the tēple of Ball, the Synagogue of errour, the assembly of the wicked, & the cōpany of the reprobat. But let vs heare the holy Fathers of this second Age & Century.

(n) *Hosea.* 2. v. 19.

The Testimonyes of the holy Fathers of this second age; That the true Church of God must needes be infallible, in proponing matters of faith to be belieued, as Apostolike Traditions.

The first Section.

S. Iustinus Martyr testifyeth that the custome of the Catholiks in his tyme was to meete vpon Sonday, to say their prayers togeather (without any singing of Psalmes in meeter) to offer vp bread and wyne mingled with water: (a) *Tum consurgimus omnes communiter & preces fundimus; & sicut ante diximus, precibus nostris peractis, panis & vinum & aqua offeruntur; is autem qui praeest, preces similiter & gratiarum actiones pro viribus fundit, populúsq; acclamat dicens, Amen.* Which custome and holy tradition of the Church doth cōtinue to this day, and hath bene without interruption, and infallibly kept euer amongst the Catholiks.

(a) *In Apolog ad Anton. Pium.*

2. S. Irenæus teacheth first, that we should be obedient to those Pastors who haue succeded one to another, saying: (b) *Quapropter eis, qui in Ecclesia sunt, Presbyteris obaudire oportet, his qui successionem habent ab Apostolis, qui cum Episcopatus successione Charisma veritatis certum, secundum placita patrum acceperunt.* And since Puritane-Ministers haue no succession, no obedience should be granted to them. 2. He recommendeth earnestly the traditions of the Catholike Church, which delyuer the same traditions to vs with infallibility: (c) *Traditionem itaq; Apostolorum in toto mundo manifestatam, in omni Ecclesia adest perspicere omnibus qui vera velint audire, & habemus annumerare eos, qui ab Apostolis instituti sunt Episcopi in Ecclesijs, & successores eorum vsq; ad nos, qui nihil tale docuerunt, neq; cogitauerunt, quale ab his deliratur. Etenim si recondita mysteria*

(b) *Lib.* 3. *aduers. hæres. cap.* 43.

(c) *Lib.* 3. *cap.* 3.

scissent Apostoli, quæ seorsum & latenter à reliquis perfectos docebunt, his vel maximè traderent ea, quibus etiam ipsas Ecclesias cōmittebant, 3. He declareth the Antiquity and infallibility of the Roman Church, to be : (d) *Maximam & antiquissimam, omnibusq; cognitam: ad quam propter potentiorem principalitatem necesse sit omnem conuenire Ecclesiam, hoc est, eos qui sunt vndiq; fideles*. 4. He deduceth the succession of the Popes of Rome from S. Peter to his tyme, and vseth the same as a most forcible argument to confound Heretiks, saying : (e) *Hac ordinatione & successione, ea quæ est ab Apostolis in Ecclesia traditio, & veritatis præconiatio, peruenit vsq; ad nos, & est plenissima hac ostensio, vnam & eandem viuificatricem fidem esse, quæ in Ecclesia ab Apostolis vsq; nunc sit conseruata & tradita in veritate.* 5. He condēneth Florinus as an heretike, by reason that he taught dyuers opinions agaynst the Church of God, against the receaued doctrine of the holy Fathers, vsing these most forcible words, which I may addresse to euery Minister in particular : (f) *Ista dogmata, Florine,* (Ramsee), *vt tecum agam humaniter, sanæ sententiæ non sunt, ista dogmata sunt Ecclesiæ repugnantia, vtpote quæ eos, qui illis obsequuntur, in maximam impietatem deijciāt: ista dogmata ne Hæretici quidem qui fuere ab Ecclesia exturbati, affirmare vnquam ausi sunt. Ista dogmata Presbyteri, qui ante nos fuerunt, quiq; erant ipsorum Apostolorum discipuli, minimè tibi tradiderunt*. Haue we not greater reason to say this to the Protestants of our tyme, who cannot proue, no not one controuerted poynt of their religion, by the expresse word of their own Scots Bible? 2. Who cannot improue any poynt of the Catholike religion by the expres word of the Bible? 3. Who cannot possible name any man, who was of their religion before Caluin & Luther? 4. Finally who cannot possible name any King or Prince of any nation, of their religion before Calnin. 6. He affirmeth that the holy traditions left to vs, by the Apostles or Apostolike men should be followed and imbraced, by reason that there be many things not conteyned in the expresse word of the Bible; & dyuers nations haue professed Christ sincerely and truly without any Bible, Scripture or written word: (g) *Quid autem* (sayth he) *si neq; Apostoli quidem Scripturas reliquissent nobis, nonne*

(d) *Ibidem.*

(e) *Ibidem.*

(f) *Euseb. lib. 5. hist. Eccles. cap. 19.*

(g) *Lib. 3. cap. 4.*

nonne oportebat ordinem sequi traditionis, quem tradiderunt ijs, quibus committebant Ecclesias? Cui ordinationi assentiunt, multa gentes Barbarorum, eorum qui in Christum credunt, sine charactere vel atramento, scriptam habentes per Spiritum in cordibus suis salutem, & veterem traditionem diligenter custodientes, in vnum deum credentes fabricatorem cæli & terræ, & omnium quæ in eis sunt, per Christum Iesum Dei filium. Hanc fidem qui sine literis crediderunt, quantum ad sermonem nostrũ, Barbari sunt: quantum autem ad sententiam & consuetudinem & conuersationẽ propter fidem perquã sapientissimi sunt, & placent Deo, conuersantes in omni iustitia & castitate & sapientia.

3. Tertullian wryteth most learnedly of the infallibility of the tradition of the Church, declaring that it was euer familiar to Heretiks to brag & boast of the Scriptures, of the word of God, of the Bible: (h) *Sed ipsi* (sayth he) *& de Scripturis agunt, & de Scripturis suadent, scripturas obtẽdunt, & hac sua audacia statim quosdam mouent: in ipso verò congressu, firmos quidem fatigant, infirmos capiunt, medios cùm scrupulo dimittunt. Hunc igitur potissimùm gradum obstruimus, non admittendo eos ad vllam de Scripturis disputationem. Si hæ sunt vires eorum: despici debet cui competat possessio Scripturarum, ne is admittatur ad eas, cùm nullo modo competit.* 2. He auoweth that it is folly to cite the Scriptures, or to take the Scriptures for iudge in disputing with the Heretikes, because first they only admit such Scriptures as pleaseth them, for Canonicall. 2. Those which they admit, they turne and explicate according to their fansy. (i) *Nihil enim proficit congressio Scripturarum, nisi planè, vt aut stomachi quis ineat euersionem aut cerebri. Ista enim hæresis non recipit quasdam Scripturas, & si quas recipit, adiectionibus & detractionibus ad dispositionem instituti sui interuertit, & si recipit, non recipit integras: & si aliquatenus integras præstat, nihilo minus aduersus expositiones commentat ac conuertit. Tantum veritati obstrepit adulter sensus, quãtum & corruptor stylus.* 3. He concludeth giuing vs a holsome lesson how to dispute with the Protestants: (k) *Ergo non ad scripturas prouocandum est, nec in his constituendum certamen, in quibus aut nulla, aut incerta victoria est, aut parum certa, &c. Ordo rerum desiderabat illud prius proponi, quod nunc solùm disputandum est: quibus competat fides ipsa, cuius sitt Scriptura, & quo, & per quos, & quãdo*

(h) *Lib. de prescript. cap. 15.*

(i) *Eodem lib. cap. 17.*

(k) *Ibidem cap. 19.*

do, & quibus sit tradita disciplina qua fiunt Christiani. Vbi enim apparuerit veritatem esse disciplinæ & fidei Christianæ, illic erit veritas Scripturarum & expositionum, & omnium traditionum Christianarum. 4. He giueth lykewyse a holesome instruction how the Catholiks (who are not well acquainted with controuersies) should answer the Protestãts who do obiect oftẽ the Scriptures: They should answere, I say, and aske of the

(l) Ibid. ca. 19. Protestants: (l) *Edant ergo origines Ecclesiarum suarum: euoluant ordinem Episcoporum suorum, ita per successiones ab initio decurrentem, vt primus ille Episcopus aliquem ex Apostolis vel Apostolicis viris, qui tamen cum Apostolis perseuerauerint, habuerit authorem & antecessorem: hoc enim modo Ecclesiæ Apostolicæ sensus suos deferunt: sicut Smyrneorum Ecclesia habens Polycarpum à Ioanne collocatum refert, sicut Romanorum Clementem à Petro ordinatum edit: confingant tale aliquod Hæretici &c.* That is, when the Protestants do aske of vs places of the Bible in proof of Purgatory, Inuocation of Saintes, we should aske of them agayne, saying, To whom haue yee, Ministers, succeded lawfully, and with imposition of hands? who sent you? who gaue you power to preach, and expone the Bible? What part of the Bible auoucheth your new Religiõ? What part of the Scripture speaketh of your extraordinary calling &c. 5. He re-

(m) Ibidem cap. 32. koneth the Apostolike Churches, and amongst the rest the Roman Church, wherof he sayth: (m) *Si autem Italiæ adiaces,*

(n) cap. 37. *habes Romam, vnde nobis quoq; authoritas præsto est. Statu felix Ecclesia, cui totam doctrinam Apostoli cum sãguine suo profuderunt, vbi Petrus passioni Dominicæ adæquatur, vbi Paulus Ioannis exitu coronatur, vbi Apostolus Ioannes posteaquã in oleum demersus, nihil passus est, sed in Insulam relegatur.* 6. He teacheth that in disputing with the Protestans or Heretiks; First of all we should aske of them: (n) *Qui estis? quando & vnde venistis? quid in meo agitis non mei? quo deniq;, Marcion, iure syluam meam cædis? qua licentia, Valentine, fontes meos transuertis? qua potestate, Appelles, limites meos commoues? mea est possessio. Quid hic cæteri ad voluntatem vestram seminatis & pascitis? Mea est possessio, olim possideo, prior possideo, habeo origines firmas ab ipsis auctoribus, quorum fuit res. Ego sum hæres Apostolorum, sicut cauerunt testamento suo, sicut fidei commiserunt, sicut adiurauerunt, ita teneo: vos certè exhæredauerunt*

semper

ſemper & abdicauerunt vt extraneos, & inimicos. Finally he affirmeth that the infallible auctority of the Church ſhould be acknowledged in the Apoſtolike traditions, which though not conteyned in the Scripture expreſly, ſhould be belieued and receaued. Of the which traditions he ſetteth down theſe in particular: (o) *Deniq; vt à Baptiſmate ingrediar, aquam adituri ibidem, ſed & aliquanto prius in Eccleſia ſub Antiſtitis manu, conteſtamur nos renunciare diabolo, & pompæ, & angelis eius. Dehinc ter mergitamur, amplius reſpondentes, quam dominus, in Euangelio determinauit; inde ſuſcepti lactis & mellis concordiam prægustamus. Exq; ea die lauacro quotidiano per totam hebdomadam abſtinemus. Euchariſtiæ ſacramentum, & in tempore victus, & omnibus mandatum à Domino etiam antelucanis cœtibus, nec de aliorum manu quàm præſidentiũ ſumimus. Oblationes pro defunctis, pro natalitijs, annua die facimus: die Dominico ieiunium nefas ducimus, vel de geniculis adorare. Eadẽ immunitate à die Paſcha in Pentecoſten vſq; gaudemus. Ad omnem progreſſum atq; promotum, ad omnem aditum & exitum, ad veſtitum & calceatum, ad lauacra, ad menſas, ad lumina, ad cubilia, ad ſedilia, quacunq; nos conuerſatio exercet, frontem crucis ſignaculo terimus.* And a little thereafter: (p) *Harum & aliarum eiuſmodi diſciplinarum ſi legem expoſtules ſcripturarum, nullam inuenies: Traditio tibi prætenditur auctrix, conſuetudo confirmatrix & fides obſeruatrix, rationem traditioni, fidei, conſuetudim patrocinaturam aut ipſe perſpicies, aut ab aliquo, qui perſpexerit diſces &c. His igitur exemplis renunciatum erit, poſſe etiam non ſcriptam traditionem in obſeruatione defendi, confirmatum conſuetudine idonea, teſte probata tunc traditionis, ex perſeuerantia obſeruationis. Conſuetudo autem etiam in ciuilibus rebus pro lege ſuſcipitur, cùm deficit lex: nec differt Scriptura, an ratione conſiſtat, quãdo & legem ratio commendet. Porro ſi lex ratione conſtat, lex erit omne iam quod ratione conſtiterit &c.*

(o) *Lib. de corona militis.*

(p) *Cap. 4.*

4. Origen in like maner teacheth vs, that when the Heretiks or Proteſtants do obiect their Bible vnto vs, we ſhould reply, preferring the antiquity of our religion and the holy antiquity of our Church: (q) *Quoties autem Canonicas proferunt Scripturas, in quibus omnis Chriſtianus conſentit & credit, videntur dicere: Ecce in domibus verbum eſt veritatis. Sed nos illis non credere debemus, nec exire à prima & Eccleſiaſtica traditione,*

(q) *Tract. 29. in Mat.*

 ne,

ne, nec aliter credere, nisi quemadmodum per successionem Ecclesiæ Dei tradiderũt nobis. 2. He teacheth, *that there be many things done and belieued in the Catholike Church, wherof the commons cannot giue reason.* (r) *In Ecclesiasticis obseruationibus sunt nonnulla huiusmodi, quæ omnibus quidem facere necesse est, nec tamen ratio eorum omnibus patet.*

(r) Hom. 5. in Num.

5. S. Cyprian setteth down the antiquity of that tradition in mingling water with wyne in the holy sacrifice, saying thus: (s) *Admonitos autem nos scias (vt in calice offerendo Dominica traditio seruetur, neq; aliud fiat à nobis, quàm quod pro nobis Dominus prior fecit) vt calix, qui in commemorationem eius offertur, mixtus vino offeratur.* He declareth also, how great & abhominable is the sinne of the Heretikes of our tymes to prefer their iudgemẽt to the iudgement of the holy church, which hath continued these sexteene hundreth yeares; to the iudgement of the holy Fathers and of all antiquity: (t) *Nec hac iacto* (sayth he speaking to Florentius, as I lykewise speake to euery Minister in particular) *sed dolens profero, cùm te iudicem Dei constituas & Christi, qui dicit ad Apostolos, ac per hos ad omnes præpositos qui Apostolis vicaria ordinatione succedunt:* (u) *Qui vos audit me audit, & qui me audit, audit eum qui me misit. Vnde enim schismata & hæreses obortæ sunt & oriuntur, nisi dum Episcopus qui vnus est & Ecclesiæ præest, superba quorundam præsumptione contemnitur, & homo dignatione Dei honoratus ab indignis hominibus iudicatur? Quis enim hic est superbiæ tumor, quæ arrogantia animi, quæ mentis inflatio, ad cognitionem suam Præpositos & Sacerdotes vocare?*

(s) Epist. 63. ad Cæcilium.

(t) Epist. 69. ad Florentium Pumpianũ.

(u) Luk. 10 v. 16.

That the Ministers haue falsified the Bible in sundry places, which do proue, that as God cannot sinne, erre, nor lye; so he will continue to performe his promises in assisting the true Church infallibly.

The second Section.

THE Ministers as they haue brought in a new Religiõ, a new doctrine, a new faith and profession; so they haue made a new Bible, a new Scripture vnknowen to all Christendome

Chriſtendome the ſpace of fyfteene hundreth yeares, and this they call Reformatiō. To this end they haue vſed in the tranſlation of their Engliſh Bibles new & prophan words againſt the vſe and cuſtome of all antiquity, tranſlating in their Bible, for Prieſt *Elder*, for Idol *Image*, and infinite others, giuing alwayes for reaſon of this abhominable proceeding: That words ſhould be taken not according to the cuſtome of all wryters, but in their owne ſignification, that is, according to the Miniſters fanſy. Conforme to this abhominable faſhion of the Miniſters, let vs take theſe words in their owne ſignification; *Báal*, for Lord, *Beelzebub*, Lord of a fly, *Diabolus* for ſtaunderer, *Angels* for Meſſengers, *πνεῦμα* for a wind (for thus the Miniſters tranſlate it *Iohn* 3. *v.* 8.) *Euchariſty* for thanks-giuing, *Baptiſmus* for waſhing, *Infernus*, or *hel* for a graue, *Anima*, or the ſoule for a Carcaſſe, *Eccleſia* or Church for Congregation or Synagogue, and *Superintendent* for Biſhop. Conforme to theſe new forged and inuented prophane words, let a Miniſter preaching in S. Giles Church in Edenburgh ſay thus to his auditors: Faithfull brethren, I that am your (a) Elder, or Superintendent, placed in this (b) Synagogue & Congregation of Edenburgh, by the holy (c) wind, for the feeding of your (d) carcaſſes, do preach vnto you in the name of (e) Baal; that except ye come to receaue (f) thanks giuing with more deuotion, and performe better your promiſe made to God in (g) waſhing, you ſhall be condemned body & carcaſſe to the (h) graue, with the ſtaunderers, I ſay with the (k) Lord of a fly, and his (l) meſſengers. How deeply, I pray you, would ſuch words ſinke into the harts of the Burgeſſes of Edenburgh, and how far different would ſuch a prophane exhortation be, from this other made by a Catholike Biſhop or Prieſt: I that am your Biſhop and Preiſt placed in this Church of Edenburgh by the holy Ghoſt, for the feeding of your ſoules, do denounce vnto yow in the name of our Lord, that except yee come to receaue the B. Sacrament, & performe better your promiſe made to God in Baptiſme, you ſhall be body & ſoule condemned to hel, your portion ſhalbe with the diuels, yea with Beelzebub, and

(a) *So the Miniſters do tranſlate Iames* 5. *v.* 14.
(b) *In the Bibles printed* 1560.
(c) *Iohn.* 3 *v.* 8.
(d) *Beza in* 2. *Acts. v.* 27.
(e) *Caſtalio the Purit.*
(f) *Idem paſsim.*
(g) *Idem paſsim.*
(h) *The Kings Bibles in the* 2. *of Acts.*
(i) *Caſtalio.*
(k) *Caſtal.*
(l) *Idem.*

and his Angels. I might giue ſundry like examples to proue the abſurdityes and great inconuenients which enſue of the Engliſh corrupted tranſlation of the Bibles, which (as ſome Proteſtants and Puritans do ſay): (m) *lead men the high way to very Atheiſme, worſe then gentility, or the ſchoole of Epicure*. Thus M. Carlile, adding this other iudgment of his of the Engliſh Bibles, *wherin the tranſlation is corrupted, the ſenſe and meaning depraued, the truth obſcured, the ignorant deceaued, and the ſimple ſupplanted*. And againe ſpeaking againſt the Miniſters who haue tranſlated the Bible, ſayth: *That in many places they detort the Scriptures from the right ſenſe, they them ſelues do loue darknes more then light, and falshood more thẽ truth*. Let vs come to the corruptions in particular.

(m) *Carl. in his booke that Chriſt went not down to hell.*

2. The firſt place corrupted by the Miniſters is that of the Prophet Dauid: (n) *In the morning I will ſtand by thee, and will ſee; becauſe thou art not a God that wilt iniquity.* Wherby the Prophet teſtifyeth, that God cannot be the author or cauſe of any ſinne; for God can do nothing contrary to his owne will, but rather he hateth iniquity, & all that worke iniquity. The Hebrew word *Chapets*, ſignifieth *volens, that will:* As the Proteſtants do tranſlate in other indifferent places, as, (o) *they are playne to him who will vnderſtand. Omnibus volentibus ea; chepet ſe hem.* The Greeke tranſlation in like maner is manifeſt. Contrary to this holy doctrine the Miniſters haue taken away the word *wilt* out of the Bible, to ſignify that deteſtable doctrine of theirs, *That God willeth ſin*, that God is the author of ſinne, and of all iniquity and abhominatiõ. To the which end they tranſlate thus, *Thou art not a God that loueth wickednes*. For ther is a great differẽce betwixt *to will a thing, and to loue the ſame*: and though the difference might ſeeme not to be ſo great, yet it is a deteſtable forme of proceding of the Miniſtry to trãſlate thus the Bible againſt the practiſe and cuſtom of al the ancient and holy Fathers. To the end that the Miniſters be not offended with me, I will ſet down their own words touching this point, whether or not God be author and cauſe of all ſinnes and abhominations. Firſt then it is certayne, that he who will ſinne, and taketh pleaſure therin, is author and cauſe therof: So

(n) *Pſalm. 5. v. 4.*

(o) *Prou. 8 v. 9.*

οὐχὶ θεὸς θέλων.

is God in the Protestants religiõ. Heare their owne words preached and pronounced at seuerall tymes by the Ministers in the order of Baptisme: (p) *God is creator of heauen and earth* (say the Ministers) *that is to say, that heauen and earth & the contents therof are so in his hand, that there is nothing done without his knowledge, neyther yet against his will.* This is that horrible and diuellish doctrine which Caluin did teach, and Knox did learne in Geneua. (q) *Il ne se fait* (sayth Caluin) *ny larcin, ny paillardise, ny homicide, que la volontè de Dieu n'entreuenne.* O destable doctrine! O abhominable religion! 2. The minister & superiour iustly is called author and cause of that sinne wherunto he induceth his seruant and subiect. In lyke manner God is author of sinne in the Ministers religion specified in the articles of their faith, thus: (r) *So then by thy saying* (sayth the Minister to the Chyld) *the power of God is not idle, but continually exercised: that nothing* (remarke the words) *is done but by him and his ordinance.* Yea (s) *God doth compell the diuels to execute his will, although it be against their intent and purpose.* O horrible blasphemy & worse thẽ Turkish doctrine! Eyther he compelleth them to do good or to do bad? good they cannot do, because they are confirmed in a reprobat sense and state: if bad, yet against their intent, is not God more the cause of the wickednes they do, yea more then they themselues in the Protestants Religion? 3. As he is iustly the cause of a mans death, who willingly and wittingly delyuereth him into his enemyes hands, by whom he is killed; So the Ministers do make God to be author of al the sinnes & abhominations of the wicked, their words be: (t) *As God of his infinite mercy doth preserue his faithfull, so lykewise he doth not only giue vp, cast off, and with draw his grace from such as he will punish: but also he delyuereth them to the diuel, committing them to his tyrãny; he stryketh them with blindnes, and giueth them vp into reprobat mynds, that they become vtterly slaues vnto sinne, and subiect to all tentations.* Can there be more abhominable words deuysed to make God author & cause of all sinnes, then the former? 4. Sin is more attributed to the chief, then to the instrumentall cause therof, by reason that the instrumentall cause doth worke subordinatly, and

(p) *In the order of baptisme of the Ministers ioined with the psal. book.*

(q) *Lib. 1. institut. c. 17. num. 5.*

(r) *In the* Articles of *the Ministers Fayth of Scotland. Sunday 3.*

(s) *In the 4. Sunday.*

(t) *In the Article of Faith. Sunday 43.*

as it were commanded by the chief and principall cause. And in this sense & meaning the Ministers do make God to be more the chief cause and author of all the sinnes and abhominations of the world, then the diuels themselues. Their words be: (u) *We confesse and believe that neyther the Diuels nor yet the wicked of the world haue any power to molest or trouble the chosen children of God, but in so farre, as it pleaseth him to vse them as instruments*. The same very blasphemous words Caluin the Sophist hath in the first booke of his diabolicall Institutions cap. 18. num. 2. Of whom Knox, Willox, Paul Messen, and such limmes of Satan did learne them in *Geneua*, the sinke and puddle of Baal, & of the Antichristian Ministers. I call them *Ministers*, by reason that as the word *Menester*, in a certaine Lãguage signifieth as it were a hotch-potch of diuers ingredients: so our Scots-Ministers haue put together, as in a hotch-potch, those heresies, which were before condẽned in al ages, giuing the name therunto of *a Reformed Religion*. Such is then the God of Caluin and of the Ministers, set down & descrybed in the former words far different from the God of the Roman Catholiks. *The false God of Caluin, and of the Ministers* (sayth *Castalio*, a prime Puritan Minister be fore cited) *is slow to mercy, prone to anger, who hath created the greatest part of the world to destruction, & hath predestinat them not only to damnation, but also to the cause of damnation, so that neyther thefts, murthers, nor Adulteryes are committed, but by his constraint and impulsion, so that not the Diuel, but the God of Caluin is the author & cause of al wickednesse. But that God, which the holy Scriptures teach, is altogether contrary to this God of Caluin, and of the Ministers &c.* And to proue this their Caluinian God out of the Scriptures, they haue falsified sundry places therof, as amongst others the foresaid: *Thou art not a God that wilt iniquity*.

(u) *In the order of Baptisme.*

3. The second corruption is that of the Prophet (x) *Dauid: The Lord is faithfull in all his words, and holy in all his works*. Wherby the Prophet assureth vs, that God is most faithfull in all his words set down in the holy Scripture, specially those: (a) *God will all men to be saued, and to come to the knowledge of the truth*. For God hath prouyded a generall medicine

(x) *Psal.* 144. v. 13. *protest.* 145

(a) 1. *Tim.* 2. v. 4.

medicine and redemption in the blood of Christ Iesus, for all those who will accept of it, in doing things set down in Gods law. Conforme to that which S. Peter also teacheth: (b) *Our Lord slacketh not his promise, as some do esteeme it: but he doth patiently for you, not willing that any perish, but that all returne to penance.* Which words of the Bible do conterpoint directly that article of the Puritanes Religion set down in their confession of Faith thus: (c) *Who of the lost sonnes of Adam hath ordeyned some as vessels of wrath to damnation, & hath chosen others as vessels of his mercy to be saued.* Because then those former words, *The Lord is faithfull &c.* declare manifestly Gods mercy and goodnes towards vs, and that he cannot be the author of any sinne or wickednes; the Ministers haue thrust them out of their Bibles, against the Greeke text of the Septuagint, and against the ancient Fathers, S. Hierome, S. Chrysostome, S. Augustine, and others, who do read them exactly as we do. What hope of saluation can the Ministers haue, who thus do corrupt the word of God, to vphold their superstitious & abhominable opiniōs against the trew God? since they haue diminished of the Scripture a whole verse, shall not that wofull sentence be accomplished in thē: (d) *If any man shall diminish of the words of the booke of this Prophecy, God shall take away his part out of the booke of life?*

(b) 2. Pet. 3. v. 9.

(c) In the confession of Fayth.

(d) Reuel. 22. v. 19.

4. The third place falsified by the Ministers is that of Ecclesiasticus, where the Ministers do make their God author of all the sinnes which Pharao cōmitted. Their words be: (e) *The Lord hardened Pharao, that he should not know him:* yet their french Bibles printed 1610. haue directly the contrary, *Le Seigneur a endurci Pharao, a ce qu'il le cogneust.* That is: *The Lord hardened Pharao that he should know him.* Turning affirmatiuely and not negatiuely as the former, which sheweth the spirit of contradiction very familiar to the Ministers. The true translation is this: *The Lord hardened Pharao, so that he did not know him.* The first translation maketh God author of Pharao his sinnes; the second, only that God did harden Pharao in taking away his graces from him by reason of his manifold sinnes: of the which hardening ensued

(e) Ecclesi. 16. v. 15.

that

that Pharao knew not God.

(f) *Hosea 13. v. 9.* 5. The fourth place falsified, is that of Hosea: (f) *Thy perdition is of thee, O Israell, only in me is thy help.* Declaring therby that the perdition, wickednes and sinnes of men do proceeed of themselues; but their good and vertue of God only, not that God can be in any way the author of sinne and iniquity, conforme to that of the Scripture: (g) *I will not the death of the impious, but that the impious conuert from his way and liue. Conuert, conuert yee from your most euill wayes.* Agayne God speaketh specially to the wicked & sinfull: (h) *come ye to me all that labour and are burthened, and I wil refresh you.* And againe: (i) *your iniquityes haue separated betwene you & your God, and your sinnes haue hid his face from you that he wil not heare.* And many such places which declare playnly that God, who is goodnes it selfe, cannot be the author of any wickednes. But the iniqnityes and sinnes of men eyther actually done or foreseene by God from all eternity, to be done freely in their owne tyme, are the cause that God doth reprobate, hardē, abandon, yea and suffer them to be giuen vp to a reprobat sense; giuing them neuertheles many good & holy inspirations, wherby they may returne, but they will not: which miserable estate of the wicked is called, *Obstinacy*, and is a sinne against the holy Ghost. The markes & tokēs wherof are easy to be seen in the Puritane Ministers. The first marke of this obstinacy & reprobation as it were, is, *A certayne inward and spirituall blindnes*, wherin willingly and wittingly men will remaine in their errours, vices, and heresies, eyther for wordly respect or fleshly libertye, as witnesseth Iob: (k) *These are they that abhorre the light, they know not the wayes therof, nor continue in the pathes therof.* The 2. marke is, a certayne spirituall deafnes, wherby willingly lykewise some men wil not heare discourses of the feare of God, of true religion, of the later day, and things to come: such men say in effect, though not in word, to God, (l) *Depart from vs, for we desire not the knowledge of thy wayes.* Of whom the Prophet in the person of God sayth: (m) *Who is blind, but my seruant? and deafe, but he to whome I haue sent my Messengers?* Which place is corrupted by the Ministers.

(g) *Ezech. 33. v. 11.*
(h) *Matth. 11. v. 28.*
(i) *Isa. 59. v. 2.*
(k) Iob.
(l) *Iob. 21. v. 14.*
(m) *Isa. 42 v. 19.*

6. The

6. The third marke is a certayne contempt of God, Godly things, & of Gods seruants, which is so manifestly seene in all the Ministers, who contemne and make no accompt of the holy Doctours, holy Councels, of the perpetuall succession and continuance of the true Church, of the prouidence of God in preseruing the Church from errour; yea not of any solide motiue, which may induce any wyse (n) Prou.
man to imbrace the truth. Such men God threatneth ter- 1. v. 24. 25.
ribly, saying: (n) *Because I haue called, and yee refused, I haue* 26.
stretched out my hand, and none would regard; but ye haue despysed all my counsell, and would none of my correction, I will also laugh at your destruction, and mock when your feare commeth. The fourth marke is the want of any feeling of Gods iudgements, of sinnes committed against God, yea reioycing as it were in sinne, iniquity & wickednes, without any outward shame (o) Prou.
or inward feeling. You shall see in this bad disposition 2. v. 14.
many Protestants, (o) *Who reioyse in doing euill, and delight in* (p) Ierem.
the frowardnes of the wicked. And the Prophet: (p) *Thou hadst* 3. v. 3.
a whores forehead, thou wouldest not be ashamed. Do not the very grounds and principles of the Protestant religion bring a man to this miserable estate? The fyfth marke is a certayne Stupidity and carelesnes of those things which (q) Hosea
appertayne to the lyfe to come, specially a carelesnes in see- 4. v. 6.
king out the true religion, as witnesseth the Prophet: (q) *Because thou hast refused knowledge, I will also refuse thee.* Of the which carelesnes and the foresaid bad dispositions & markes, procedeth as it were an impossibility, or rather a great difficulty in such persons to find out the true Religion, the (r) Ierem.
true faith & profession, saith the Prophet: (r) *Can the black-* 13. v. 23.
More change his skin, or the Leopard his spots? then may yee also do good, that are accustomed to do euill. All these former marks are easy to be seen in many Protestantes, and generally in the Ministers, whose sinne is, in that the greater before God, by reason that many of them do know the truth and will neyther imbrace it, nor suffer others to imbrace it. Which detestable sin of theirs, (s) *is written with a pen of Iron, & with* (s) Ierem.
the poynt of a diamond, and grauen vpon the table of their hart, and 17. v. 1.
conscience, which shall accuse and condemne them at the later

later day.

(t) 1. Tim. 2. v. 4.

7. The fifth place corrupted is that of S. Paul (t) *God will all men to be saued, and to come to the knowledge of the truth*. And consequently he hath created none to be damned and reprobat, as the Ministers did teach before. Who to cōfirme that their blasphemous doctrine, do translate obscurly, yet perniciously, the foresaid sentence thus: *God will that all men should be saued, & come to the knowledge of the truth*: referring the matter to the *future will of God*, and not to the present. Beza lykewise vitiously translateth thus: *Qui quosuis homines vult saluari.* Taking away the force of the generall proposition. In the Greeke, and Syriake *decullehun*, i. all men. The words are so playne, that playner cannot be: the reason of the Catholike verity is euident, for since (u) *Christ* died for *sinnes according to the Scriptures, and not for our sinnes only*, (x) *but also for the sinnes of the whole world*; what profit could it haue bene for the reprobate, if God had created them to damnation, if God had not a will to saue them? Truly since the Ministers haue so boldly and effrontedly falsified those so playne words of the Bible, what can be looked for at their hands, when the words be obscure and indifferent? If they in this their Idolatrous translation do abandon all the holy Fathers and writers, what meruaile they think themselues the only wyse & learned? But in effect professing themselues to be thus wyse, (y) *They become fooles, for they haue turned the glory of the incorruptible word of God to their owne imaginations, wherfore also God hath giuen them vp to their hartes lust, vnto vncleannes, to defyle their owne bodyes betwene themselues*, By reason that they turned the word of God into a lye. If I would produce all the places of the Bible which the Ministers haue falsified, to mainteyne this and other articles of their abhominable Idolatry and superstitious doctrine, whole volumes of Bookes might be framed therof, bigger without comparyson then six Bibles. But since my health is greatly weakned, specially since my last imprisonmēt, I cannot performe that which I intēded, to refute the greatest part of the Protestants falsifications: declaring therby consequently that the Scots, or English Bible is no wayes the word of God.

πάντας ἀνθρώπους θέλει σωθῆναι

(u) 1. Cor. 15. v. 3.

(x) 1. Iohn 2. v. 2.

(y) Rom. 1. v. 22. & 24.

The

The conclusion of this Second Century, or hundreth yeares. Togeather with a Challenge to M. Andrew Rāsey Minister of Edenburgh, requiring of him a Catalogue to be made of the professours of his Religion, for these two former Ages, or Centuryes.

HAuing thus set downe the doctrine & Professours of the Catholike Religion for these two former Ages (as godwilling I am to do in the ensuing Ages) I challenge M. Andrew Ramsey Minister of Edenburgh, to deuise and set down the very wordes and sentences of his professours in euery Age as making for the defence of his hereticall Religion, as I haue set downe in the two preceding Ages the names & sentences of the Professours of the Catholike Religion, in defence of the same. Which I know he cannot do. For if there had bene any man in any of these former or ensuing Ages, professing the Protestants or Puritans Religion, assuredly some history-writer had made mention of him by way of prayse or disprayse, since other men and matter of lesse moment, haue bene recorded and noted by history-writers. The reason of this any petition is. Since God hath appoynted Pastours to be alwayes in the true Church & Religion vnto the worlds end, that men should be preserued from wauering in Fayth, and from being carryed about with euery wind of false doctrine; If the Protestants cannot name me, no not one man of their Religion who was in these two former, or ensuing Ages, vnto the coming of Luther; it followeth of necessity that their Religion is nothing else, but a new inuention of Luther & Caluin, and a rapsody or rable of ragged heretikes.

2. If the Ministers will reply that the Apostles were of their Religiō: I answere first, that I haue refuted before that foolish saying at lēgth, & they cannot produce no not one place of all the Apostles writs, wherby in playne termes, expresse wordes and formal text, they shall be able to proue any debatable poynt of their Religion, or improue any debatable poynt of our Catholik Religion. 2. I answer, that all

all the heretikes who be now a dayes differing amongst themselues in essentiall poynts, as Lutheranes, Caluinists, Anabaptists, Zuynglians, Vbiquitists, Trinitaryes, & such infinite number, they say all that they are of the Apostles Religion, deceauing therby the simple people, condemning notwithstanding one another of manifest heresie and diabolicall Idolatry. 3. I answere that it is in question and debate betwixt vs and the Protestants, whether they be of the Apostles Religion, wherfore ignorantly and beggarly they presuppose which is in question. That which I aske then of M. Ramsey is, that he will name me any wryter of these two former Ages, setting downe his wordes & writings, as I haue done, who being after the Apostles immediatly, or mediatly, hath made mention of any debatable poynt of this Religion, as professing the same, and consenting with him in that vnity of Fayth, which is required to true Religion.

3. To the better vnderstanding of the which petition of mine it is to be remarked: (a) *That the Church of God is a carefull keeper of true Religiō, which is cōmitted to her charge, for she neuer changeth or altereth it in any thing: she diminisheth nothing, nothing she addeth, because God promised that* (b) *the spirit of truth should teach all truth vnto the Church.* Wherfore since that all the holy Fathers named in these two former Ages, and to be named in the ensuing Ages, did constantly belieue, that the true Church of God was euer to continue, that she should not erre in matters of Fayth, that all truth in her was to be foūd as in a rich Treasure house: They in lyke manner did belieue constātly, *fide saltem implicita*, whatsoeuer then & now the Catholike Church doth teach and professe: they did all say with holy Irenæus: (c) *We must heare and obey that Church, those Priests, who haue succession of their Episcopall function, haue receaued the Charisma of truth.* And forasmuch as these former & ensuing holy Pastours were euer ready to submit their particular opinions to the Fayth and Iudgement of the holy Church, to imbrace that as a poynt of Fayth which the Church taught and resolued; neither can particular opinion, or errour of some of them hinder their vnity in Fayth with

(a) *Vincēt. Lyrin. lib. contra hæres. cap.* 32.
(b) *Iohn.* 16. *v.* 13.
(c) *Lib.* 4. *cap.* 43.

with vs, nor yet can we be sayd to belieue any thing, which they belieued not: because they euer submitted their iudgement to the iudgement of the true Church, which then was visible; & which was euer to continue. Contrarywise all heretikes which hath bene and be, as they would neuer submit their iudgement to any Church, which then was, or now is, hauing alwayes for the last ground of their Religion, *Their owne particular, and inward spirit, and perswasion*, as they haue not, nor euer had any vnity in Fayth; so euery one condemneth another of heresy, of errour and infidelity. This doctrine with the rest of the holy Fathers S. Augustin doth teache: (d) *Those* (sayth he) *who in the Church of Christ do hold some vnsound and peruerse opinions, if beyng admonished to come to wholesome and right beliefe, they resist contumaciously, and will not amend, but do persist to defend their pestilent and deadly doctrines, they are made heretike.* The same sayth Origē: (e) *That man is to be accompted an heretike, who professeth himselfe to belieue Christ, and yet belieueth something which is different from that, which the definition of Ecclesiasticall tradition conteyneth.* And Beza himselfe, though a Puritane: (f) *He is an heretike who doth so go away from wholesome doctrine, as condemning God, and the iudgement of the Church, persisteth in his opinion and violateth the concord of the Church.* Because pertinacy, which is proper to all heretikes consisteth in holding opinions contrary to the knowne opinion of the Church of God.

(d) Aug. l. de ciuit. c. 5

(e) In cap. 3 ad Titū. apud Pamph. in Apolog. praefat. Origē.

(f) Beza in notis super Act. 5. v. 17.

4. Finally, as I haue set downe in these two former Ages manifestly the beliefe and Religion of the Catholike Roman Church, so the Protestants themselues do auow that the Roman Church the first six hundreth yeares was the only true Church; confirming therby in generall all which I haue set down in particular. Thus Whitaker a prim Minister: (g) *The Roman Church*, sayth he, *during the first six hundreth yeares after Christ, was pure and flourishing, and inuiolably taught, and defended the Fayth deliuered by the Apostles.* Which purity of the Roman Church gaue occasion to Tertullian to prouoke the Heretikes of his tyme with the succession of the Bishops of Rome, and the Roman Church: (h) *For that*, sayth M. Fulk, *the Church of Rome retayned by succession, vntill*

(g) Lib. de Antichristo cont. Sanderum pag. 35. & sequent.

(h) In his confutatiō of Purgatory pag. 374.

 Ter-

Tertullians dayes, that Fayth which it did first receaue from the Apostles. The which tyme he extendeth not only to Irenæus Cyprian, Tertullian, and Optatus tyme and Age; but lykewise to S. Hierome, and Augustins Age, saying thus: (i) *That those men specially named the Church of Rome, it was because the Church of Rome at that time, as it was founded by the Apostles, so it continued in the doctrine of the Apostles*. And Caluin himselfe: (k) *It was a thing notorious, & without doubt, that after the Apostles Age, vntill the tyme of those holy Fathers* (that is, of S. Augustine, S. Chrysostome &c.) *who were 440. yeares after Christ, no change was made in doctrine, neyther at Rome, nor at other cittyes*: which verity sundry other Protestants accordingly do teach. If thẽ the Roman Church, faith and religion was only the true religion the first four hundreth yeares, much more the first two hundreth yeares. Which doctrine of two hundreth or foure hundreth yeares is the selfe same for which we Catholiks are now persecuted in England Scotland & Irland as is notorious, and which hath continued from the Apostles to our dayes without any interruption at all; and for the which our Blessed Queene Mary, his Highnesse dearest & most holy mother, the last of fourscore Catholike Kings and Queenes of Scotland, suffered martyrdome. Wherfore, deare Countreymen, let vs loue our Lord and God, but let vs loue also this his Church: him as our Father, her as our mother: for he who hath not the Catholike and Roman church for his Mother, assuredly shall neuer haue God of heauen for his Father.

(i) *Ibid. p. 373. and in his Retentiue &c. pag. 85.*

(k) *Caluin in his French Institutions anno 1562.*

The end of the third Part, or second Century.

Aduertisement.

By reason that these bookes were printed by men who had no great skil in the Scottish language, sundry small errours haue escaped, which the learned and charitable Reader will, I hope, the more easily excuse, and correct.

Errata.

IN the first Part, in the Preface to the Reader, read *Carpere vel noli*. In the second Part, line 28. read, *these*. Pag. 2. in the margent, *dele* these words, *See these words in the Bible*. Pag. 23. lin. 3. read, *which hath byn vsed*. Pag. 27. l. 12. *dele* these words, *Quem & citat Beza*. Pag. 44. l. 1. read, *these*. Ibid. in the margent, *dele* these words, *Serm. de Annuntiat*. Pag. 45. l. 3. read, *Carne sola*. Pag. 72. l. 3. read, *recludunt*. Ibid. l. 7. read *additus*. Pag. 73. l. 3. read *Bruma*. Ibid. l. 34. read *solo*. Pag. 81. l. 30. read *Biblet*. Pag. 93. l. 30. read *meritorious*.

The Errours of the third Part, if any haue escaped, the Courteous Reader, I trust, will of himselfe correct.

FINIS.

PIETRO TERAMANO

Esmudiad Eglwys . . . Loreto

1635

DECHREVAD A RHYFEDHVS

ESMVDIAD EGLVVYS YR ARGLVVYDHES

FAIR O LORETO.

EGLVVYS Loreto oedh gynt yn stafelh o duy 'r fendigedig Fair forvvyn Yn ninas Nazareth, yn agos at Gaersalem, Yn Yr hon i ganvvyd, i magvvyd, ag ai cyfarchvvyd gan Yr Angel; Yn hon hefyd i càd drvvy ràdyr Ysbryd glàn i mab IESV, ag ai dygvvyd i fyny hyd Yn dheudhegmlvvydh oed. Yr stafelh hon Ynol derchafeiad Yn Harglvvydh an achubvvr, a gasegrodh yr Apostolion Yn Eglvvys, i anrhydedh Yr Arglvvydhes Fair forvvyn; a S.LVK a liniodh i lhún, sydh Yr avvr hon yn bresenol ag Yn vveledigavvl yno. Yr oedh cyrchfa mavvr a duvviol bermdora ati or gvvledydh o amgylch, tra 'r oedhynt Yn Gatholig, ond gvvedi Ydhynt vvneithyr Ygar a phydh Grist a dilin athravvieth Mahomet, Yr Angylion ai 'smudasont i Slafonia ag ai gosodasont vvrth Dref a elvvyr Flvvmen lhe ni chafodh barch dhyledys: O hervvydh hyny 'r Angylion eilvvaith ai cariasont dros y mór i lvvyn o goed Yn svvydh Recanati, o heidho gvvraig fonhedhig a elvvyd Loreta; ond o achos amryvv ledrad ar Y phordh favvr, ai dugasont odhiuno hefyd, i funydh Y dhau frodyr, Yn Yr vnrhyvv svvydh Recanati. Ag Yn dhivvaitha o ran Ymrafaelion Y brodyr Ynghylch Y rhodhion ar ophrvvmion, ai cariasont or mynydh heb i silfaeneu, i Yslys y phordh gyphredyn, yn agos ir fan lhe i mae hi 'r avvr hon yn sefylh: yn envvog, o ran lhavver o arvvidhion rhadeu, a gvvrthieu gorchestavvl. O hervvydh hynny Dynasvvyr Recanati, yn mavvr ryfedhu i rhinvvedh ai amgylchasont a chaireu cadarn; etto ni vvydheu neb o ble gynta i 's mudvvyd, hyd y flvvydhyn M. CC. XC. VI. pan amrithiodh yr Arglvvydhes Fair i vvr duvviol drvvy i gvvsc, ir hvvn yr anirgelodh y gvvirionedh: ag ynteu ai manegodh i vvyr o audurdod o fevvn y profins yma. Ag er mvvyn cael profedigaeth or vveledigaeth yma depholvvyd XVI. o vvyr o gredit i fynd i Dhinas Nazareth: yr 'hain a dhugasont genthynt fesur yr eglvvys, ag ai cavvsont i fod yn cytuno ai sylfeineu oedh yno; yn yr 'hain ir oedh Yn scrifenedig i bod hi yno ag ymadel ar lhe; Gvvedi hyn, y gvvyr yma a dhymchvvelasont ivv cartref, gan hai Y gvvirionedh dros y gvvledydh, ag o hynny alhan fo gaed gvvybod mae 'r eglvvys yma oedh stafelh yr Arglvvydhes Fair forvvyn, a Christnogion a dheghreuasont fod Yn dhefosionavvl ir lhe, ag a fuont felhy'n vvastadol hyd Y dydh hedhivv, o ran Y mavvr vvyrthieu i mae hi beunydh Yn i vvneythyd Yno. Vn Pavvl de Sylfa crefydhvvr ag ermit o favvr santeidhrvvydh, hvvn oedh Yn trigo mevvn bvvth, Yn agos at Yr eglvvys, ir hon 'r oedh Yn m'ynd bob dydh i blygen, a dhvvedodh, vveled o hono, dros Ysbàd deg-mlvvynedh, ar yr VIII dydh o fis Medi, dvvy avvr cyn dydh, oleini mavvr Yn descyn arni or nefoedh: Sef, Y fendigedig Fair forvvyn, hon (medheu ef) syn ymdhangos yno ar gyfan y dydh y ganvvyd. Ag i gydarnhau y cvvbl, dau vvr rinvvedhol o Dhinas Recanati a dhovvedasont, lavver gvvaith imi Brefect a Rheolvvr Terreman a Phresvvylvvr yr eglvvys hon, fal i mae yn callyn. Y nailh a elvvyd Pavvl Renalduci o dhovvedodh vveled o dàd i hendaid, pan i cariodh yr angylion hi dros y mór ir lhvvyn Coed a fonvvyd or blaen, lhe 'r aeth yn fynych ivv gvveled. y lhalh a elvvyd Phrancis Prior hefyd a dhovvedodh darfod ivv dàd a oedh CXX. mlvvydh oed fynych gyrchu yno. Ag i brofi 'mhelhach i bod yno, fo fanegodh, fod gan dad i hendaid duy'n agos ati, lhe 'r oedh yn trigo, a darfod ir Angylion yn i amser ef i 'symud odhiuno i funydh y dhau frodyr fal i dovvedbvvyd or blaen.

I favvl tragvvydhol ag anrhydedh y fendigedig Fair Forvvyn;

IN LORETO Per Francesco Serafini. M. DC. XXX V.

Con licenza de' Superiori.